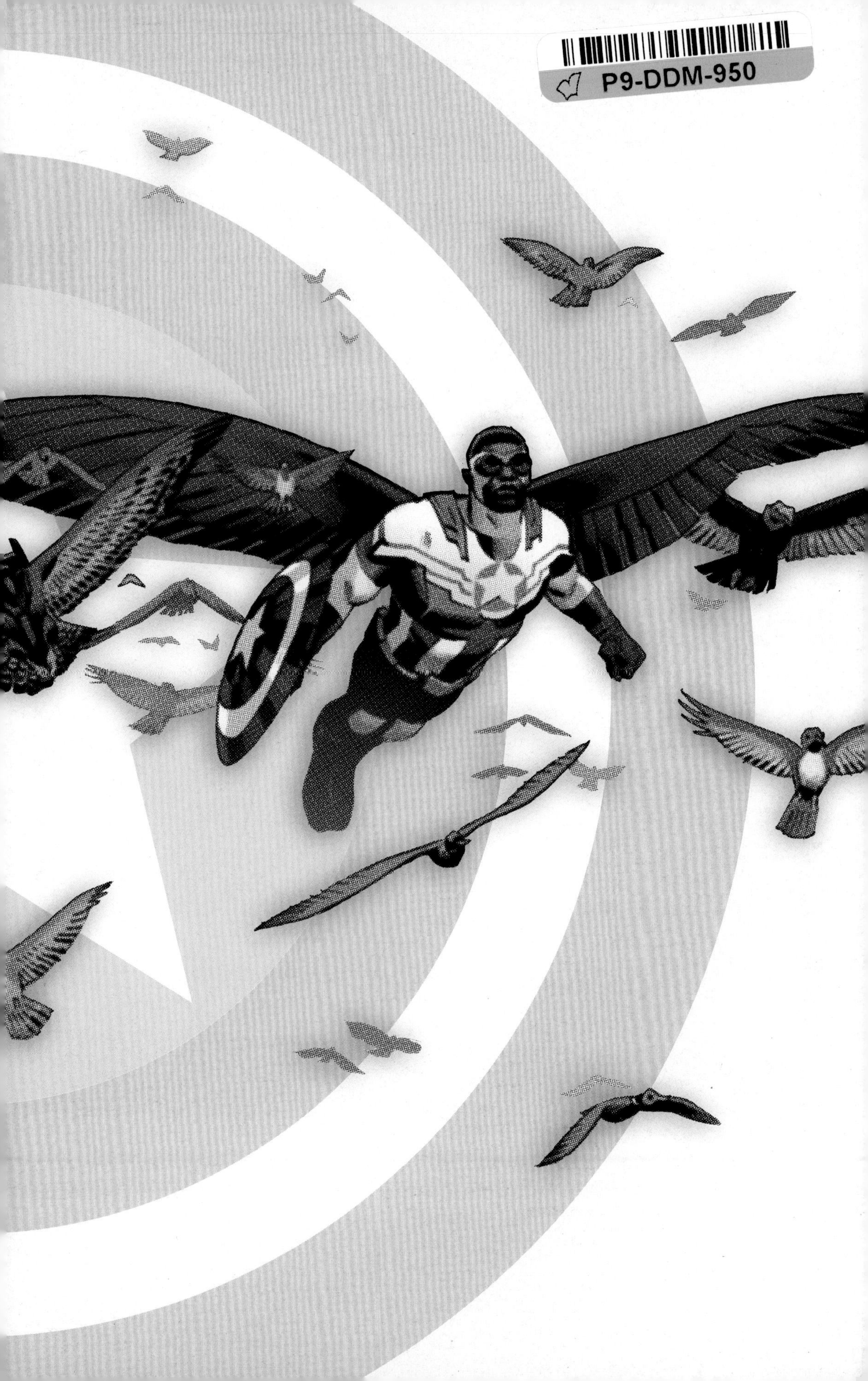

NOT MY CAPTAIN AMERICA

writer
NICK SPENCER

#1–3
artists **DANIEL ACUÑA**
with MIKE CHOI (#3)

#4–5
artist **PAUL RENAUD**
color artist ROMULO FAJARDO

#6
penciler **JOE BENNETT**
inker BELARDINO BRABO
color artist ROMULO FAJARDO

letterer **VC's JOE CARAMAGNA**
cover art **DANIEL ACUÑA** (#1–3, #5)
PAUL RENAUD (#4)
OSCAR JIMÉNEZ (#6)

assistant editor **ALANNA SMITH**
editors **TOM BREVOORT** with **KATIE KUBERT**

Captain America created by Joe Simon & Jack Kirby

collection editor SARAH BRUNSTAD
associate manager, digital assets JOE HOCHSTEIN
associate managing editor ALEX STARBUCK
editors, special projects JENNIFER GRÜNWALD & MARK D. BEAZLEY
vp, production & special projects JEFF YOUNGQUIST
book design ADAM DEL RE

svp print, sales & marketing DAVID GABRIEL
editor in chief AXEL ALONSO
chief creative officer JOE QUESADA
publisher DAN BUCKLEY
executive producer ALAN FINE

CAPTAIN AMERICA: SAM WILSON — NOT MY CAPTAIN AMERICA. Contains material originally published in magazine form as CAPTAIN AMERICA: SAM WILSON #1-6. First printing 2016. ISBN# 978-0-7851-9640-2. Published by MARVEL WORLDWIDE, INC., a subsidiary of MARVEL ENTERTAINMENT, LLC. OFFICE OF PUBLICATION: 135 West 50th Street, New York, NY 10020. Copyright © 2016 MARVEL No similarity between any of the names, characters, persons, and/or institutions in this magazine with those of any living or dead person or institution is intended, and any such similarity which may exist is purely coincidental. **Printed in Canada.** ALAN FINE, President, Marvel Entertainment; DAN BUCKLEY, President, TV, Publishing & Brand Management; JOE QUESADA, Chief Creative Officer; TOM BREVOORT, SVP of Publishing; DAVID BOGART, SVP of Business Affairs & Operations, Publishing & Partnership; C.B. CEBULSKI, VP of Brand Management & Development, Asia; DAVID GABRIEL, SVP of Sales & Marketing, Publishing; JEFF YOUNGQUIST, VP of Production & Special Projects; DAN CARR, Executive Director of Publishing Technology; ALEX MORALES, Director of Publishing Operations; SUSAN CRESPI, Production Manager; STAN LEE, Chairman Emeritus. For information regarding advertising in Marvel Comics or on Marvel.com, please contact Vit DeBellis, Integrated Sales Manager, at vdebellis@marvel.com. For Marvel subscription inquiries, please call 888-511-5480. **Manufactured between 2/26/2016 and 4/4/2016 by SOLISCO PRINTERS, SCOTT, QC, CANADA.**

10 9 8 7 6 5 4 3 2 1

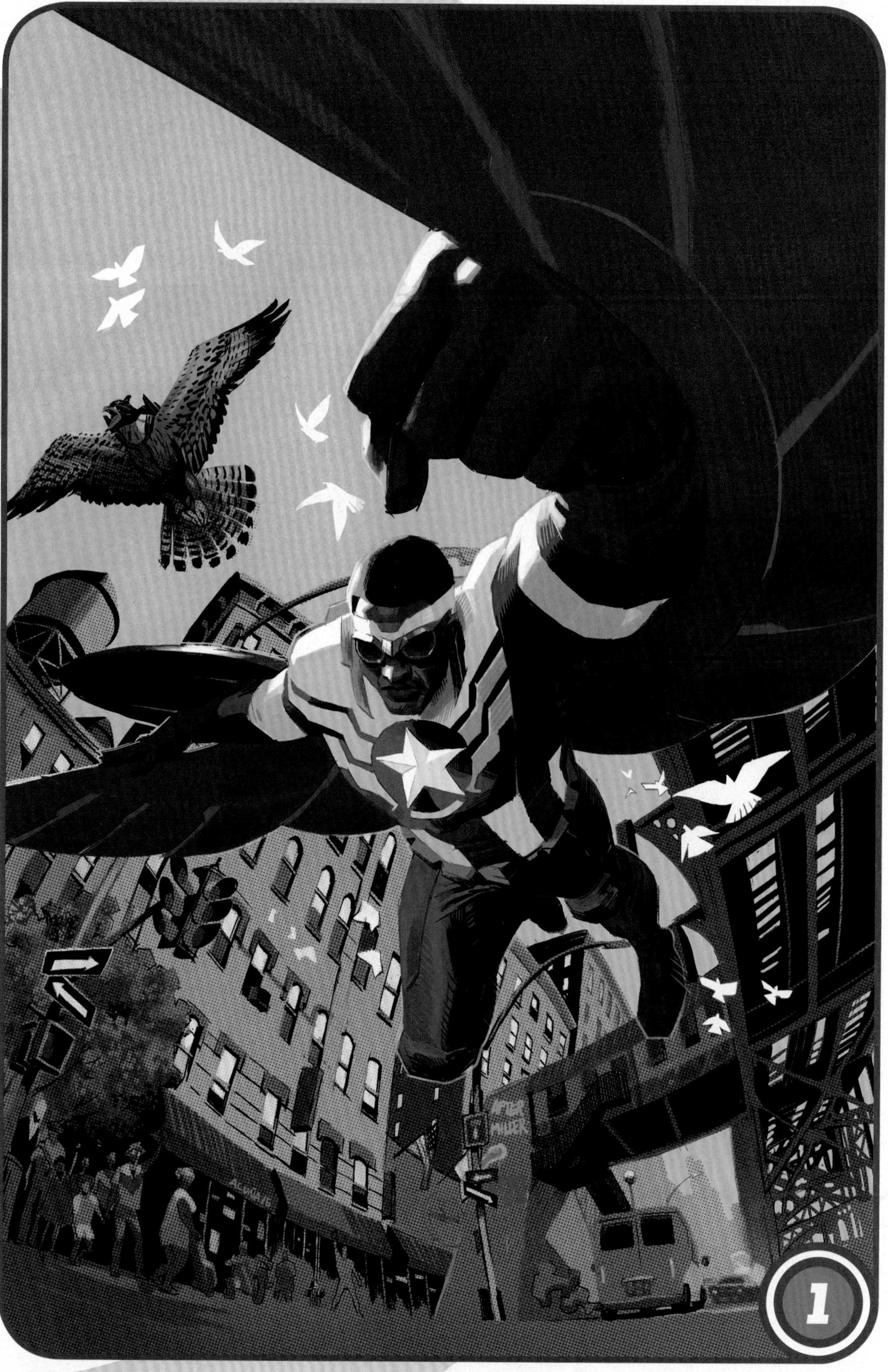
1

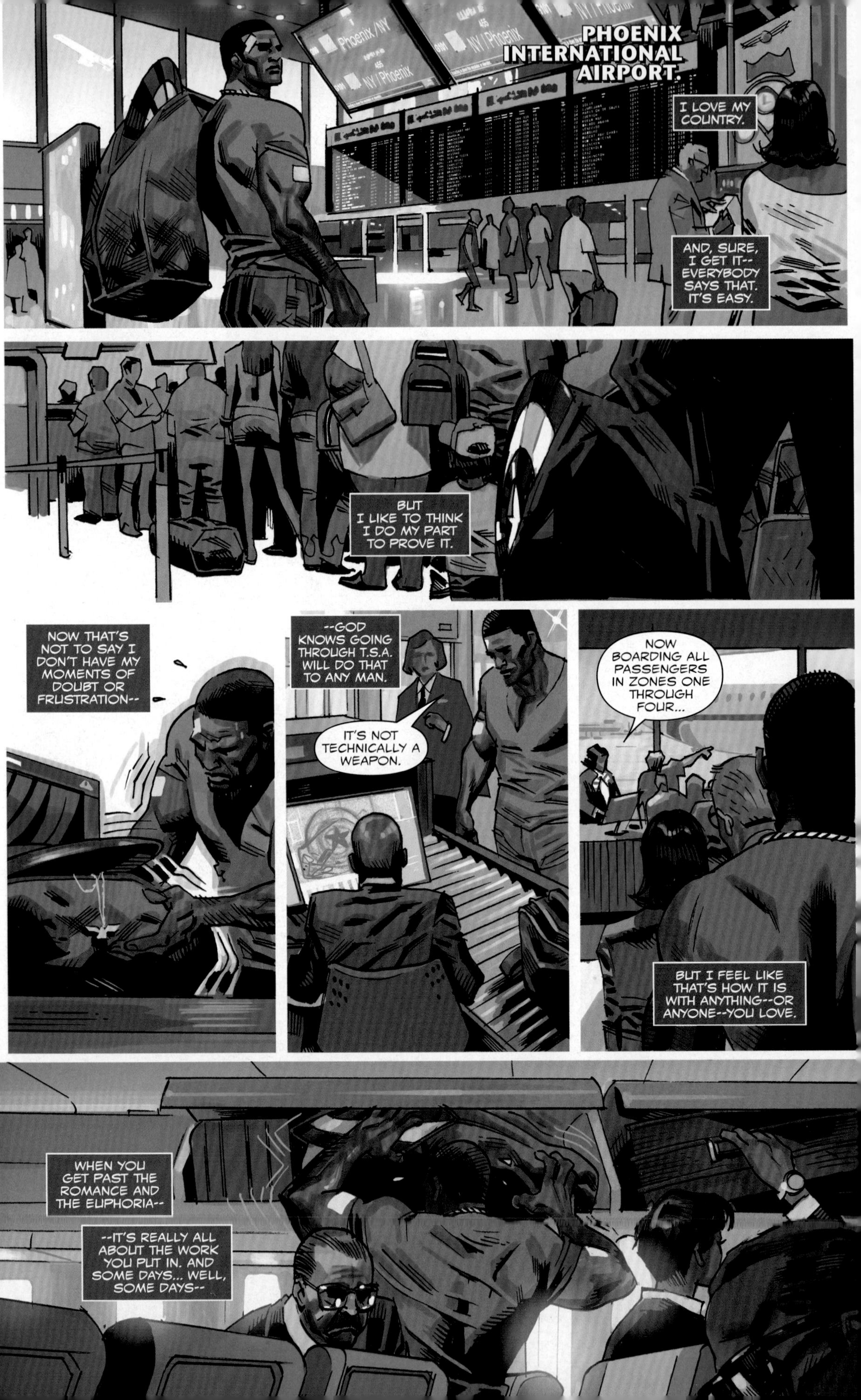

PHOENIX INTERNATIONAL AIRPORT.
I LOVE MY COUNTRY.
AND, SURE, I GET IT-- EVERYBODY SAYS THAT. IT'S EASY.
BUT I LIKE TO THINK I DO MY PART TO PROVE IT.
NOW THAT'S NOT TO SAY I DON'T HAVE MY MOMENTS OF DOUBT OR FRUSTRATION--
--GOD KNOWS GOING THROUGH T.S.A. WILL DO THAT TO ANY MAN.
IT'S NOT TECHNICALLY A WEAPON.
NOW BOARDING ALL PASSENGERS IN ZONES ONE THROUGH FOUR...
BUT I FEEL LIKE THAT'S HOW IT IS WITH ANYTHING--OR ANYONE--YOU LOVE.
WHEN YOU GET PAST THE ROMANCE AND THE EUPHORIA--
--IT'S REALLY ALL ABOUT THE WORK YOU PUT IN. AND SOME DAYS... WELL, SOME DAYS--

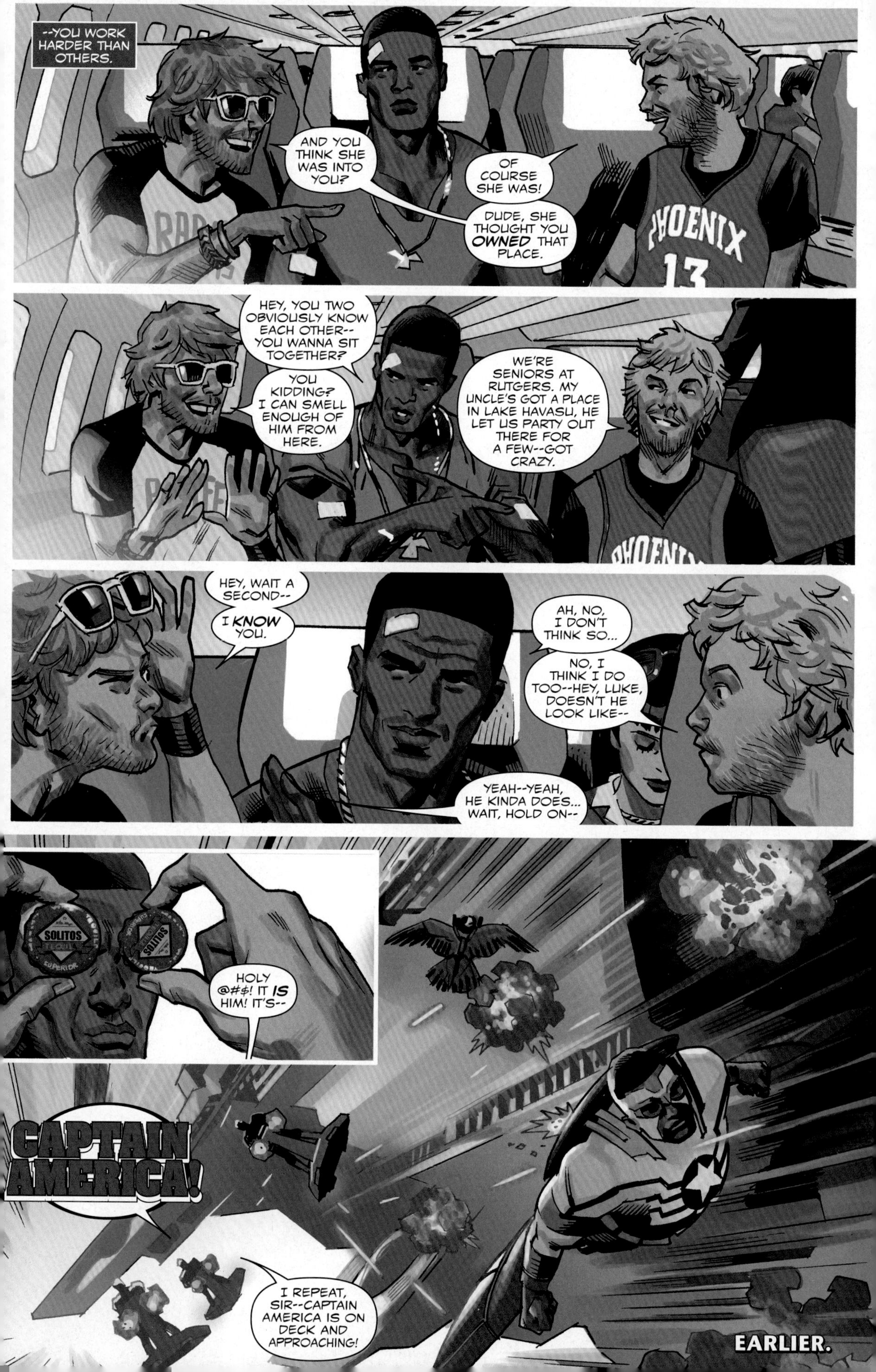
--YOU WORK HARDER THAN OTHERS.
AND YOU THINK SHE WAS INTO YOU?
OF COURSE SHE WAS!
DUDE, SHE THOUGHT YOU OWNED THAT PLACE.
PHOENIX 13
HEY, YOU TWO OBVIOUSLY KNOW EACH OTHER-- YOU WANNA SIT TOGETHER?
YOU KIDDING? I CAN SMELL ENOUGH OF HIM FROM HERE.
WE'RE SENIORS AT RUTGERS. MY UNCLE'S GOT A PLACE IN LAKE HAVASU, HE LET US PARTY OUT THERE FOR A FEW--GOT CRAZY.
HEY, WAIT A SECOND--
I KNOW YOU.
AH, NO, I DON'T THINK SO...
NO, I THINK I DO TOO--HEY, LUKE, DOESN'T HE LOOK LIKE--
YEAH--YEAH, HE KINDA DOES... WAIT, HOLD ON--
SOLITOS
HOLY @#$! IT IS HIM! IT'S--
CAPTAIN AMERICA!
I REPEAT, SIR--CAPTAIN AMERICA IS ON DECK AND APPROACHING!
EARLIER.

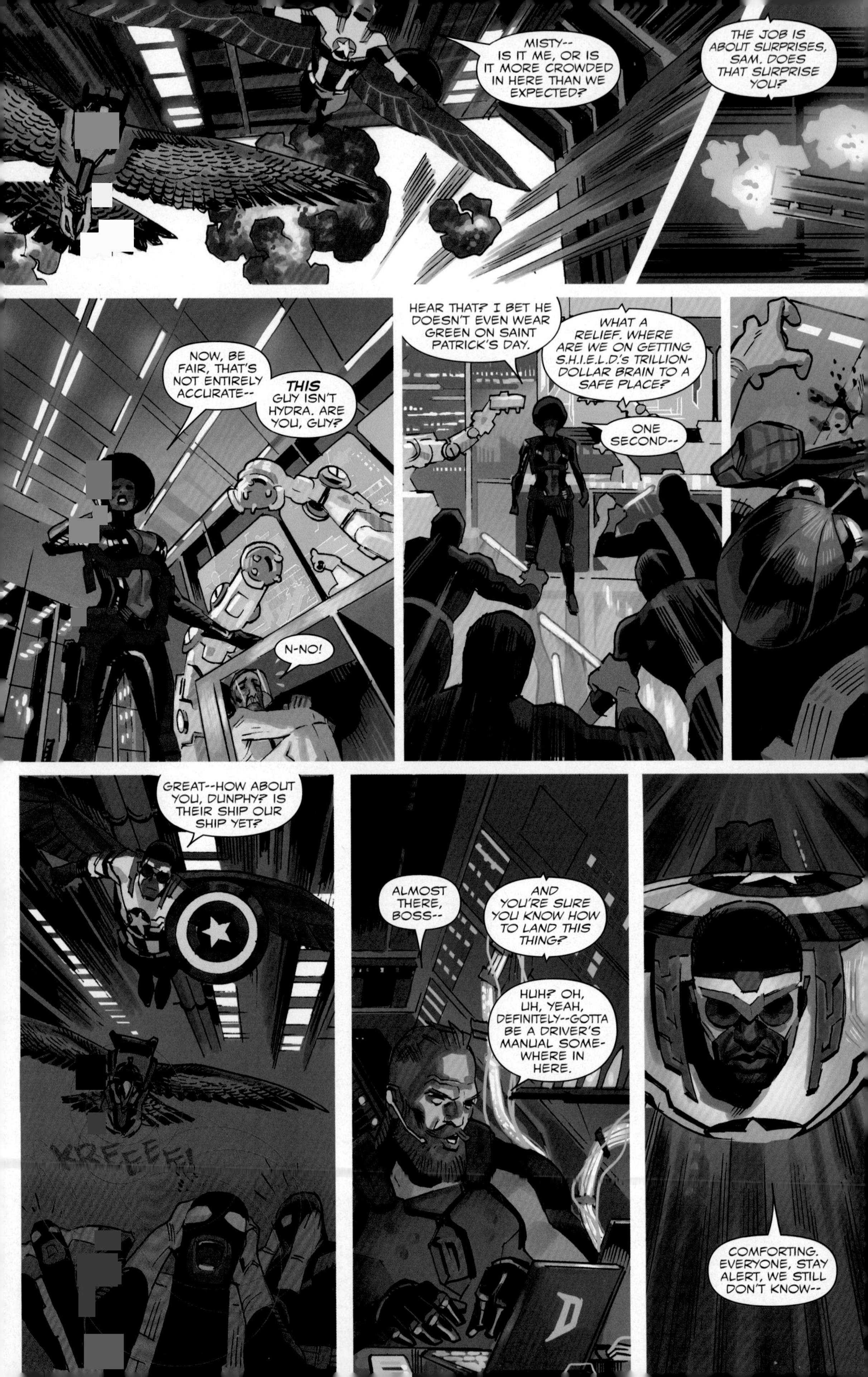
MISTY-- IS IT ME, OR IS IT MORE CROWDED IN HERE THAN WE EXPECTED?
THE JOB IS ABOUT SURPRISES, SAM. DOES THAT SURPRISE YOU?
NOW, BE FAIR, THAT'S NOT ENTIRELY ACCURATE--
THIS GUY ISN'T HYDRA. ARE YOU, GUY?
N-NO!
HEAR THAT? I BET HE DOESN'T EVEN WEAR GREEN ON SAINT PATRICK'S DAY.
WHAT A RELIEF. WHERE ARE WE ON GETTING S.H.I.E.L.D.'s TRILLION-DOLLAR BRAIN TO A SAFE PLACE?
ONE SECOND--
GREAT--HOW ABOUT YOU, DUNPHY? IS THEIR SHIP OUR SHIP YET?
ALMOST THERE, BOSS--
AND YOU'RE SURE YOU KNOW HOW TO LAND THIS THING?
HUH? OH, UH, YEAH, DEFINITELY--GOTTA BE A DRIVER'S MANUAL SOME-WHERE IN HERE.
COMFORTING. EVERYONE, STAY ALERT, WE STILL DON'T KNOW--

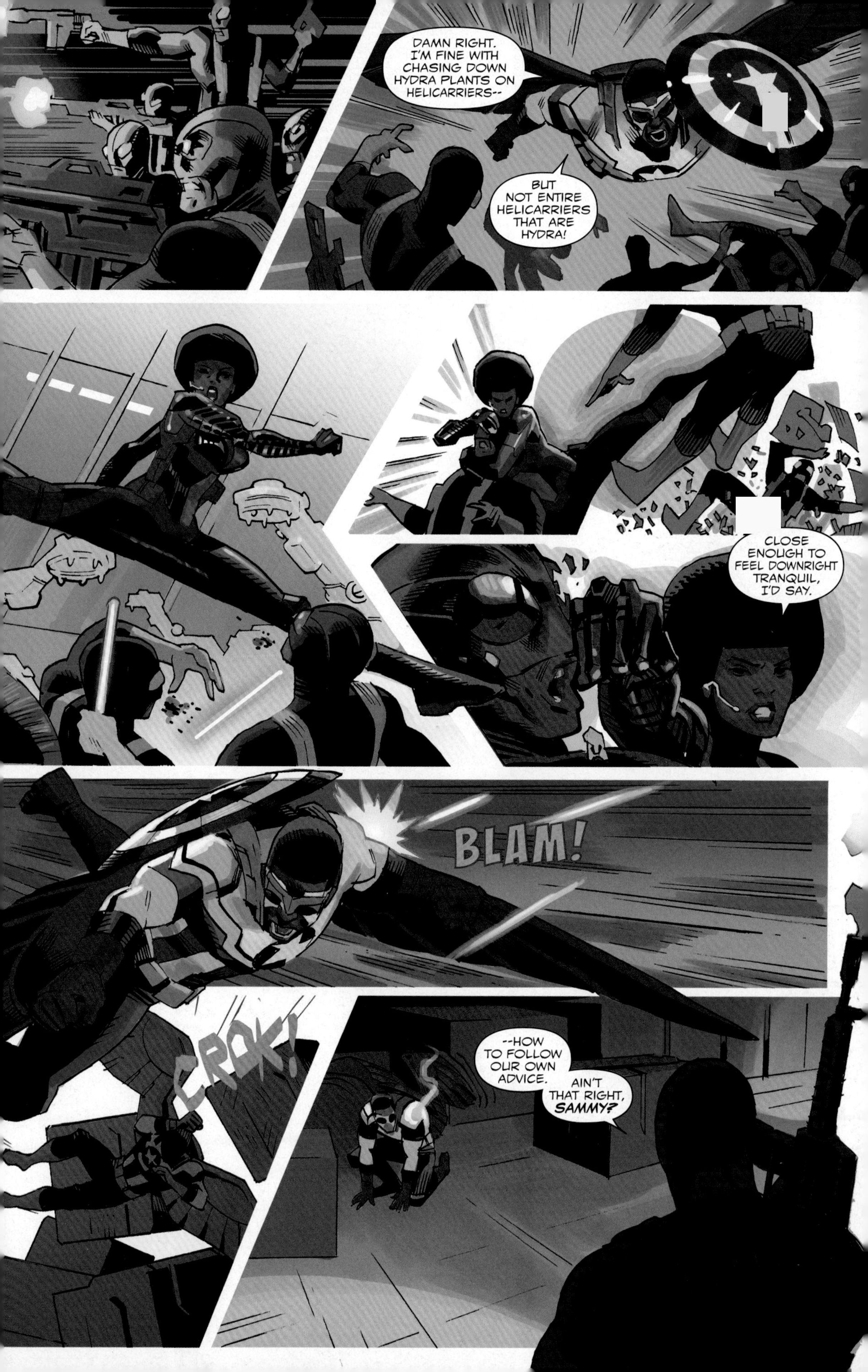
DAMN RIGHT. I'M FINE WITH CHASING DOWN HYDRA PLANTS ON HELICARRIERS--
BUT NOT ENTIRE HELICARRIERS THAT ARE HYDRA!
CLOSE ENOUGH TO FEEL DOWNRIGHT TRANQUIL, I'D SAY.
BLAM!
CRAK!
--HOW TO FOLLOW OUR OWN ADVICE.
AIN'T THAT RIGHT, SAMMY?

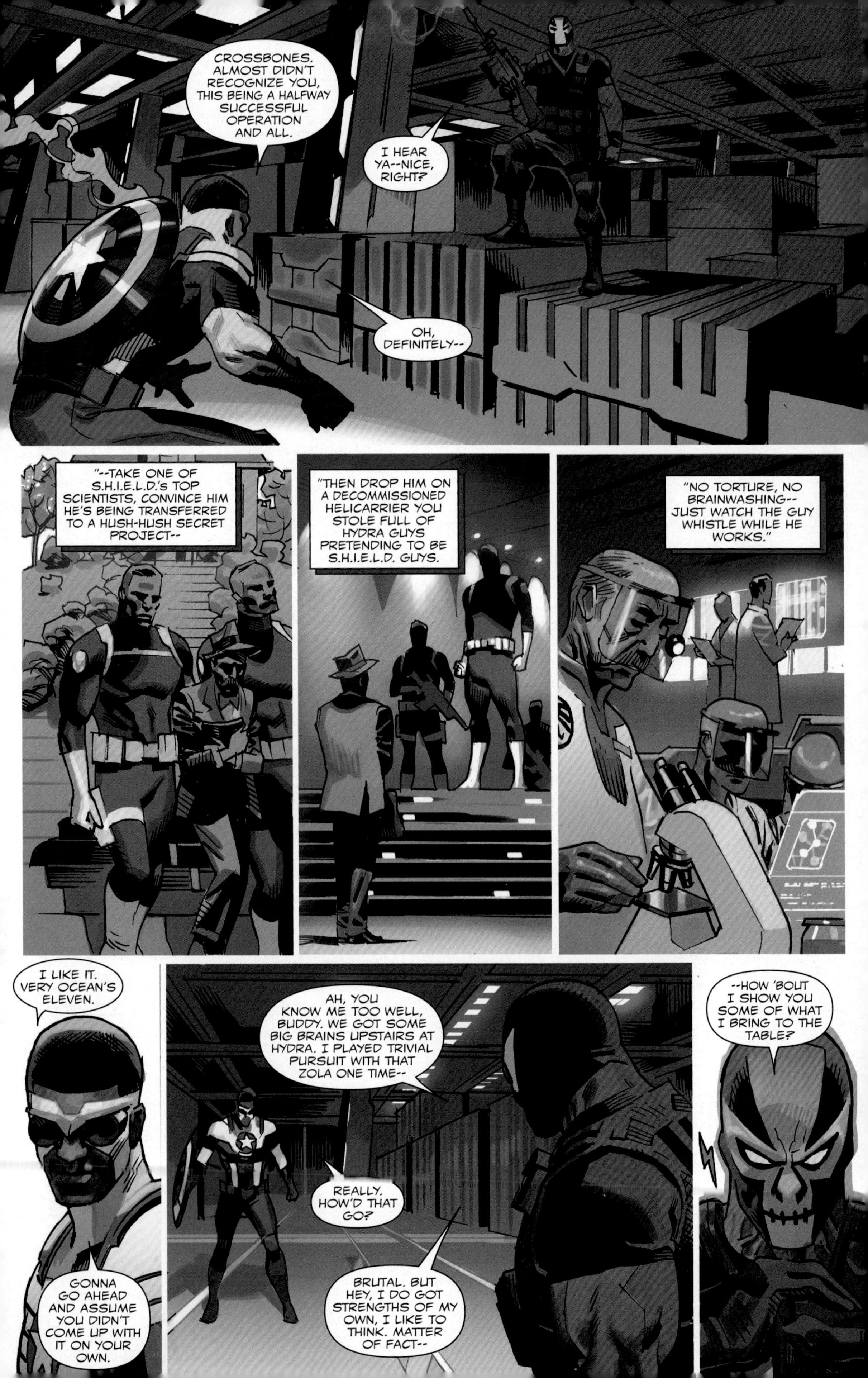
CROSSBONES. ALMOST DIDN'T RECOGNIZE YOU, THIS BEING A HALFWAY SUCCESSFUL OPERATION AND ALL.
I HEAR YA--NICE, RIGHT?
OH, DEFINITELY--
"--TAKE ONE OF S.H.I.E.L.D.'s TOP SCIENTISTS, CONVINCE HIM HE'S BEING TRANSFERRED TO A HUSH-HUSH SECRET PROJECT--
"THEN DROP HIM ON A DECOMMISSIONED HELICARRIER YOU STOLE FULL OF HYDRA GUYS PRETENDING TO BE S.H.I.E.L.D. GUYS.
"NO TORTURE, NO BRAINWASHING--JUST WATCH THE GUY WHISTLE WHILE HE WORKS."
I LIKE IT. VERY OCEAN'S ELEVEN.
GONNA GO AHEAD AND ASSUME YOU DIDN'T COME UP WITH IT ON YOUR OWN.
AH, YOU KNOW ME TOO WELL, BUDDY. WE GOT SOME BIG BRAINS UPSTAIRS AT HYDRA. I PLAYED TRIVIAL PURSUIT WITH THAT ZOLA ONE TIME--
REALLY. HOW'D THAT GO?
BRUTAL. BUT HEY, I DO GOT STRENGTHS OF MY OWN, I LIKE TO THINK. MATTER OF FACT--
--HOW 'BOUT I SHOW YOU SOME OF WHAT I BRING TO THE TABLE?

"HOLD UP, I DON'T GET THIS--"

--CAPTAIN AMERICA FLIES **COMMERCIAL?**

FORGET THAT--CAPTAIN AMERICA FLIES **COACH.**

NOT EVEN A WINDOW SEAT. DUDE, WHERE'S YOUR QUINJET?

CLEARLY YOU'VE NEVER SEEN THE FUEL BILL ON ONE OF THOSE THINGS.

I THOUGHT YOU COULD FLY--

THAT'S RIGHT! WITH THE WINGS! *KAA! KAA!*

PHOENIX TO NEW YORK IS A LITTLE FAR FOR THAT KIND OF TRAVEL.

EXCUSE ME, GENTLEMEN--

--WOULD YOU LIKE ANYTHING? WATER? SNACKS?

LADY, DO YOU KNOW WHO THIS IS?!

FELLAS, IT'S ALL RIGHT--

S'CAPTAIN AMERICA! THE NEW ONE!

HMMPH.

WHICH IS A RESPONSE YOU MIGHT THINK I DON'T GET TOO OFTEN. BUT THEN--

OOF!

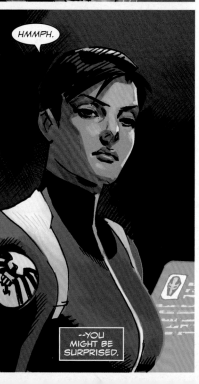

HMMPH.

--YOU MIGHT BE SURPRISED.

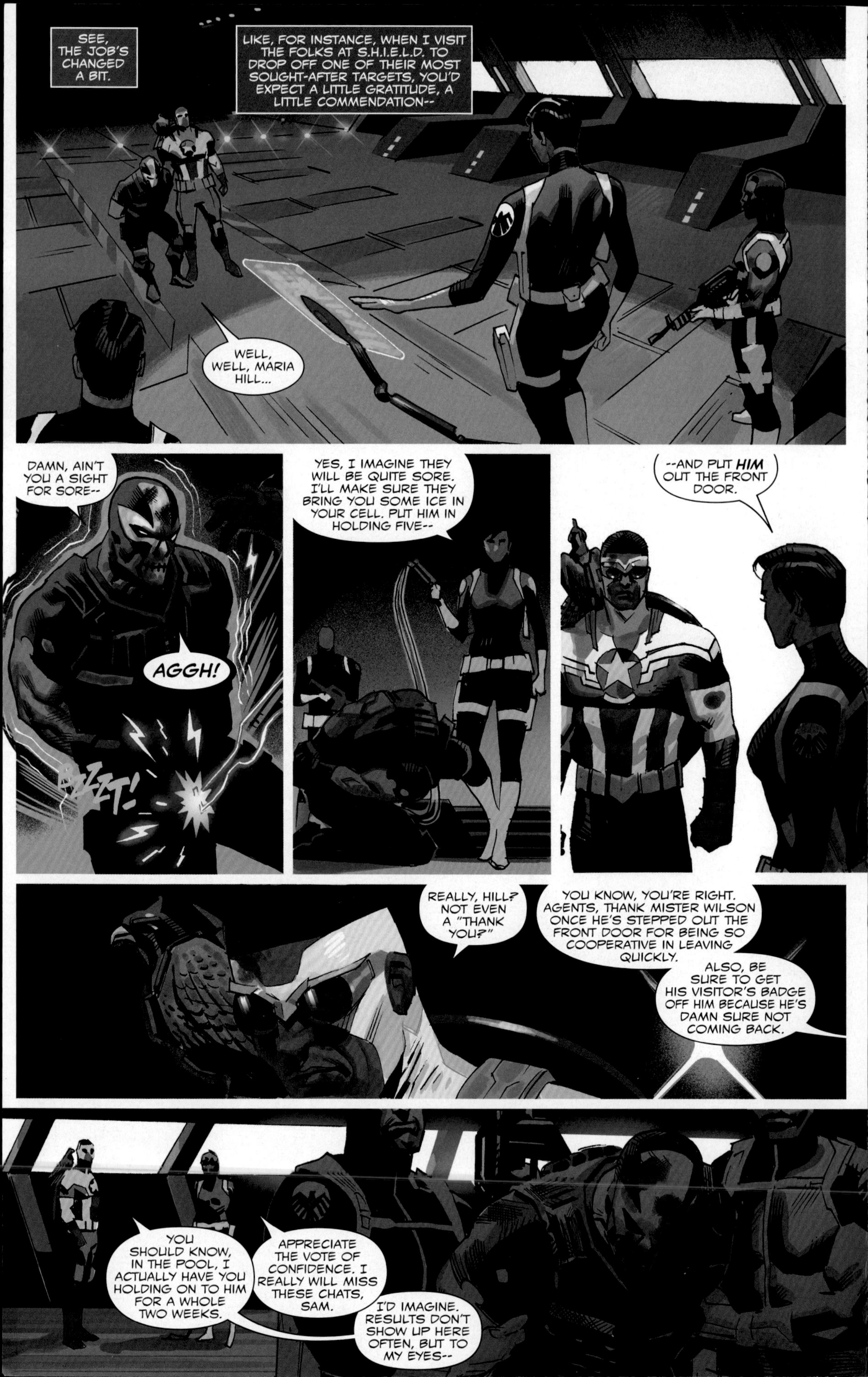
SEE, THE JOB'S CHANGED A BIT.
LIKE, FOR INSTANCE, WHEN I VISIT THE FOLKS AT S.H.I.E.L.D. TO DROP OFF ONE OF THEIR MOST SOUGHT-AFTER TARGETS, YOU'D EXPECT A LITTLE GRATITUDE, A LITTLE COMMENDATION--
WELL, WELL, MARIA HILL...
DAMN, AIN'T YOU A SIGHT FOR SORE--
AGGH!
YES, I IMAGINE THEY WILL BE QUITE SORE. I'LL MAKE SURE THEY BRING YOU SOME ICE IN YOUR CELL. PUT HIM IN HOLDING FIVE--
--AND PUT *HIM* OUT THE FRONT DOOR.
REALLY, HILL? NOT EVEN A "THANK YOU?"
YOU KNOW, YOU'RE RIGHT. AGENTS, THANK MISTER WILSON ONCE HE'S STEPPED OUT THE FRONT DOOR FOR BEING SO COOPERATIVE IN LEAVING QUICKLY.
ALSO, BE SURE TO GET HIS VISITOR'S BADGE OFF HIM BECAUSE HE'S DAMN SURE NOT COMING BACK.
YOU SHOULD KNOW, IN THE POOL, I ACTUALLY HAVE YOU HOLDING ON TO HIM FOR A WHOLE TWO WEEKS.
APPRECIATE THE VOTE OF CONFIDENCE. I REALLY WILL MISS THESE CHATS, SAM.
I'D IMAGINE. RESULTS DON'T SHOW UP HERE OFTEN, BUT TO MY EYES--

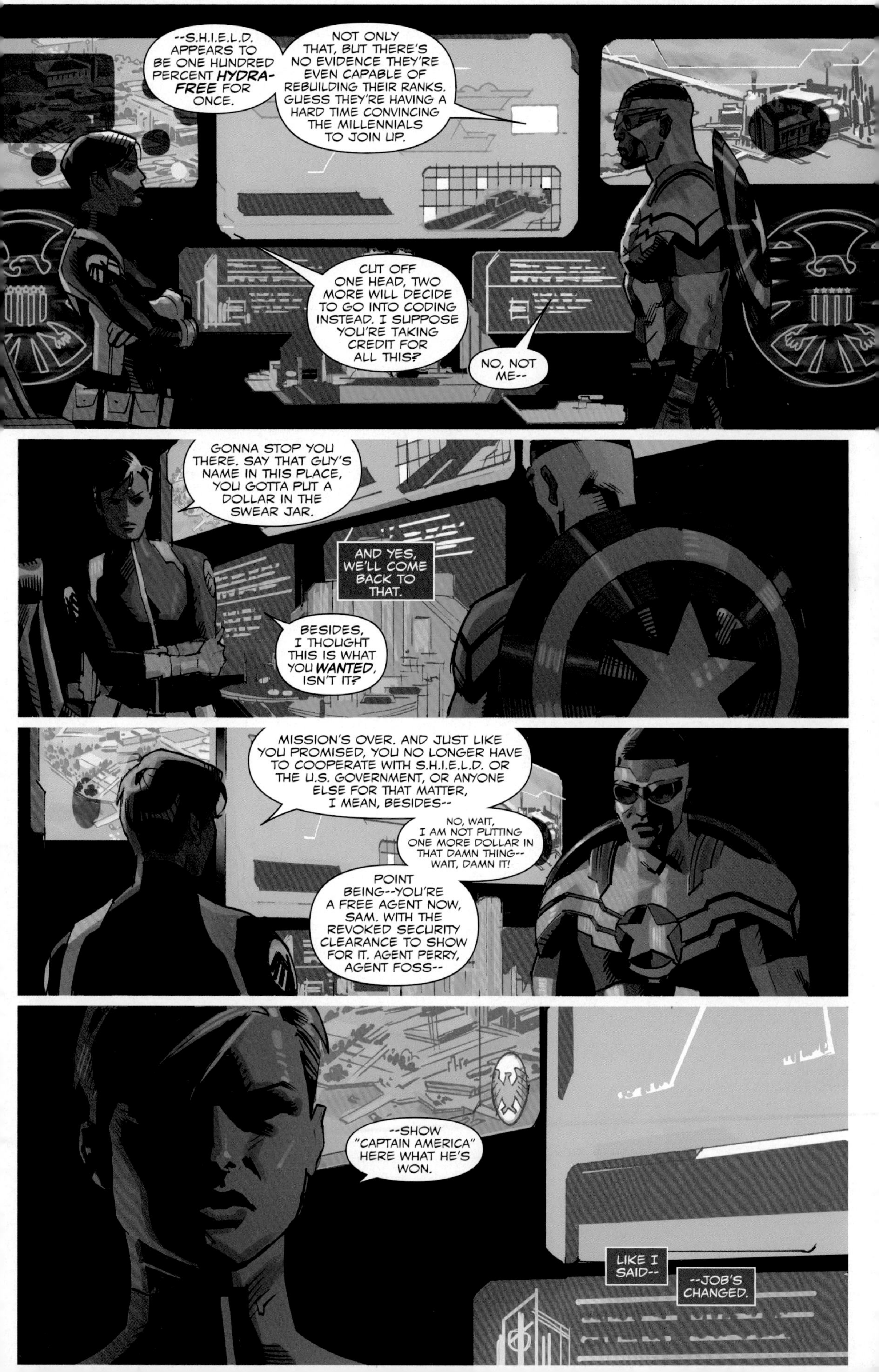

--S.H.I.E.L.D. APPEARS TO BE ONE HUNDRED PERCENT HYDRA-FREE FOR ONCE.
NOT ONLY THAT, BUT THERE'S NO EVIDENCE THEY'RE EVEN CAPABLE OF REBUILDING THEIR RANKS. GUESS THEY'RE HAVING A HARD TIME CONVINCING THE MILLENNIALS TO JOIN UP.
CUT OFF ONE HEAD, TWO MORE WILL DECIDE TO GO INTO CODING INSTEAD. I SUPPOSE YOU'RE TAKING CREDIT FOR ALL THIS?
NO, NOT ME--
GONNA STOP YOU THERE. SAY THAT GUY'S NAME IN THIS PLACE, YOU GOTTA PUT A DOLLAR IN THE SWEAR JAR.
AND YES, WE'LL COME BACK TO THAT.
BESIDES, I THOUGHT THIS IS WHAT YOU WANTED, ISN'T IT?
MISSION'S OVER. AND JUST LIKE YOU PROMISED, YOU NO LONGER HAVE TO COOPERATE WITH S.H.I.E.L.D. OR THE U.S. GOVERNMENT, OR ANYONE ELSE FOR THAT MATTER, I MEAN, BESIDES--
NO, WAIT, I AM NOT PUTTING ONE MORE DOLLAR IN THAT DAMN THING-- WAIT, DAMN IT!
POINT BEING--YOU'RE A FREE AGENT NOW, SAM. WITH THE REVOKED SECURITY CLEARANCE TO SHOW FOR IT. AGENT PERRY, AGENT FOSS--
--SHOW "CAPTAIN AMERICA" HERE WHAT HE'S WON.
LIKE I SAID--
--JOB'S CHANGED.

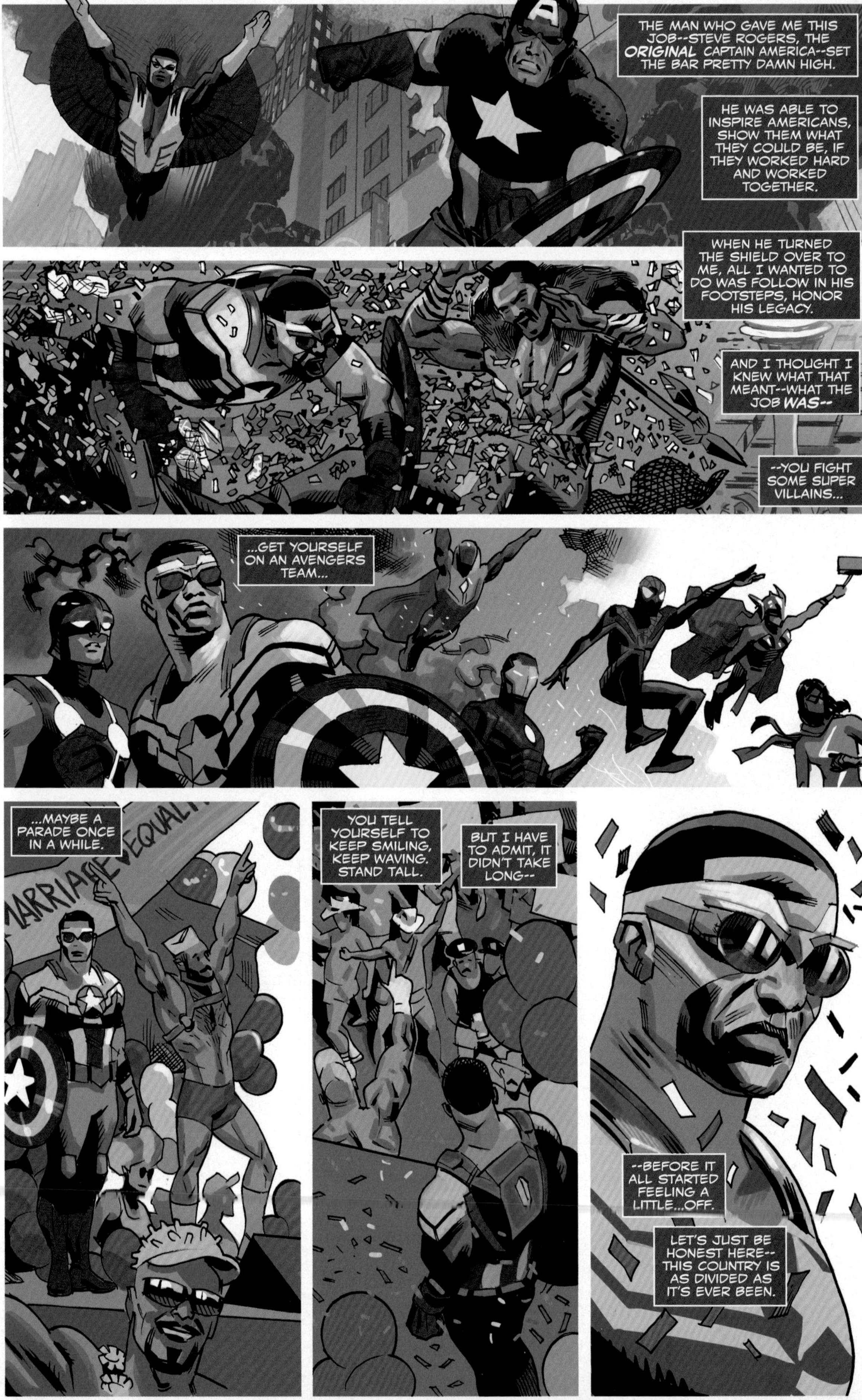
THE MAN WHO GAVE ME THIS JOB--STEVE ROGERS, THE ORIGINAL CAPTAIN AMERICA--SET THE BAR PRETTY DAMN HIGH.
HE WAS ABLE TO INSPIRE AMERICANS, SHOW THEM WHAT THEY COULD BE, IF THEY WORKED HARD AND WORKED TOGETHER.
WHEN HE TURNED THE SHIELD OVER TO ME, ALL I WANTED TO DO WAS FOLLOW IN HIS FOOTSTEPS, HONOR HIS LEGACY.
AND I THOUGHT I KNEW WHAT THAT MEANT--WHAT THE JOB WAS--
--YOU FIGHT SOME SUPER VILLAINS...
...GET YOURSELF ON AN AVENGERS TEAM...
...MAYBE A PARADE ONCE IN A WHILE.
YOU TELL YOURSELF TO KEEP SMILING, KEEP WAVING. STAND TALL.
BUT I HAVE TO ADMIT, IT DIDN'T TAKE LONG--
--BEFORE IT ALL STARTED FEELING A LITTLE...OFF.
LET'S JUST BE HONEST HERE--THIS COUNTRY IS AS DIVIDED AS IT'S EVER BEEN.

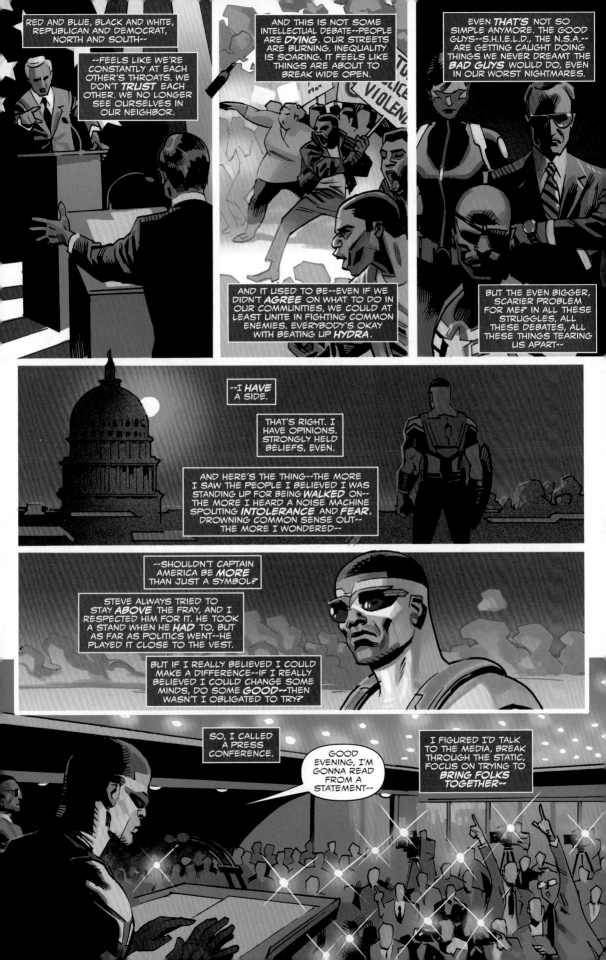

RED AND BLUE, BLACK AND WHITE, REPUBLICAN AND DEMOCRAT, NORTH AND SOUTH--

--FEELS LIKE WE'RE CONSTANTLY AT EACH OTHER'S THROATS. WE DON'T *TRUST* EACH OTHER. WE NO LONGER SEE OURSELVES IN OUR NEIGHBOR.

AND THIS IS NOT SOME INTELLECTUAL DEBATE--PEOPLE ARE *DYING*. OUR STREETS ARE BURNING. INEQUALITY IS SOARING. IT FEELS LIKE THINGS ARE ABOUT TO BREAK WIDE OPEN.

AND IT USED TO BE--EVEN IF WE DIDN'T *AGREE* ON WHAT TO DO IN OUR COMMUNITIES, WE COULD AT LEAST UNITE IN FIGHTING COMMON ENEMIES. EVERYBODY'S OKAY WITH BEATING UP *HYDRA*.

EVEN *THAT'S* NOT SO SIMPLE ANYMORE. THE GOOD GUYS--S.H.I.E.L.D., THE N.S.A.-- ARE GETTING CAUGHT DOING THINGS WE NEVER DREAMT THE *BAD GUYS* WOULD DO, EVEN IN OUR WORST NIGHTMARES.

BUT THE EVEN BIGGER, SCARIER PROBLEM FOR ME? IN ALL THESE STRUGGLES, ALL THESE DEBATES, ALL THESE THINGS TEARING US APART--

--I *HAVE* A SIDE.

THAT'S RIGHT. I HAVE OPINIONS. STRONGLY HELD BELIEFS, EVEN.

AND HERE'S THE THING--THE MORE I SAW THE PEOPLE I BELIEVED I WAS STANDING UP FOR BEING *WALKED* ON-- THE MORE I HEARD A NOISE MACHINE SPOUTING *INTOLERANCE* AND *FEAR*, DROWNING COMMON SENSE OUT-- THE MORE I WONDERED--

--SHOULDN'T CAPTAIN AMERICA BE *MORE* THAN JUST A SYMBOL?

STEVE ALWAYS TRIED TO STAY *ABOVE* THE FRAY, AND I RESPECTED HIM FOR IT. HE TOOK A STAND WHEN HE *HAD* TO, BUT AS FAR AS POLITICS WENT--HE PLAYED IT CLOSE TO THE VEST.

BUT IF I REALLY BELIEVED I COULD MAKE A DIFFERENCE--IF I REALLY BELIEVED I COULD CHANGE SOME MINDS, DO SOME *GOOD*--THEN WASN'T I OBLIGATED TO TRY?

SO, I CALLED A PRESS CONFERENCE.

GOOD EVENING, I'M GONNA READ FROM A STATEMENT--

I FIGURED I'D TALK TO THE MEDIA, BREAK THROUGH THE STATIC, FOCUS ON TRYING TO *BRING FOLKS TOGETHER*--

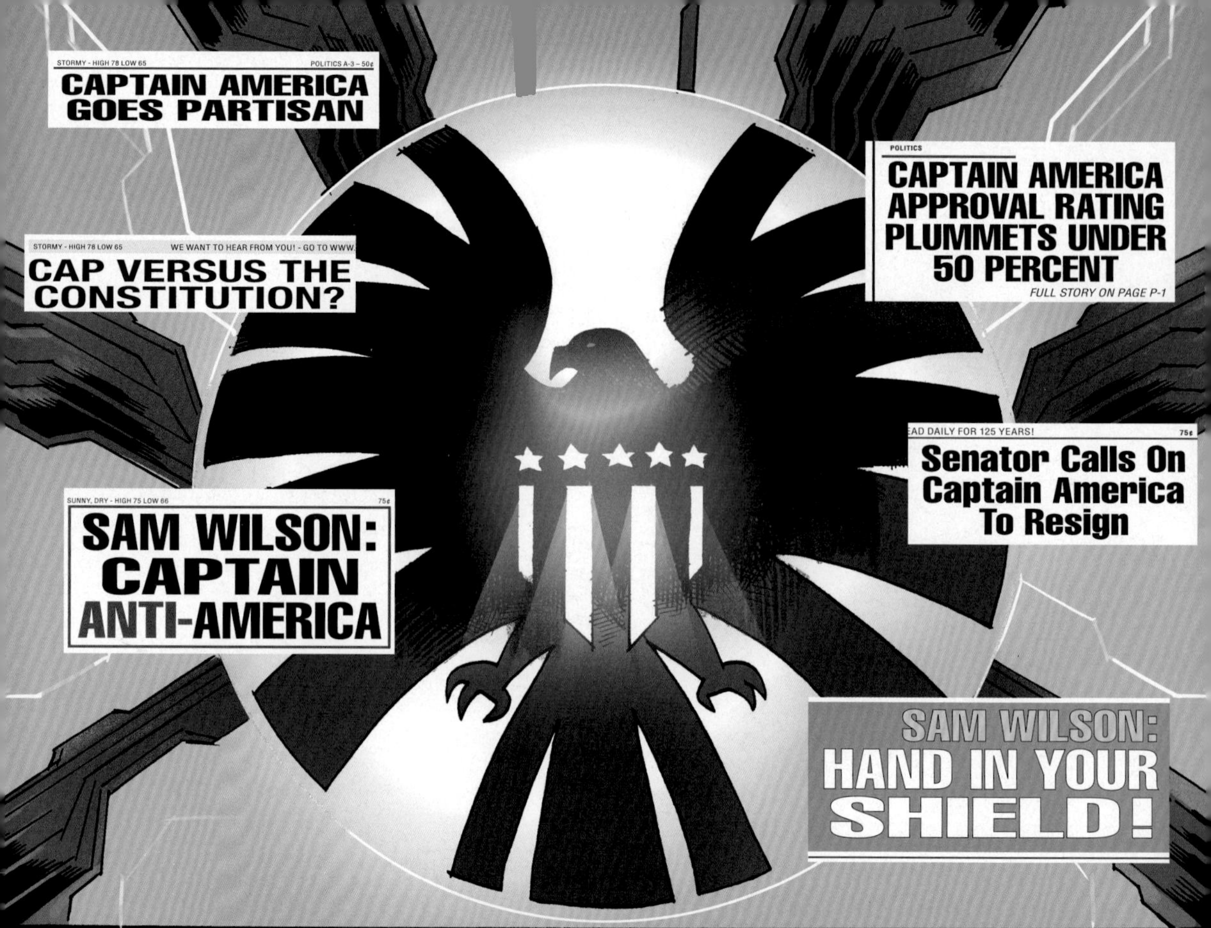
STORMY - HIGH 78 LOW 65 POLITICS A-3 – 50¢
CAPTAIN AMERICA GOES PARTISAN
STORMY - HIGH 78 LOW 65 WE WANT TO HEAR FROM YOU! - GO TO WWW.
CAP VERSUS THE CONSTITUTION?
SUNNY, DRY - HIGH 75 LOW 66 75¢
SAM WILSON: CAPTAIN ANTI-AMERICA
POLITICS
CAPTAIN AMERICA APPROVAL RATING PLUMMETS UNDER 50 PERCENT
FULL STORY ON PAGE P-1
EAD DAILY FOR 125 YEARS! 75¢
Senator Calls On Captain America To Resign
SAM WILSON: HAND IN YOUR SHIELD!

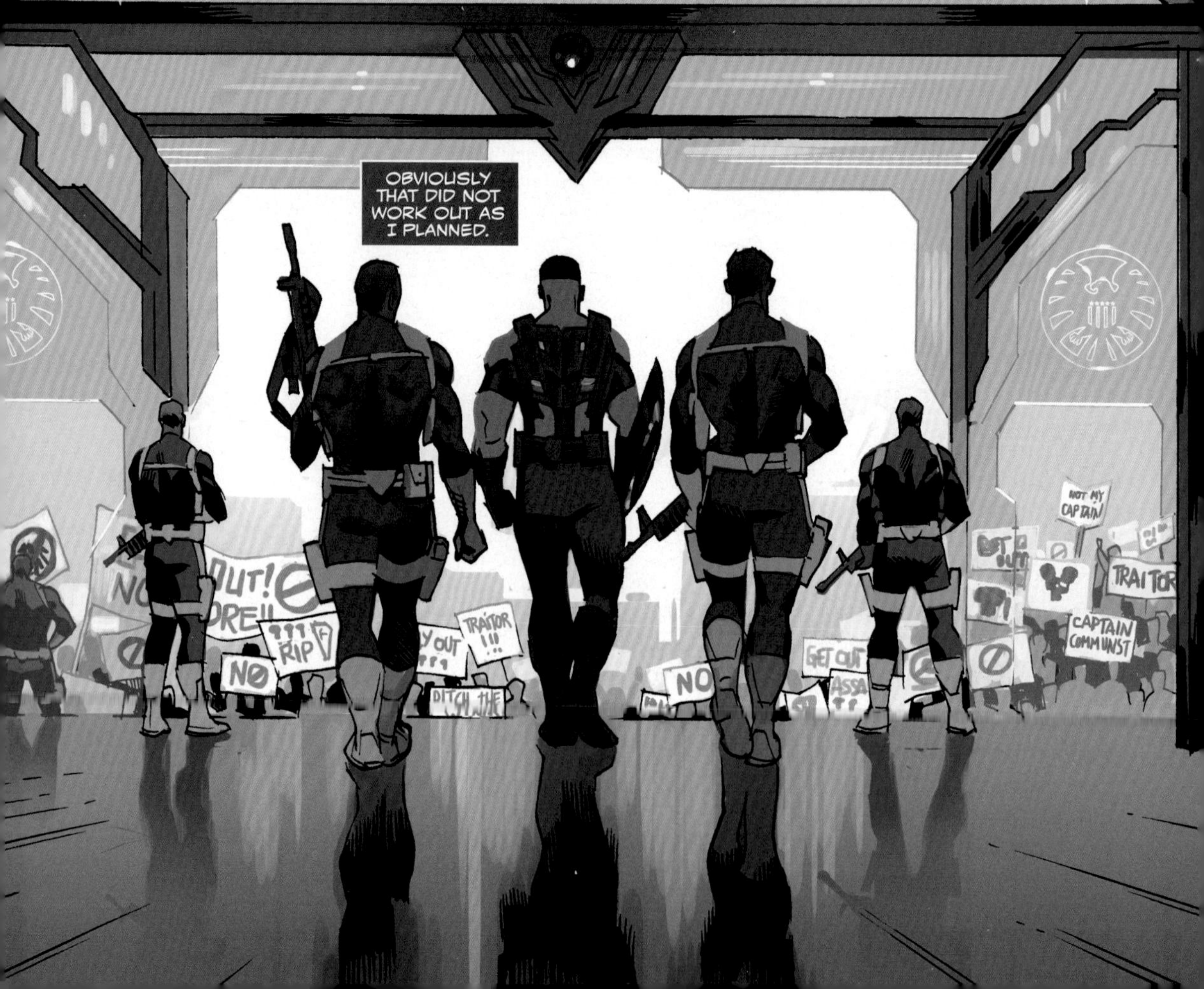
OBVIOUSLY THAT DID NOT WORK OUT AS I PLANNED.
NOT MY CAPTAIN
TRAITOR
CAPTAIN COMMUNST
TRAITOR !!!
GET OUT
NO

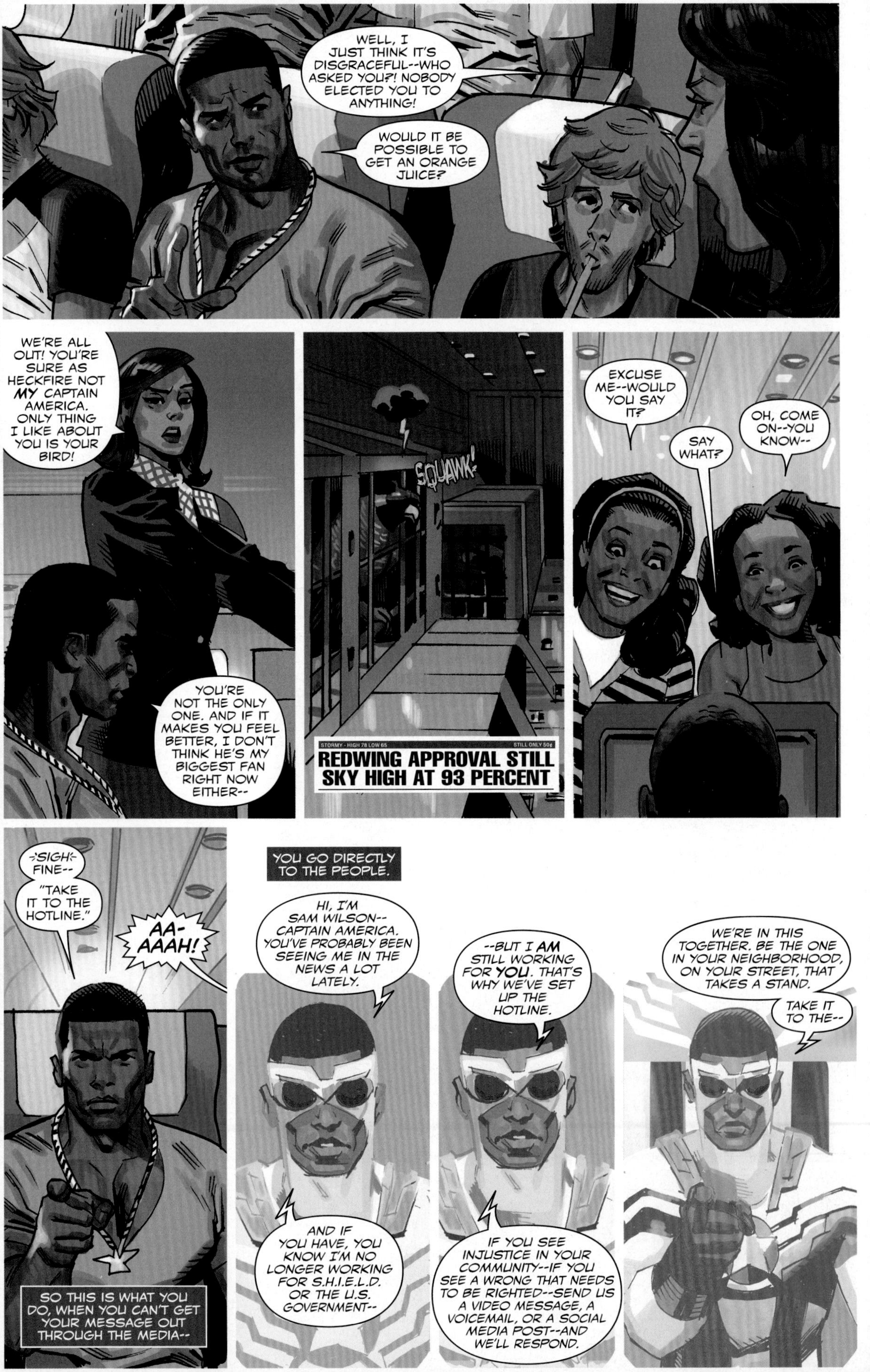
WELL, I JUST THINK IT'S DISGRACEFUL--WHO ASKED YOU?! NOBODY ELECTED YOU TO ANYTHING!
WOULD IT BE POSSIBLE TO GET AN ORANGE JUICE?
WE'RE ALL OUT! YOU'RE SURE AS HECKFIRE NOT MY CAPTAIN AMERICA. ONLY THING I LIKE ABOUT YOU IS YOUR BIRD!
YOU'RE NOT THE ONLY ONE. AND IF IT MAKES YOU FEEL BETTER, I DON'T THINK HE'S MY BIGGEST FAN RIGHT NOW EITHER--
SQUAWK!
STORMY - HIGH 78 LOW 65
STILL ONLY 50¢
REDWING APPROVAL STILL SKY HIGH AT 93 PERCENT
EXCUSE ME--WOULD YOU SAY IT?
SAY WHAT?
OH, COME ON--YOU KNOW--
-SIGH- FINE--
"TAKE IT TO THE HOTLINE."
AA-AAAH!
SO THIS IS WHAT YOU DO, WHEN YOU CAN'T GET YOUR MESSAGE OUT THROUGH THE MEDIA--
YOU GO DIRECTLY TO THE PEOPLE.
HI, I'M SAM WILSON--CAPTAIN AMERICA. YOU'VE PROBABLY BEEN SEEING ME IN THE NEWS A LOT LATELY.
AND IF YOU HAVE, YOU KNOW I'M NO LONGER WORKING FOR S.H.I.E.L.D. OR THE U.S. GOVERNMENT--
--BUT I AM STILL WORKING FOR YOU. THAT'S WHY WE'VE SET UP THE HOTLINE.
IF YOU SEE INJUSTICE IN YOUR COMMUNITY--IF YOU SEE A WRONG THAT NEEDS TO BE RIGHTED--SEND US A VIDEO MESSAGE, A VOICEMAIL, OR A SOCIAL MEDIA POST--AND WE'LL RESPOND.
WE'RE IN THIS TOGETHER. BE THE ONE IN YOUR NEIGHBORHOOD, ON YOUR STREET, THAT TAKES A STAND.
TAKE IT TO THE--

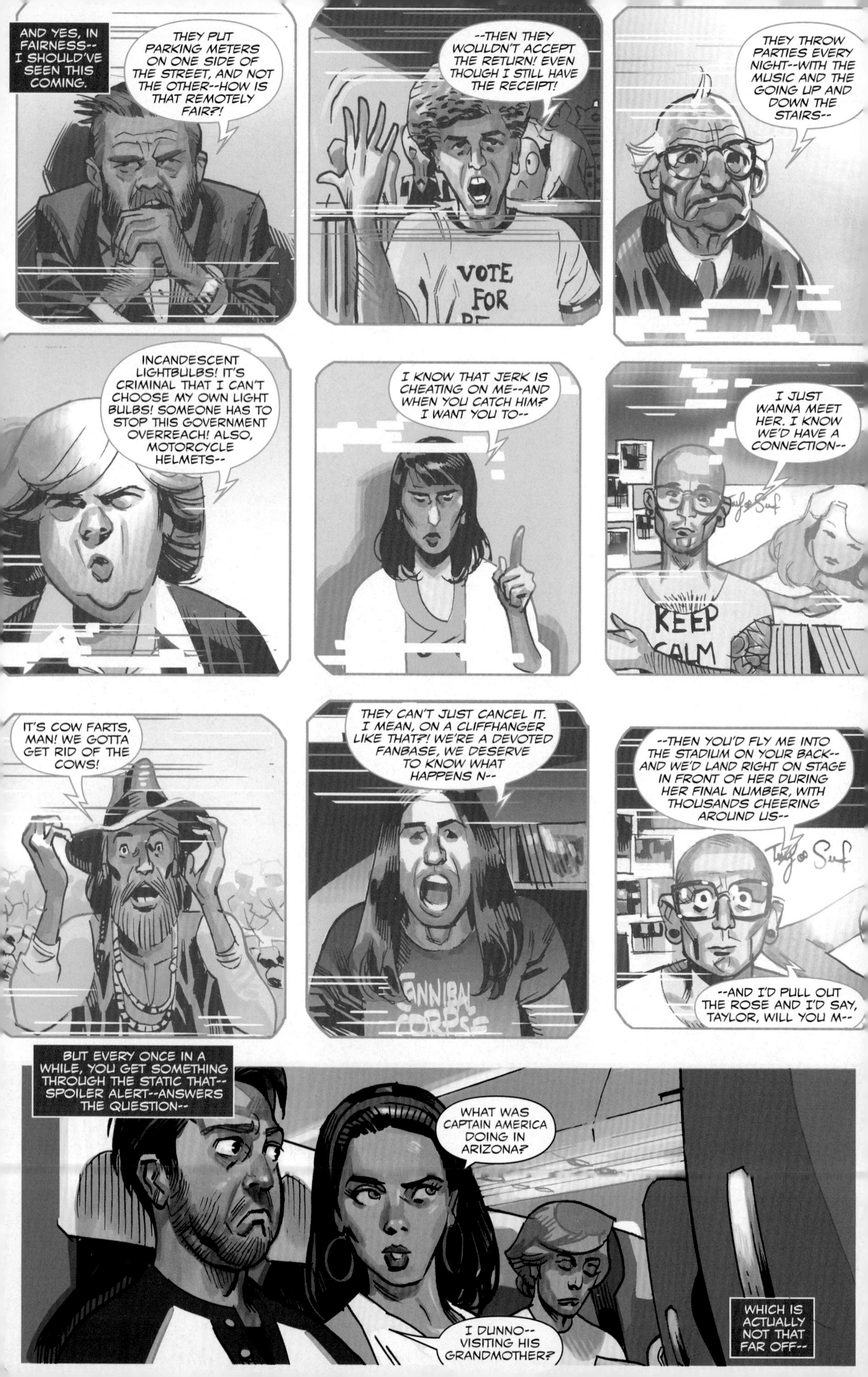

AND YES, IN FAIRNESS-- I SHOULD'VE SEEN THIS COMING.
THEY PUT PARKING METERS ON ONE SIDE OF THE STREET, AND NOT THE OTHER--HOW IS THAT REMOTELY FAIR?!
--THEN THEY WOULDN'T ACCEPT THE RETURN! EVEN THOUGH I STILL HAVE THE RECEIPT!
VOTE FOR
THEY THROW PARTIES EVERY NIGHT--WITH THE MUSIC AND THE GOING UP AND DOWN THE STAIRS--
INCANDESCENT LIGHTBULBS! IT'S CRIMINAL THAT I CAN'T CHOOSE MY OWN LIGHT BULBS! SOMEONE HAS TO STOP THIS GOVERNMENT OVERREACH! ALSO, MOTORCYCLE HELMETS--
I KNOW THAT JERK IS CHEATING ON ME--AND WHEN YOU CATCH HIM? I WANT YOU TO--
I JUST WANNA MEET HER. I KNOW WE'D HAVE A CONNECTION--
KEEP CALM
IT'S COW FARTS, MAN! WE GOTTA GET RID OF THE COWS!
THEY CAN'T JUST CANCEL IT. I MEAN, ON A CLIFFHANGER LIKE THAT?! WE'RE A DEVOTED FANBASE, WE DESERVE TO KNOW WHAT HAPPENS N--
--THEN YOU'D FLY ME INTO THE STADIUM ON YOUR BACK--AND WE'D LAND RIGHT ON STAGE IN FRONT OF HER DURING HER FINAL NUMBER, WITH THOUSANDS CHEERING AROUND US--
--AND I'D PULL OUT THE ROSE AND I'D SAY, TAYLOR, WILL YOU M--
BUT EVERY ONCE IN A WHILE, YOU GET SOMETHING THROUGH THE STATIC THAT--SPOILER ALERT--ANSWERS THE QUESTION--
WHAT WAS CAPTAIN AMERICA DOING IN ARIZONA?
I DUNNO-- VISITING HIS GRANDMOTHER?
WHICH IS ACTUALLY NOT THAT FAR OFF--

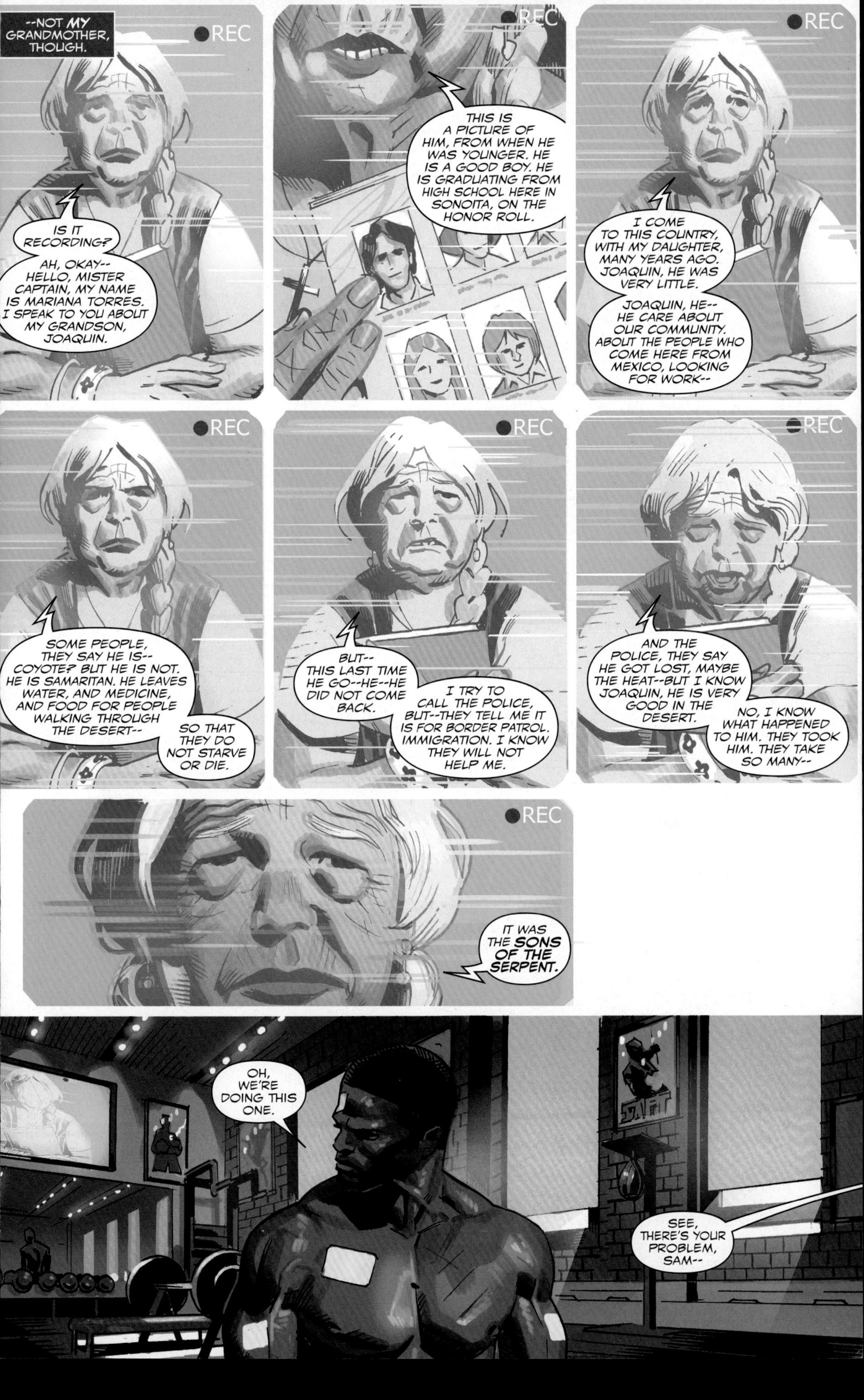
--NOT MY GRANDMOTHER, THOUGH.
REC
IS IT RECORDING?
AH, OKAY-- HELLO, MISTER CAPTAIN, MY NAME IS MARIANA TORRES. I SPEAK TO YOU ABOUT MY GRANDSON, JOAQUIN.
REC
THIS IS A PICTURE OF HIM, FROM WHEN HE WAS YOUNGER. HE IS A GOOD BOY. HE IS GRADUATING FROM HIGH SCHOOL HERE IN SONOITA, ON THE HONOR ROLL.
REC
I COME TO THIS COUNTRY, WITH MY DAUGHTER, MANY YEARS AGO. JOAQUIN, HE WAS VERY LITTLE.
JOAQUIN, HE-- HE CARE ABOUT OUR COMMUNITY. ABOUT THE PEOPLE WHO COME HERE FROM MEXICO, LOOKING FOR WORK--
REC
SOME PEOPLE, THEY SAY HE IS-- COYOTE? BUT HE IS NOT. HE IS SAMARITAN. HE LEAVES WATER, AND MEDICINE, AND FOOD FOR PEOPLE WALKING THROUGH THE DESERT--
SO THAT THEY DO NOT STARVE OR DIE.
REC
BUT-- THIS LAST TIME HE GO--HE--HE DID NOT COME BACK.
I TRY TO CALL THE POLICE, BUT--THEY TELL ME IT IS FOR BORDER PATROL. IMMIGRATION. I KNOW THEY WILL NOT HELP ME.
REC
AND THE POLICE, THEY SAY HE GOT LOST, MAYBE THE HEAT--BUT I KNOW JOAQUIN, HE IS VERY GOOD IN THE DESERT.
NO, I KNOW WHAT HAPPENED TO HIM. THEY TOOK HIM. THEY TAKE SO MANY--
REC
IT WAS THE SONS OF THE SERPENT.
OH, WE'RE DOING THIS ONE.
SEE, THERE'S YOUR PROBLEM, SAM--

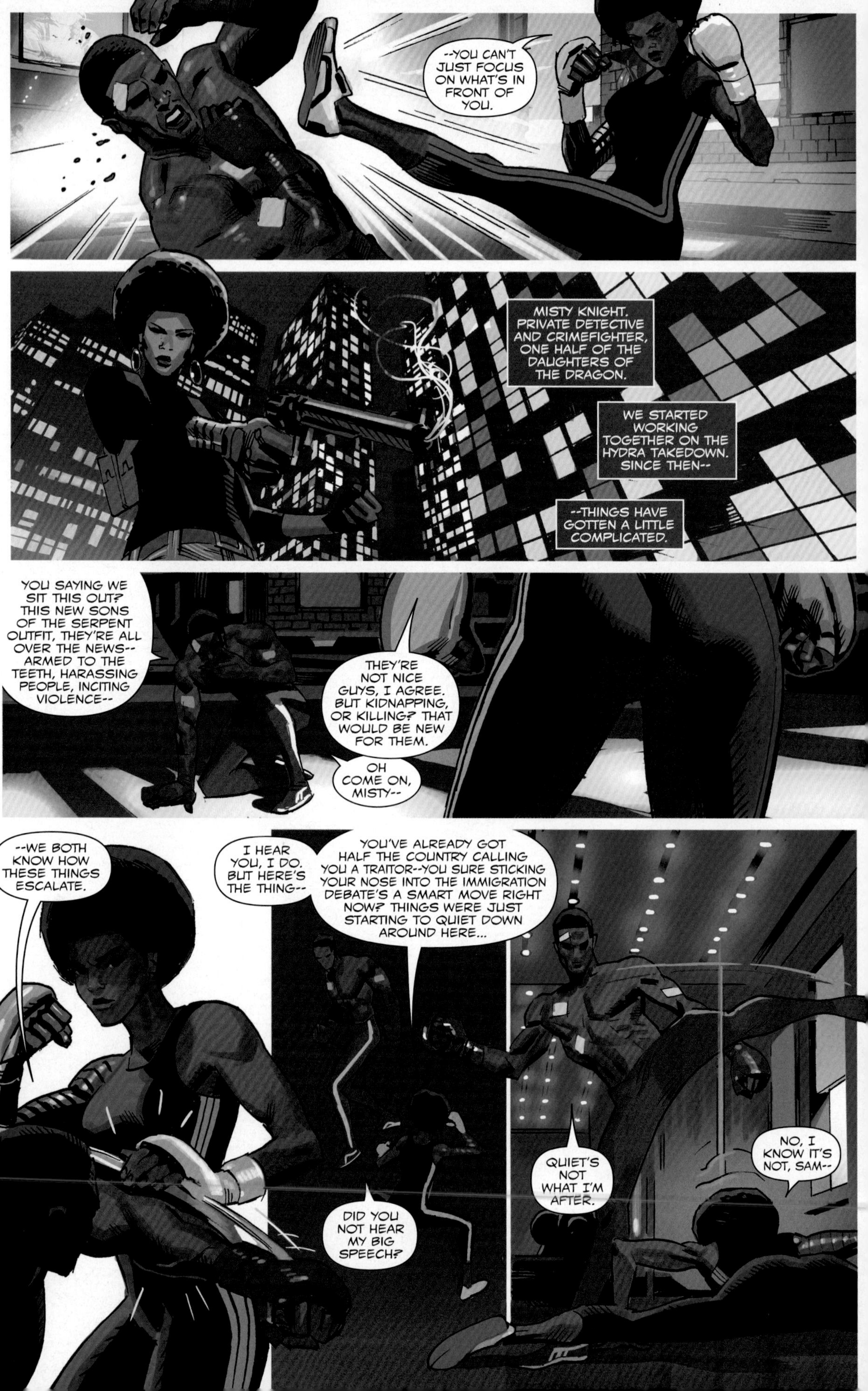
--YOU CAN'T JUST FOCUS ON WHAT'S IN FRONT OF YOU.
MISTY KNIGHT. PRIVATE DETECTIVE AND CRIMEFIGHTER, ONE HALF OF THE DAUGHTERS OF THE DRAGON.
WE STARTED WORKING TOGETHER ON THE HYDRA TAKEDOWN. SINCE THEN--
--THINGS HAVE GOTTEN A LITTLE COMPLICATED.
YOU SAYING WE SIT THIS OUT? THIS NEW SONS OF THE SERPENT OUTFIT, THEY'RE ALL OVER THE NEWS--ARMED TO THE TEETH, HARASSING PEOPLE, INCITING VIOLENCE--
THEY'RE NOT NICE GUYS, I AGREE. BUT KIDNAPPING, OR KILLING? THAT WOULD BE NEW FOR THEM.
OH COME ON, MISTY--
--WE BOTH KNOW HOW THESE THINGS ESCALATE.
I HEAR YOU, I DO. BUT HERE'S THE THING--
YOU'VE ALREADY GOT HALF THE COUNTRY CALLING YOU A TRAITOR--YOU SURE STICKING YOUR NOSE INTO THE IMMIGRATION DEBATE'S A SMART MOVE RIGHT NOW? THINGS WERE JUST STARTING TO QUIET DOWN AROUND HERE...
DID YOU NOT HEAR MY BIG SPEECH?
QUIET'S NOT WHAT I'M AFTER.
NO, I KNOW IT'S NOT, SAM--

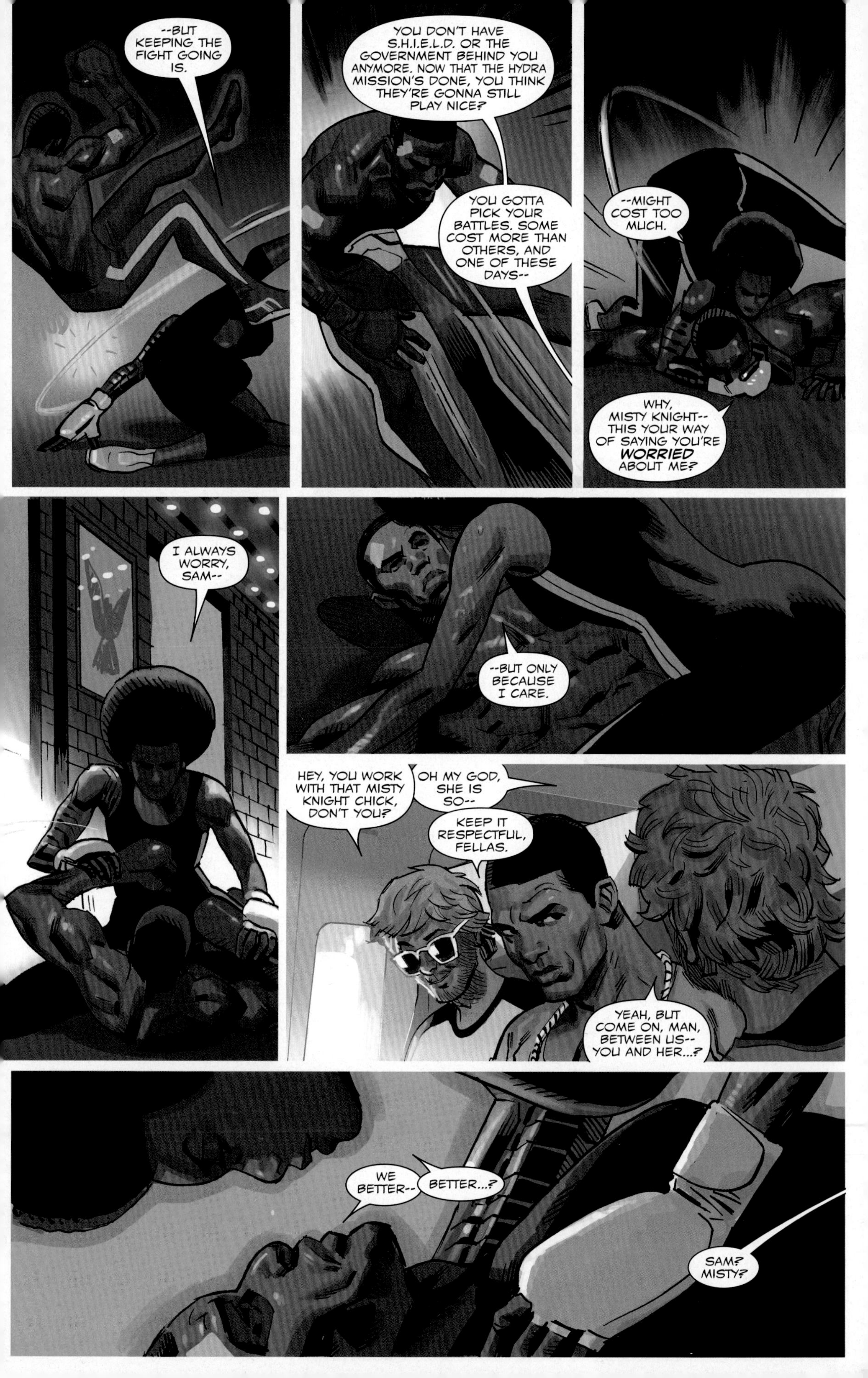
--BUT KEEPING THE FIGHT GOING IS.
YOU DON'T HAVE S.H.I.E.L.D. OR THE GOVERNMENT BEHIND YOU ANYMORE. NOW THAT THE HYDRA MISSION'S DONE, YOU THINK THEY'RE GONNA STILL PLAY NICE?
YOU GOTTA PICK YOUR BATTLES. SOME COST MORE THAN OTHERS, AND ONE OF THESE DAYS--
--MIGHT COST TOO MUCH.
WHY, MISTY KNIGHT-- THIS YOUR WAY OF SAYING YOU'RE **WORRIED** ABOUT ME?
I ALWAYS WORRY, SAM--
--BUT ONLY BECAUSE I CARE.
HEY, YOU WORK WITH THAT MISTY KNIGHT CHICK, DON'T YOU?
OH MY GOD, SHE IS SO--
KEEP IT RESPECTFUL, FELLAS.
YEAH, BUT COME ON, MAN, BETWEEN US-- YOU AND HER...?
WE BETTER--
BETTER...?
SAM? MISTY?

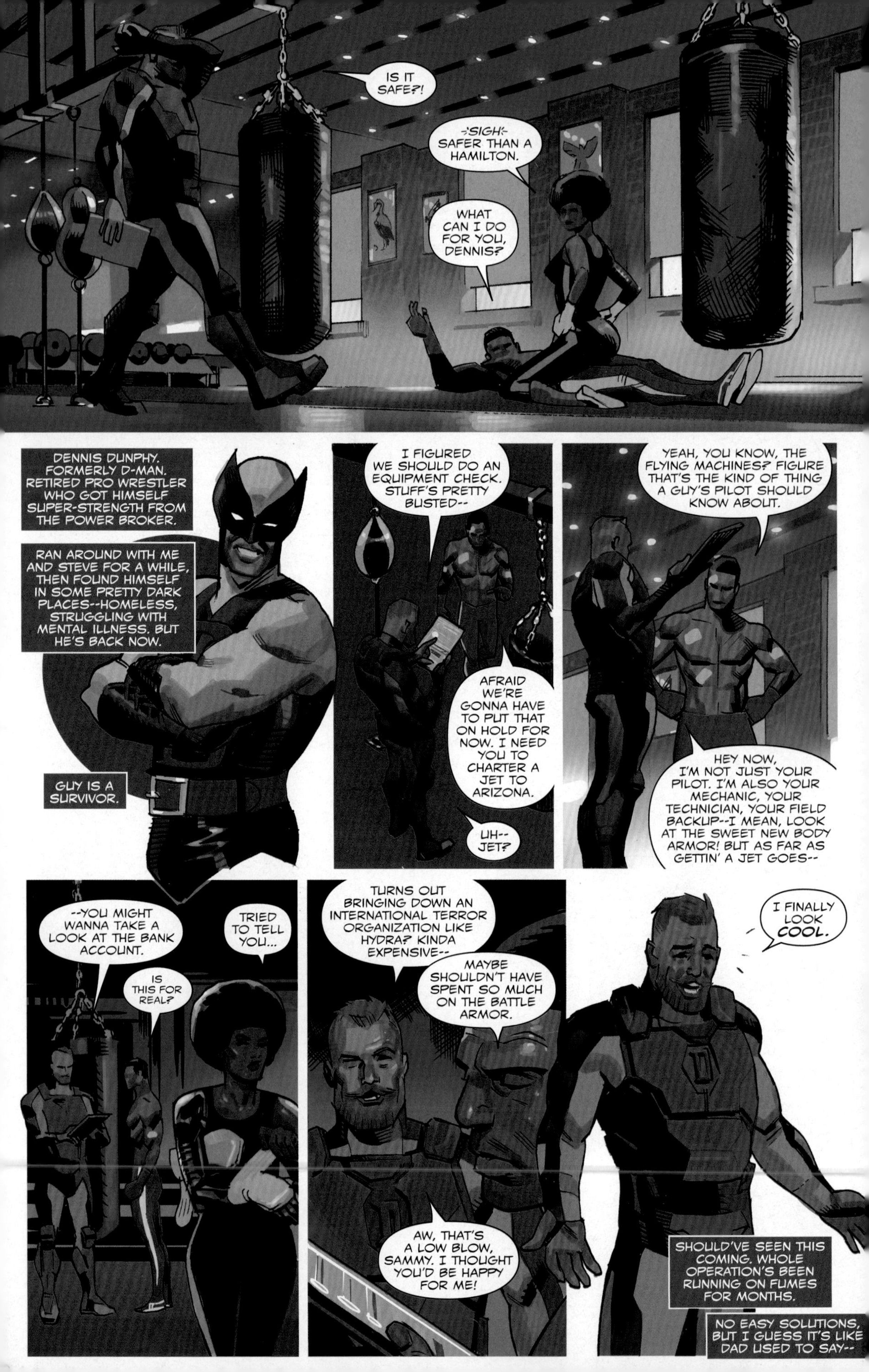
IS IT SAFE?!
-SIGH- SAFER THAN A HAMILTON.
WHAT CAN I DO FOR YOU, DENNIS?
DENNIS DUNPHY. FORMERLY D-MAN. RETIRED PRO WRESTLER WHO GOT HIMSELF SUPER-STRENGTH FROM THE POWER BROKER.
RAN AROUND WITH ME AND STEVE FOR A WHILE, THEN FOUND HIMSELF IN SOME PRETTY DARK PLACES--HOMELESS, STRUGGLING WITH MENTAL ILLNESS. BUT HE'S BACK NOW.
GUY IS A SURVIVOR.
I FIGURED WE SHOULD DO AN EQUIPMENT CHECK. STUFF'S PRETTY BUSTED--
AFRAID WE'RE GONNA HAVE TO PUT THAT ON HOLD FOR NOW. I NEED YOU TO CHARTER A JET TO ARIZONA.
UH-- JET?
YEAH, YOU KNOW, THE FLYING MACHINES? FIGURE THAT'S THE KIND OF THING A GUY'S PILOT SHOULD KNOW ABOUT.
HEY NOW, I'M NOT JUST YOUR PILOT. I'M ALSO YOUR MECHANIC, YOUR TECHNICIAN, YOUR FIELD BACKUP--I MEAN, LOOK AT THE SWEET NEW BODY ARMOR! BUT AS FAR AS GETTIN' A JET GOES--
--YOU MIGHT WANNA TAKE A LOOK AT THE BANK ACCOUNT.
TRIED TO TELL YOU...
IS THIS FOR REAL?
TURNS OUT BRINGING DOWN AN INTERNATIONAL TERROR ORGANIZATION LIKE HYDRA? KINDA EXPENSIVE--
MAYBE SHOULDN'T HAVE SPENT SO MUCH ON THE BATTLE ARMOR.
AW, THAT'S A LOW BLOW, SAMMY. I THOUGHT YOU'D BE HAPPY FOR ME!
I FINALLY LOOK COOL.
SHOULD'VE SEEN THIS COMING. WHOLE OPERATION'S BEEN RUNNING ON FUMES FOR MONTHS.
NO EASY SOLUTIONS, BUT I GUESS IT'S LIKE DAD USED TO SAY--

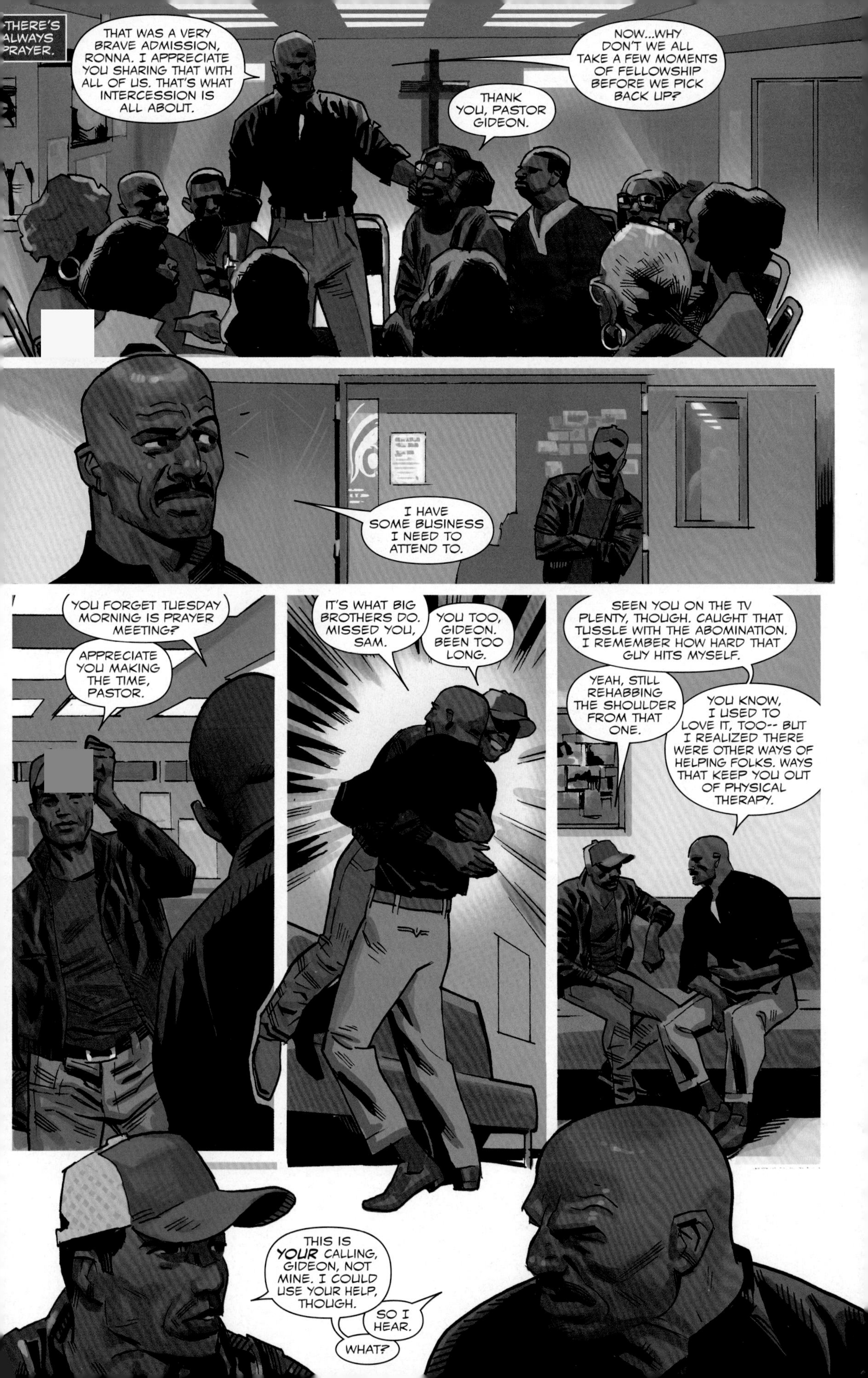
THERE'S ALWAYS PRAYER.
THAT WAS A VERY BRAVE ADMISSION, RONNA. I APPRECIATE YOU SHARING THAT WITH ALL OF US. THAT'S WHAT INTERCESSION IS ALL ABOUT.
THANK YOU, PASTOR GIDEON.
NOW...WHY DON'T WE ALL TAKE A FEW MOMENTS OF FELLOWSHIP BEFORE WE PICK BACK UP?
I HAVE SOME BUSINESS I NEED TO ATTEND TO.
YOU FORGET TUESDAY MORNING IS PRAYER MEETING?
APPRECIATE YOU MAKING THE TIME, PASTOR.
IT'S WHAT BIG BROTHERS DO. MISSED YOU, SAM.
YOU TOO, GIDEON. BEEN TOO LONG.
SEEN YOU ON THE TV PLENTY, THOUGH. CAUGHT THAT TUSSLE WITH THE ABOMINATION. I REMEMBER HOW HARD THAT GUY HITS MYSELF.
YEAH, STILL REHABBING THE SHOULDER FROM THAT ONE.
YOU KNOW, I USED TO LOVE IT, TOO-- BUT I REALIZED THERE WERE OTHER WAYS OF HELPING FOLKS. WAYS THAT KEEP YOU OUT OF PHYSICAL THERAPY.
THIS IS YOUR CALLING, GIDEON, NOT MINE. I COULD USE YOUR HELP, THOUGH.
SO I HEAR.
WHAT?

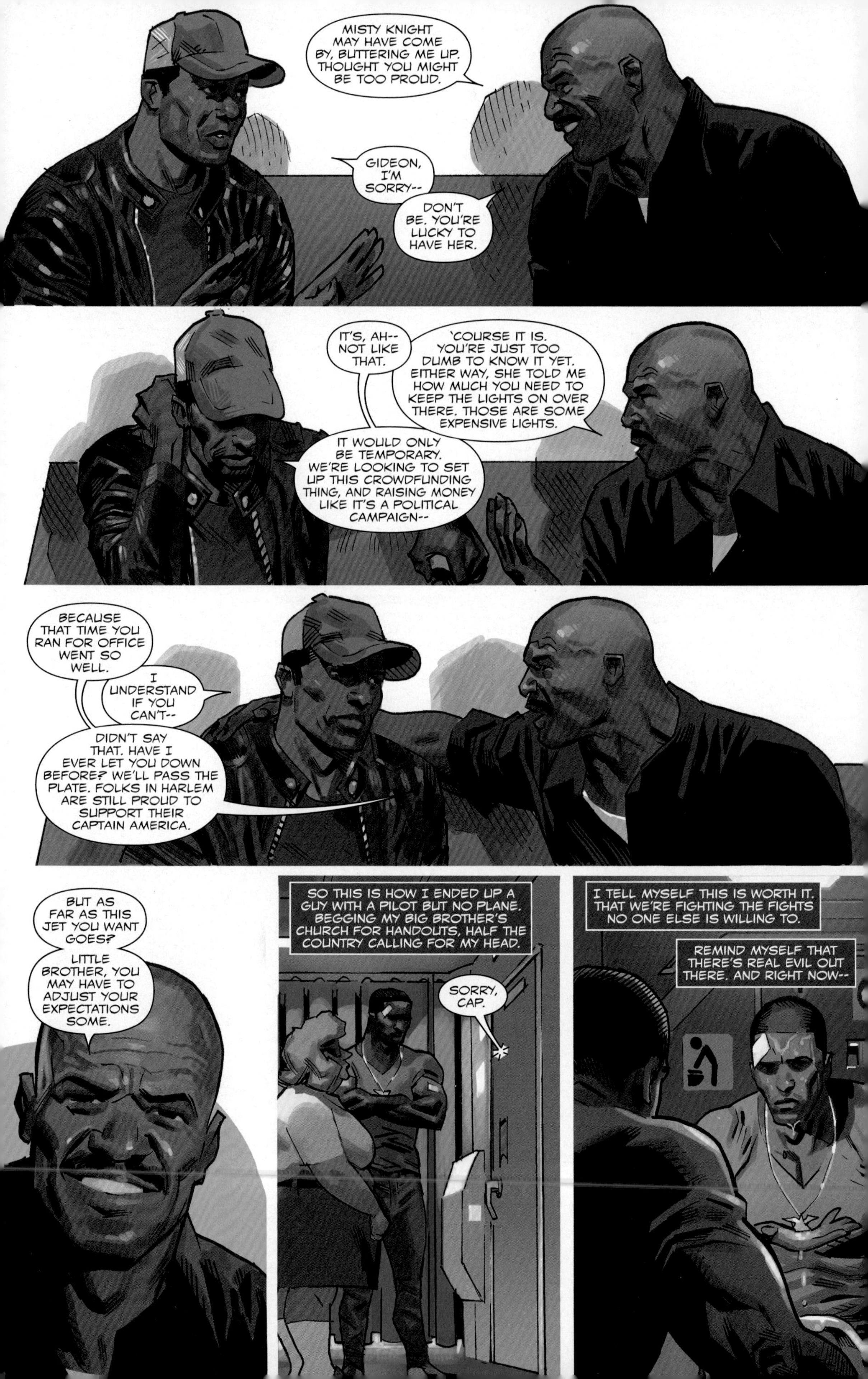
MISTY KNIGHT MAY HAVE COME BY, BUTTERING ME UP. THOUGHT YOU MIGHT BE TOO PROUD.
GIDEON, I'M SORRY--
DON'T BE. YOU'RE LUCKY TO HAVE HER.
IT'S, AH-- NOT LIKE THAT.
'COURSE IT IS. YOU'RE JUST TOO DUMB TO KNOW IT YET. EITHER WAY, SHE TOLD ME HOW MUCH YOU NEED TO KEEP THE LIGHTS ON OVER THERE. THOSE ARE SOME EXPENSIVE LIGHTS.
IT WOULD ONLY BE TEMPORARY. WE'RE LOOKING TO SET UP THIS CROWDFUNDING THING, AND RAISING MONEY LIKE IT'S A POLITICAL CAMPAIGN--
BECAUSE THAT TIME YOU RAN FOR OFFICE WENT SO WELL.
I UNDERSTAND IF YOU CAN'T--
DIDN'T SAY THAT. HAVE I EVER LET YOU DOWN BEFORE? WE'LL PASS THE PLATE. FOLKS IN HARLEM ARE STILL PROUD TO SUPPORT THEIR CAPTAIN AMERICA.
BUT AS FAR AS THIS JET YOU WANT GOES?
LITTLE BROTHER, YOU MAY HAVE TO ADJUST YOUR EXPECTATIONS SOME.
SO THIS IS HOW I ENDED UP A GUY WITH A PILOT BUT NO PLANE. BEGGING MY BIG BROTHER'S CHURCH FOR HANDOUTS, HALF THE COUNTRY CALLING FOR MY HEAD.
SORRY, CAP.
I TELL MYSELF THIS IS WORTH IT. THAT WE'RE FIGHTING THE FIGHTS NO ONE ELSE IS WILLING TO.
REMIND MYSELF THAT THERE'S REAL EVIL OUT THERE. AND RIGHT NOW--

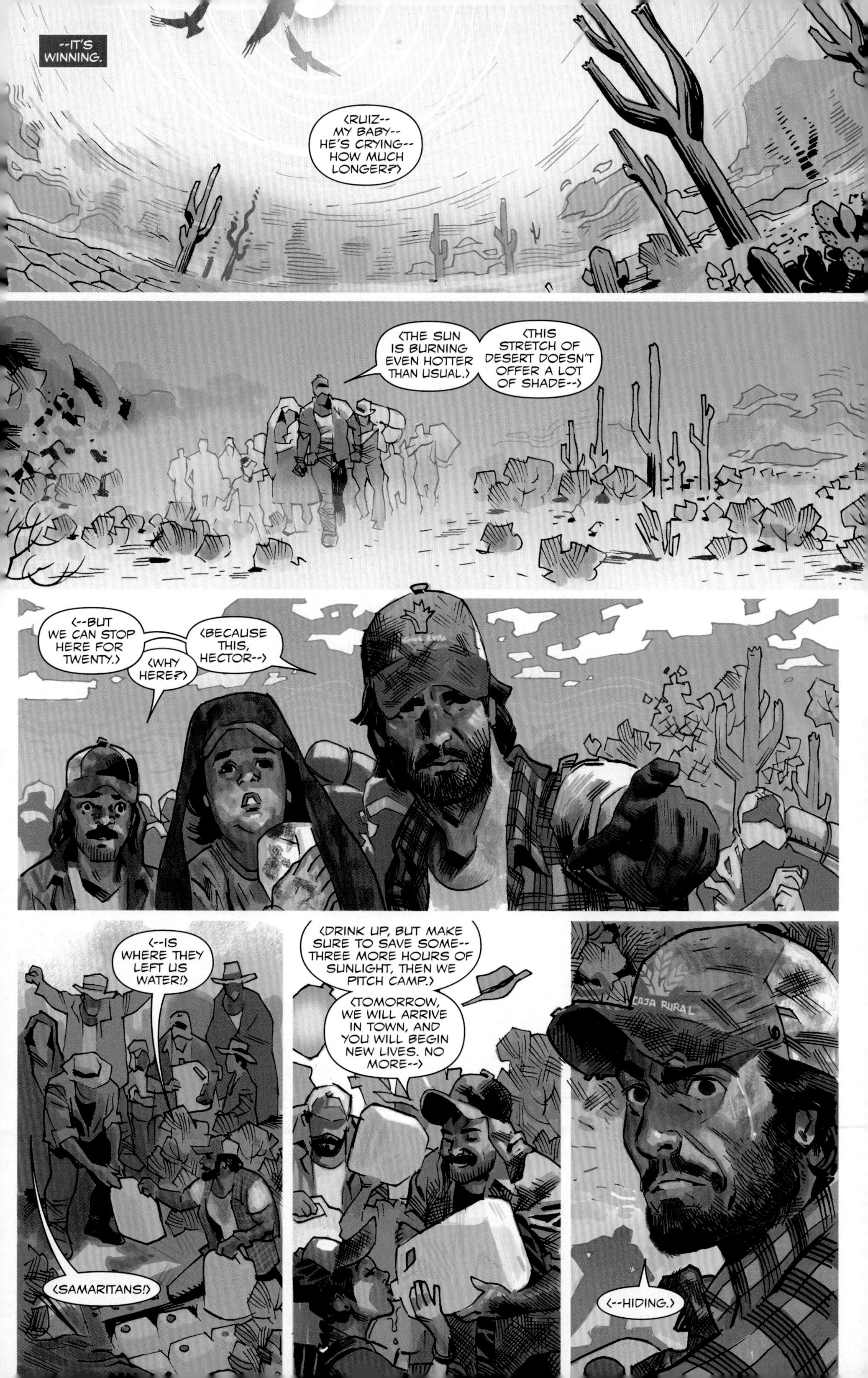
--IT'S WINNING.
‹RUIZ-- MY BABY-- HE'S CRYING-- HOW MUCH LONGER?›
‹THE SUN IS BURNING EVEN HOTTER THAN USUAL.›
‹THIS STRETCH OF DESERT DOESN'T OFFER A LOT OF SHADE--›
‹--BUT WE CAN STOP HERE FOR TWENTY.›
‹WHY HERE?›
‹BECAUSE THIS, HECTOR--›
‹--IS WHERE THEY LEFT US WATER!›
‹SAMARITANS!›
‹DRINK UP, BUT MAKE SURE TO SAVE SOME-- THREE MORE HOURS OF SUNLIGHT, THEN WE PITCH CAMP.›
‹TOMORROW, WE WILL ARRIVE IN TOWN, AND YOU WILL BEGIN NEW LIVES. NO MORE--›
CAJA RURAL
‹--HIDING.›

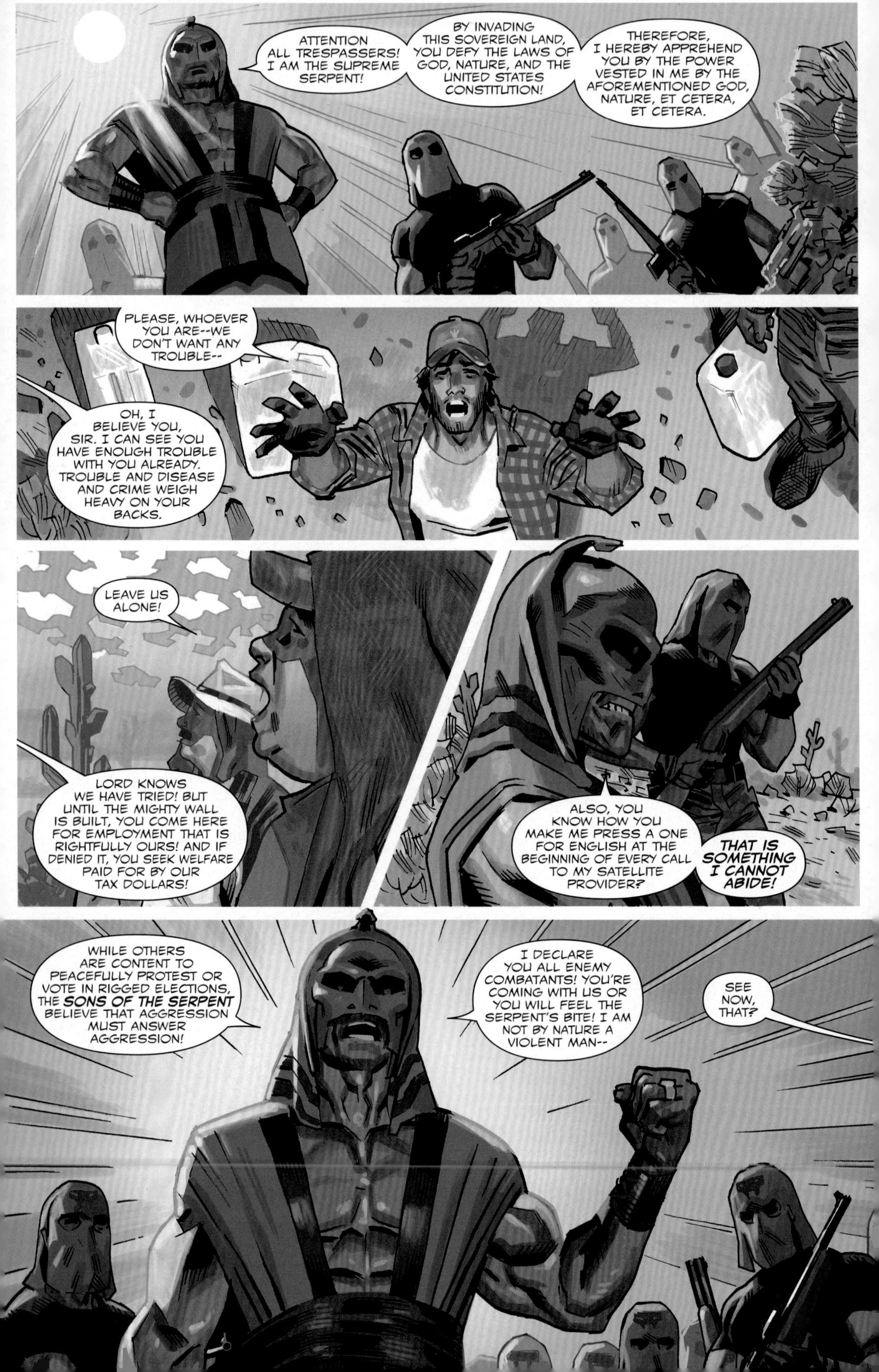
ATTENTION ALL TRESPASSERS! I AM THE SUPREME SERPENT!
BY INVADING THIS SOVEREIGN LAND, YOU DEFY THE LAWS OF GOD, NATURE, AND THE UNITED STATES CONSTITUTION!
THEREFORE, I HEREBY APPREHEND YOU BY THE POWER VESTED IN ME BY THE AFOREMENTIONED GOD, NATURE, ET CETERA, ET CETERA.
PLEASE, WHOEVER YOU ARE--WE DON'T WANT ANY TROUBLE--
OH, I BELIEVE YOU, SIR. I CAN SEE YOU HAVE ENOUGH TROUBLE WITH YOU ALREADY. TROUBLE AND DISEASE AND CRIME WEIGH HEAVY ON YOUR BACKS.
LEAVE US ALONE!
LORD KNOWS WE HAVE TRIED! BUT UNTIL THE MIGHTY WALL IS BUILT, YOU COME HERE FOR EMPLOYMENT THAT IS RIGHTFULLY OURS! AND IF DENIED IT, YOU SEEK WELFARE PAID FOR BY OUR TAX DOLLARS!
ALSO, YOU KNOW HOW YOU MAKE ME PRESS A ONE FOR ENGLISH AT THE BEGINNING OF EVERY CALL TO MY SATELLITE PROVIDER?
THAT IS SOMETHING I CANNOT ABIDE!
WHILE OTHERS ARE CONTENT TO PEACEFULLY PROTEST OR VOTE IN RIGGED ELECTIONS, THE SONS OF THE SERPENT BELIEVE THAT AGGRESSION MUST ANSWER AGGRESSION!
I DECLARE YOU ALL ENEMY COMBATANTS! YOU'RE COMING WITH US OR YOU WILL FEEL THE SERPENT'S BITE! I AM NOT BY NATURE A VIOLENT MAN--
SEE NOW, THAT?

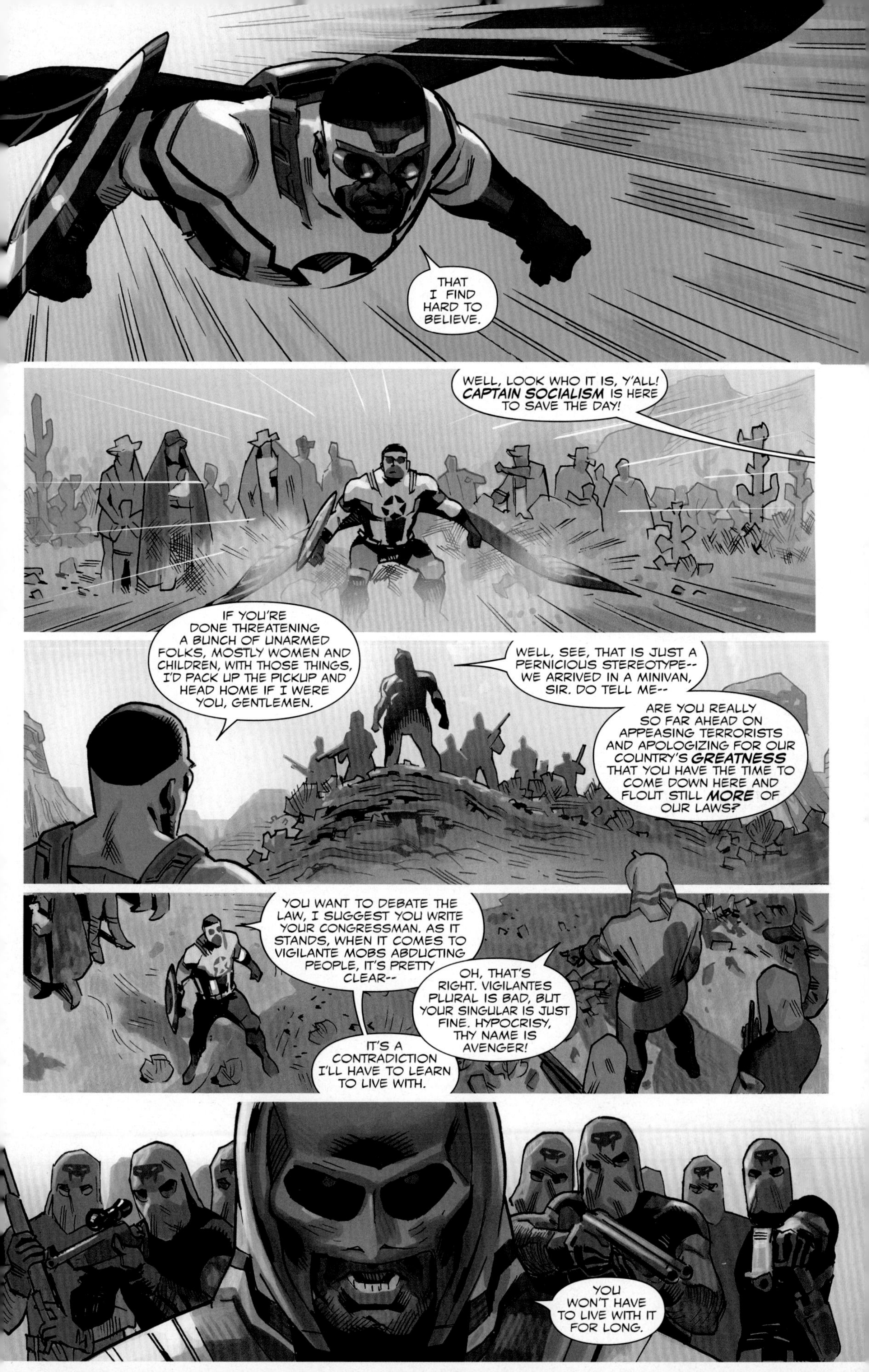
THAT I FIND HARD TO BELIEVE.
WELL, LOOK WHO IT IS, Y'ALL! CAPTAIN SOCIALISM IS HERE TO SAVE THE DAY!
IF YOU'RE DONE THREATENING A BUNCH OF UNARMED FOLKS, MOSTLY WOMEN AND CHILDREN, WITH THOSE THINGS, I'D PACK UP THE PICKUP AND HEAD HOME IF I WERE YOU, GENTLEMEN.
WELL, SEE, THAT IS JUST A PERNICIOUS STEREOTYPE-- WE ARRIVED IN A MINIVAN, SIR. DO TELL ME--
ARE YOU REALLY SO FAR AHEAD ON APPEASING TERRORISTS AND APOLOGIZING FOR OUR COUNTRY'S GREATNESS THAT YOU HAVE THE TIME TO COME DOWN HERE AND FLOUT STILL MORE OF OUR LAWS?
YOU WANT TO DEBATE THE LAW, I SUGGEST YOU WRITE YOUR CONGRESSMAN. AS IT STANDS, WHEN IT COMES TO VIGILANTE MOBS ABDUCTING PEOPLE, IT'S PRETTY CLEAR--
OH, THAT'S RIGHT. VIGILANTES PLURAL IS BAD, BUT YOUR SINGULAR IS JUST FINE. HYPOCRISY, THY NAME IS AVENGER!
IT'S A CONTRADICTION I'LL HAVE TO LEARN TO LIVE WITH.
YOU WON'T HAVE TO LIVE WITH IT FOR LONG.

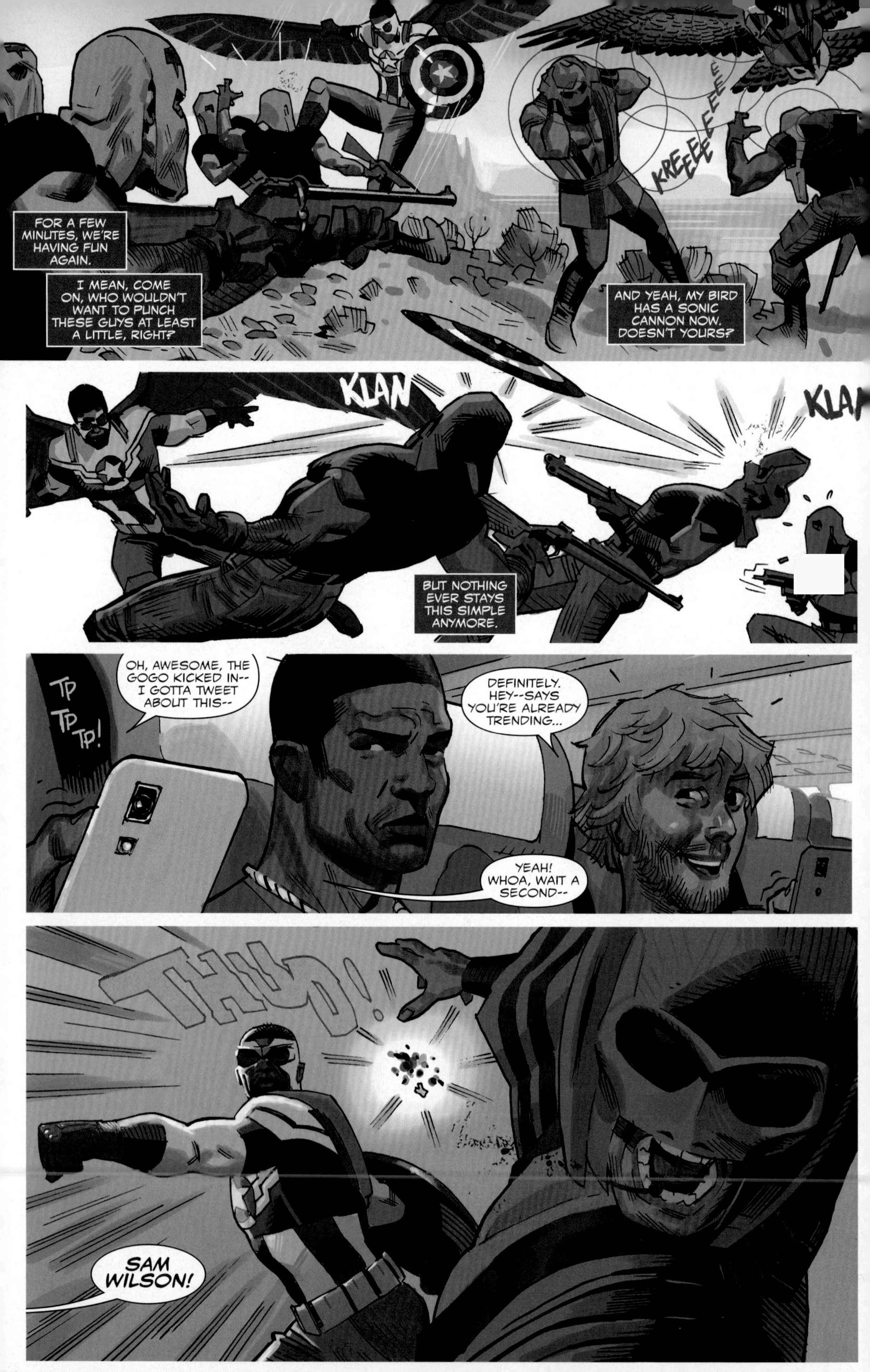

FOR A FEW MINUTES, WE'RE HAVING FUN AGAIN.
I MEAN, COME ON, WHO WOULDN'T WANT TO PUNCH THESE GUYS AT LEAST A LITTLE, RIGHT?
KREEEEEEEE
AND YEAH, MY BIRD HAS A SONIC CANNON NOW. DOESN'T YOURS?
KLAN
KLAN
BUT NOTHING EVER STAYS THIS SIMPLE ANYMORE.
TP TP TP!
OH, AWESOME, THE GOGO KICKED IN-- I GOTTA TWEET ABOUT THIS--
DEFINITELY. HEY--SAYS YOU'RE ALREADY TRENDING...
YEAH! WHOA, WAIT A SECOND--
THUD!
SAM WILSON!

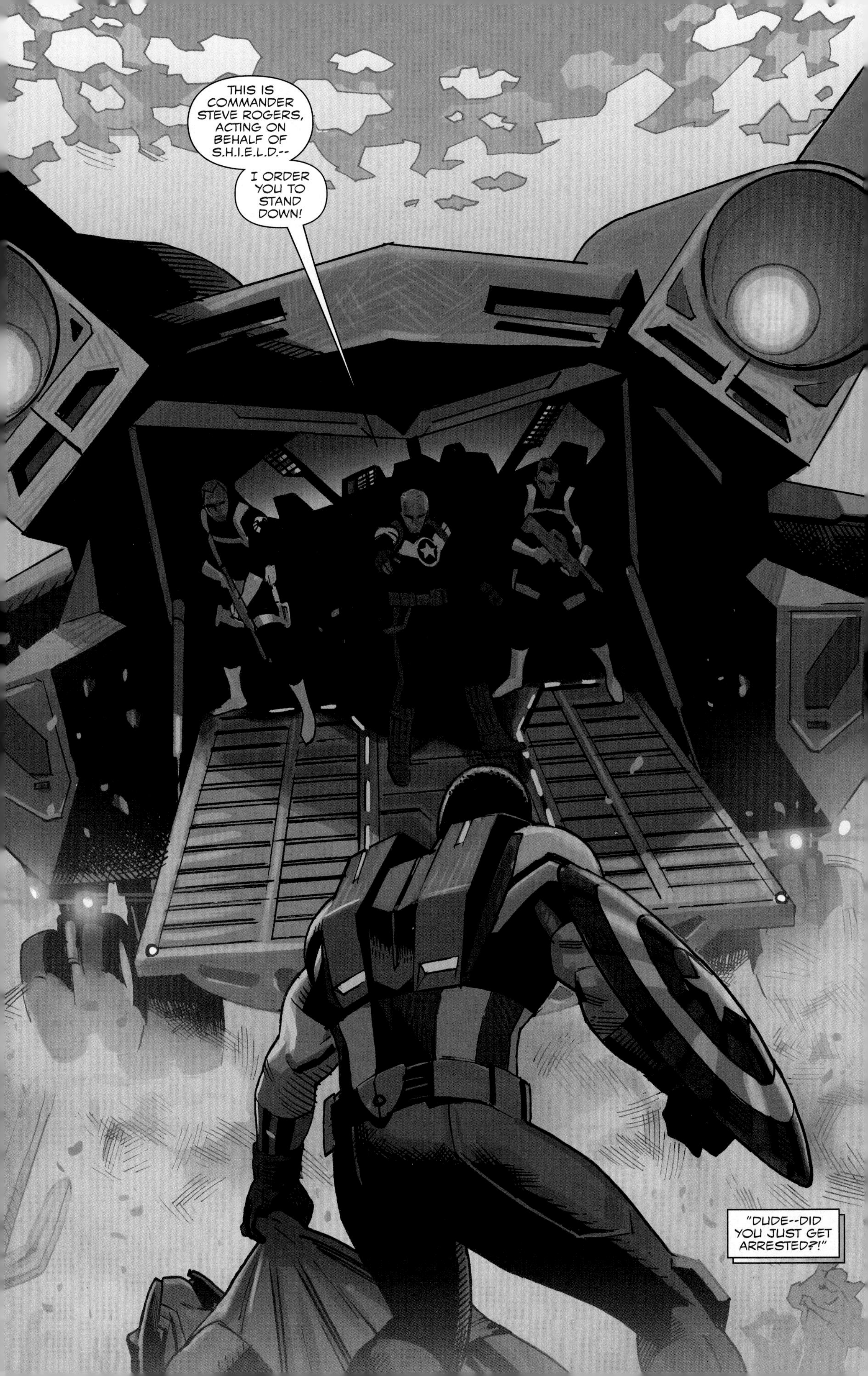
THIS IS COMMANDER STEVE ROGERS, ACTING ON BEHALF OF S.H.I.E.L.D.--
I ORDER YOU TO STAND DOWN!
"DUDE--DID YOU JUST GET ARRESTED?!"

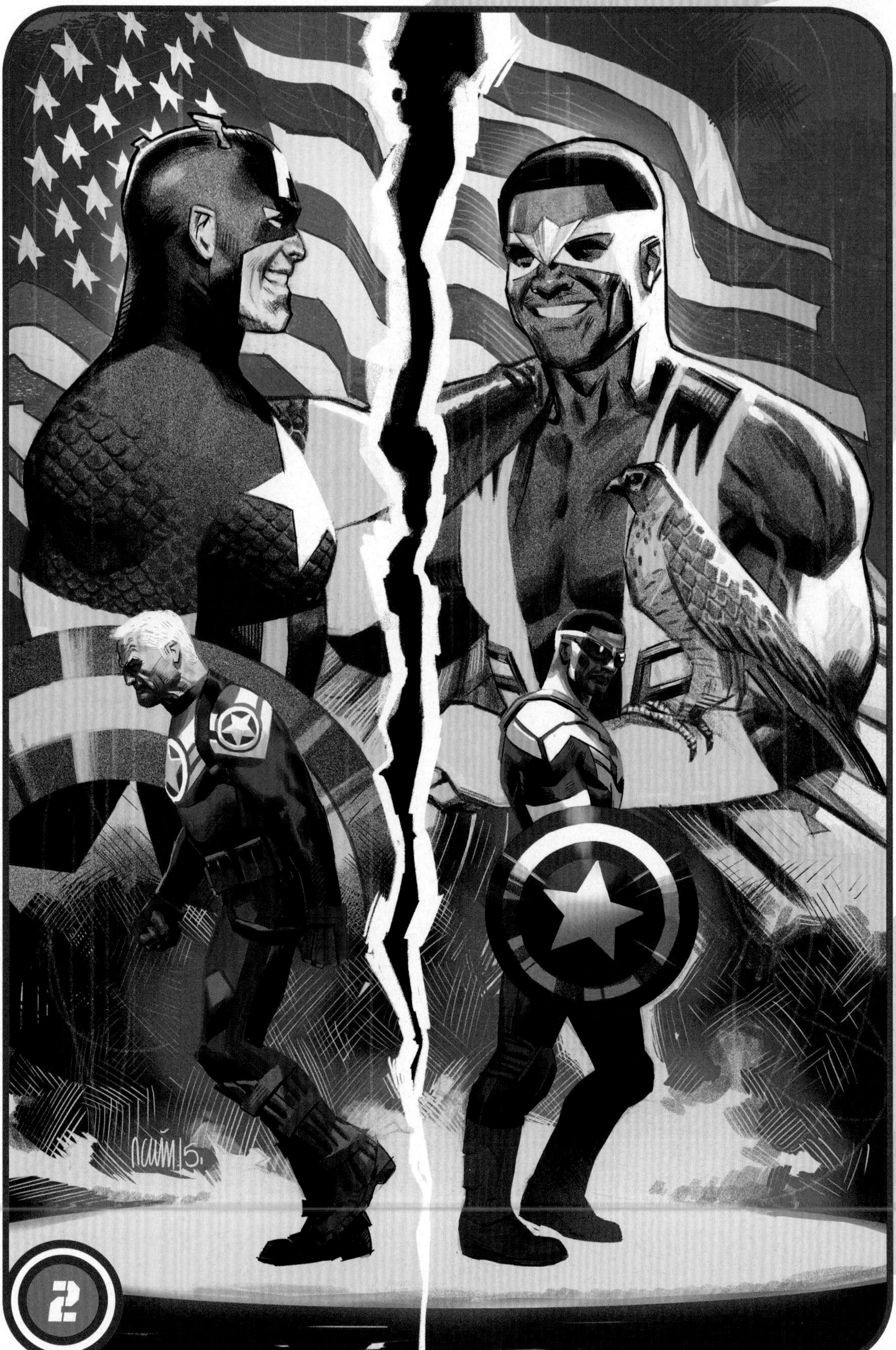
2

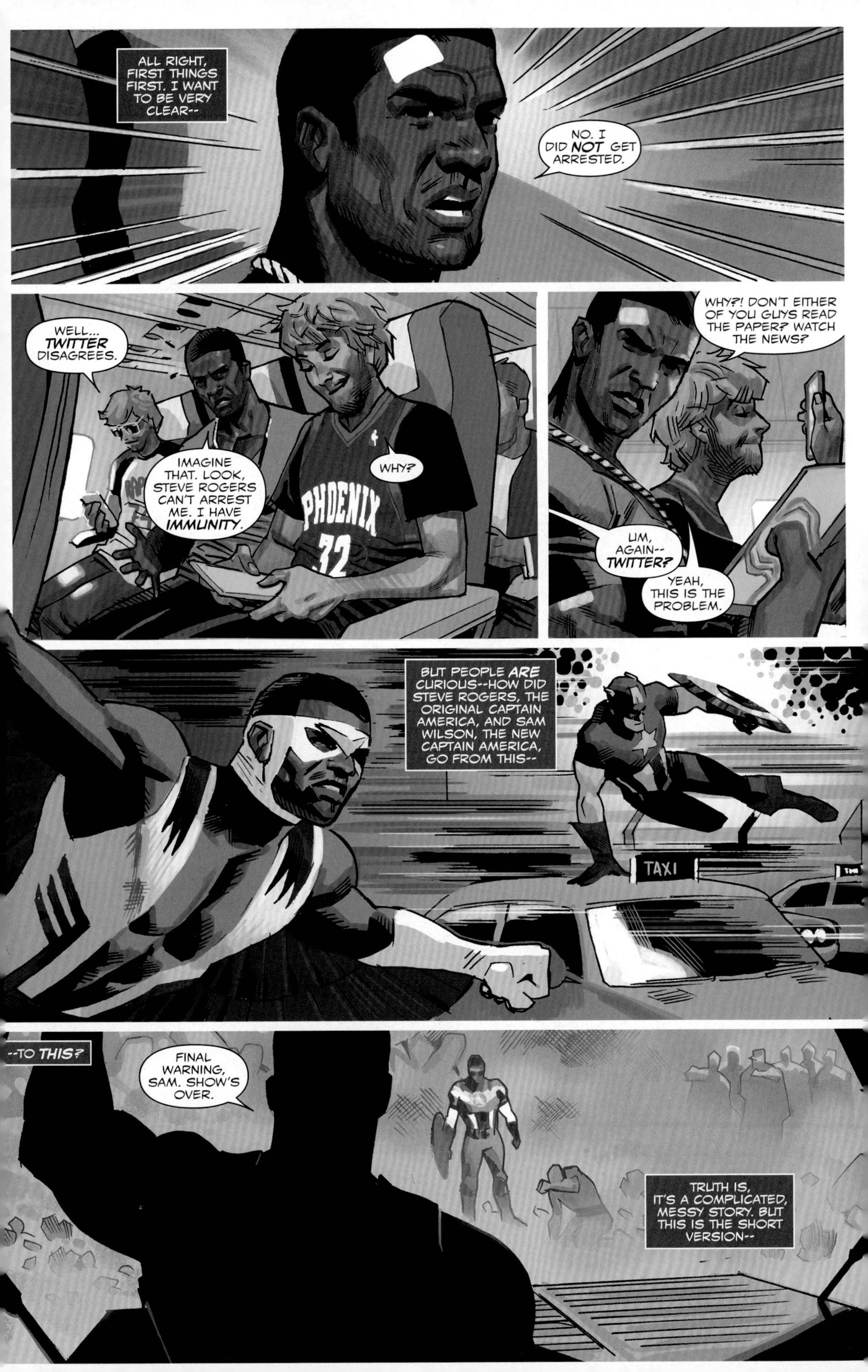
ALL RIGHT, FIRST THINGS FIRST. I WANT TO BE VERY CLEAR--
NO. I DID NOT GET ARRESTED.
WELL... TWITTER DISAGREES.
IMAGINE THAT. LOOK, STEVE ROGERS CAN'T ARREST ME. I HAVE IMMUNITY.
WHY?
PHOENIX 32
WHY?! DON'T EITHER OF YOU GUYS READ THE PAPER? WATCH THE NEWS?
UM, AGAIN-- TWITTER?
YEAH, THIS IS THE PROBLEM.
BUT PEOPLE ARE CURIOUS--HOW DID STEVE ROGERS, THE ORIGINAL CAPTAIN AMERICA, AND SAM WILSON, THE NEW CAPTAIN AMERICA, GO FROM THIS--
TAXI
--TO THIS?
FINAL WARNING, SAM. SHOW'S OVER.
TRUTH IS, IT'S A COMPLICATED, MESSY STORY. BUT THIS IS THE SHORT VERSION--

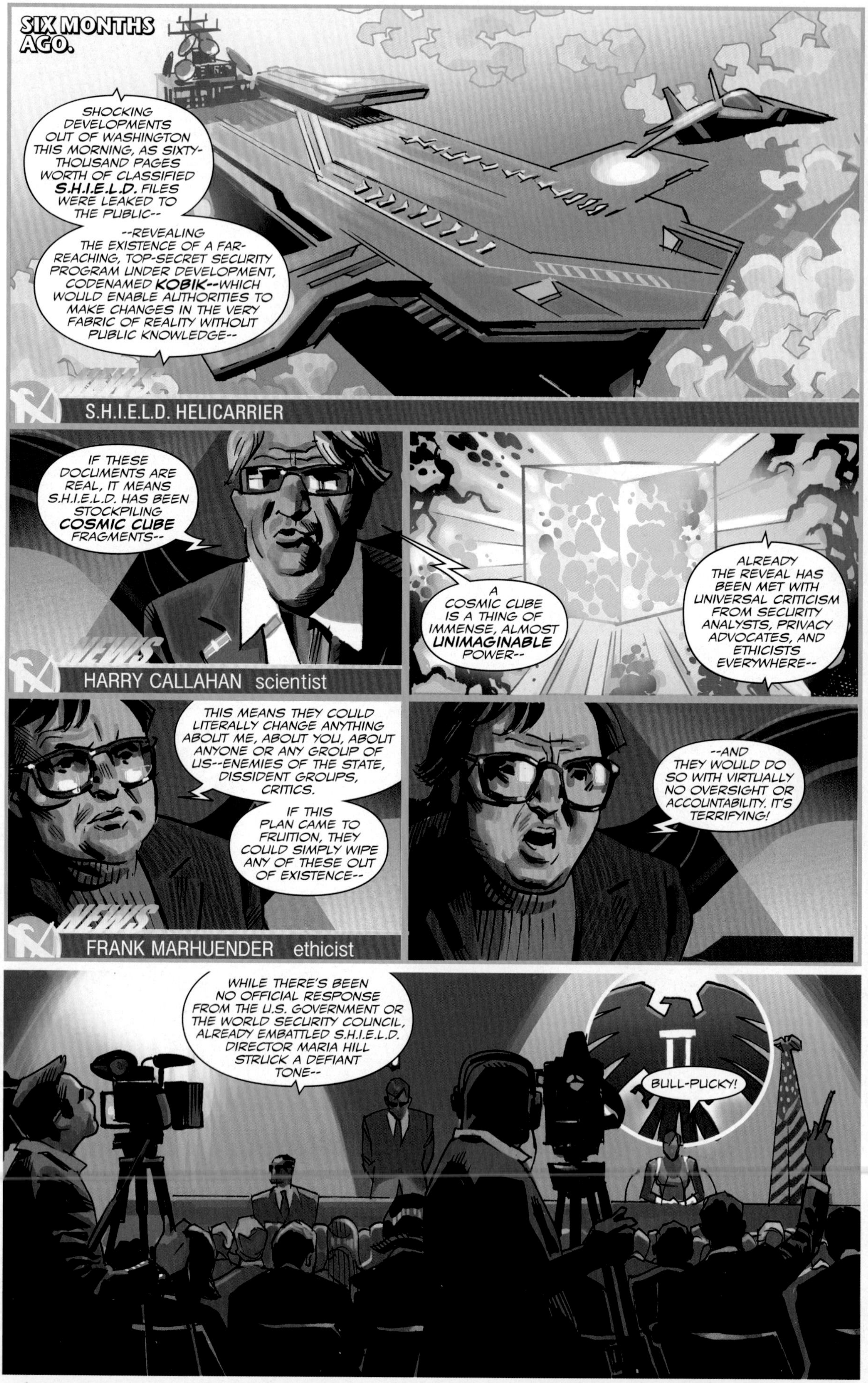
SIX MONTHS AGO.
SHOCKING DEVELOPMENTS OUT OF WASHINGTON THIS MORNING, AS SIXTY-THOUSAND PAGES WORTH OF CLASSIFIED S.H.I.E.L.D. FILES WERE LEAKED TO THE PUBLIC--
--REVEALING THE EXISTENCE OF A FAR-REACHING, TOP-SECRET SECURITY PROGRAM UNDER DEVELOPMENT, CODENAMED KOBIK--WHICH WOULD ENABLE AUTHORITIES TO MAKE CHANGES IN THE VERY FABRIC OF REALITY WITHOUT PUBLIC KNOWLEDGE--
NEWS
S.H.I.E.L.D. HELICARRIER
IF THESE DOCUMENTS ARE REAL, IT MEANS S.H.I.E.L.D. HAS BEEN STOCKPILING COSMIC CUBE FRAGMENTS--
A COSMIC CUBE IS A THING OF IMMENSE, ALMOST UNIMAGINABLE POWER--
NEWS
HARRY CALLAHAN scientist
ALREADY THE REVEAL HAS BEEN MET WITH UNIVERSAL CRITICISM FROM SECURITY ANALYSTS, PRIVACY ADVOCATES, AND ETHICISTS EVERYWHERE--
THIS MEANS THEY COULD LITERALLY CHANGE ANYTHING ABOUT ME, ABOUT YOU, ABOUT ANYONE OR ANY GROUP OF US--ENEMIES OF THE STATE, DISSIDENT GROUPS, CRITICS.
IF THIS PLAN CAME TO FRUITION, THEY COULD SIMPLY WIPE ANY OF THESE OUT OF EXISTENCE--
NEWS
FRANK MARHUENDER ethicist
--AND THEY WOULD DO SO WITH VIRTUALLY NO OVERSIGHT OR ACCOUNTABILITY. IT'S TERRIFYING!
WHILE THERE'S BEEN NO OFFICIAL RESPONSE FROM THE U.S. GOVERNMENT OR THE WORLD SECURITY COUNCIL, ALREADY EMBATTLED S.H.I.E.L.D. DIRECTOR MARIA HILL STRUCK A DEFIANT TONE--
BULL-PUCKY!

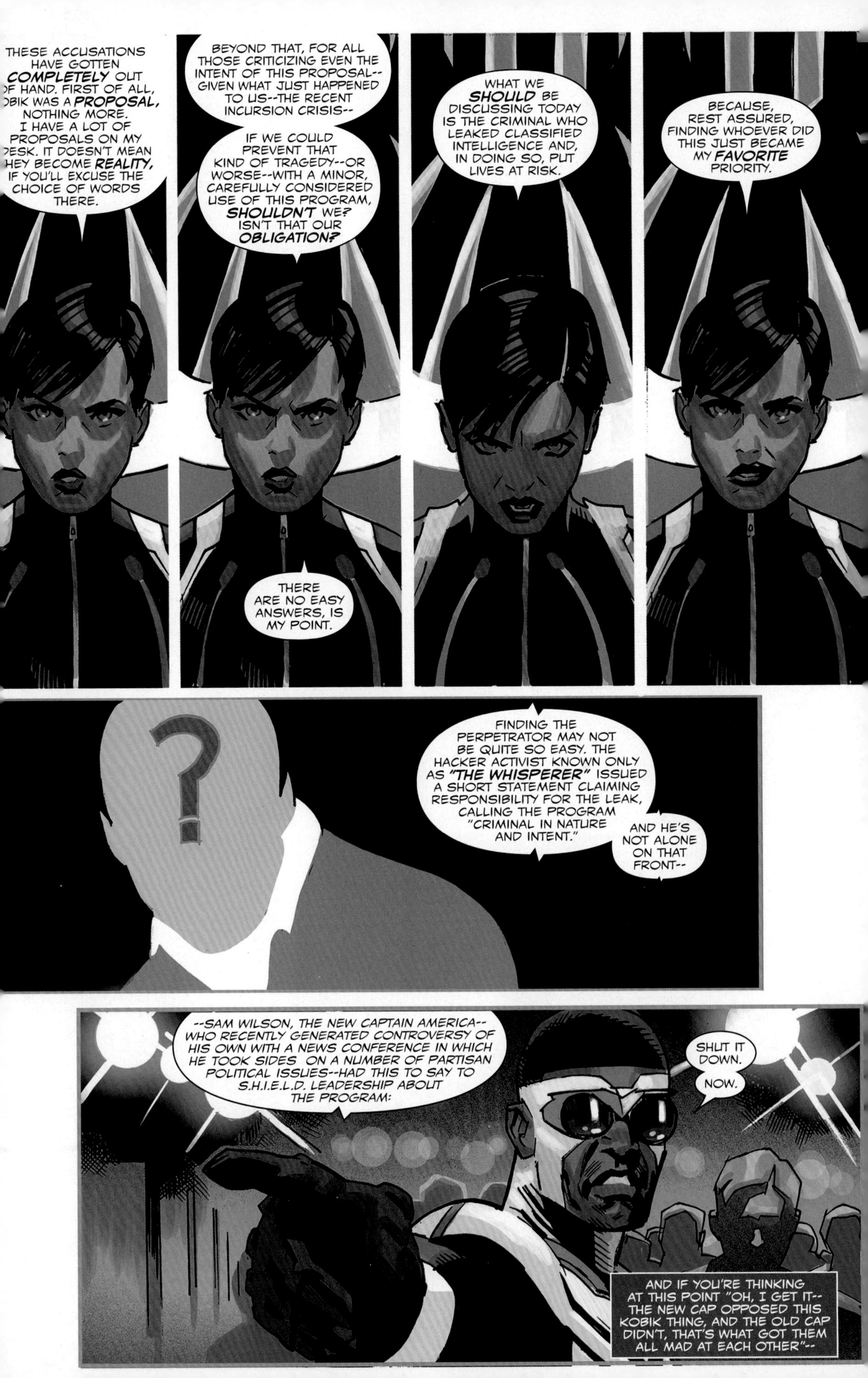
THESE ACCUSATIONS HAVE GOTTEN COMPLETELY OUT OF HAND. FIRST OF ALL, KOBIK WAS A PROPOSAL, NOTHING MORE. I HAVE A LOT OF PROPOSALS ON MY DESK. IT DOESN'T MEAN THEY BECOME REALITY, IF YOU'LL EXCUSE THE CHOICE OF WORDS THERE.
BEYOND THAT, FOR ALL THOSE CRITICIZING EVEN THE INTENT OF THIS PROPOSAL--GIVEN WHAT JUST HAPPENED TO US--THE RECENT INCURSION CRISIS--
IF WE COULD PREVENT THAT KIND OF TRAGEDY--OR WORSE--WITH A MINOR, CAREFULLY CONSIDERED USE OF THIS PROGRAM, SHOULDN'T WE? ISN'T THAT OUR OBLIGATION?
THERE ARE NO EASY ANSWERS, IS MY POINT.
WHAT WE SHOULD BE DISCUSSING TODAY IS THE CRIMINAL WHO LEAKED CLASSIFIED INTELLIGENCE AND, IN DOING SO, PUT LIVES AT RISK.
BECAUSE, REST ASSURED, FINDING WHOEVER DID THIS JUST BECAME MY FAVORITE PRIORITY.
FINDING THE PERPETRATOR MAY NOT BE QUITE SO EASY. THE HACKER ACTIVIST KNOWN ONLY AS "THE WHISPERER" ISSUED A SHORT STATEMENT CLAIMING RESPONSIBILITY FOR THE LEAK, CALLING THE PROGRAM "CRIMINAL IN NATURE AND INTENT."
AND HE'S NOT ALONE ON THAT FRONT--
--SAM WILSON, THE NEW CAPTAIN AMERICA--WHO RECENTLY GENERATED CONTROVERSY OF HIS OWN WITH A NEWS CONFERENCE IN WHICH HE TOOK SIDES ON A NUMBER OF PARTISAN POLITICAL ISSUES--HAD THIS TO SAY TO S.H.I.E.L.D. LEADERSHIP ABOUT THE PROGRAM:
SHUT IT DOWN.
NOW.
AND IF YOU'RE THINKING AT THIS POINT "OH, I GET IT--THE NEW CAP OPPOSED THIS KOBIK THING, AND THE OLD CAP DIDN'T, THAT'S WHAT GOT THEM ALL MAD AT EACH OTHER"--

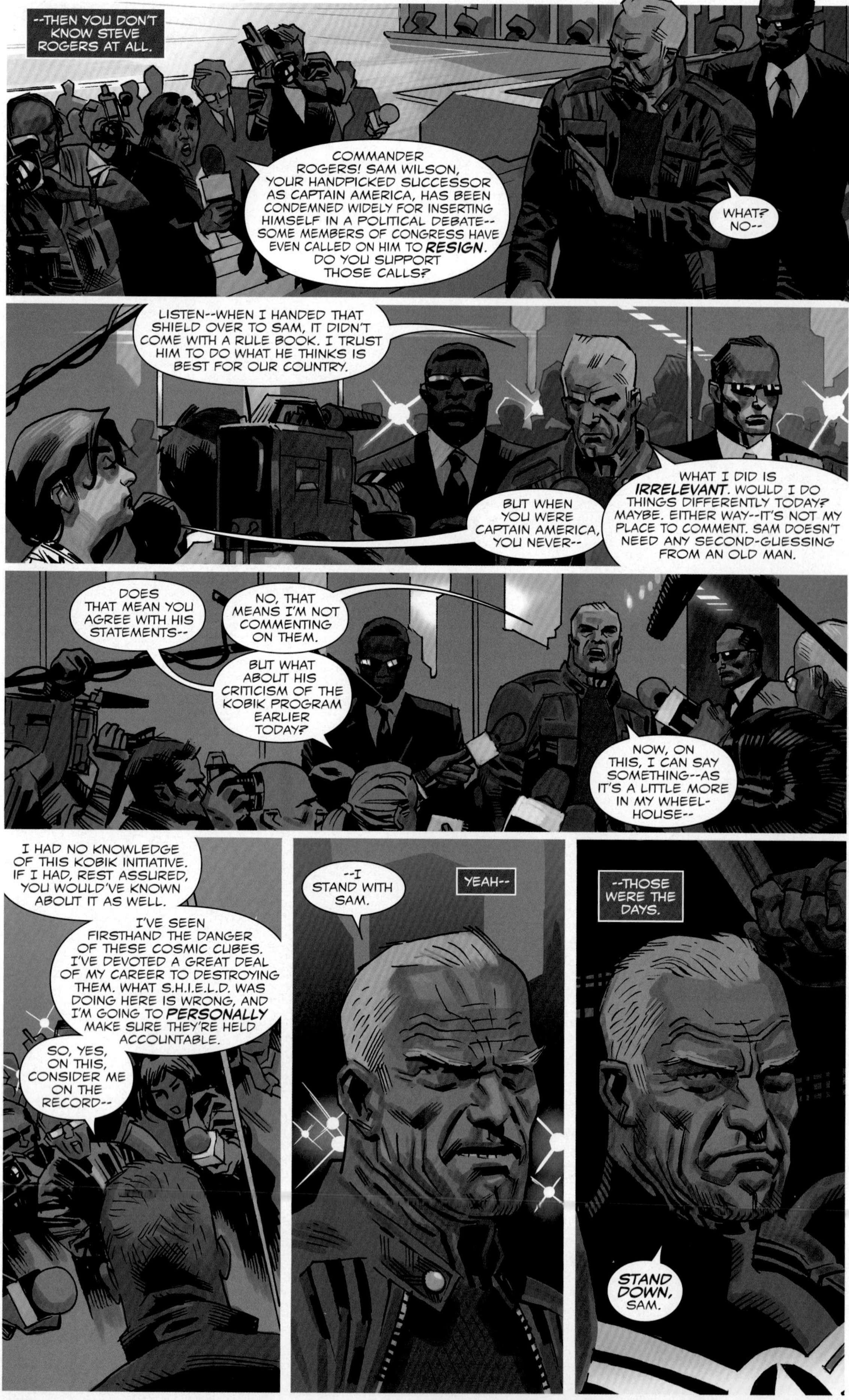
--THEN YOU DON'T KNOW STEVE ROGERS AT ALL.
COMMANDER ROGERS! SAM WILSON, YOUR HANDPICKED SUCCESSOR AS CAPTAIN AMERICA, HAS BEEN CONDEMNED WIDELY FOR INSERTING HIMSELF IN A POLITICAL DEBATE-- SOME MEMBERS OF CONGRESS HAVE EVEN CALLED ON HIM TO RESIGN. DO YOU SUPPORT THOSE CALLS?
WHAT? NO--
LISTEN--WHEN I HANDED THAT SHIELD OVER TO SAM, IT DIDN'T COME WITH A RULE BOOK. I TRUST HIM TO DO WHAT HE THINKS IS BEST FOR OUR COUNTRY.
BUT WHEN YOU WERE CAPTAIN AMERICA, YOU NEVER--
WHAT I DID IS IRRELEVANT. WOULD I DO THINGS DIFFERENTLY TODAY? MAYBE. EITHER WAY--IT'S NOT MY PLACE TO COMMENT. SAM DOESN'T NEED ANY SECOND-GUESSING FROM AN OLD MAN.
DOES THAT MEAN YOU AGREE WITH HIS STATEMENTS--
NO, THAT MEANS I'M NOT COMMENTING ON THEM.
BUT WHAT ABOUT HIS CRITICISM OF THE KOBIK PROGRAM EARLIER TODAY?
NOW, ON THIS, I CAN SAY SOMETHING--AS IT'S A LITTLE MORE IN MY WHEEL-HOUSE--
I HAD NO KNOWLEDGE OF THIS KOBIK INITIATIVE. IF I HAD, REST ASSURED, YOU WOULD'VE KNOWN ABOUT IT AS WELL.
I'VE SEEN FIRSTHAND THE DANGER OF THESE COSMIC CUBES. I'VE DEVOTED A GREAT DEAL OF MY CAREER TO DESTROYING THEM. WHAT S.H.I.E.L.D. WAS DOING HERE IS WRONG, AND I'M GOING TO PERSONALLY MAKE SURE THEY'RE HELD ACCOUNTABLE.
SO, YES, ON THIS, CONSIDER ME ON THE RECORD--
--I STAND WITH SAM.
YEAH--
--THOSE WERE THE DAYS.
STAND DOWN, SAM.

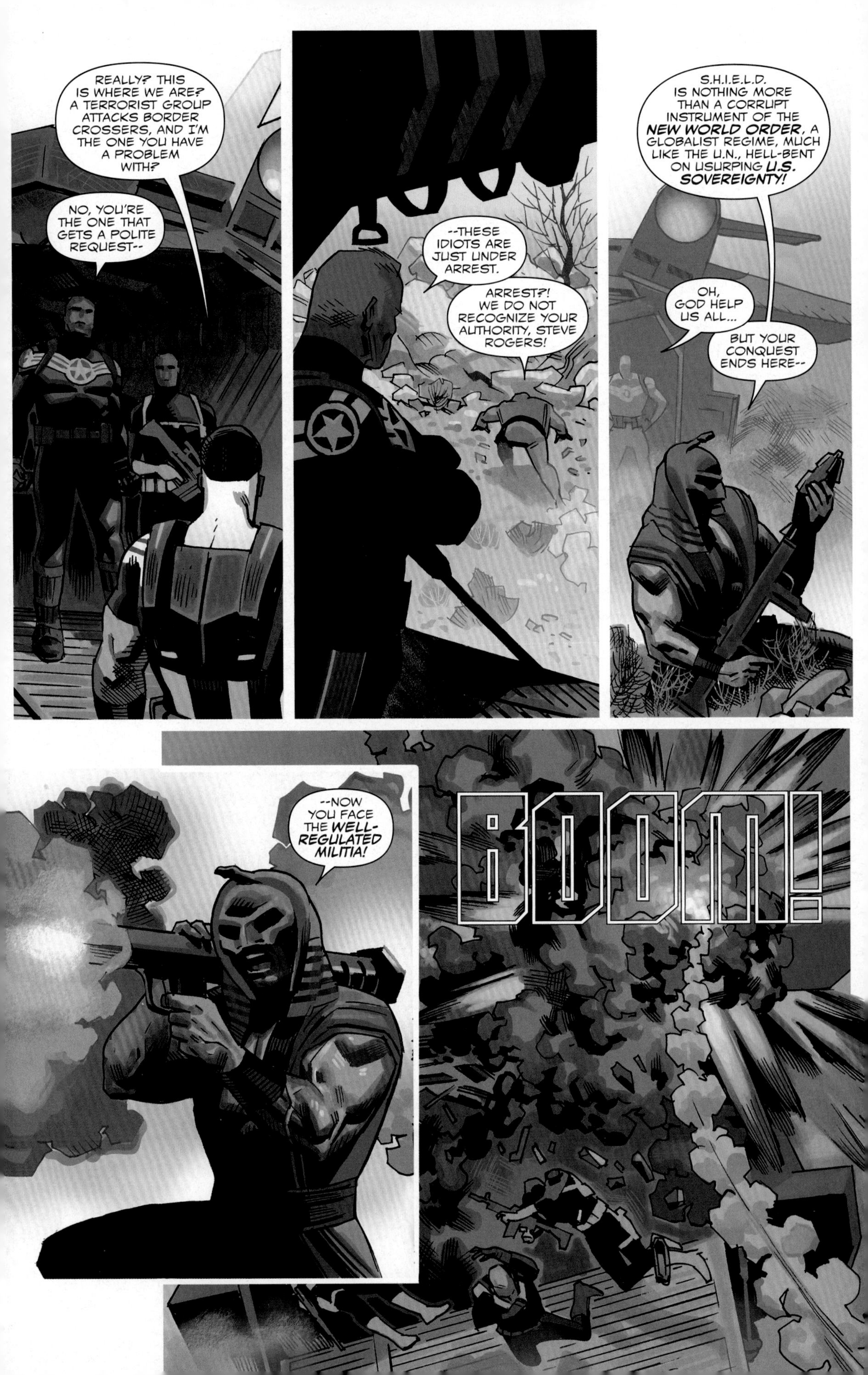

REALLY? THIS IS WHERE WE ARE? A TERRORIST GROUP ATTACKS BORDER CROSSERS, AND I'M THE ONE YOU HAVE A PROBLEM WITH?
NO, YOU'RE THE ONE THAT GETS A POLITE REQUEST--
--THESE IDIOTS ARE JUST UNDER ARREST.
ARREST?! WE DO NOT RECOGNIZE YOUR AUTHORITY, STEVE ROGERS!
S.H.I.E.L.D. IS NOTHING MORE THAN A CORRUPT INSTRUMENT OF THE NEW WORLD ORDER, A GLOBALIST REGIME, MUCH LIKE THE U.N., HELL-BENT ON USURPING U.S. SOVEREIGNTY!
OH, GOD HELP US ALL...
BUT YOUR CONQUEST ENDS HERE--
--NOW YOU FACE THE WELL-REGULATED MILITIA!
BOOM!

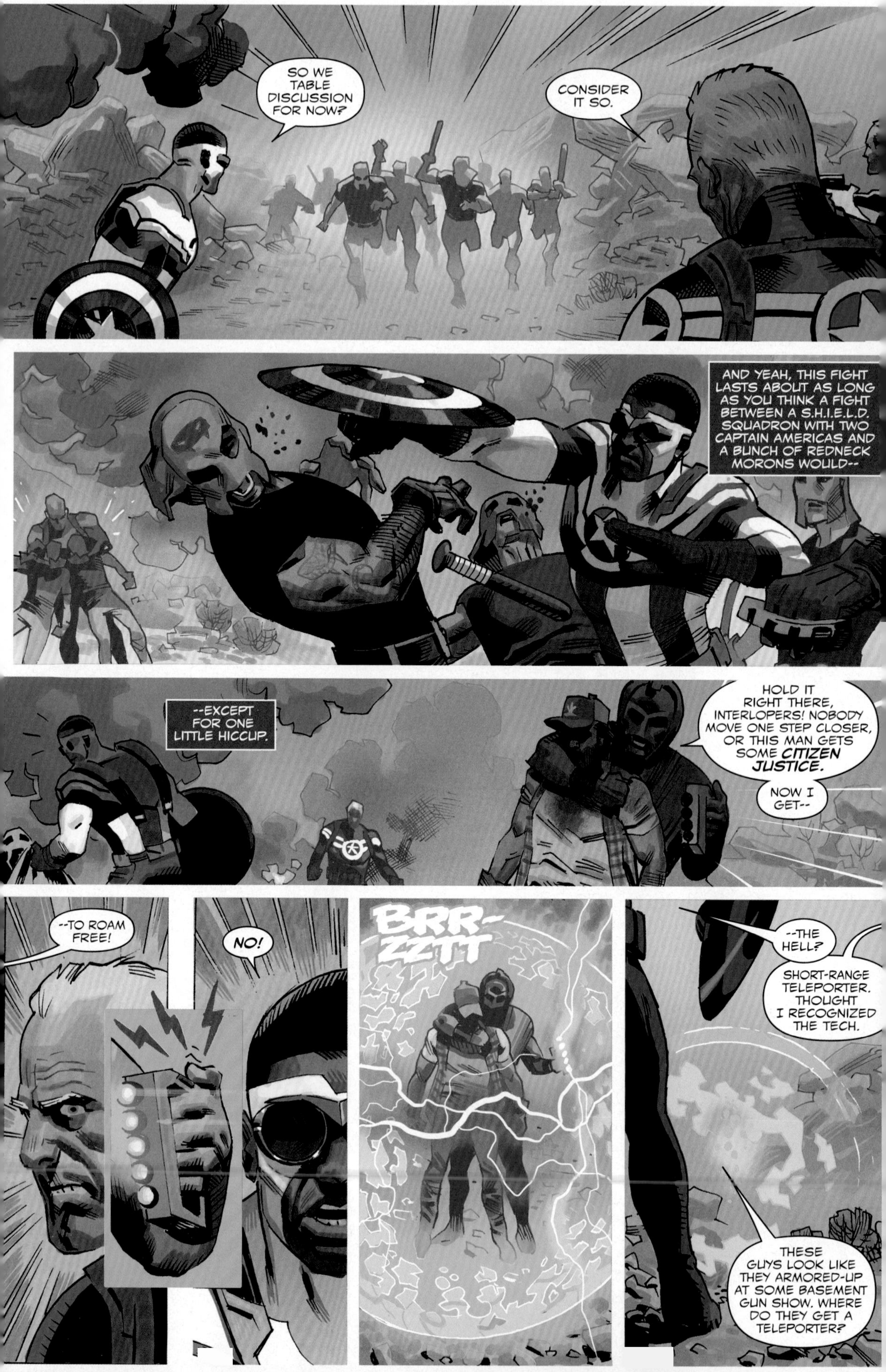
SO WE TABLE DISCUSSION FOR NOW?
CONSIDER IT SO.
AND YEAH, THIS FIGHT LASTS ABOUT AS LONG AS YOU THINK A FIGHT BETWEEN A S.H.I.E.L.D. SQUADRON WITH TWO CAPTAIN AMERICAS AND A BUNCH OF REDNECK MORONS WOULD--
--EXCEPT FOR ONE LITTLE HICCUP.
HOLD IT RIGHT THERE, INTERLOPERS! NOBODY MOVE ONE STEP CLOSER, OR THIS MAN GETS SOME CITIZEN JUSTICE.
NOW I GET--
--TO ROAM FREE!
NO!
BRR-ZZTT
--THE HELL?
SHORT-RANGE TELEPORTER. THOUGHT I RECOGNIZED THE TECH.
THESE GUYS LOOK LIKE THEY ARMORED-UP AT SOME BASEMENT GUN SHOW. WHERE DO THEY GET A TELEPORTER?

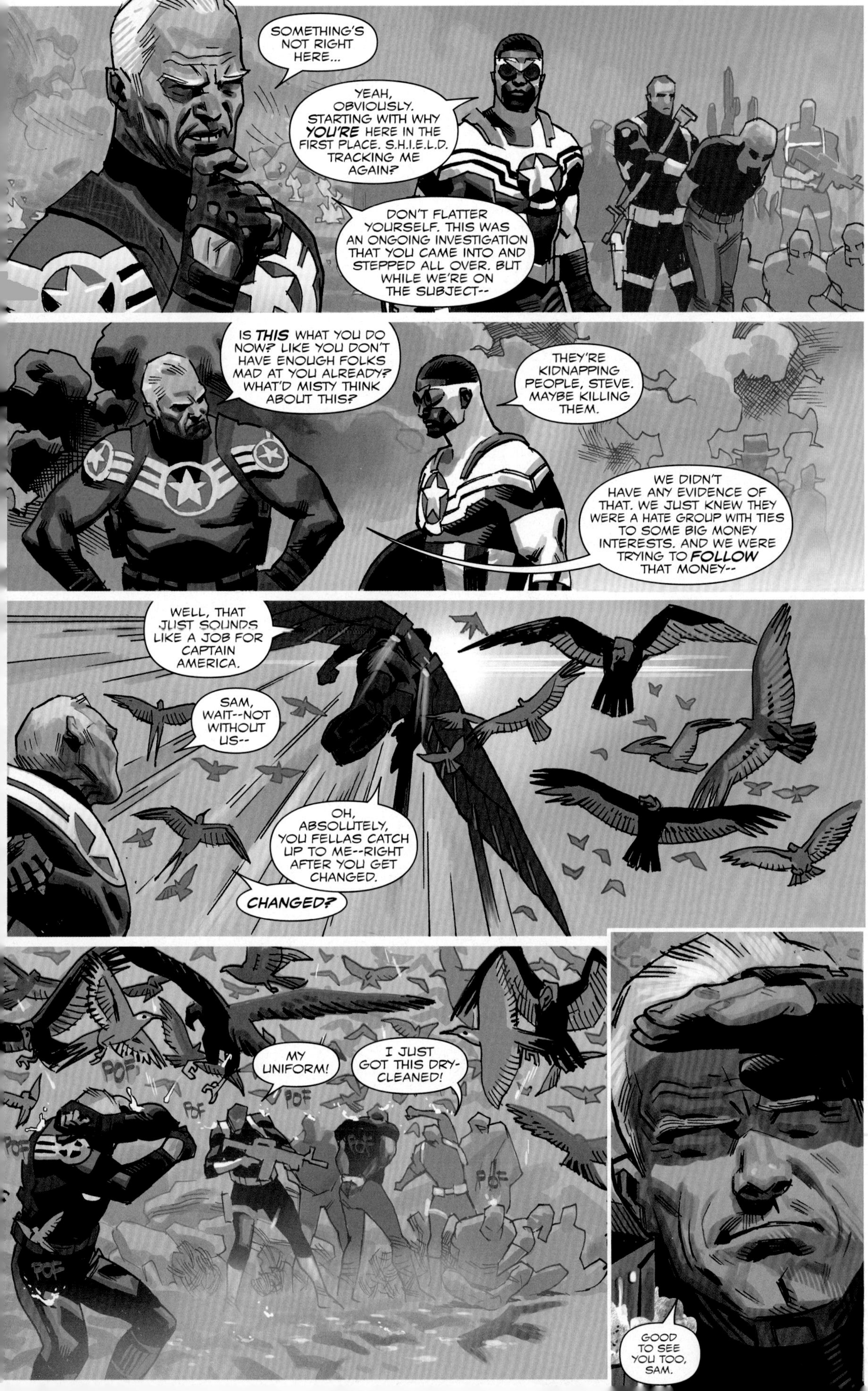
SOMETHING'S NOT RIGHT HERE...
YEAH, OBVIOUSLY. STARTING WITH WHY YOU'RE HERE IN THE FIRST PLACE. S.H.I.E.L.D. TRACKING ME AGAIN?
DON'T FLATTER YOURSELF. THIS WAS AN ONGOING INVESTIGATION THAT YOU CAME INTO AND STEPPED ALL OVER. BUT WHILE WE'RE ON THE SUBJECT--
IS THIS WHAT YOU DO NOW? LIKE YOU DON'T HAVE ENOUGH FOLKS MAD AT YOU ALREADY? WHAT'D MISTY THINK ABOUT THIS?
THEY'RE KIDNAPPING PEOPLE, STEVE. MAYBE KILLING THEM.
WE DIDN'T HAVE ANY EVIDENCE OF THAT. WE JUST KNEW THEY WERE A HATE GROUP WITH TIES TO SOME BIG MONEY INTERESTS. AND WE WERE TRYING TO FOLLOW THAT MONEY--
WELL, THAT JUST SOUNDS LIKE A JOB FOR CAPTAIN AMERICA.
SAM, WAIT--NOT WITHOUT US--
OH, ABSOLUTELY, YOU FELLAS CATCH UP TO ME--RIGHT AFTER YOU GET CHANGED.
CHANGED?
POF
MY UNIFORM!
I JUST GOT THIS DRY-CLEANED!
POF
POF
GOOD TO SEE YOU TOO, SAM.

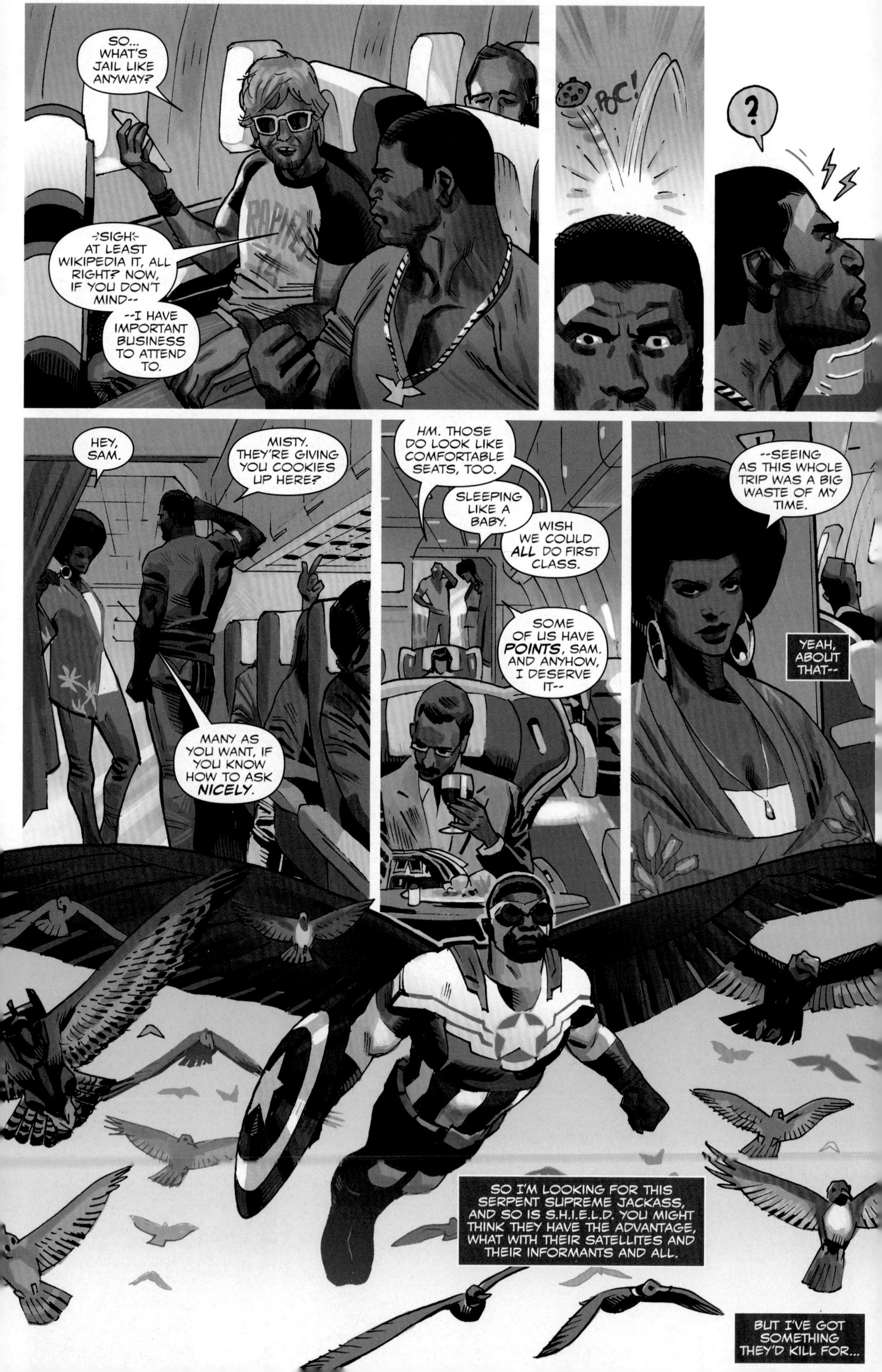
SO... WHAT'S JAIL LIKE ANYWAY?
-SIGH- AT LEAST WIKIPEDIA IT, ALL RIGHT? NOW, IF YOU DON'T MIND--
--I HAVE IMPORTANT BUSINESS TO ATTEND TO.
POC!
?
HEY, SAM.
MISTY. THEY'RE GIVING YOU COOKIES UP HERE?
MANY AS YOU WANT, IF YOU KNOW HOW TO ASK NICELY.
HM. THOSE DO LOOK LIKE COMFORTABLE SEATS, TOO.
SLEEPING LIKE A BABY.
WISH WE COULD ALL DO FIRST CLASS.
SOME OF US HAVE POINTS, SAM. AND ANYHOW, I DESERVE IT--
--SEEING AS THIS WHOLE TRIP WAS A BIG WASTE OF MY TIME.
YEAH, ABOUT THAT--
SO I'M LOOKING FOR THIS SERPENT SUPREME JACKASS, AND SO IS S.H.I.E.L.D. YOU MIGHT THINK THEY HAVE THE ADVANTAGE, WHAT WITH THEIR SATELLITES AND THEIR INFORMANTS AND ALL.
BUT I'VE GOT SOMETHING THEY'D KILL FOR...

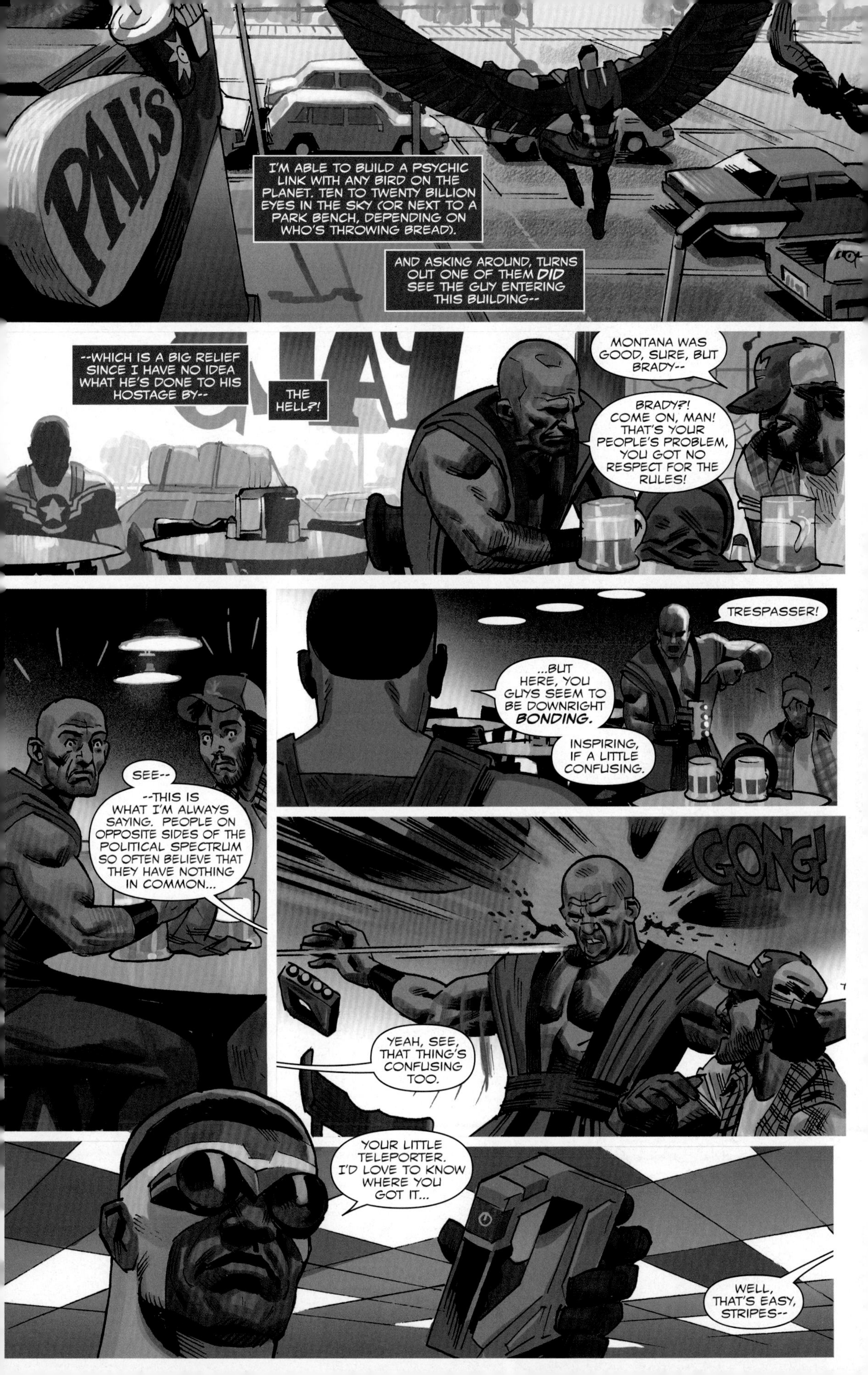
PAL'S
I'M ABLE TO BUILD A PSYCHIC LINK WITH ANY BIRD ON THE PLANET. TEN TO TWENTY BILLION EYES IN THE SKY (OR NEXT TO A PARK BENCH, DEPENDING ON WHO'S THROWING BREAD).
AND ASKING AROUND, TURNS OUT ONE OF THEM DID SEE THE GUY ENTERING THIS BUILDING--
--WHICH IS A BIG RELIEF SINCE I HAVE NO IDEA WHAT HE'S DONE TO HIS HOSTAGE BY--
THE HELL?!
MONTANA WAS GOOD, SURE, BUT BRADY--
BRADY?! COME ON, MAN! THAT'S YOUR PEOPLE'S PROBLEM, YOU GOT NO RESPECT FOR THE RULES!
SEE--
--THIS IS WHAT I'M ALWAYS SAYING. PEOPLE ON OPPOSITE SIDES OF THE POLITICAL SPECTRUM SO OFTEN BELIEVE THAT THEY HAVE NOTHING IN COMMON...
...BUT HERE, YOU GUYS SEEM TO BE DOWNRIGHT BONDING.
INSPIRING, IF A LITTLE CONFUSING.
TRESPASSER!
GONG!
YEAH, SEE, THAT THING'S CONFUSING TOO.
YOUR LITTLE TELEPORTER. I'D LOVE TO KNOW WHERE YOU GOT IT...
WELL, THAT'S EASY, STRIPES--

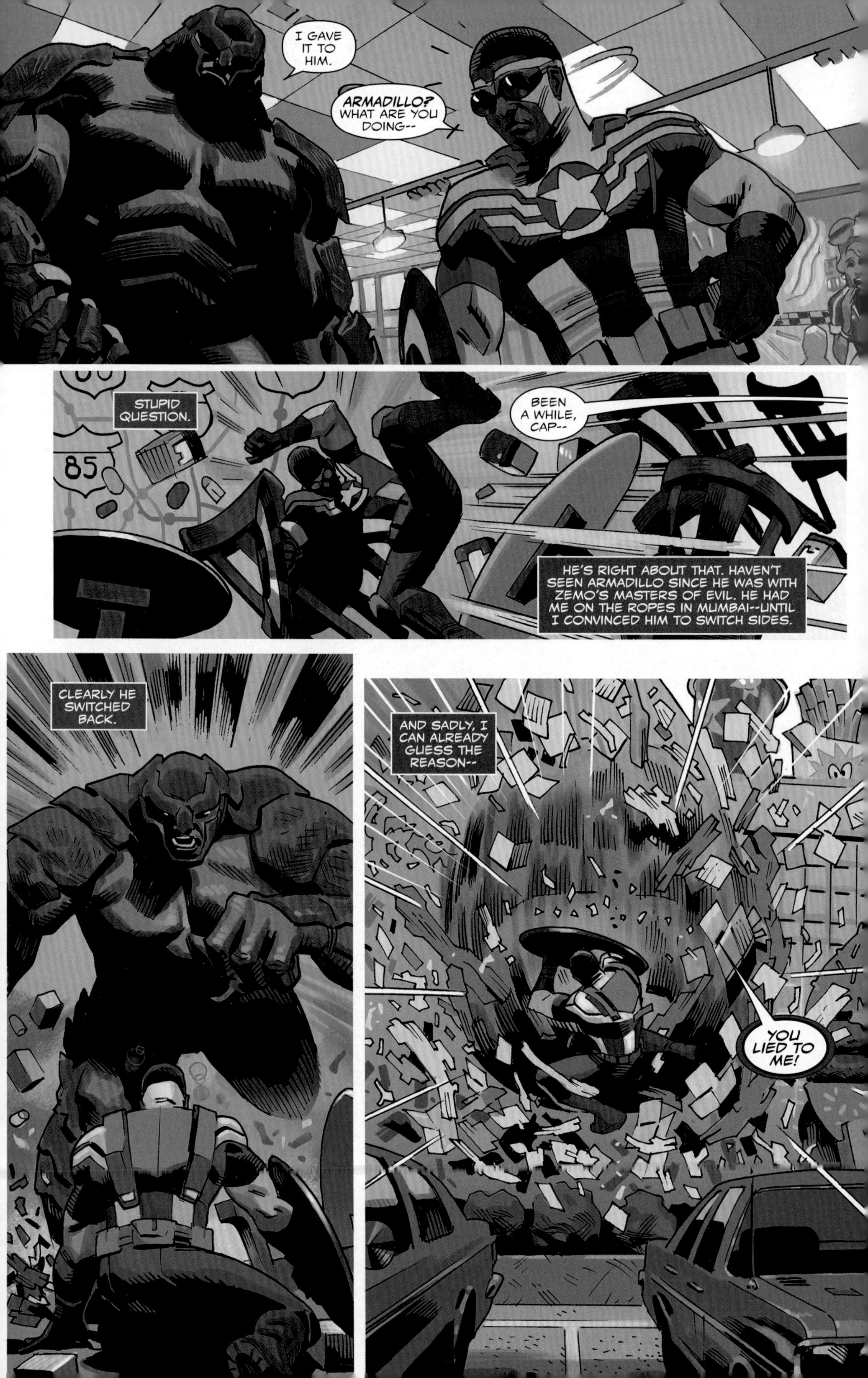
I GAVE IT TO HIM.
ARMADILLO? WHAT ARE YOU DOING--
STUPID QUESTION.
BEEN A WHILE, CAP--
85
HE'S RIGHT ABOUT THAT. HAVEN'T SEEN ARMADILLO SINCE HE WAS WITH ZEMO'S MASTERS OF EVIL. HE HAD ME ON THE ROPES IN MUMBAI--UNTIL I CONVINCED HIM TO SWITCH SIDES.
CLEARLY HE SWITCHED BACK.
AND SADLY, I CAN ALREADY GUESS THE REASON--
YOU LIED TO ME!

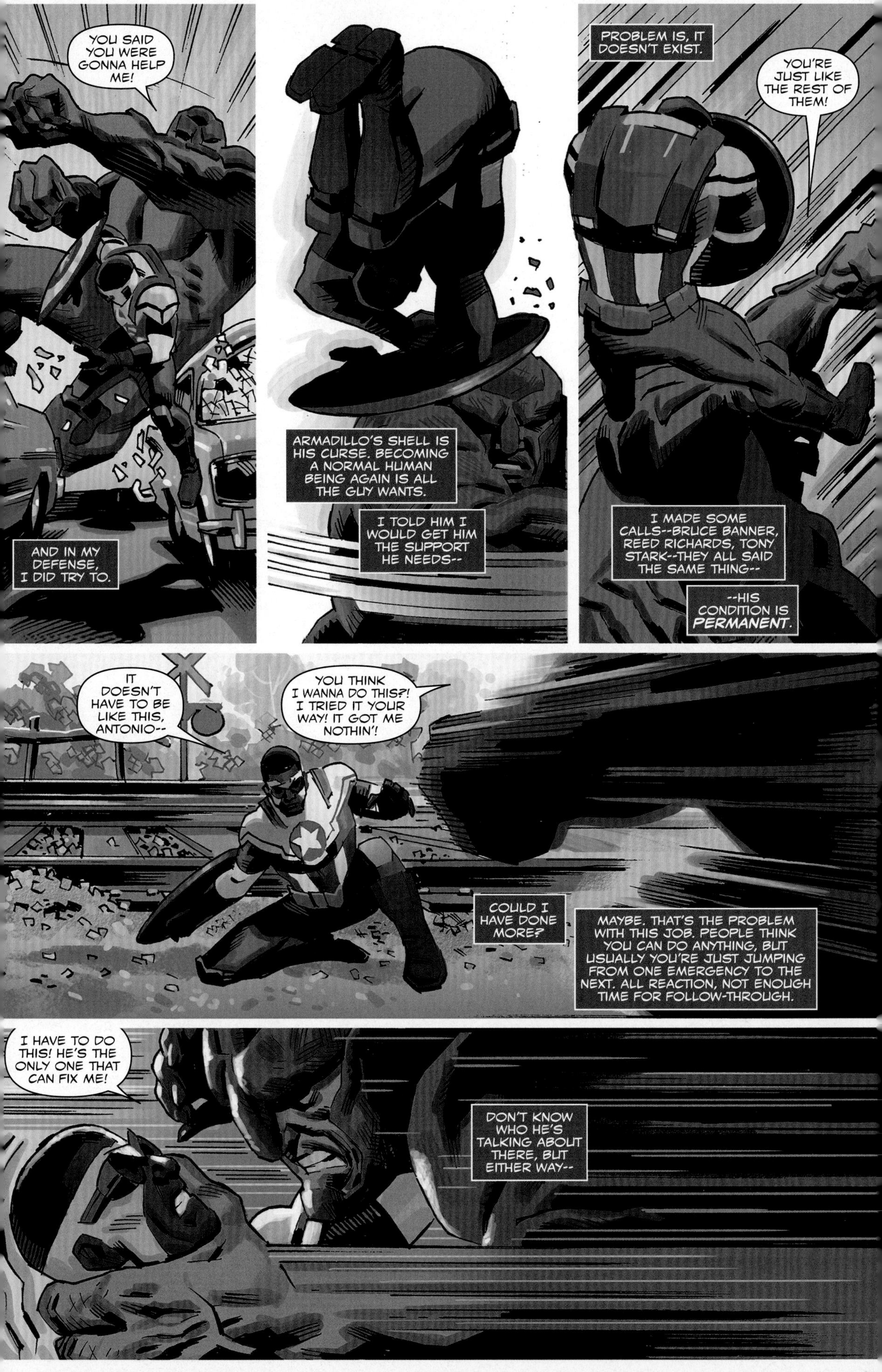
YOU SAID YOU WERE GONNA HELP ME!
AND IN MY DEFENSE, I DID TRY TO.
ARMADILLO'S SHELL IS HIS CURSE. BECOMING A NORMAL HUMAN BEING AGAIN IS ALL THE GUY WANTS.
I TOLD HIM I WOULD GET HIM THE SUPPORT HE NEEDS--
PROBLEM IS, IT DOESN'T EXIST.
YOU'RE JUST LIKE THE REST OF THEM!
I MADE SOME CALLS--BRUCE BANNER, REED RICHARDS, TONY STARK--THEY ALL SAID THE SAME THING--
--HIS CONDITION IS *PERMANENT*.
IT DOESN'T HAVE TO BE LIKE THIS, ANTONIO--
YOU THINK I WANNA DO THIS?! I TRIED IT YOUR WAY! IT GOT ME NOTHIN'!
COULD I HAVE DONE MORE?
MAYBE. THAT'S THE PROBLEM WITH THIS JOB. PEOPLE THINK YOU CAN DO ANYTHING, BUT USUALLY YOU'RE JUST JUMPING FROM ONE EMERGENCY TO THE NEXT. ALL REACTION, NOT ENOUGH TIME FOR FOLLOW-THROUGH.
I HAVE TO DO THIS! HE'S THE ONLY ONE THAT CAN FIX ME!
DON'T KNOW WHO HE'S TALKING ABOUT THERE, BUT EITHER WAY--

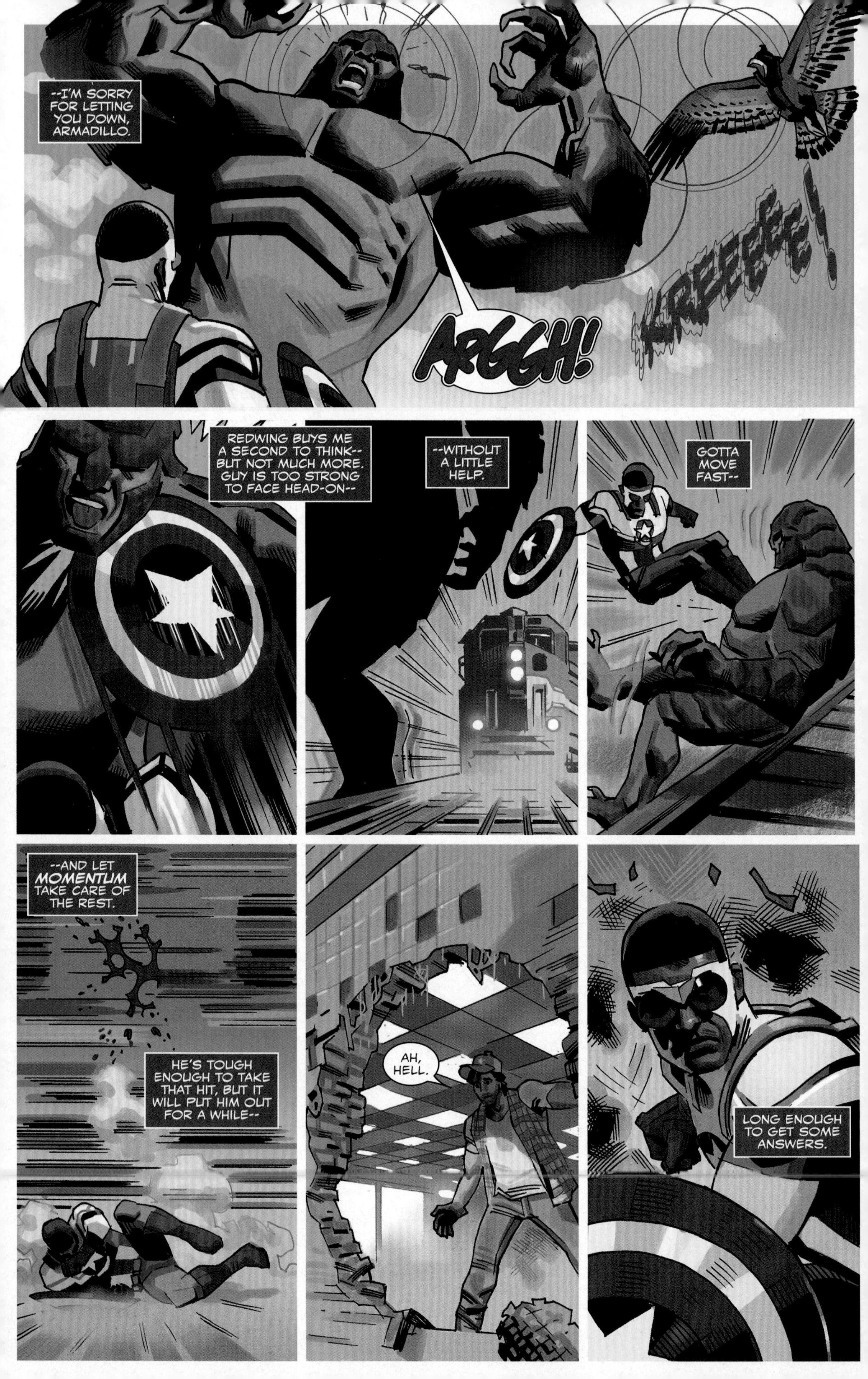

--I'M SORRY FOR LETTING YOU DOWN, ARMADILLO.
ARGGH!
KREEEEE!
REDWING BUYS ME A SECOND TO THINK-- BUT NOT MUCH MORE. GUY IS TOO STRONG TO FACE HEAD-ON--
--WITHOUT A LITTLE HELP.
GOTTA MOVE FAST--
--AND LET MOMENTUM TAKE CARE OF THE REST.
HE'S TOUGH ENOUGH TO TAKE THAT HIT, BUT IT WILL PUT HIM OUT FOR A WHILE--
AH, HELL.
LONG ENOUGH TO GET SOME ANSWERS.

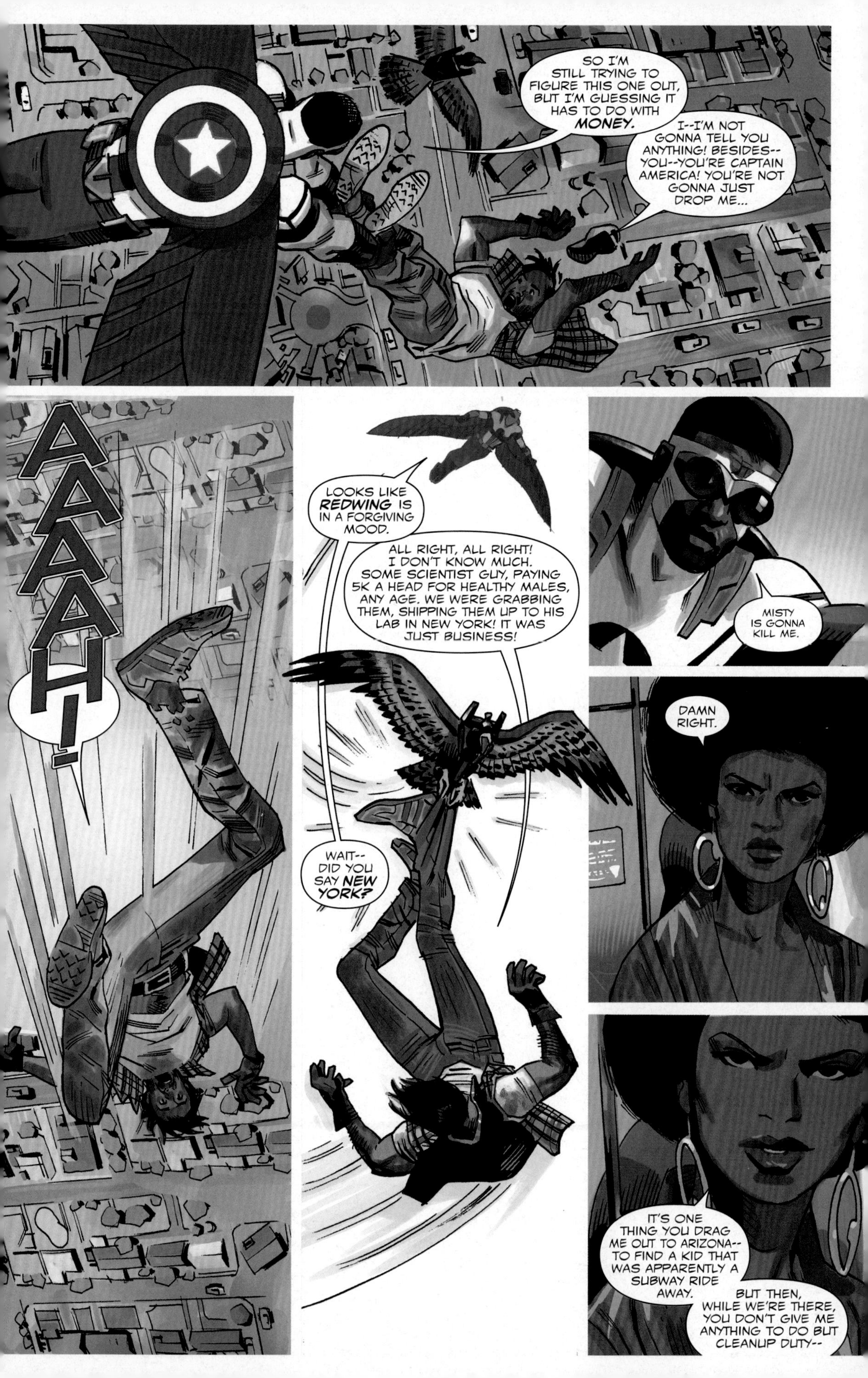
SO I'M STILL TRYING TO FIGURE THIS ONE OUT, BUT I'M GUESSING IT HAS TO DO WITH MONEY.
I--I'M NOT GONNA TELL YOU ANYTHING! BESIDES-- YOU--YOU'RE CAPTAIN AMERICA! YOU'RE NOT GONNA JUST DROP ME...
AAAAH!
LOOKS LIKE REDWING IS IN A FORGIVING MOOD.
ALL RIGHT, ALL RIGHT! I DON'T KNOW MUCH. SOME SCIENTIST GUY, PAYING 5K A HEAD FOR HEALTHY MALES, ANY AGE. WE WERE GRABBING THEM, SHIPPING THEM UP TO HIS LAB IN NEW YORK! IT WAS JUST BUSINESS!
WAIT-- DID YOU SAY NEW YORK?
MISTY IS GONNA KILL ME.
DAMN RIGHT.
IT'S ONE THING YOU DRAG ME OUT TO ARIZONA-- TO FIND A KID THAT WAS APPARENTLY A SUBWAY RIDE AWAY.
BUT THEN, WHILE WE'RE THERE, YOU DON'T GIVE ME ANYTHING TO DO BUT CLEANUP DUTY--

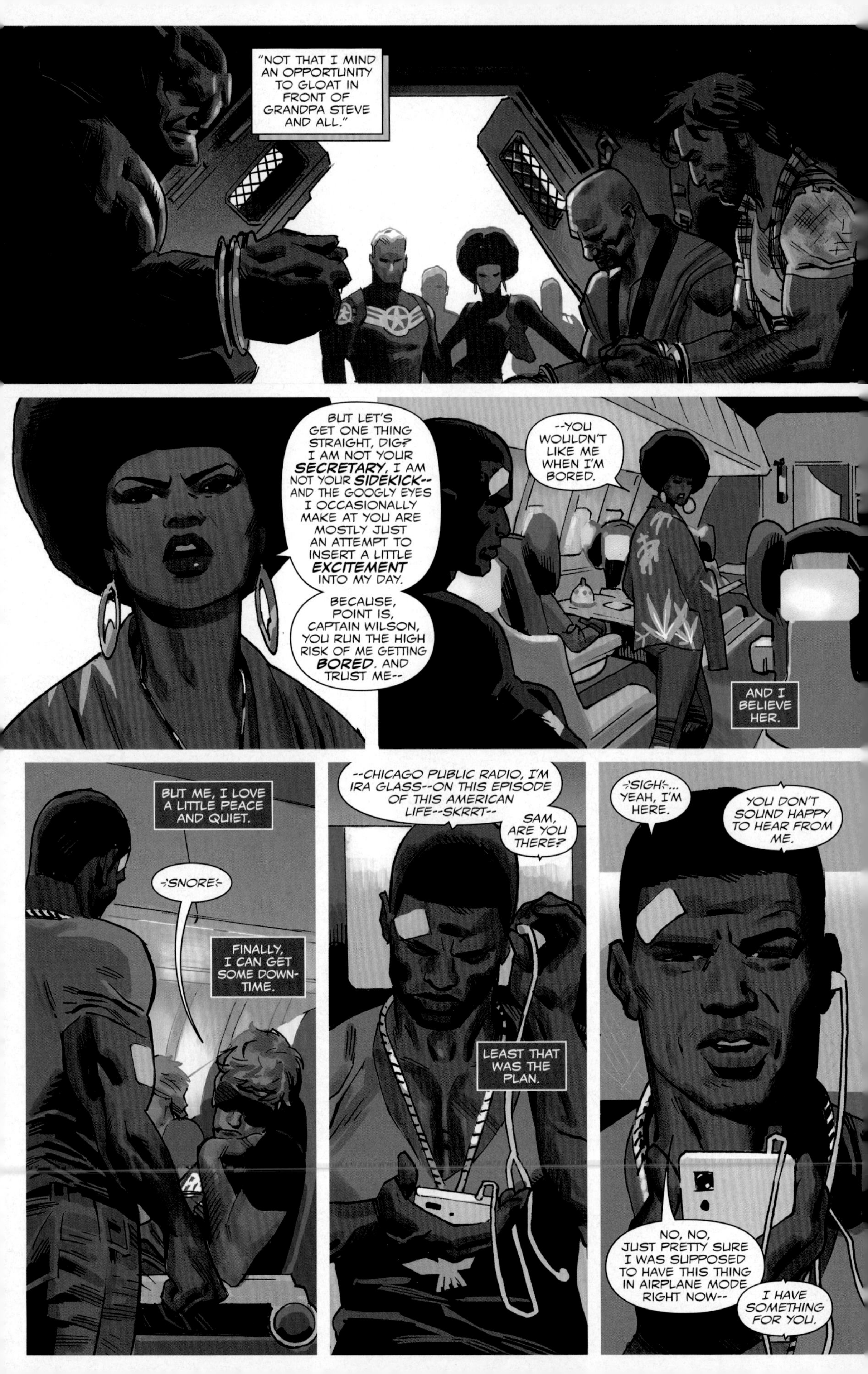
"NOT THAT I MIND AN OPPORTUNITY TO GLOAT IN FRONT OF GRANDPA STEVE AND ALL."
BUT LET'S GET ONE THING STRAIGHT, DIG? I AM NOT YOUR SECRETARY, I AM NOT YOUR SIDEKICK-- AND THE GOOGLY EYES I OCCASIONALLY MAKE AT YOU ARE MOSTLY JUST AN ATTEMPT TO INSERT A LITTLE EXCITEMENT INTO MY DAY.
BECAUSE, POINT IS, CAPTAIN WILSON, YOU RUN THE HIGH RISK OF ME GETTING BORED. AND TRUST ME--
--YOU WOULDN'T LIKE ME WHEN I'M BORED.
AND I BELIEVE HER.
BUT ME, I LOVE A LITTLE PEACE AND QUIET.
-SNORE-
FINALLY, I CAN GET SOME DOWN-TIME.
--CHICAGO PUBLIC RADIO, I'M IRA GLASS--ON THIS EPISODE OF THIS AMERICAN LIFE--SKRRT--
SAM, ARE YOU THERE?
LEAST THAT WAS THE PLAN.
-SIGH-... YEAH, I'M HERE.
YOU DON'T SOUND HAPPY TO HEAR FROM ME.
NO, NO, JUST PRETTY SURE I WAS SUPPOSED TO HAVE THIS THING IN AIRPLANE MODE RIGHT NOW--
I HAVE SOMETHING FOR YOU.

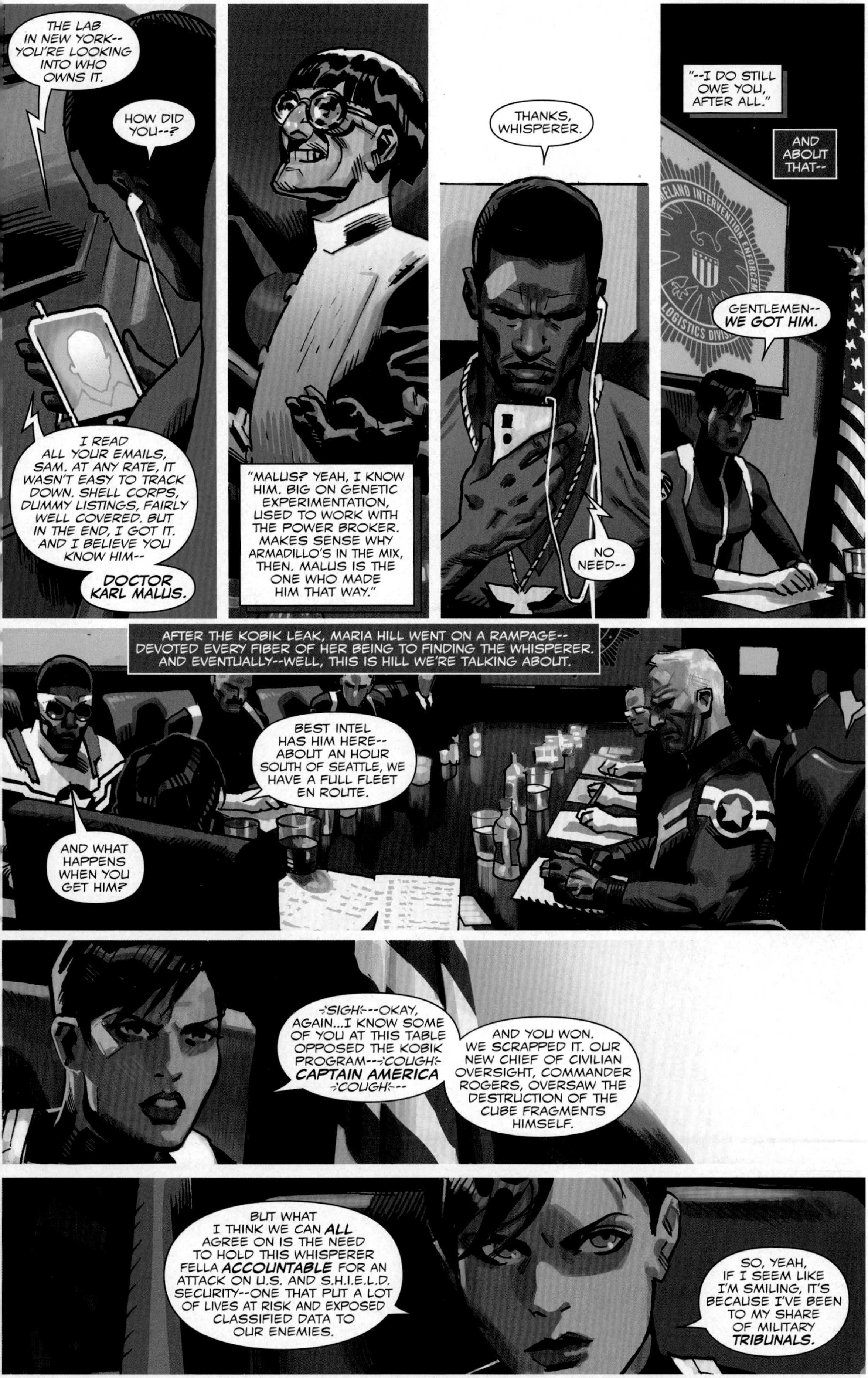
THE LAB IN NEW YORK-- YOU'RE LOOKING INTO WHO OWNS IT.
HOW DID YOU--?
I READ ALL YOUR EMAILS, SAM. AT ANY RATE, IT WASN'T EASY TO TRACK DOWN. SHELL CORPS, DUMMY LISTINGS, FAIRLY WELL COVERED. BUT IN THE END, I GOT IT. AND I BELIEVE YOU KNOW HIM--
DOCTOR KARL MALUS.
"MALUS? YEAH, I KNOW HIM. BIG ON GENETIC EXPERIMENTATION, USED TO WORK WITH THE POWER BROKER. MAKES SENSE WHY ARMADILLO'S IN THE MIX, THEN. MALUS IS THE ONE WHO MADE HIM THAT WAY."
THANKS, WHISPERER.
NO NEED--
"--I DO STILL OWE YOU, AFTER ALL."
AND ABOUT THAT--
GENTLEMEN-- WE GOT HIM.
AFTER THE KOBIK LEAK, MARIA HILL WENT ON A RAMPAGE-- DEVOTED EVERY FIBER OF HER BEING TO FINDING THE WHISPERER. AND EVENTUALLY--WELL, THIS IS HILL WE'RE TALKING ABOUT.
BEST INTEL HAS HIM HERE-- ABOUT AN HOUR SOUTH OF SEATTLE. WE HAVE A FULL FLEET EN ROUTE.
AND WHAT HAPPENS WHEN YOU GET HIM?
SIGH--OKAY, AGAIN...I KNOW SOME OF YOU AT THIS TABLE OPPOSED THE KOBIK PROGRAM--*COUGH* CAPTAIN AMERICA *COUGH*--
AND YOU WON. WE SCRAPPED IT. OUR NEW CHIEF OF CIVILIAN OVERSIGHT, COMMANDER ROGERS, OVERSAW THE DESTRUCTION OF THE CUBE FRAGMENTS HIMSELF.
BUT WHAT I THINK WE CAN ALL AGREE ON IS THE NEED TO HOLD THIS WHISPERER FELLA ACCOUNTABLE FOR AN ATTACK ON U.S. AND S.H.I.E.L.D. SECURITY--ONE THAT PUT A LOT OF LIVES AT RISK AND EXPOSED CLASSIFIED DATA TO OUR ENEMIES.
SO, YEAH, IF I SEEM LIKE I'M SMILING, IT'S BECAUSE I'VE BEEN TO MY SHARE OF MILITARY TRIBUNALS.

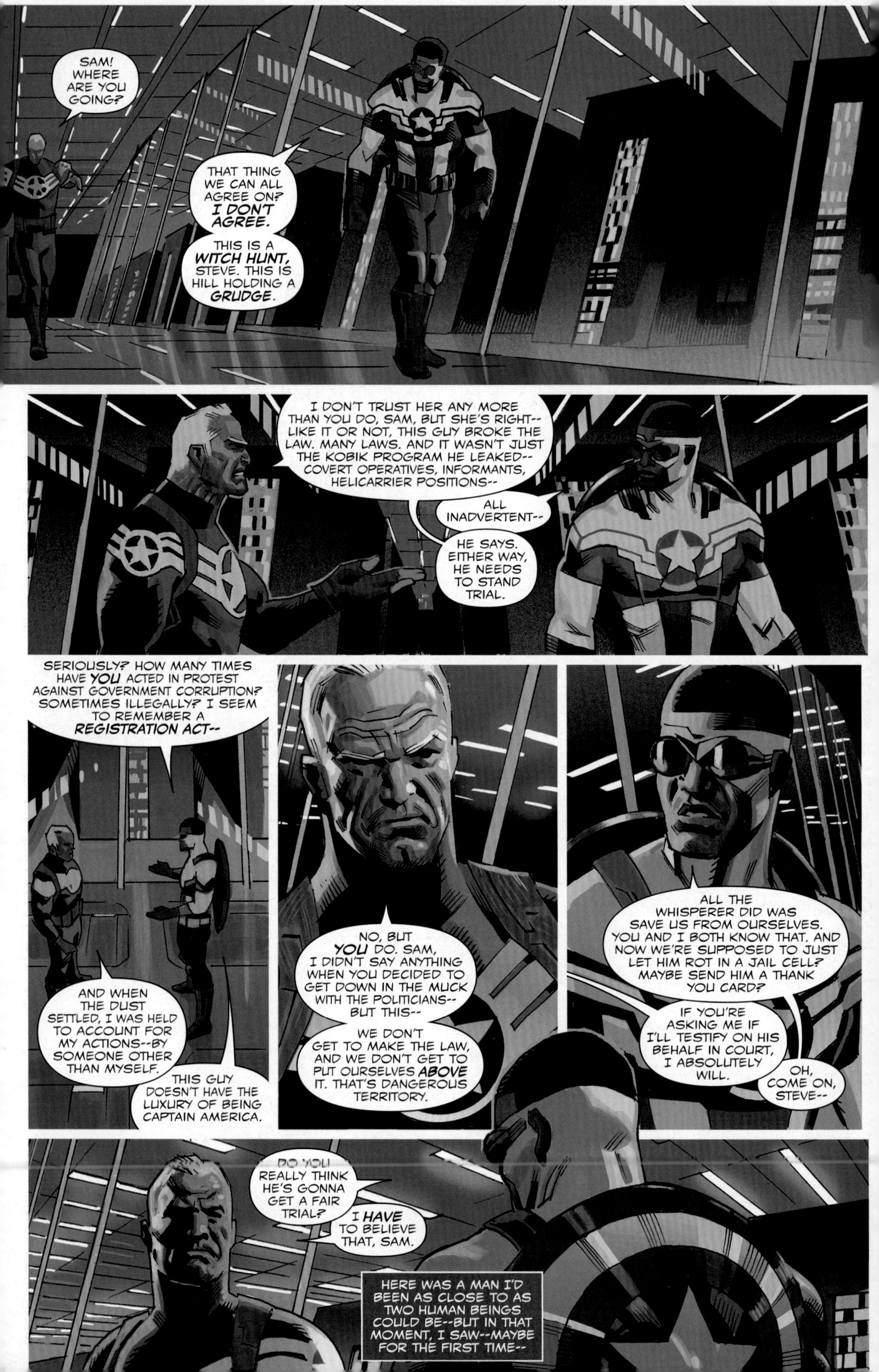
SAM! WHERE ARE YOU GOING?
THAT THING WE CAN ALL AGREE ON? I DON'T AGREE.
THIS IS A WITCH HUNT, STEVE. THIS IS HILL HOLDING A GRUDGE.
I DON'T TRUST HER ANY MORE THAN YOU DO, SAM, BUT SHE'S RIGHT--LIKE IT OR NOT, THIS GUY BROKE THE LAW. MANY LAWS. AND IT WASN'T JUST THE KOBIK PROGRAM HE LEAKED--COVERT OPERATIVES, INFORMANTS, HELICARRIER POSITIONS--
ALL INADVERTENT--
HE SAYS. EITHER WAY, HE NEEDS TO STAND TRIAL.
SERIOUSLY? HOW MANY TIMES HAVE YOU ACTED IN PROTEST AGAINST GOVERNMENT CORRUPTION? SOMETIMES ILLEGALLY? I SEEM TO REMEMBER A REGISTRATION ACT--
AND WHEN THE DUST SETTLED, I WAS HELD TO ACCOUNT FOR MY ACTIONS--BY SOMEONE OTHER THAN MYSELF.
THIS GUY DOESN'T HAVE THE LUXURY OF BEING CAPTAIN AMERICA.
NO, BUT YOU DO. SAM, I DIDN'T SAY ANYTHING WHEN YOU DECIDED TO GET DOWN IN THE MUCK WITH THE POLITICIANS--BUT THIS--
WE DON'T GET TO MAKE THE LAW, AND WE DON'T GET TO PUT OURSELVES ABOVE IT. THAT'S DANGEROUS TERRITORY.
ALL THE WHISPERER DID WAS SAVE US FROM OURSELVES. YOU AND I BOTH KNOW THAT. AND NOW WE'RE SUPPOSED TO JUST LET HIM ROT IN A JAIL CELL? MAYBE SEND HIM A THANK YOU CARD?
IF YOU'RE ASKING ME IF I'LL TESTIFY ON HIS BEHALF IN COURT, I ABSOLUTELY WILL.
OH, COME ON, STEVE--
DO YOU REALLY THINK HE'S GONNA GET A FAIR TRIAL?
I HAVE TO BELIEVE THAT, SAM.
HERE WAS A MAN I'D BEEN AS CLOSE TO AS TWO HUMAN BEINGS COULD BE--BUT IN THAT MOMENT, I SAW--MAYBE FOR THE FIRST TIME--

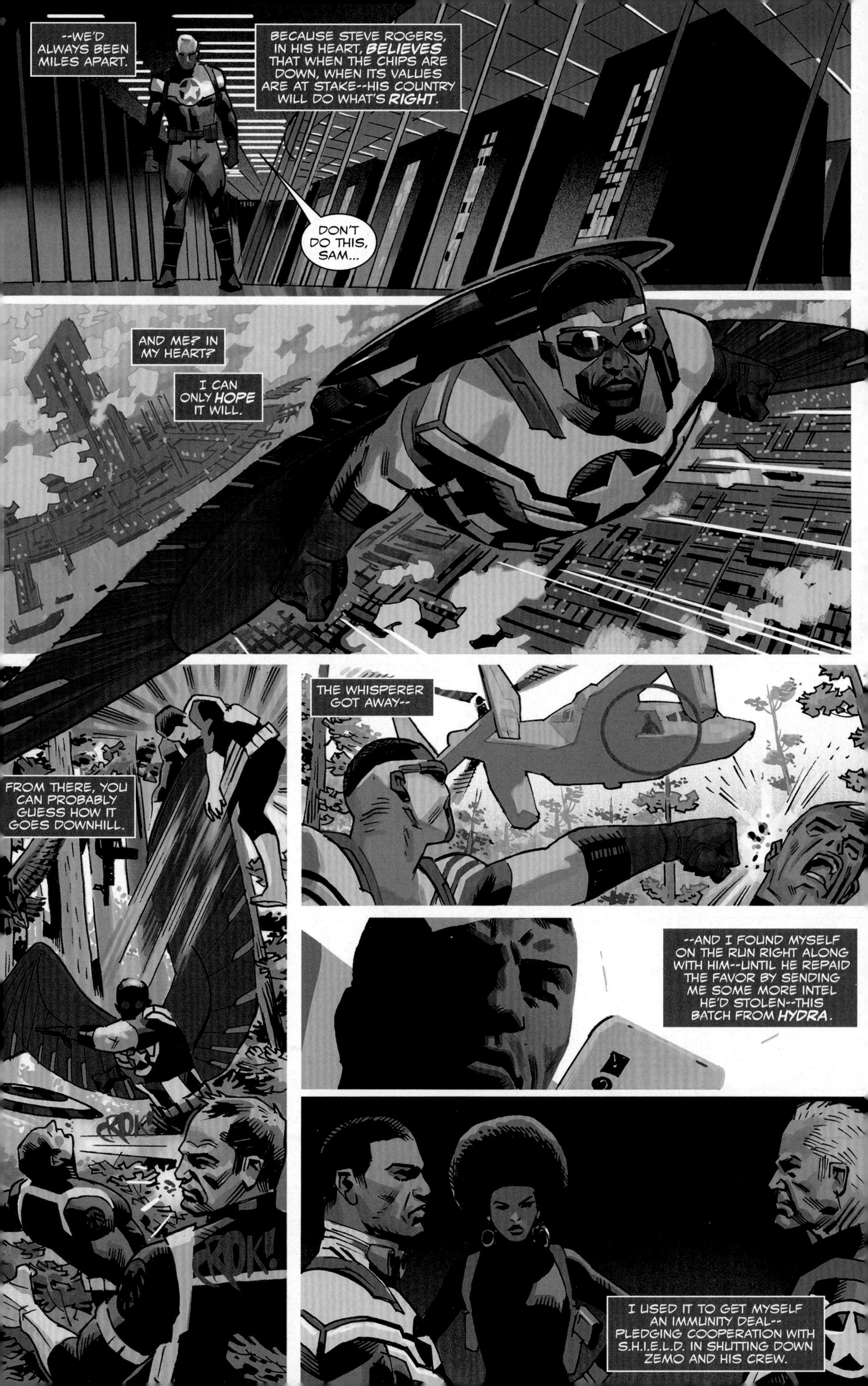
--WE'D ALWAYS BEEN MILES APART.
BECAUSE STEVE ROGERS, IN HIS HEART, BELIEVES THAT WHEN THE CHIPS ARE DOWN, WHEN ITS VALUES ARE AT STAKE--HIS COUNTRY WILL DO WHAT'S RIGHT.
DON'T DO THIS, SAM...
AND ME? IN MY HEART?
I CAN ONLY HOPE IT WILL.
FROM THERE, YOU CAN PROBABLY GUESS HOW IT GOES DOWNHILL.
KROK!
KROK!
THE WHISPERER GOT AWAY--
--AND I FOUND MYSELF ON THE RUN RIGHT ALONG WITH HIM--UNTIL HE REPAID THE FAVOR BY SENDING ME SOME MORE INTEL HE'D STOLEN--THIS BATCH FROM HYDRA.
I USED IT TO GET MYSELF AN IMMUNITY DEAL--PLEDGING COOPERATION WITH S.H.I.E.L.D. IN SHUTTING DOWN ZEMO AND HIS CREW.

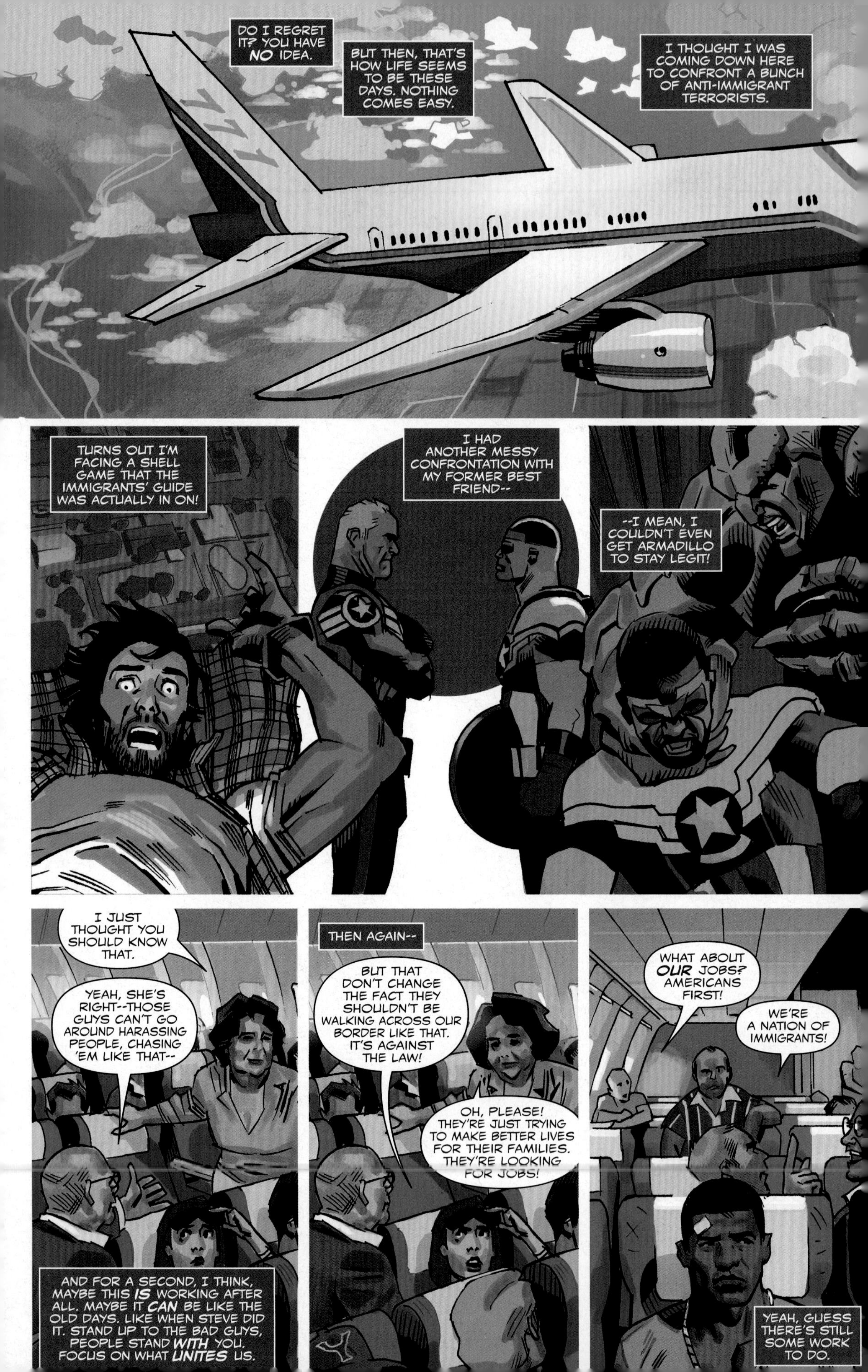
DO I REGRET IT? YOU HAVE NO IDEA.
BUT THEN, THAT'S HOW LIFE SEEMS TO BE THESE DAYS. NOTHING COMES EASY.
I THOUGHT I WAS COMING DOWN HERE TO CONFRONT A BUNCH OF ANTI-IMMIGRANT TERRORISTS.
TURNS OUT I'M FACING A SHELL GAME THAT THE IMMIGRANTS' GUIDE WAS ACTUALLY IN ON!
I HAD ANOTHER MESSY CONFRONTATION WITH MY FORMER BEST FRIEND--
--I MEAN, I COULDN'T EVEN GET ARMADILLO TO STAY LEGIT!
I JUST THOUGHT YOU SHOULD KNOW THAT.
YEAH, SHE'S RIGHT--THOSE GUYS CAN'T GO AROUND HARASSING PEOPLE, CHASING 'EM LIKE THAT--
AND FOR A SECOND, I THINK, MAYBE THIS IS WORKING AFTER ALL. MAYBE IT CAN BE LIKE THE OLD DAYS. LIKE WHEN STEVE DID IT. STAND UP TO THE BAD GUYS, PEOPLE STAND WITH YOU. FOCUS ON WHAT UNITES US.
THEN AGAIN--
BUT THAT DON'T CHANGE THE FACT THEY SHOULDN'T BE WALKING ACROSS OUR BORDER LIKE THAT. IT'S AGAINST THE LAW!
OH, PLEASE! THEY'RE JUST TRYING TO MAKE BETTER LIVES FOR THEIR FAMILIES. THEY'RE LOOKING FOR JOBS!
WHAT ABOUT OUR JOBS? AMERICANS FIRST!
WE'RE A NATION OF IMMIGRANTS!
YEAH, GUESS THERE'S STILL SOME WORK TO DO.

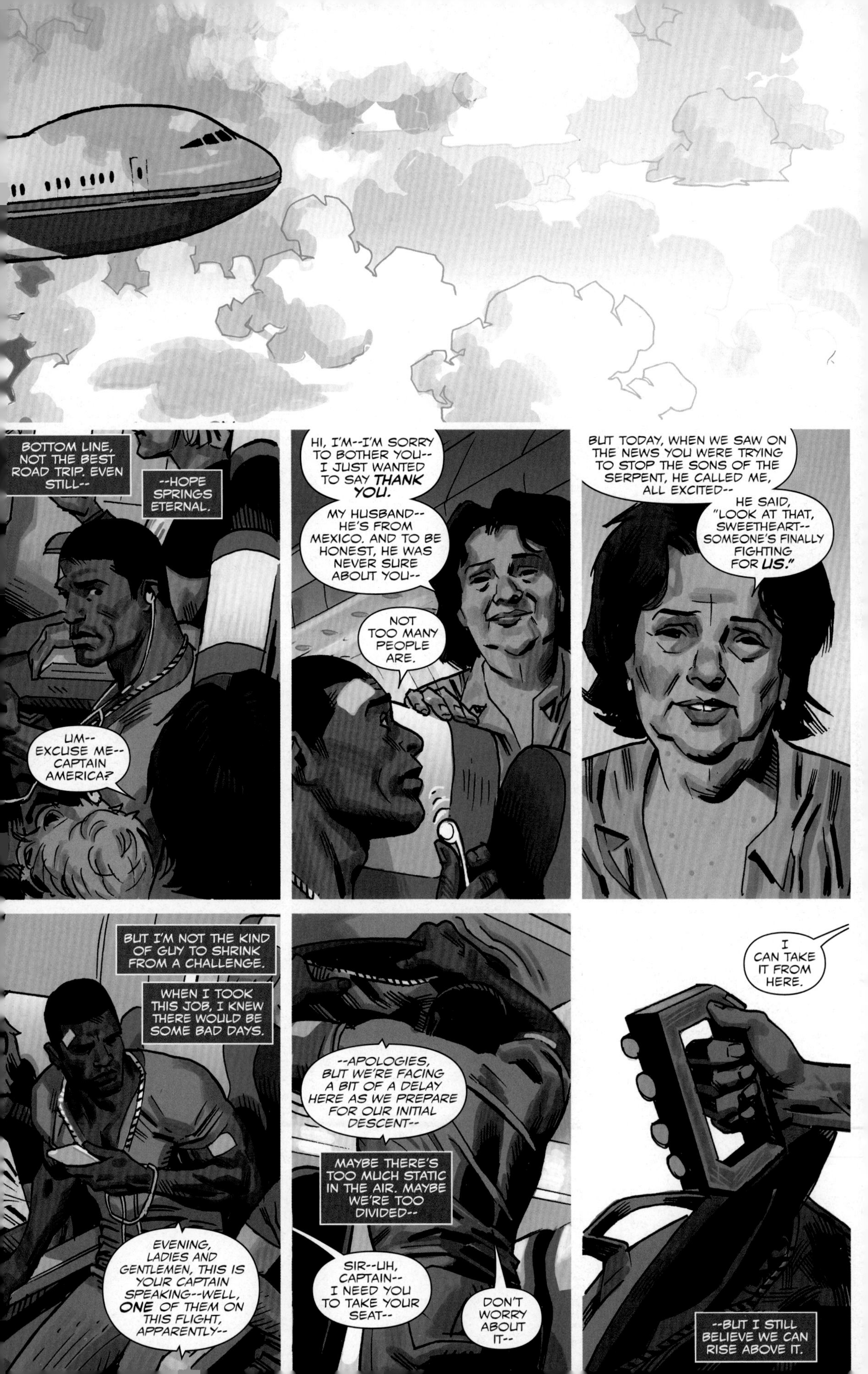
BOTTOM LINE, NOT THE BEST ROAD TRIP. EVEN STILL--
--HOPE SPRINGS ETERNAL.
UM--EXCUSE ME--CAPTAIN AMERICA?
HI, I'M--I'M SORRY TO BOTHER YOU--I JUST WANTED TO SAY THANK YOU.
MY HUSBAND--HE'S FROM MEXICO. AND TO BE HONEST, HE WAS NEVER SURE ABOUT YOU--
NOT TOO MANY PEOPLE ARE.
BUT TODAY, WHEN WE SAW ON THE NEWS YOU WERE TRYING TO STOP THE SONS OF THE SERPENT, HE CALLED ME, ALL EXCITED--
HE SAID, "LOOK AT THAT, SWEETHEART--SOMEONE'S FINALLY FIGHTING FOR US."
BUT I'M NOT THE KIND OF GUY TO SHRINK FROM A CHALLENGE.
WHEN I TOOK THIS JOB, I KNEW THERE WOULD BE SOME BAD DAYS.
EVENING, LADIES AND GENTLEMEN, THIS IS YOUR CAPTAIN SPEAKING--WELL, ONE OF THEM ON THIS FLIGHT, APPARENTLY--
--APOLOGIES, BUT WE'RE FACING A BIT OF A DELAY HERE AS WE PREPARE FOR OUR INITIAL DESCENT--
MAYBE THERE'S TOO MUCH STATIC IN THE AIR. MAYBE WE'RE TOO DIVIDED--
SIR--UH, CAPTAIN--I NEED YOU TO TAKE YOUR SEAT--
DON'T WORRY ABOUT IT--
I CAN TAKE IT FROM HERE.
--BUT I STILL BELIEVE WE CAN RISE ABOVE IT.

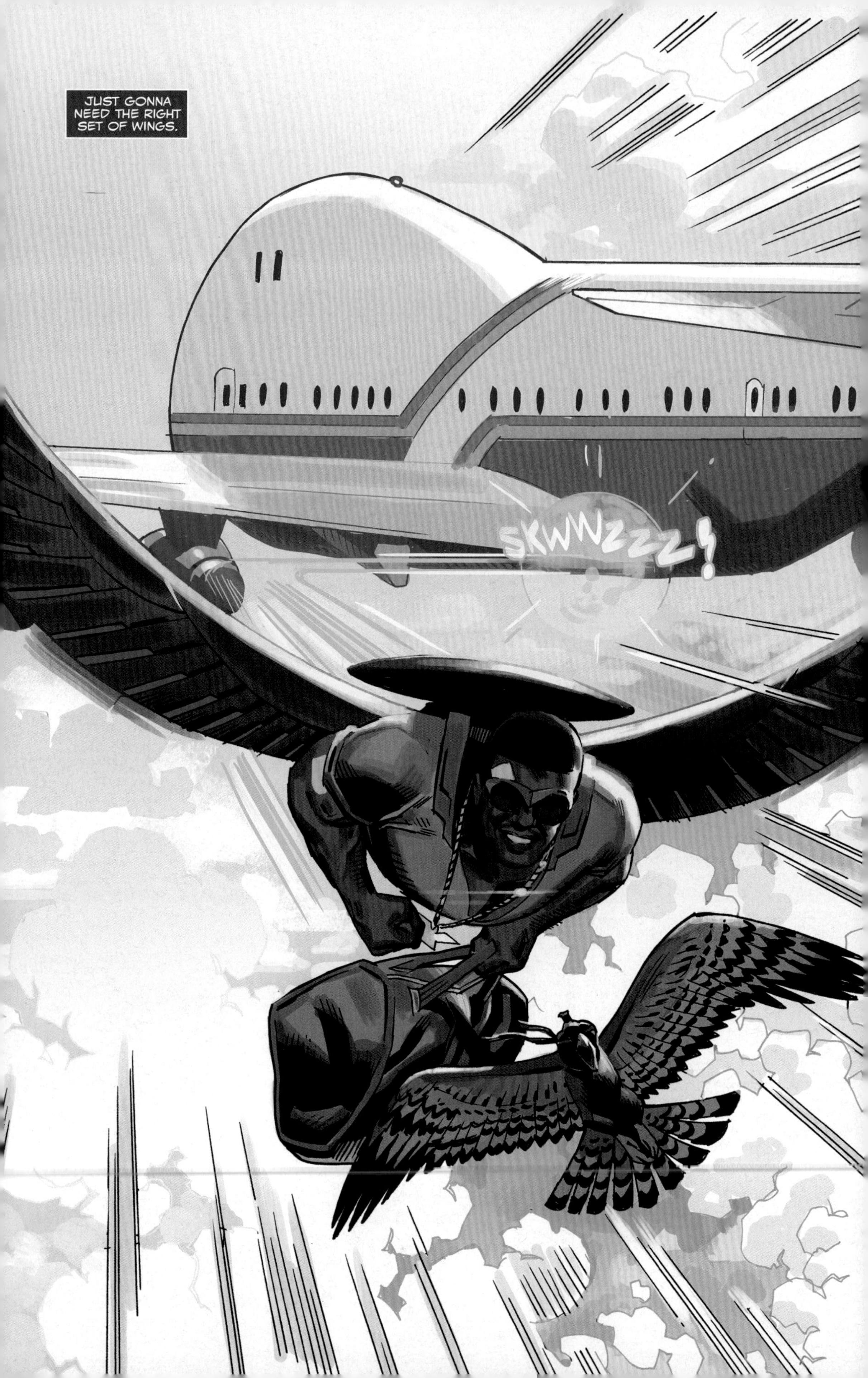
JUST GONNA NEED THE RIGHT SET OF WINGS.
SKWWZZZZ!

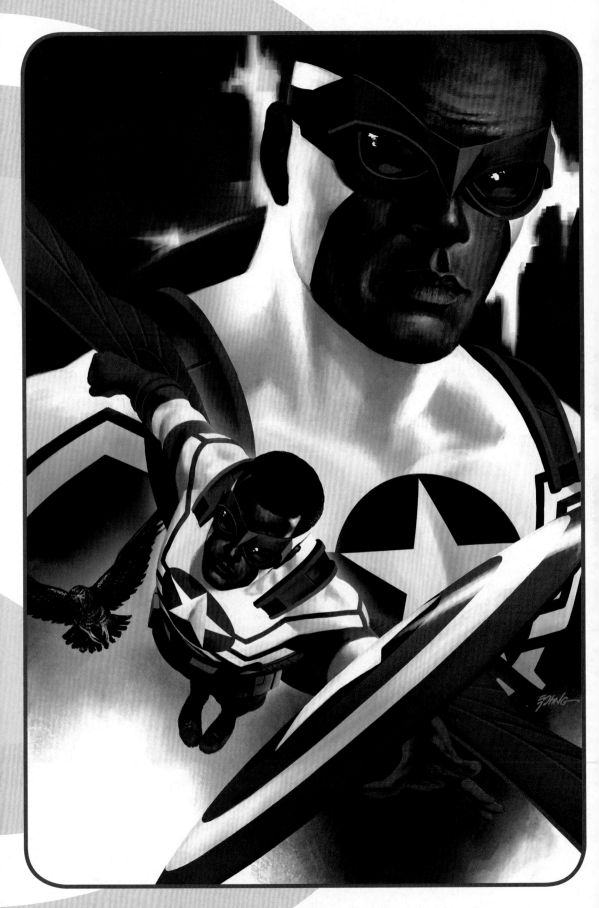

#3 variant by **STEVE EPTING**

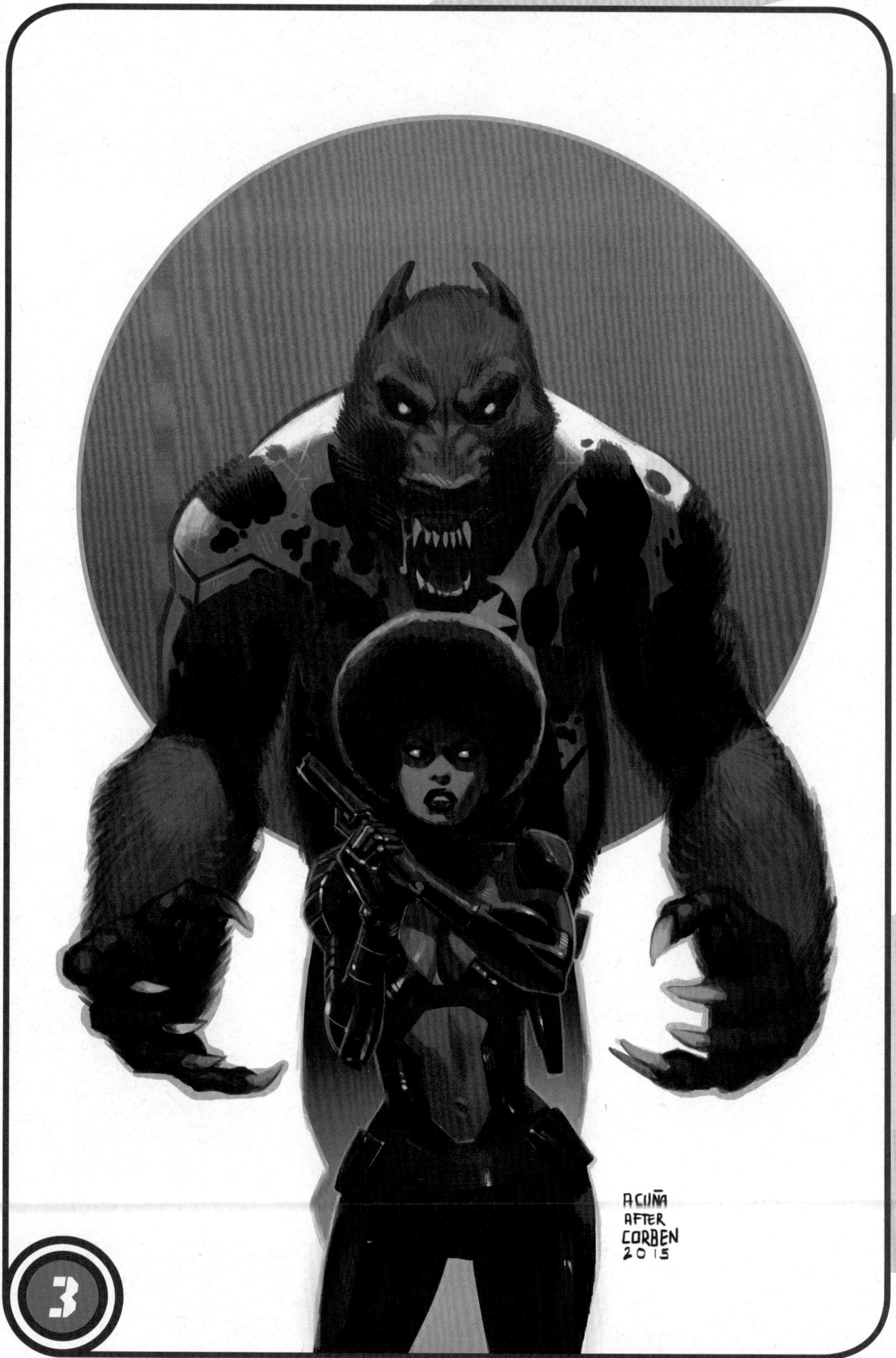
ACUÑA
AFTER
CORBEN
2015
3

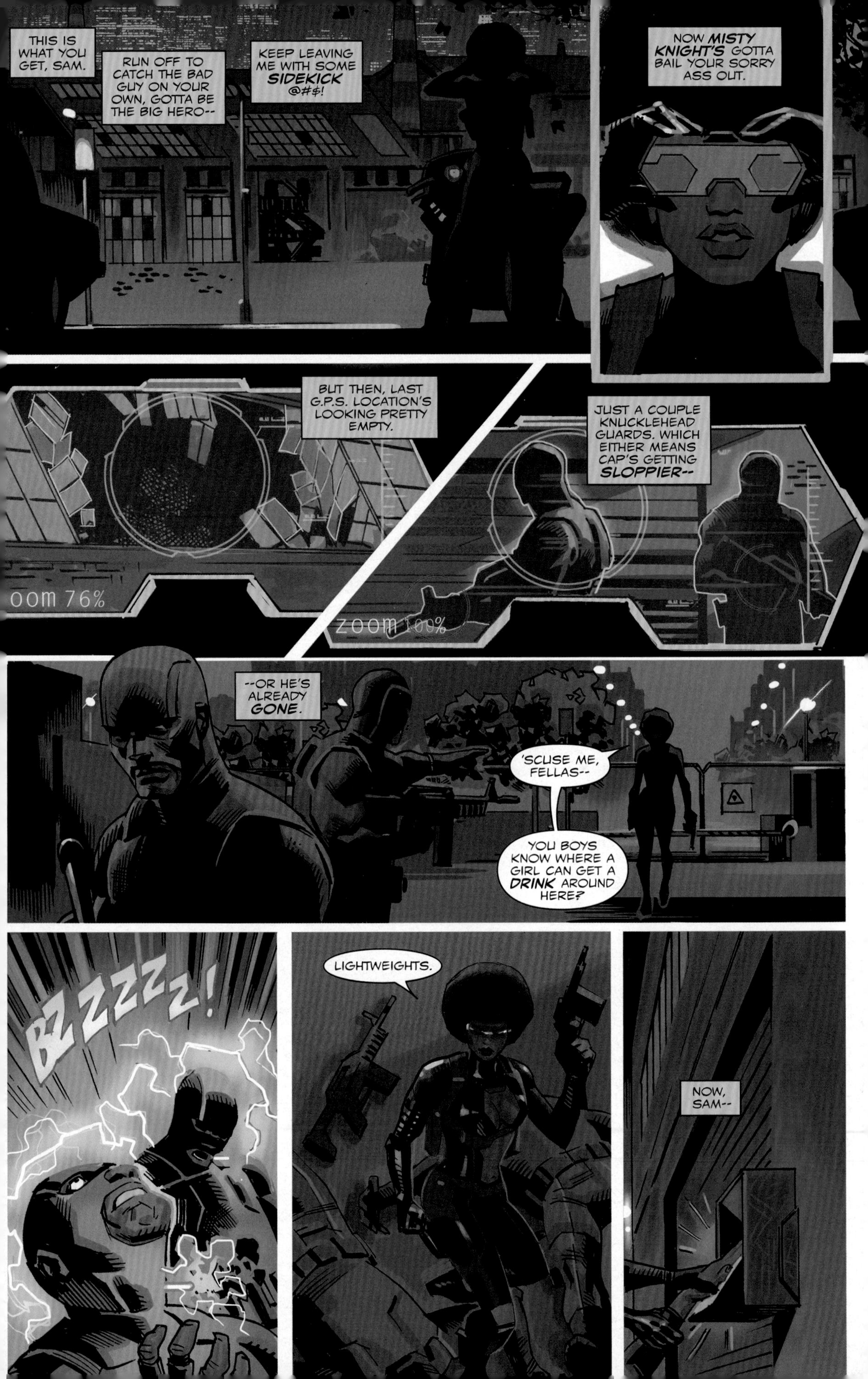

THIS IS WHAT YOU GET, SAM.
RUN OFF TO CATCH THE BAD GUY ON YOUR OWN, GOTTA BE THE BIG HERO--
KEEP LEAVING ME WITH SOME SIDEKICK @#$!
NOW MISTY KNIGHT'S GOTTA BAIL YOUR SORRY ASS OUT.
BUT THEN, LAST G.P.S. LOCATION'S LOOKING PRETTY EMPTY.
OOM 76%
JUST A COUPLE KNUCKLEHEAD GUARDS. WHICH EITHER MEANS CAP'S GETTING SLOPPIER--
ZOOM 100%
--OR HE'S ALREADY GONE.
'SCUSE ME, FELLAS--
YOU BOYS KNOW WHERE A GIRL CAN GET A DRINK AROUND HERE?
BZZZZZ!
LIGHTWEIGHTS.
NOW, SAM--

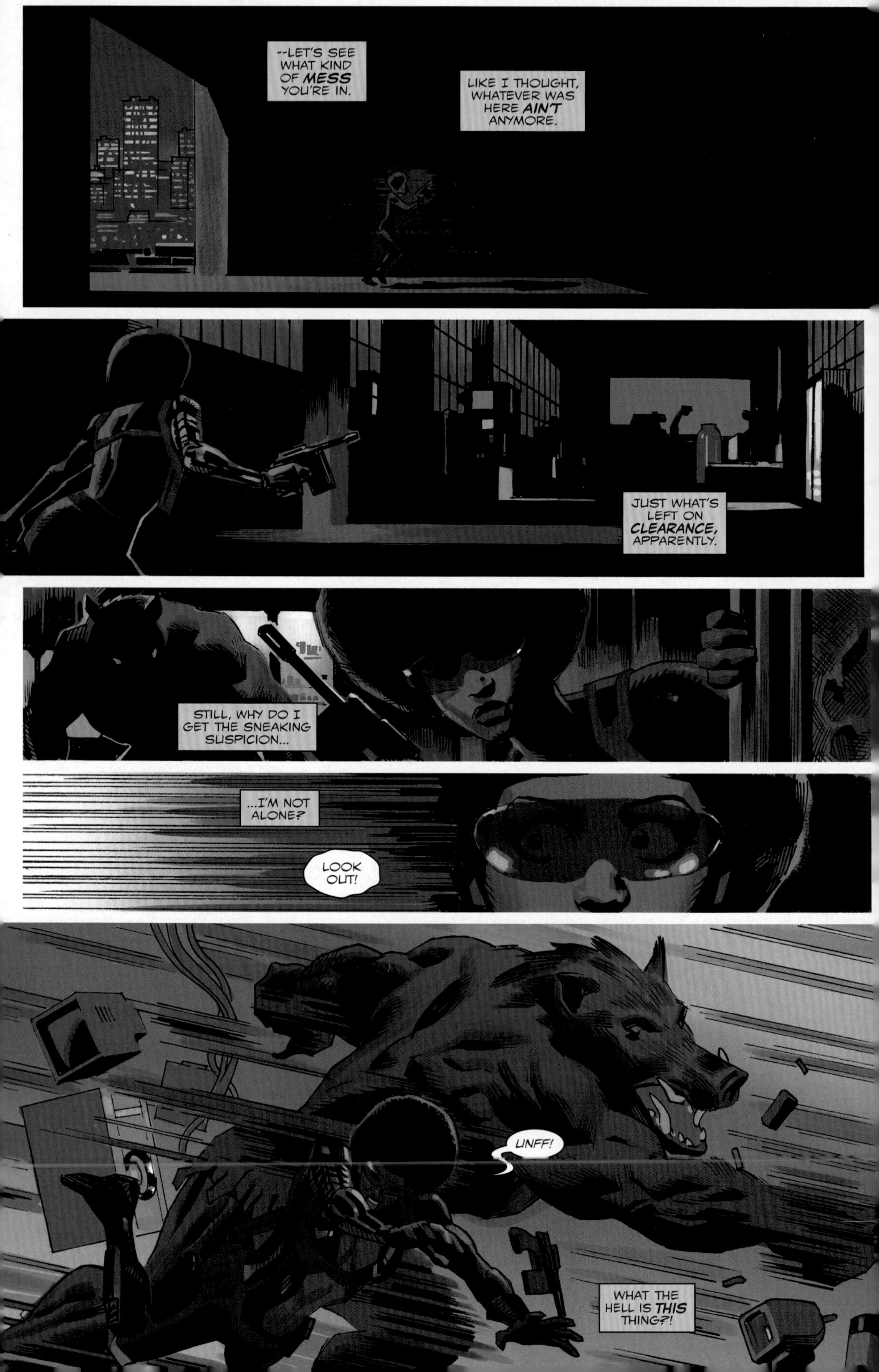
--LET'S SEE WHAT KIND OF MESS YOU'RE IN.
LIKE I THOUGHT, WHATEVER WAS HERE AIN'T ANYMORE.
JUST WHAT'S LEFT ON CLEARANCE, APPARENTLY.
STILL, WHY DO I GET THE SNEAKING SUSPICION...
...I'M NOT ALONE?
LOOK OUT!
UNFF!
WHAT THE HELL IS THIS THING?!

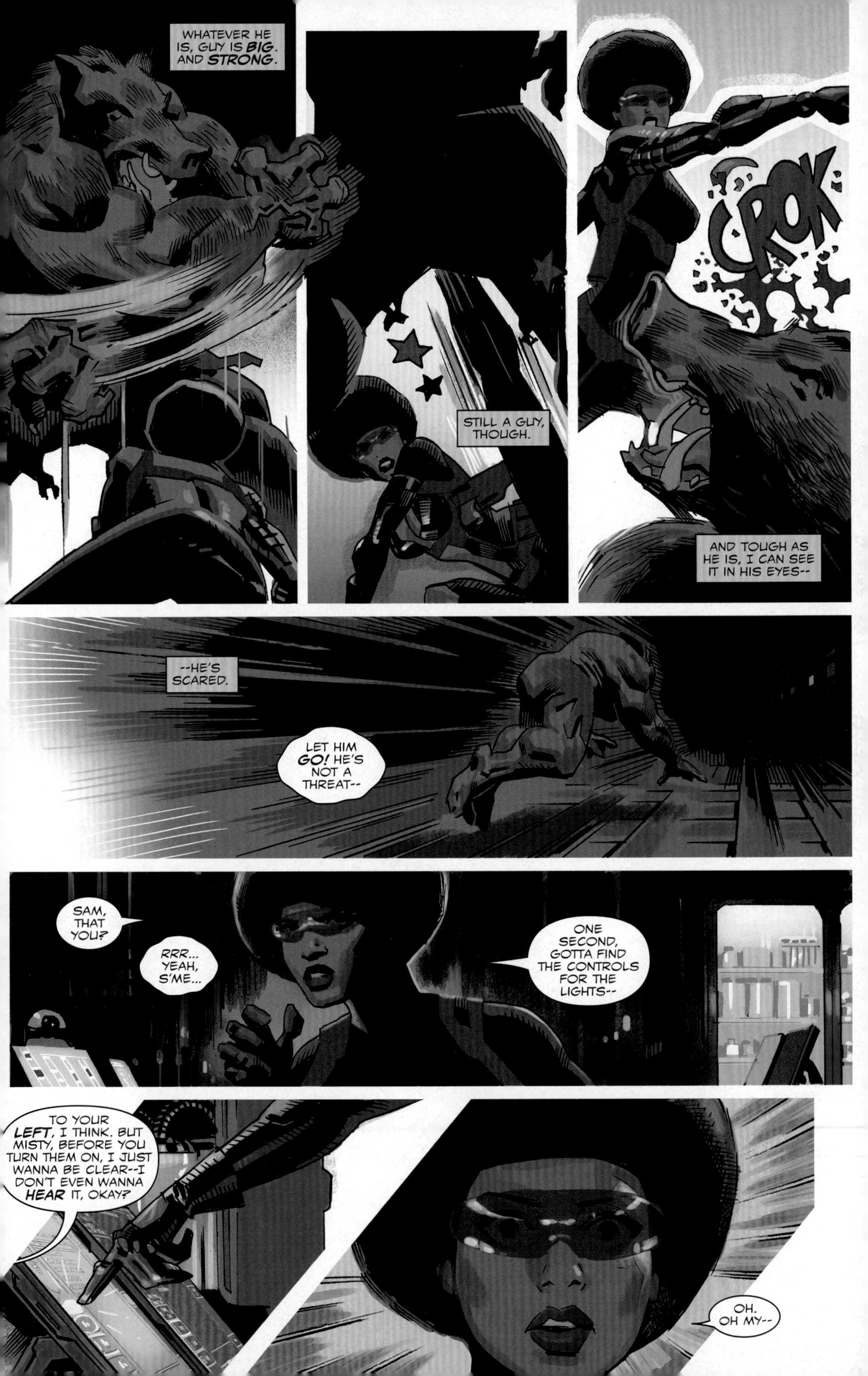
WHATEVER HE IS, GUY IS BIG. AND STRONG.
STILL A GUY, THOUGH.
CROK
AND TOUGH AS HE IS, I CAN SEE IT IN HIS EYES--
--HE'S SCARED.
LET HIM GO! HE'S NOT A THREAT--
SAM, THAT YOU?
RRR... YEAH, S'ME...
ONE SECOND, GOTTA FIND THE CONTROLS FOR THE LIGHTS--
TO YOUR LEFT, I THINK. BUT MISTY, BEFORE YOU TURN THEM ON, I JUST WANNA BE CLEAR--I DON'T EVEN WANNA HEAR IT, OKAY?
OH. OH MY--

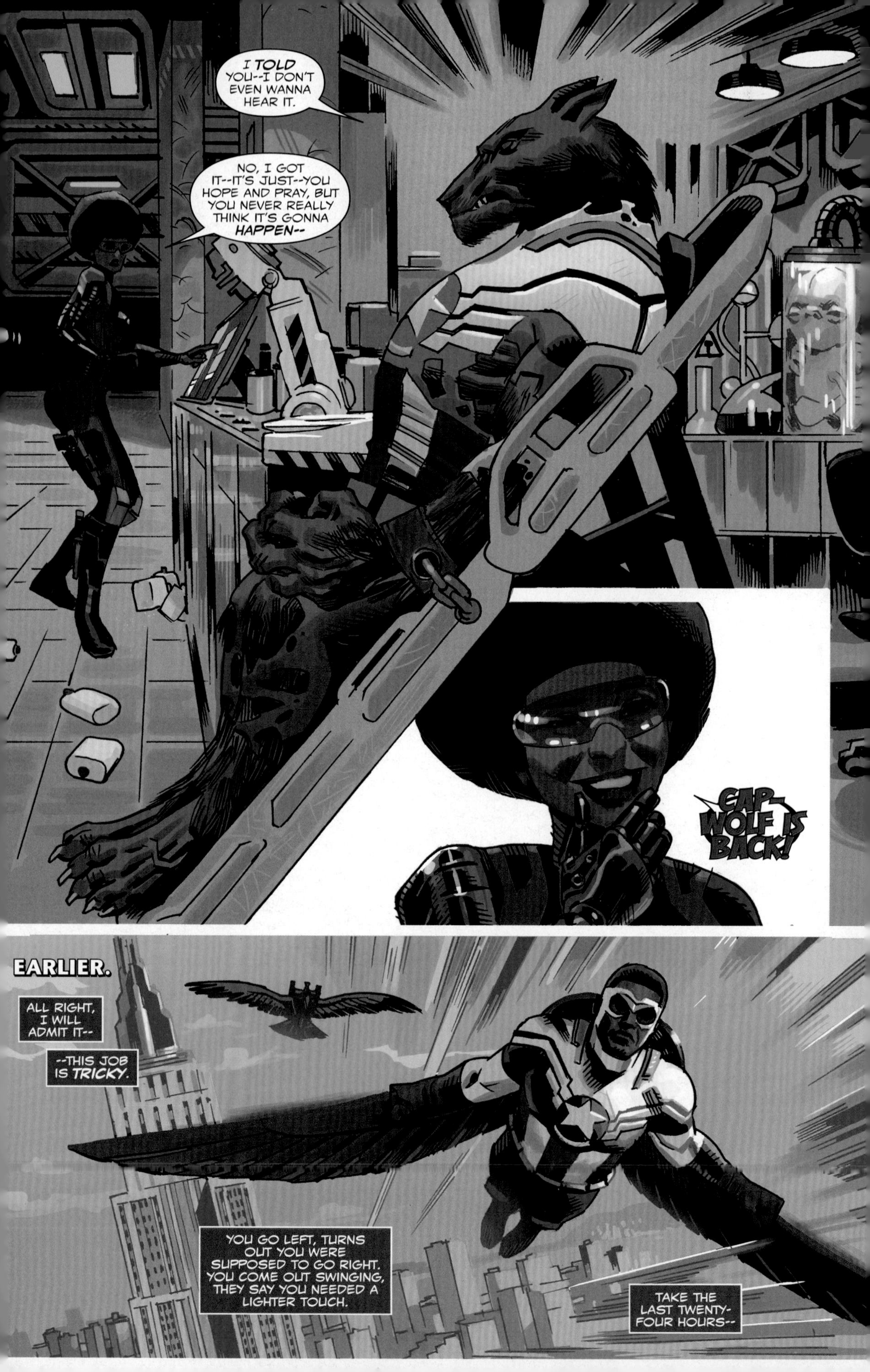
I TOLD YOU--I DON'T EVEN WANNA HEAR IT.
NO, I GOT IT--IT'S JUST--YOU HOPE AND PRAY, BUT YOU NEVER REALLY THINK IT'S GONNA HAPPEN--
CAP-WOLF IS BACK!
EARLIER.
ALL RIGHT, I WILL ADMIT IT--
--THIS JOB IS TRICKY.
YOU GO LEFT, TURNS OUT YOU WERE SUPPOSED TO GO RIGHT. YOU COME OUT SWINGING, THEY SAY YOU NEEDED A LIGHTER TOUCH.
TAKE THE LAST TWENTY-FOUR HOURS--

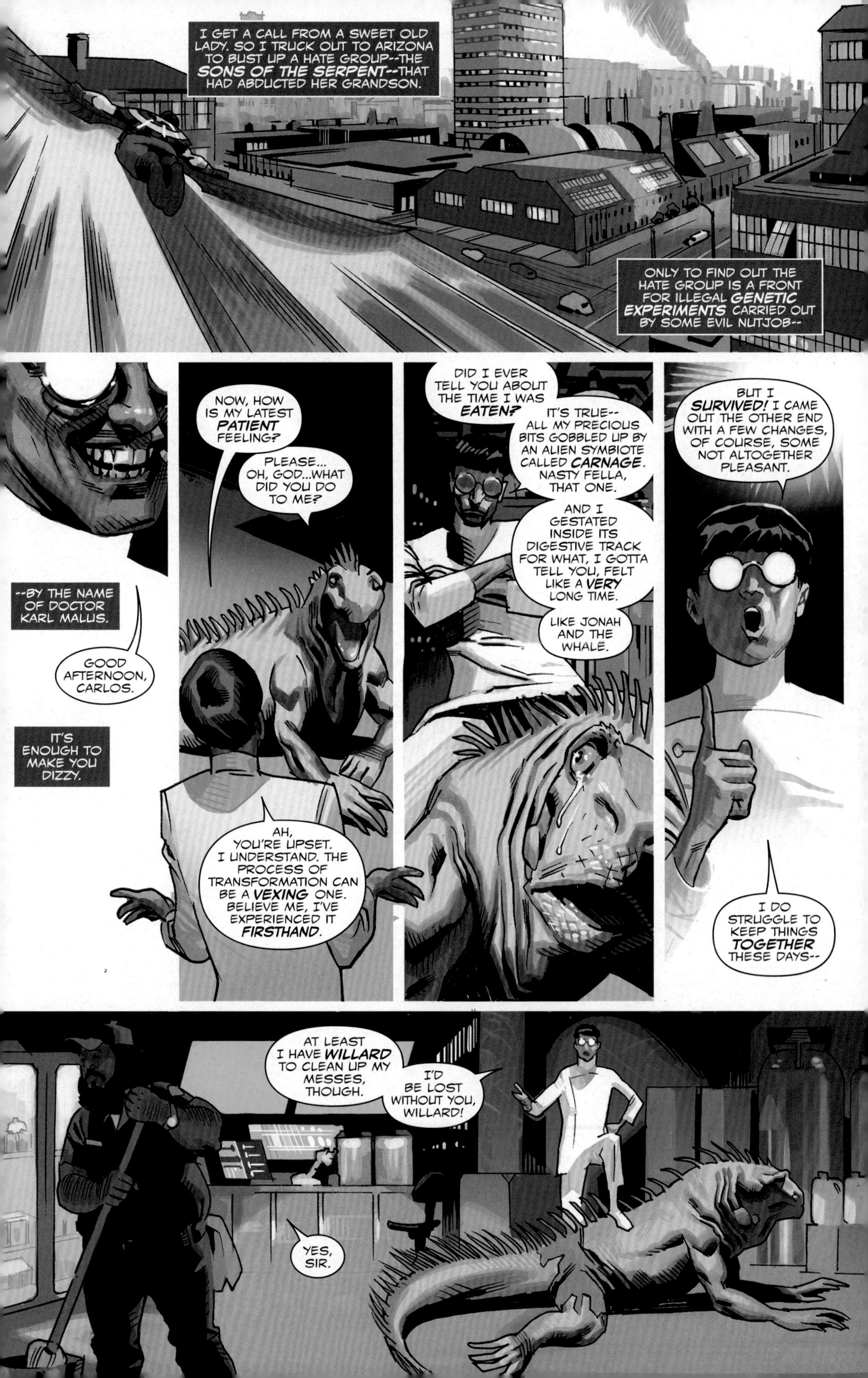

I GET A CALL FROM A SWEET OLD LADY. SO I TRUCK OUT TO ARIZONA TO BUST UP A HATE GROUP--THE SONS OF THE SERPENT--THAT HAD ABDUCTED HER GRANDSON.
ONLY TO FIND OUT THE HATE GROUP IS A FRONT FOR ILLEGAL GENETIC EXPERIMENTS CARRIED OUT BY SOME EVIL NUTJOB--
--BY THE NAME OF DOCTOR KARL MALUS.
GOOD AFTERNOON, CARLOS.
IT'S ENOUGH TO MAKE YOU DIZZY.
NOW, HOW IS MY LATEST PATIENT FEELING?
PLEASE... OH, GOD...WHAT DID YOU DO TO ME?
AH, YOU'RE UPSET. I UNDERSTAND. THE PROCESS OF TRANSFORMATION CAN BE A VEXING ONE. BELIEVE ME, I'VE EXPERIENCED IT FIRSTHAND.
DID I EVER TELL YOU ABOUT THE TIME I WAS EATEN?
IT'S TRUE-- ALL MY PRECIOUS BITS GOBBLED UP BY AN ALIEN SYMBIOTE CALLED CARNAGE. NASTY FELLA, THAT ONE.
AND I GESTATED INSIDE ITS DIGESTIVE TRACK FOR WHAT, I GOTTA TELL YOU, FELT LIKE A VERY LONG TIME.
LIKE JONAH AND THE WHALE.
BUT I SURVIVED! I CAME OUT THE OTHER END WITH A FEW CHANGES, OF COURSE, SOME NOT ALTOGETHER PLEASANT.
I DO STRUGGLE TO KEEP THINGS TOGETHER THESE DAYS--
AT LEAST I HAVE WILLARD TO CLEAN UP MY MESSES, THOUGH.
I'D BE LOST WITHOUT YOU, WILLARD!
YES, SIR.

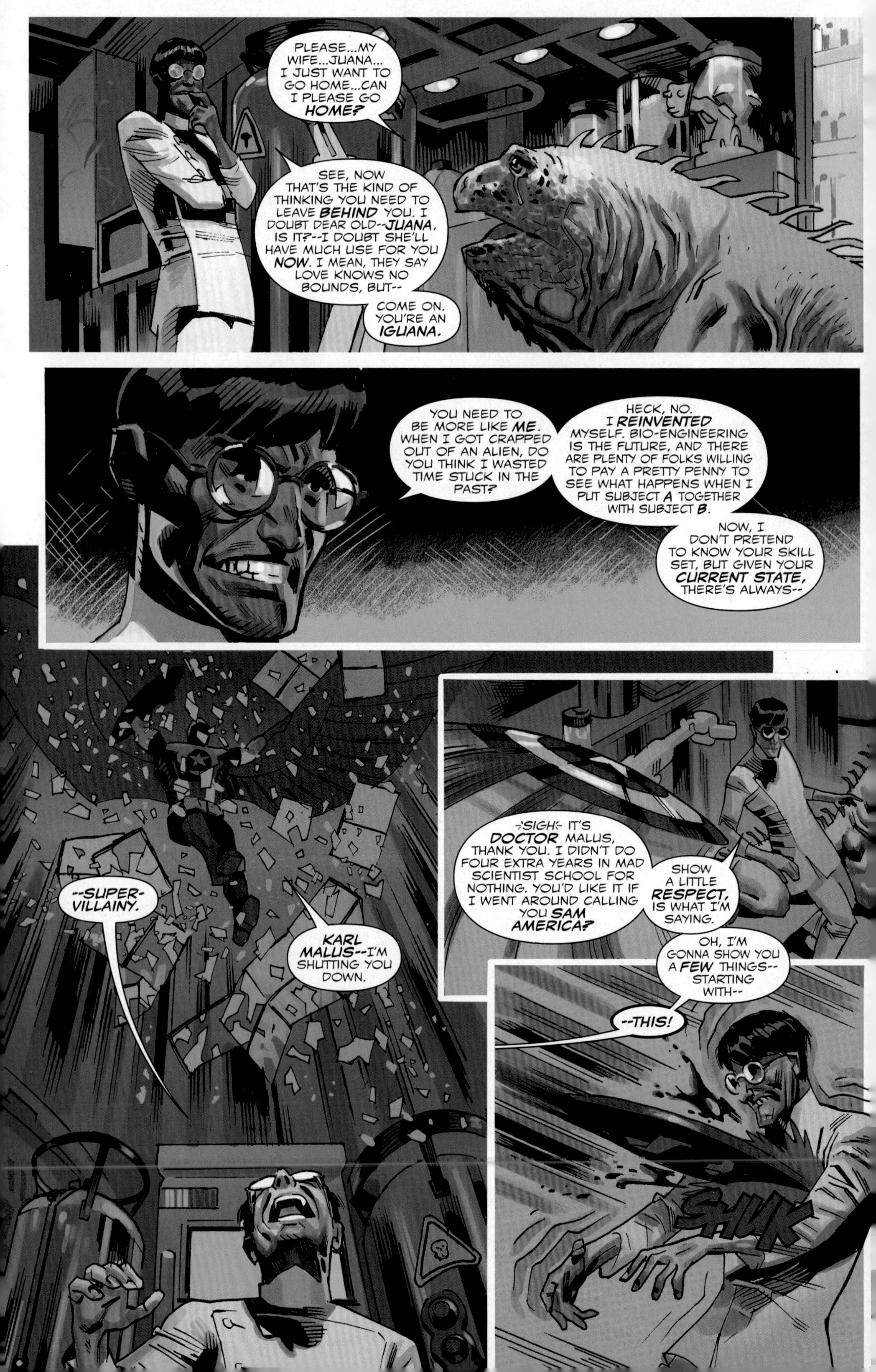
PLEASE...MY WIFE...JUANA... I JUST WANT TO GO HOME...CAN I PLEASE GO HOME?
SEE, NOW THAT'S THE KIND OF THINKING YOU NEED TO LEAVE BEHIND YOU. I DOUBT DEAR OLD--JUANA, IS IT?--I DOUBT SHE'LL HAVE MUCH USE FOR YOU NOW. I MEAN, THEY SAY LOVE KNOWS NO BOUNDS, BUT--
COME ON. YOU'RE AN IGUANA.
YOU NEED TO BE MORE LIKE ME. WHEN I GOT CRAPPED OUT OF AN ALIEN, DO YOU THINK I WASTED TIME STUCK IN THE PAST?
HECK, NO. I REINVENTED MYSELF. BIO-ENGINEERING IS THE FUTURE, AND THERE ARE PLENTY OF FOLKS WILLING TO PAY A PRETTY PENNY TO SEE WHAT HAPPENS WHEN I PUT SUBJECT A TOGETHER WITH SUBJECT B.
NOW, I DON'T PRETEND TO KNOW YOUR SKILL SET, BUT GIVEN YOUR CURRENT STATE, THERE'S ALWAYS--
--SUPER-VILLAINY.
KARL MALUS--I'M SHUTTING YOU DOWN.
SIGH IT'S DOCTOR MALUS, THANK YOU. I DIDN'T DO FOUR EXTRA YEARS IN MAD SCIENTIST SCHOOL FOR NOTHING. YOU'D LIKE IT IF I WENT AROUND CALLING YOU SAM AMERICA?
SHOW A LITTLE RESPECT, IS WHAT I'M SAYING.
OH, I'M GONNA SHOW YOU A FEW THINGS-- STARTING WITH--
--THIS!
SHUK

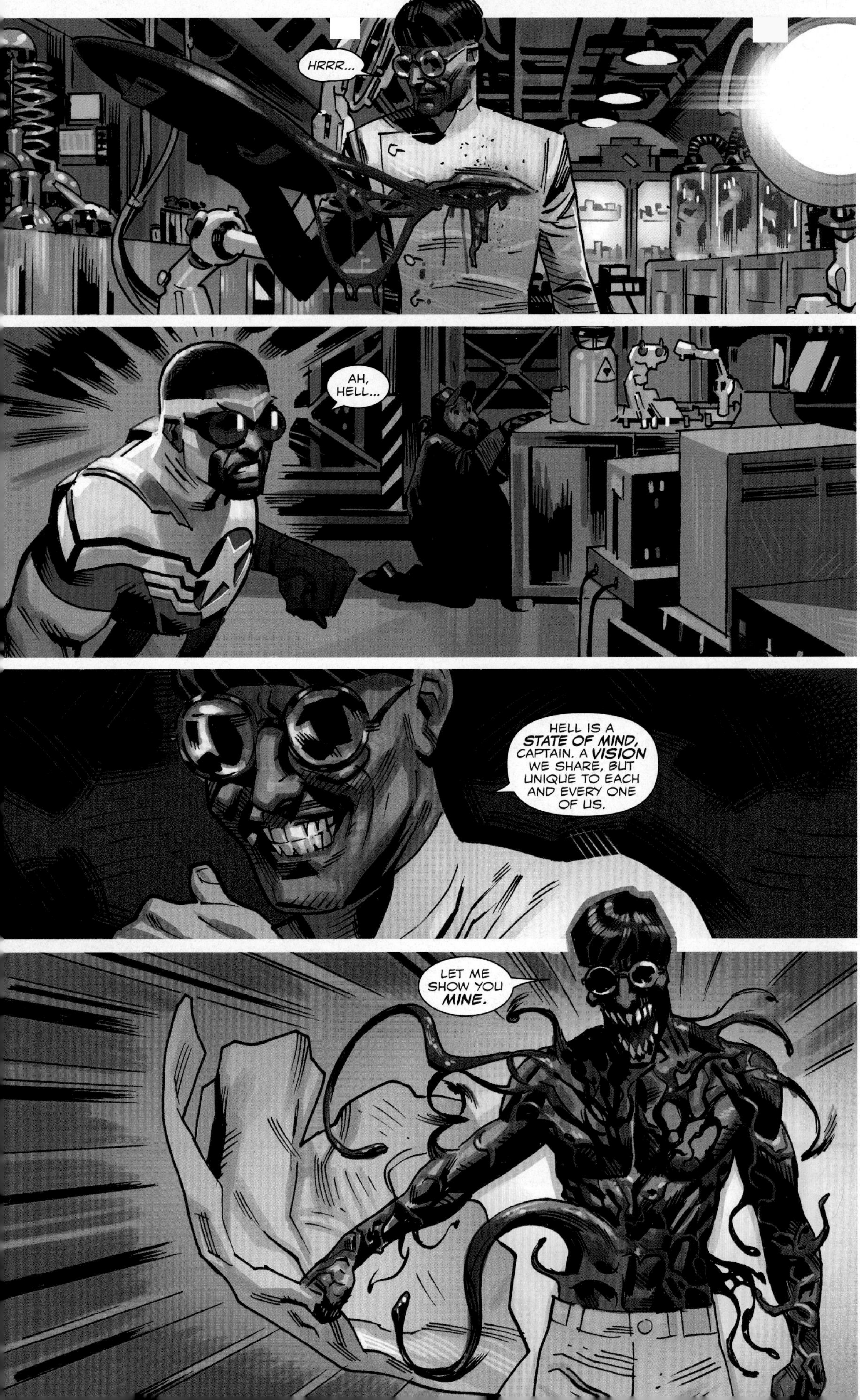
HRRR...
AH, HELL...
HELL IS A **STATE OF MIND,** CAPTAIN. A **VISION** WE SHARE, BUT UNIQUE TO EACH AND EVERY ONE OF US.
LET ME SHOW YOU **MINE.**

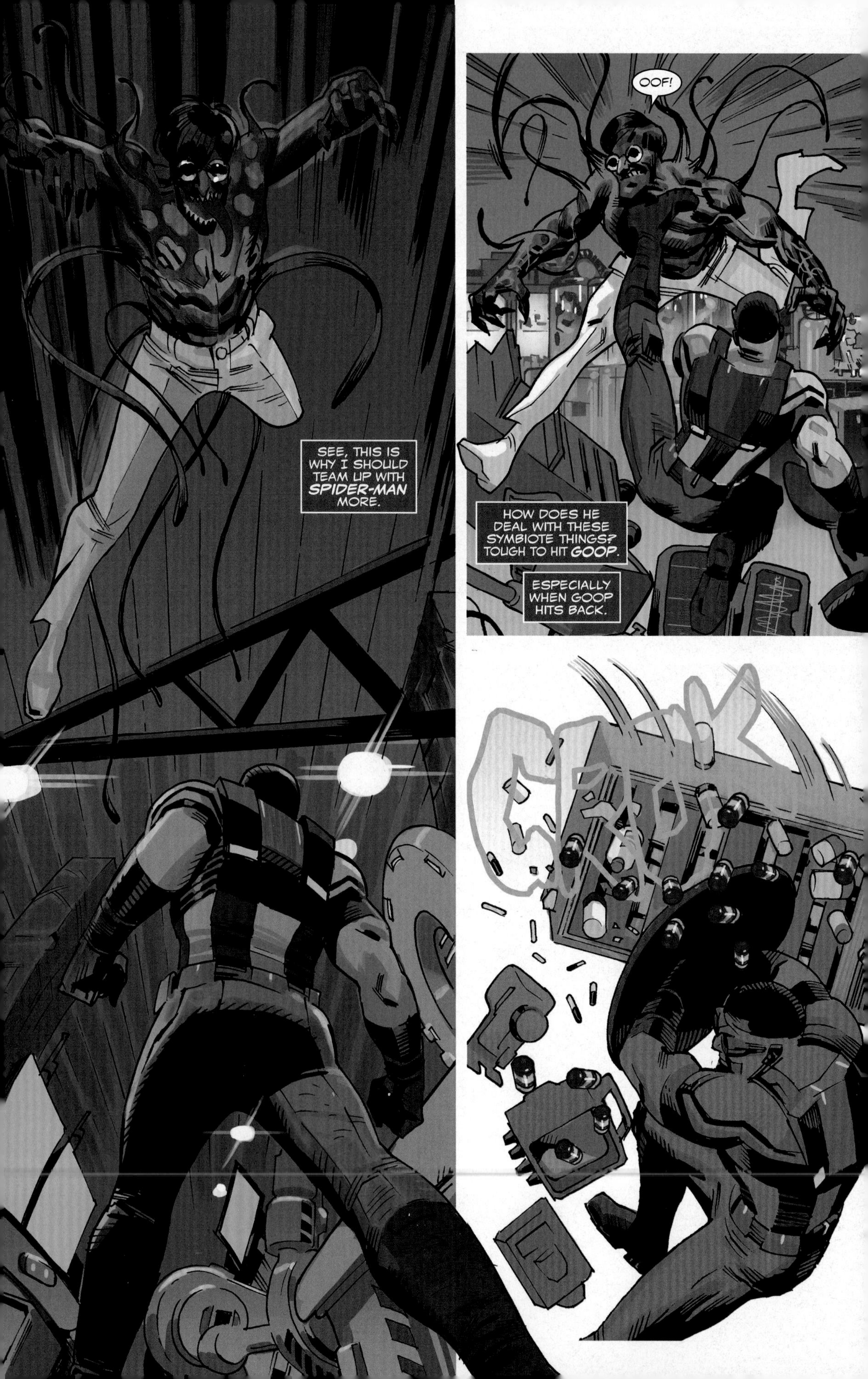
SEE, THIS IS WHY I SHOULD TEAM UP WITH SPIDER-MAN MORE.
OOF!
HOW DOES HE DEAL WITH THESE SYMBIOTE THINGS? TOUGH TO HIT GOOP.
ESPECIALLY WHEN GOOP HITS BACK.

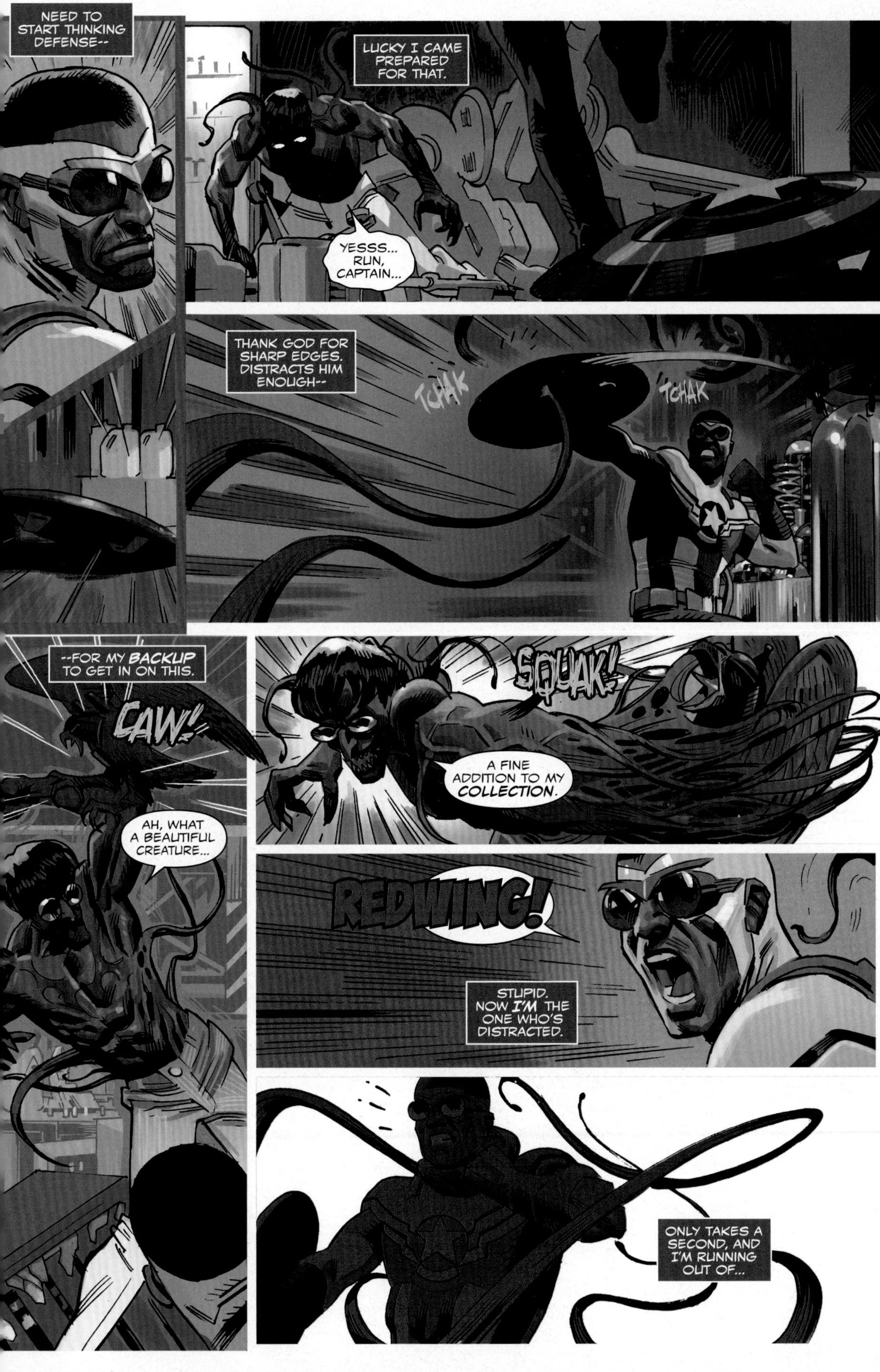
NEED TO START THINKING DEFENSE--
LUCKY I CAME PREPARED FOR THAT.
YESSS... RUN, CAPTAIN...
THANK GOD FOR SHARP EDGES. DISTRACTS HIM ENOUGH--
TCHAK
TCHAK
--FOR MY BACKUP TO GET IN ON THIS.
CAW!
AH, WHAT A BEAUTIFUL CREATURE...
SQUAK!
A FINE ADDITION TO MY COLLECTION.
REDWING!
STUPID. NOW I'M THE ONE WHO'S DISTRACTED.
ONLY TAKES A SECOND, AND I'M RUNNING OUT OF...

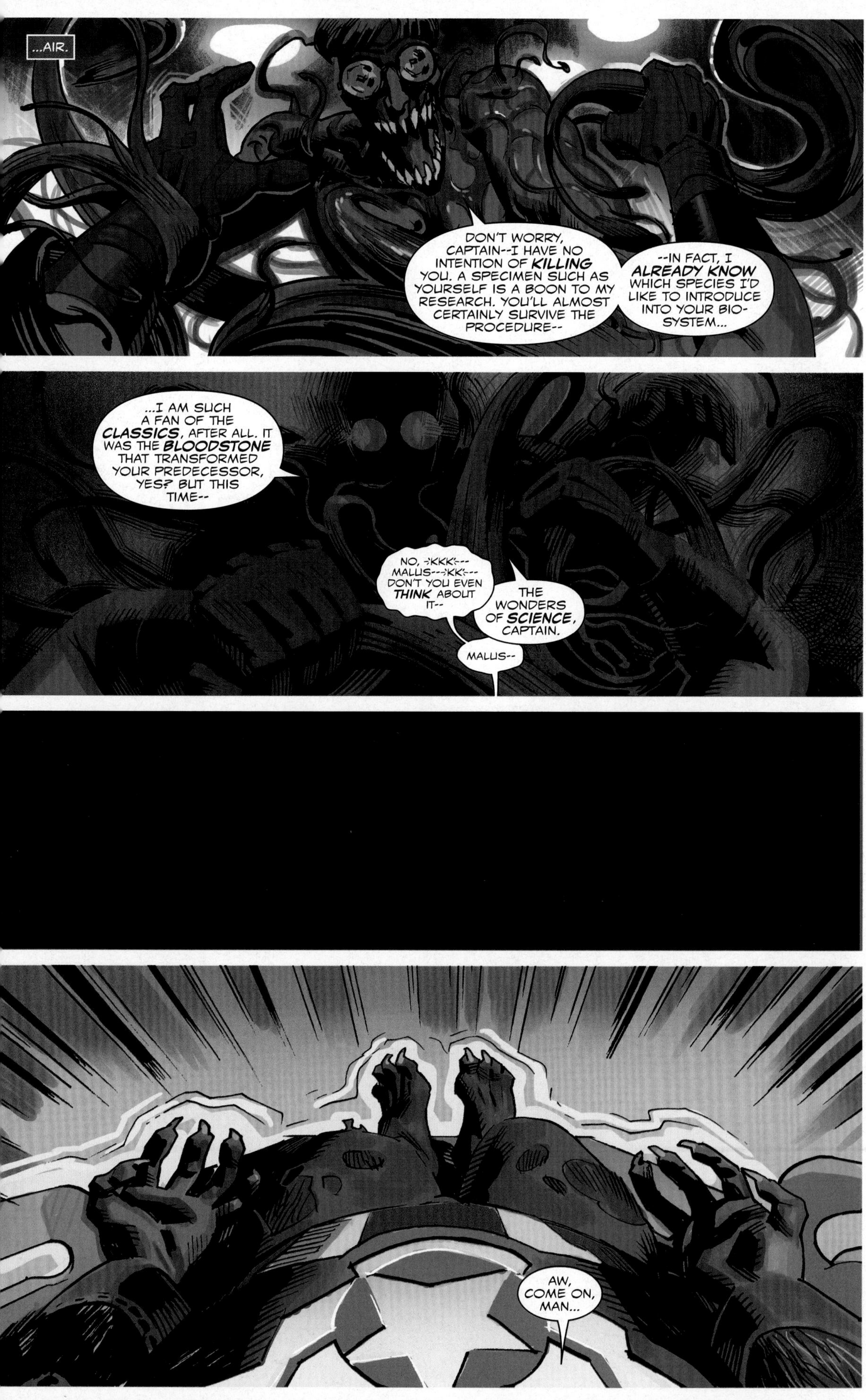
...AIR.
DON'T WORRY, CAPTAIN--I HAVE NO INTENTION OF **KILLING** YOU. A SPECIMEN SUCH AS YOURSELF IS A BOON TO MY RESEARCH. YOU'LL ALMOST CERTAINLY SURVIVE THE PROCEDURE--
--IN FACT, I **ALREADY KNOW** WHICH SPECIES I'D LIKE TO INTRODUCE INTO YOUR BIO-SYSTEM...
...I AM SUCH A FAN OF THE **CLASSICS**, AFTER ALL. IT WAS THE **BLOODSTONE** THAT TRANSFORMED YOUR PREDECESSOR, YES? BUT THIS TIME--
NO, --KKK--- MALUS---KK--- DON'T YOU EVEN **THINK** ABOUT IT--
THE WONDERS OF **SCIENCE**, CAPTAIN.
MALUS--
AW, COME ON, MAN...

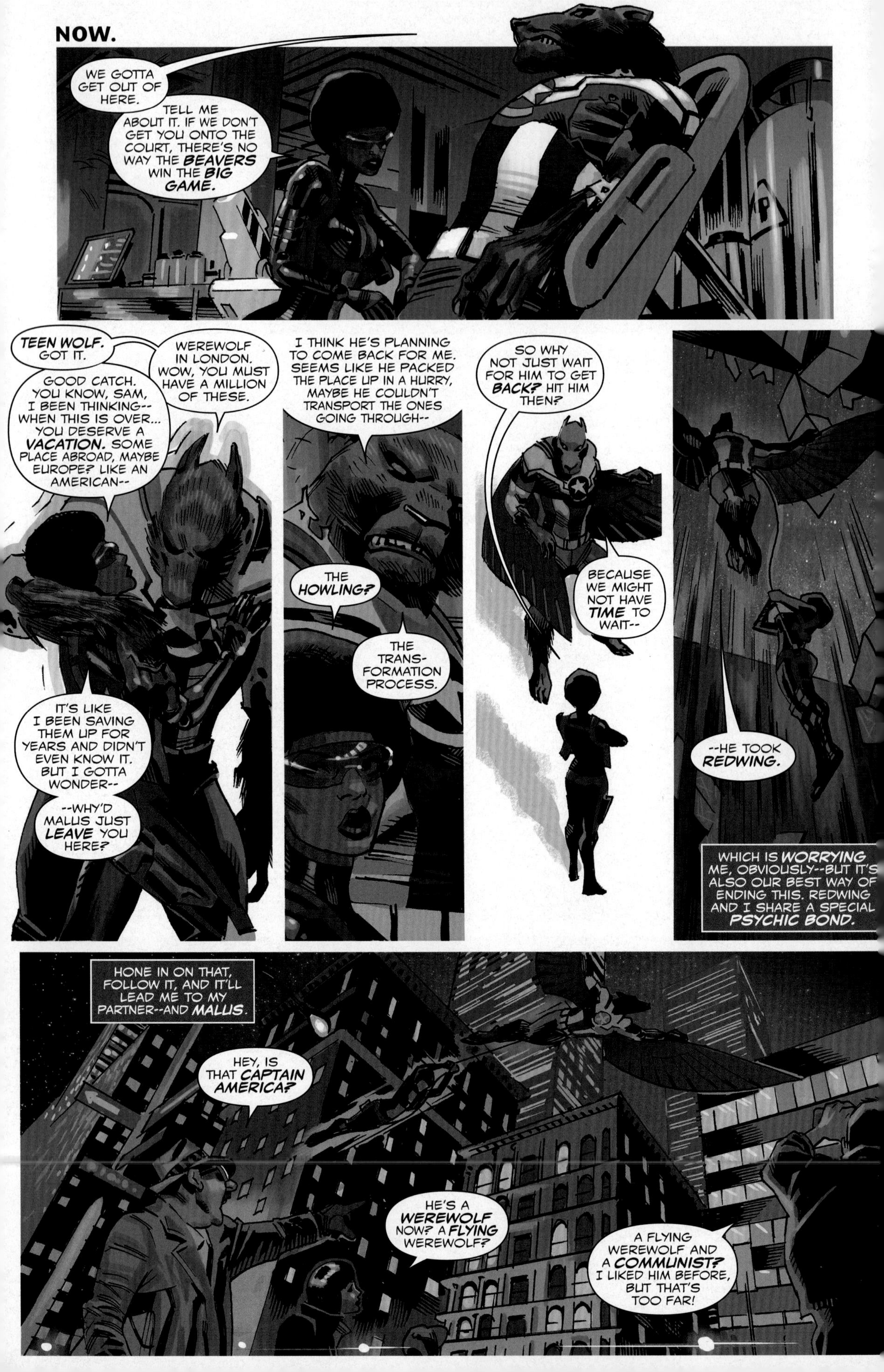
NOW.
WE GOTTA GET OUT OF HERE.
TELL ME ABOUT IT. IF WE DON'T GET YOU ONTO THE COURT, THERE'S NO WAY THE BEAVERS WIN THE BIG GAME.
TEEN WOLF. GOT IT.
WEREWOLF IN LONDON. WOW, YOU MUST HAVE A MILLION OF THESE.
GOOD CATCH. YOU KNOW, SAM, I BEEN THINKING-- WHEN THIS IS OVER... YOU DESERVE A VACATION. SOME PLACE ABROAD, MAYBE EUROPE? LIKE AN AMERICAN--
IT'S LIKE I BEEN SAVING THEM UP FOR YEARS AND DIDN'T EVEN KNOW IT. BUT I GOTTA WONDER--
--WHY'D MALUS JUST LEAVE YOU HERE?
I THINK HE'S PLANNING TO COME BACK FOR ME. SEEMS LIKE HE PACKED THE PLACE UP IN A HURRY, MAYBE HE COULDN'T TRANSPORT THE ONES GOING THROUGH--
THE HOWLING?
THE TRANS-FORMATION PROCESS.
SO WHY NOT JUST WAIT FOR HIM TO GET BACK? HIT HIM THEN?
BECAUSE WE MIGHT NOT HAVE TIME TO WAIT--
--HE TOOK REDWING.
WHICH IS WORRYING ME, OBVIOUSLY--BUT IT'S ALSO OUR BEST WAY OF ENDING THIS. REDWING AND I SHARE A SPECIAL PSYCHIC BOND.
HONE IN ON THAT, FOLLOW IT, AND IT'LL LEAD ME TO MY PARTNER--AND MALUS.
HEY, IS THAT CAPTAIN AMERICA?
HE'S A WEREWOLF NOW? A FLYING WEREWOLF?
A FLYING WEREWOLF AND A COMMUNIST? I LIKED HIM BEFORE, BUT THAT'S TOO FAR!

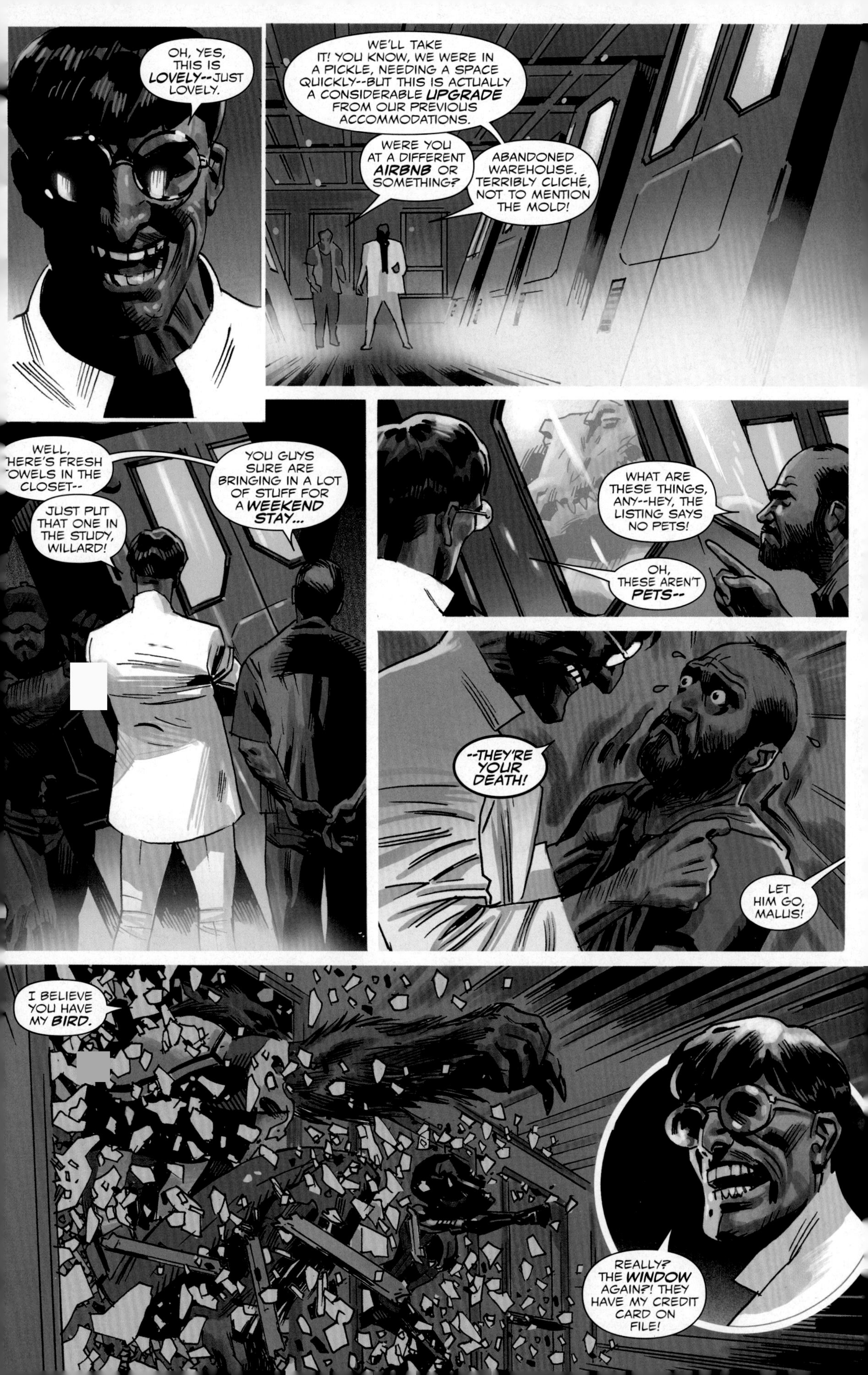
OH, YES, THIS IS LOVELY--JUST LOVELY.
WE'LL TAKE IT! YOU KNOW, WE WERE IN A PICKLE, NEEDING A SPACE QUICKLY--BUT THIS IS ACTUALLY A CONSIDERABLE UPGRADE FROM OUR PREVIOUS ACCOMMODATIONS.
WERE YOU AT A DIFFERENT AIRBNB OR SOMETHING?
ABANDONED WAREHOUSE. TERRIBLY CLICHÉ, NOT TO MENTION THE MOLD!
WELL, HERE'S FRESH OWELS IN THE CLOSET--
JUST PUT THAT ONE IN THE STUDY, WILLARD!
YOU GUYS SURE ARE BRINGING IN A LOT OF STUFF FOR A WEEKEND STAY...
WHAT ARE THESE THINGS, ANY--HEY, THE LISTING SAYS NO PETS!
OH, THESE AREN'T PETS--
--THEY'RE YOUR DEATH!
LET HIM GO, MALUS!
I BELIEVE YOU HAVE MY BIRD.
REALLY? THE WINDOW AGAIN?! THEY HAVE MY CREDIT CARD ON FILE!

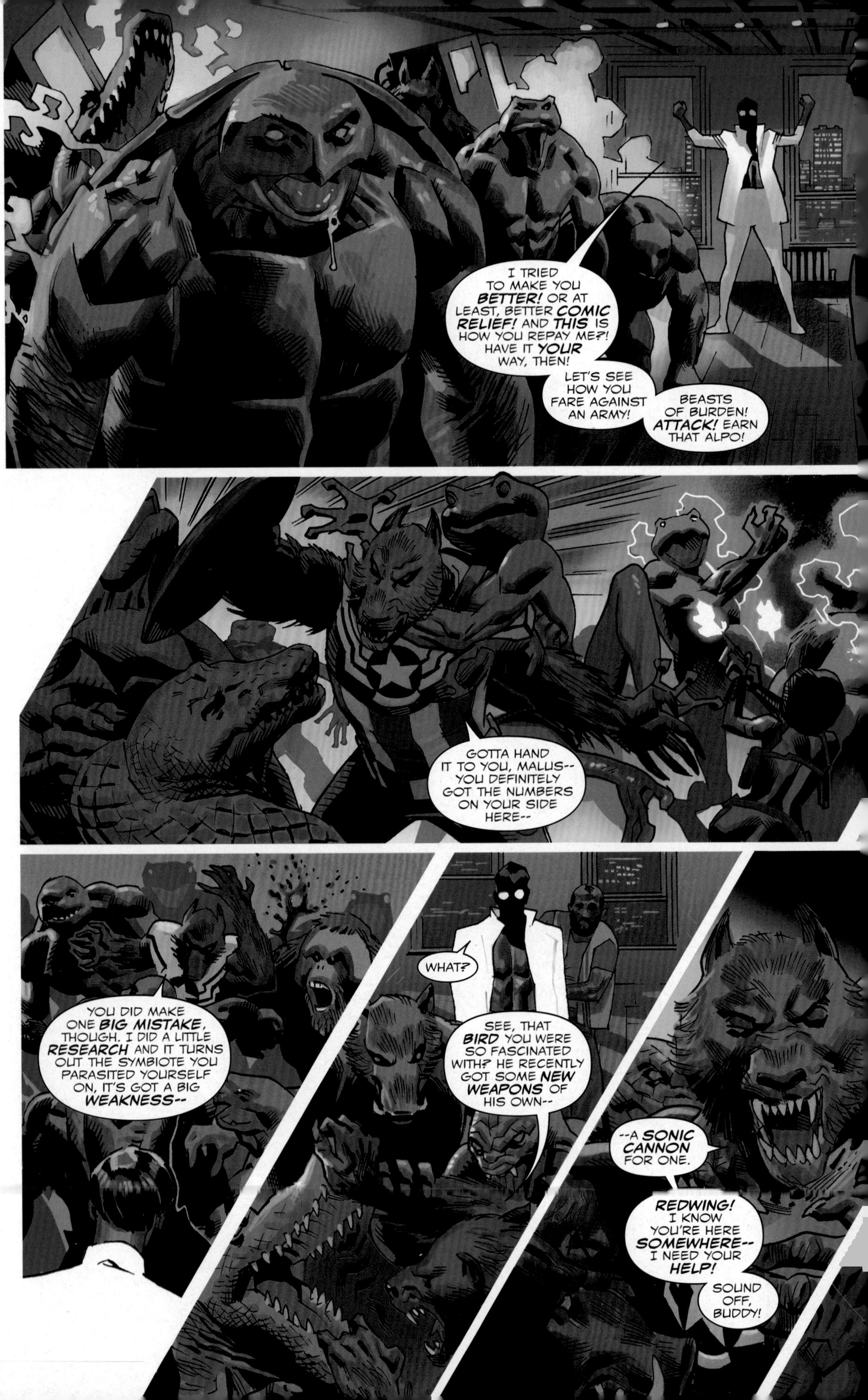
I TRIED TO MAKE YOU BETTER! OR AT LEAST, BETTER COMIC RELIEF! AND THIS IS HOW YOU REPAY ME?! HAVE IT YOUR WAY, THEN!
LET'S SEE HOW YOU FARE AGAINST AN ARMY!
BEASTS OF BURDEN! ATTACK! EARN THAT ALPO!
GOTTA HAND IT TO YOU, MALUS-- YOU DEFINITELY GOT THE NUMBERS ON YOUR SIDE HERE--
YOU DID MAKE ONE BIG MISTAKE, THOUGH. I DID A LITTLE RESEARCH AND IT TURNS OUT THE SYMBIOTE YOU PARASITED YOURSELF ON, IT'S GOT A BIG WEAKNESS--
WHAT?
SEE, THAT BIRD YOU WERE SO FASCINATED WITH? HE RECENTLY GOT SOME NEW WEAPONS OF HIS OWN--
--A SONIC CANNON FOR ONE.
REDWING! I KNOW YOU'RE HERE SOMEWHERE-- I NEED YOUR HELP!
SOUND OFF, BUDDY!

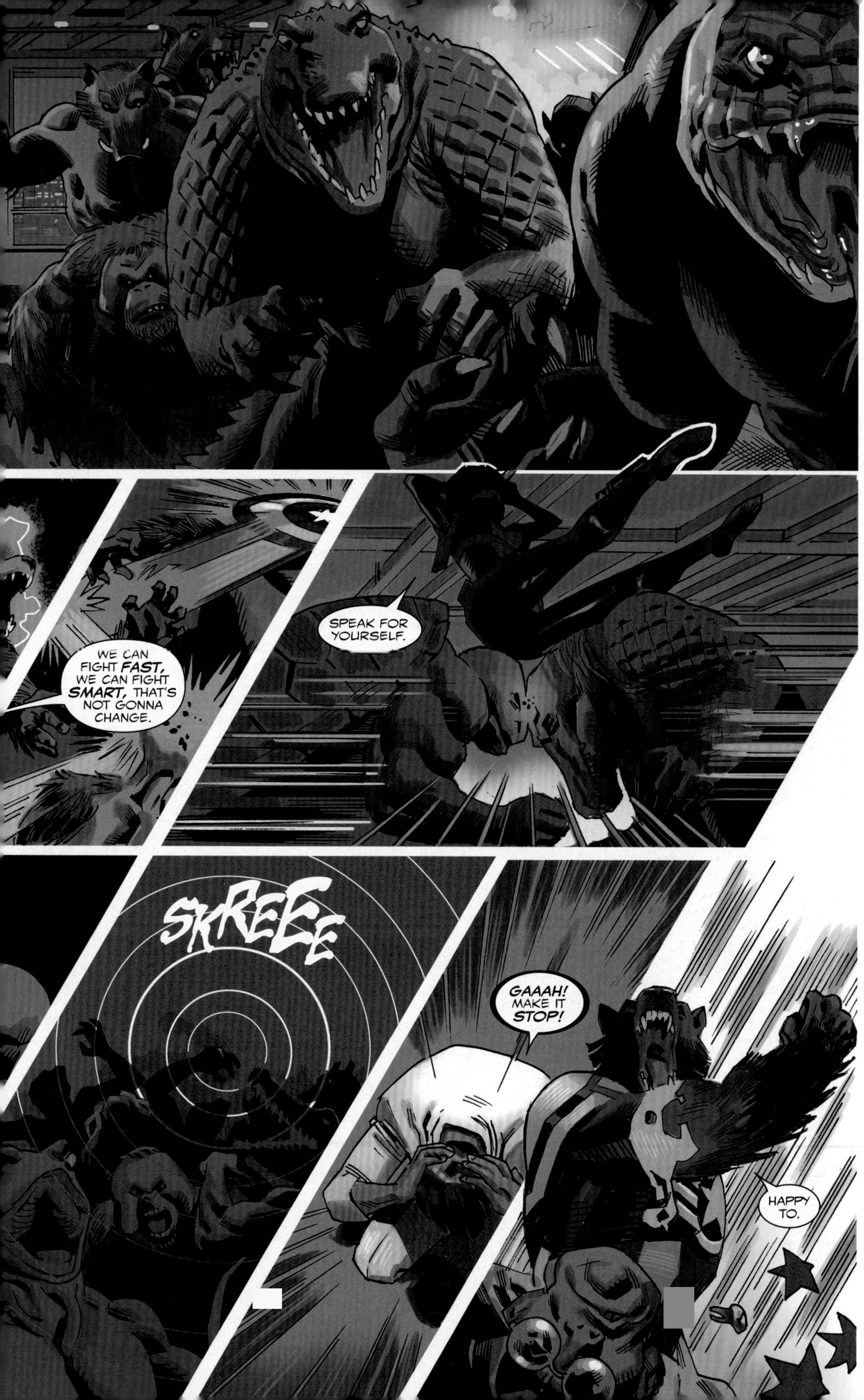
WE CAN FIGHT FAST, WE CAN FIGHT SMART, THAT'S NOT GONNA CHANGE.
SPEAK FOR YOURSELF.
SKREEE
GAAAH! MAKE IT STOP!
HAPPY TO.

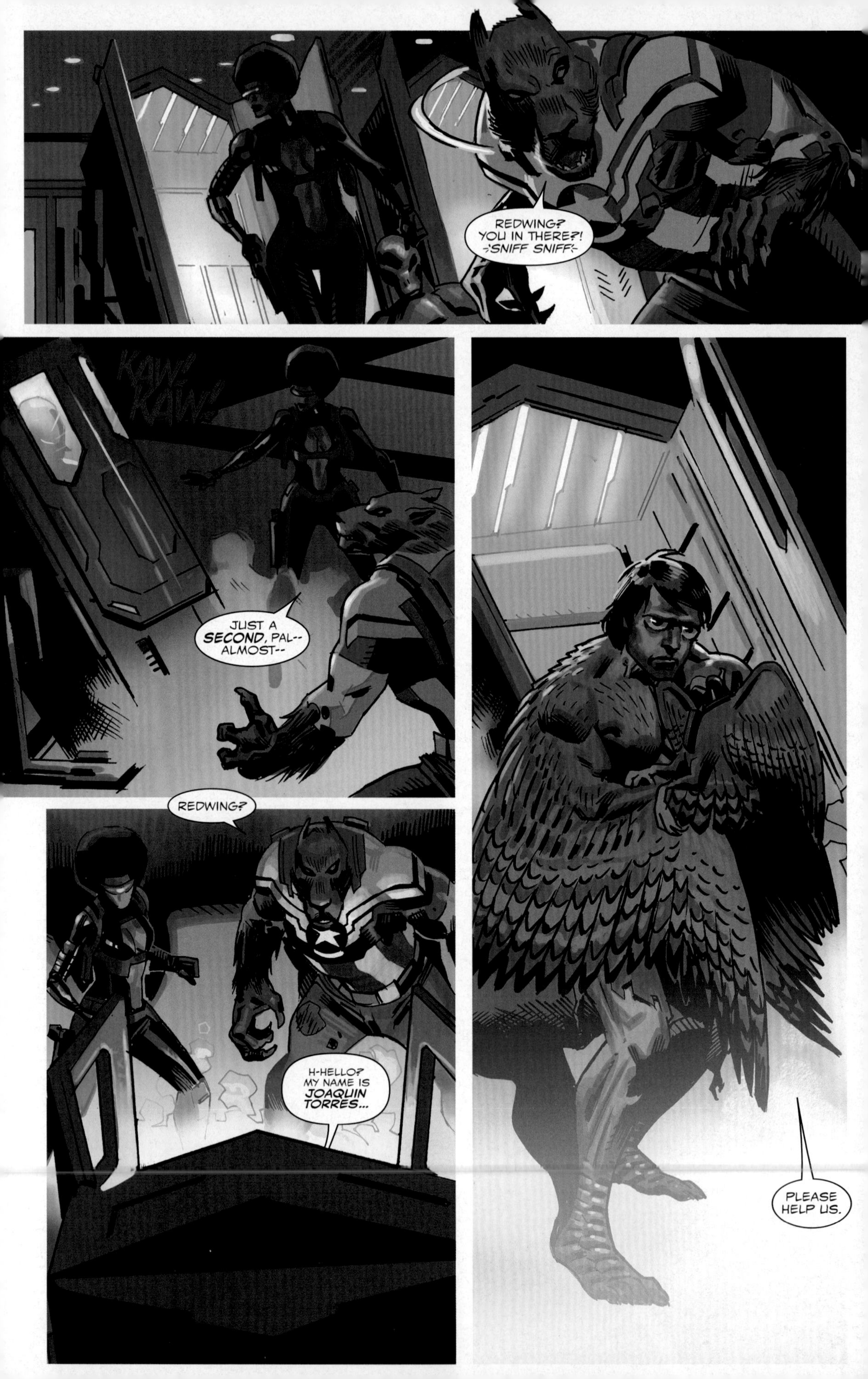
REDWING? YOU IN THERE?! -SNIFF SNIFF-
KAW! KAW!
JUST A SECOND, PAL-- ALMOST--
REDWING?
H-HELLO? MY NAME IS JOAQUIN TORRES...
PLEASE HELP US.

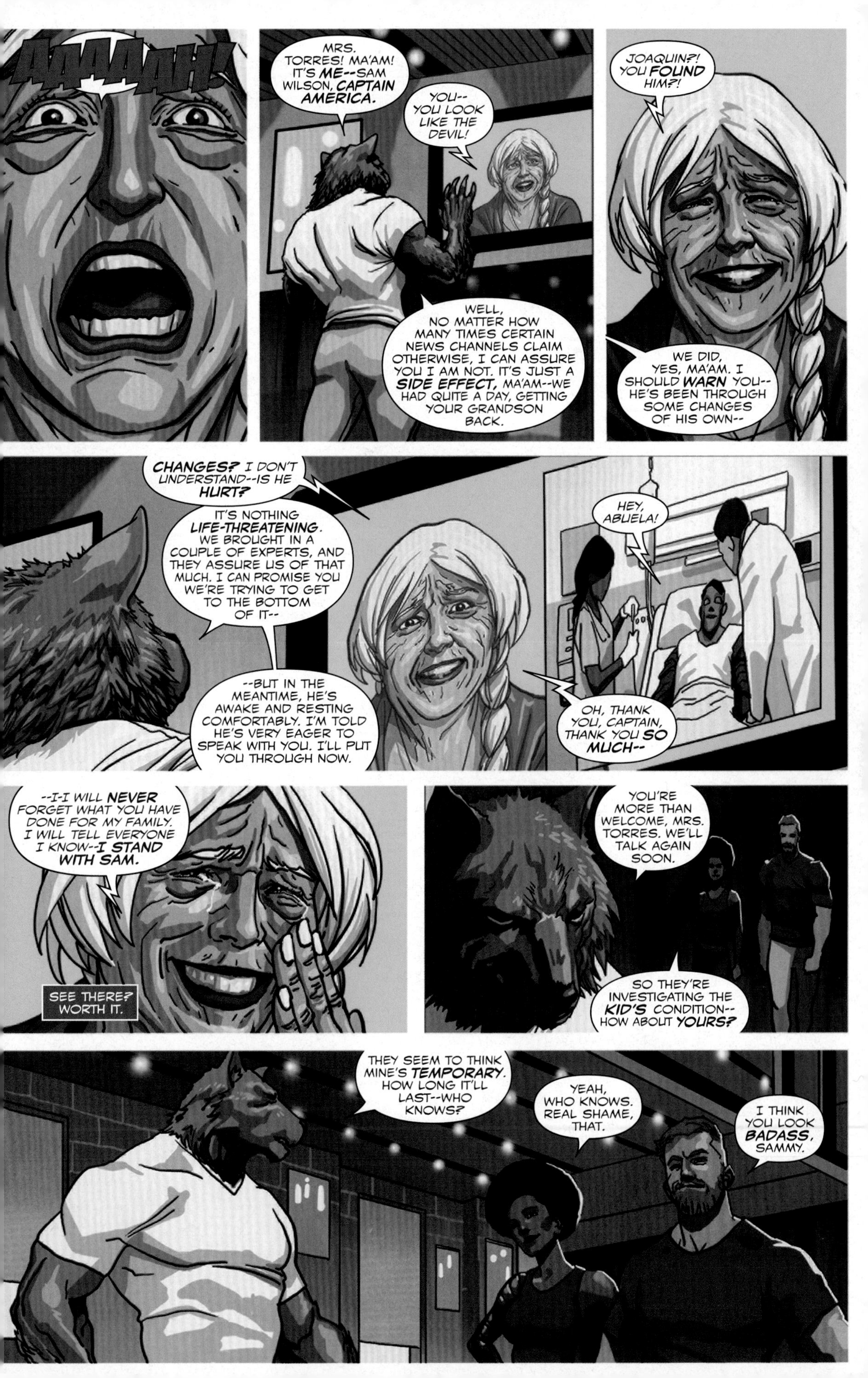
AAAAAH!
MRS. TORRES! MA'AM! IT'S ME--SAM WILSON, CAPTAIN AMERICA.
YOU--YOU LOOK LIKE THE DEVIL!
WELL, NO MATTER HOW MANY TIMES CERTAIN NEWS CHANNELS CLAIM OTHERWISE, I CAN ASSURE YOU I AM NOT. IT'S JUST A SIDE EFFECT, MA'AM--WE HAD QUITE A DAY, GETTING YOUR GRANDSON BACK.
JOAQUIN?! YOU FOUND HIM?!
WE DID, YES, MA'AM. I SHOULD WARN YOU--HE'S BEEN THROUGH SOME CHANGES OF HIS OWN--
CHANGES? I DON'T UNDERSTAND--IS HE HURT?
IT'S NOTHING LIFE-THREATENING. WE BROUGHT IN A COUPLE OF EXPERTS, AND THEY ASSURE US OF THAT MUCH. I CAN PROMISE YOU WE'RE TRYING TO GET TO THE BOTTOM OF IT--
--BUT IN THE MEANTIME, HE'S AWAKE AND RESTING COMFORTABLY. I'M TOLD HE'S VERY EAGER TO SPEAK WITH YOU. I'LL PUT YOU THROUGH NOW.
HEY, ABUELA!
OH, THANK YOU, CAPTAIN, THANK YOU SO MUCH--
--I-I WILL NEVER FORGET WHAT YOU HAVE DONE FOR MY FAMILY. I WILL TELL EVERYONE I KNOW--I STAND WITH SAM.
SEE THERE? WORTH IT.
YOU'RE MORE THAN WELCOME, MRS. TORRES. WE'LL TALK AGAIN SOON.
SO THEY'RE INVESTIGATING THE KID'S CONDITION--HOW ABOUT YOURS?
THEY SEEM TO THINK MINE'S TEMPORARY. HOW LONG IT'LL LAST--WHO KNOWS?
YEAH, WHO KNOWS. REAL SHAME, THAT.
I THINK YOU LOOK BADASS, SAMMY.

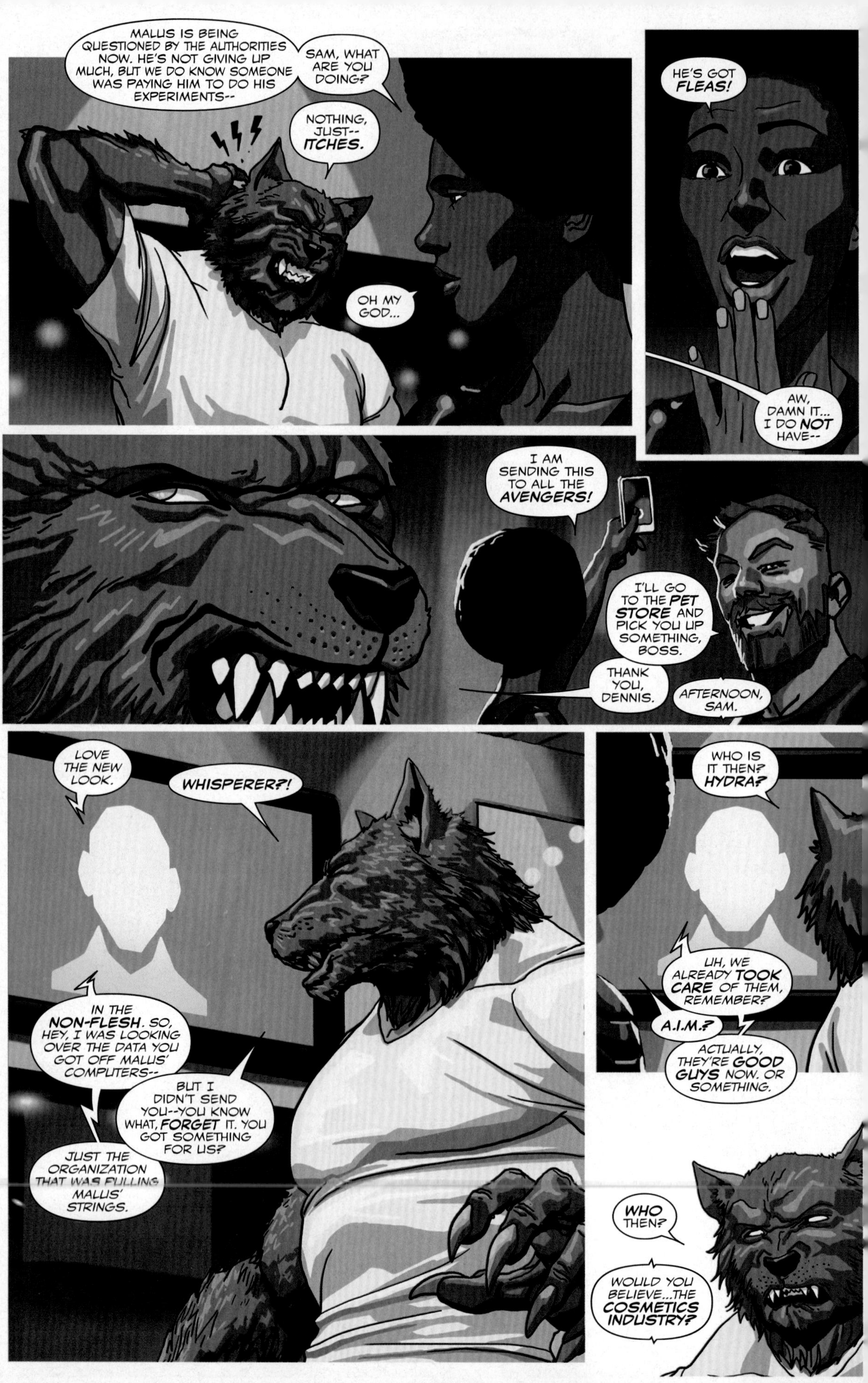
MALUS IS BEING QUESTIONED BY THE AUTHORITIES NOW. HE'S NOT GIVING UP MUCH, BUT WE DO KNOW SOMEONE WAS PAYING HIM TO DO HIS EXPERIMENTS--
SAM, WHAT ARE YOU DOING?
NOTHING, JUST-- ITCHES.
OH MY GOD...
HE'S GOT FLEAS!
AW, DAMN IT... I DO NOT HAVE--
I AM SENDING THIS TO ALL THE AVENGERS!
I'LL GO TO THE PET STORE AND PICK YOU UP SOMETHING, BOSS.
THANK YOU, DENNIS.
AFTERNOON, SAM.
LOVE THE NEW LOOK.
WHISPERER?!
IN THE NON-FLESH. SO, HEY, I WAS LOOKING OVER THE DATA YOU GOT OFF MALUS' COMPUTERS--
BUT I DIDN'T SEND YOU--YOU KNOW WHAT, FORGET IT. YOU GOT SOMETHING FOR US?
JUST THE ORGANIZATION THAT WAS PULLING MALUS' STRINGS.
WHO IS IT THEN? HYDRA?
UH, WE ALREADY TOOK CARE OF THEM, REMEMBER?
A.I.M.?
ACTUALLY, THEY'RE GOOD GUYS NOW. OR SOMETHING.
WHO THEN?
WOULD YOU BELIEVE...THE COSMETICS INDUSTRY?

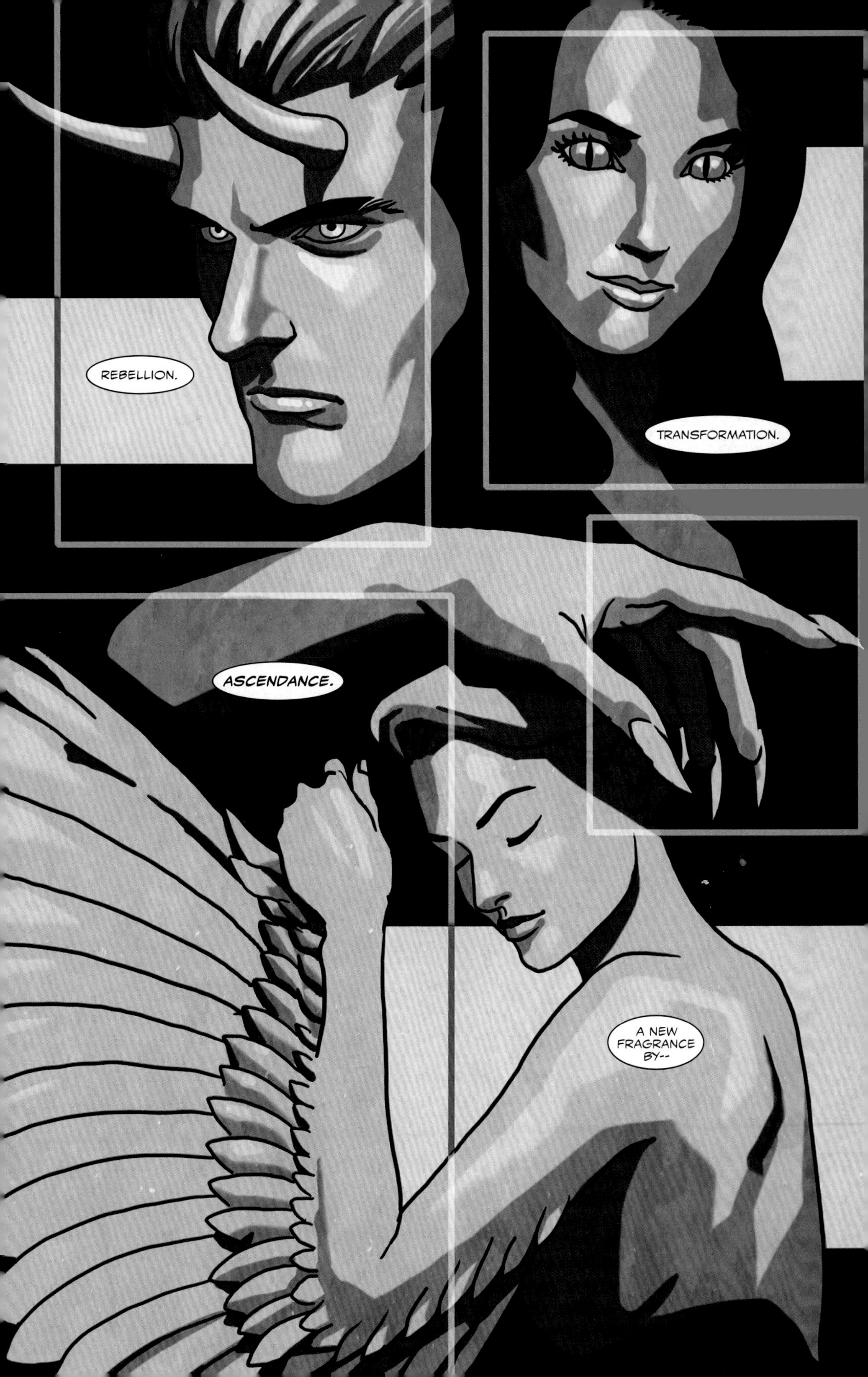
REBELLION.
TRANSFORMATION.
ASCENDANCE.
A NEW FRAGRANCE BY--

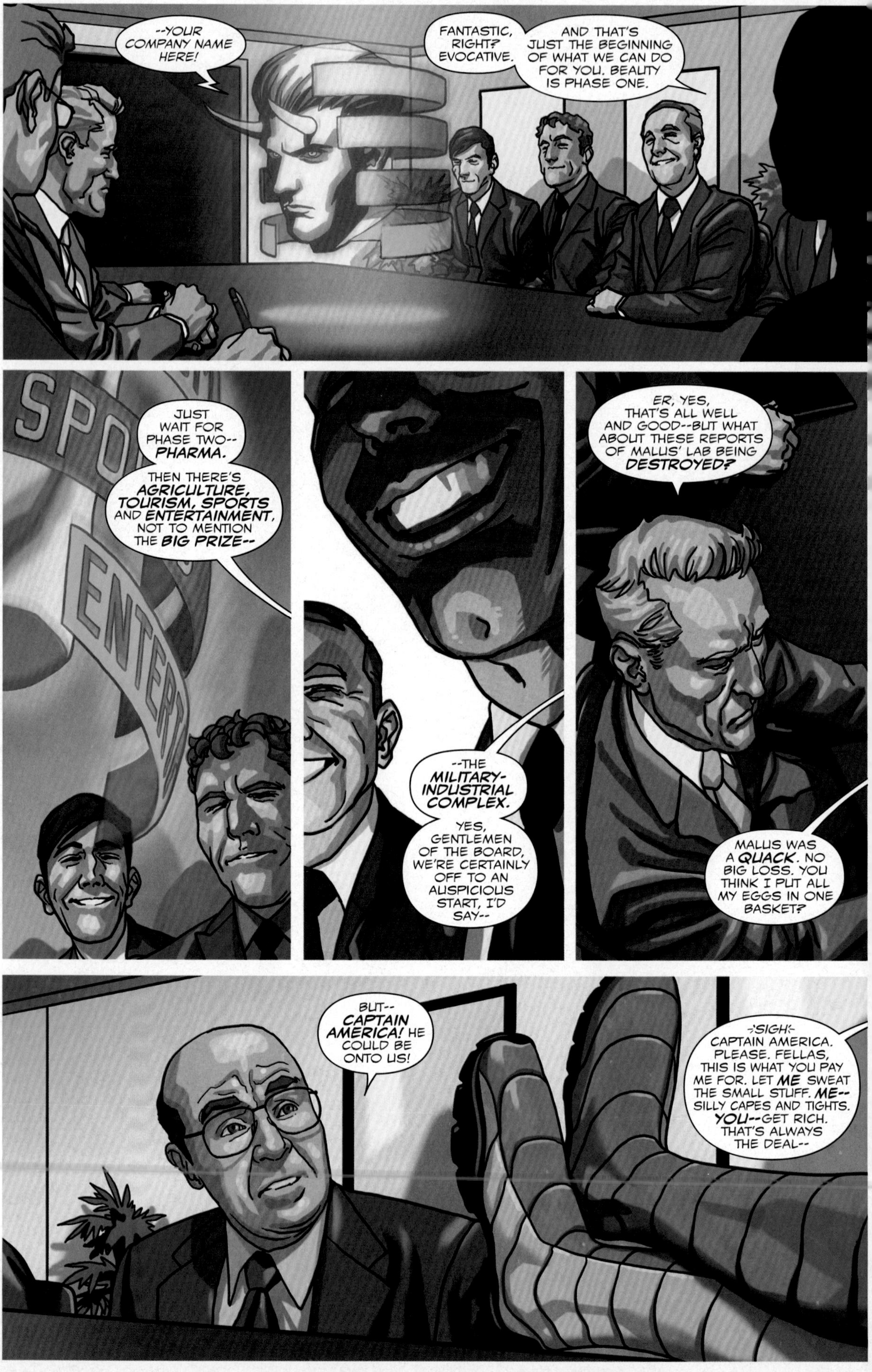
--YOUR COMPANY NAME HERE!
FANTASTIC, RIGHT? EVOCATIVE.
AND THAT'S JUST THE BEGINNING OF WHAT WE CAN DO FOR YOU. BEAUTY IS PHASE ONE.
JUST WAIT FOR PHASE TWO-- PHARMA.
THEN THERE'S AGRICULTURE, TOURISM, SPORTS AND ENTERTAINMENT, NOT TO MENTION THE BIG PRIZE--
--THE MILITARY-INDUSTRIAL COMPLEX.
YES, GENTLEMEN OF THE BOARD, WE'RE CERTAINLY OFF TO AN AUSPICIOUS START, I'D SAY--
ER, YES, THAT'S ALL WELL AND GOOD--BUT WHAT ABOUT THESE REPORTS OF MALUS' LAB BEING DESTROYED?
MALUS WAS A QUACK. NO BIG LOSS. YOU THINK I PUT ALL MY EGGS IN ONE BASKET?
BUT-- CAPTAIN AMERICA! HE COULD BE ONTO US!
SIGH CAPTAIN AMERICA. PLEASE. FELLAS, THIS IS WHAT YOU PAY ME FOR. LET ME SWEAT THE SMALL STUFF. ME-- SILLY CAPES AND TIGHTS. YOU--GET RICH. THAT'S ALWAYS THE DEAL--

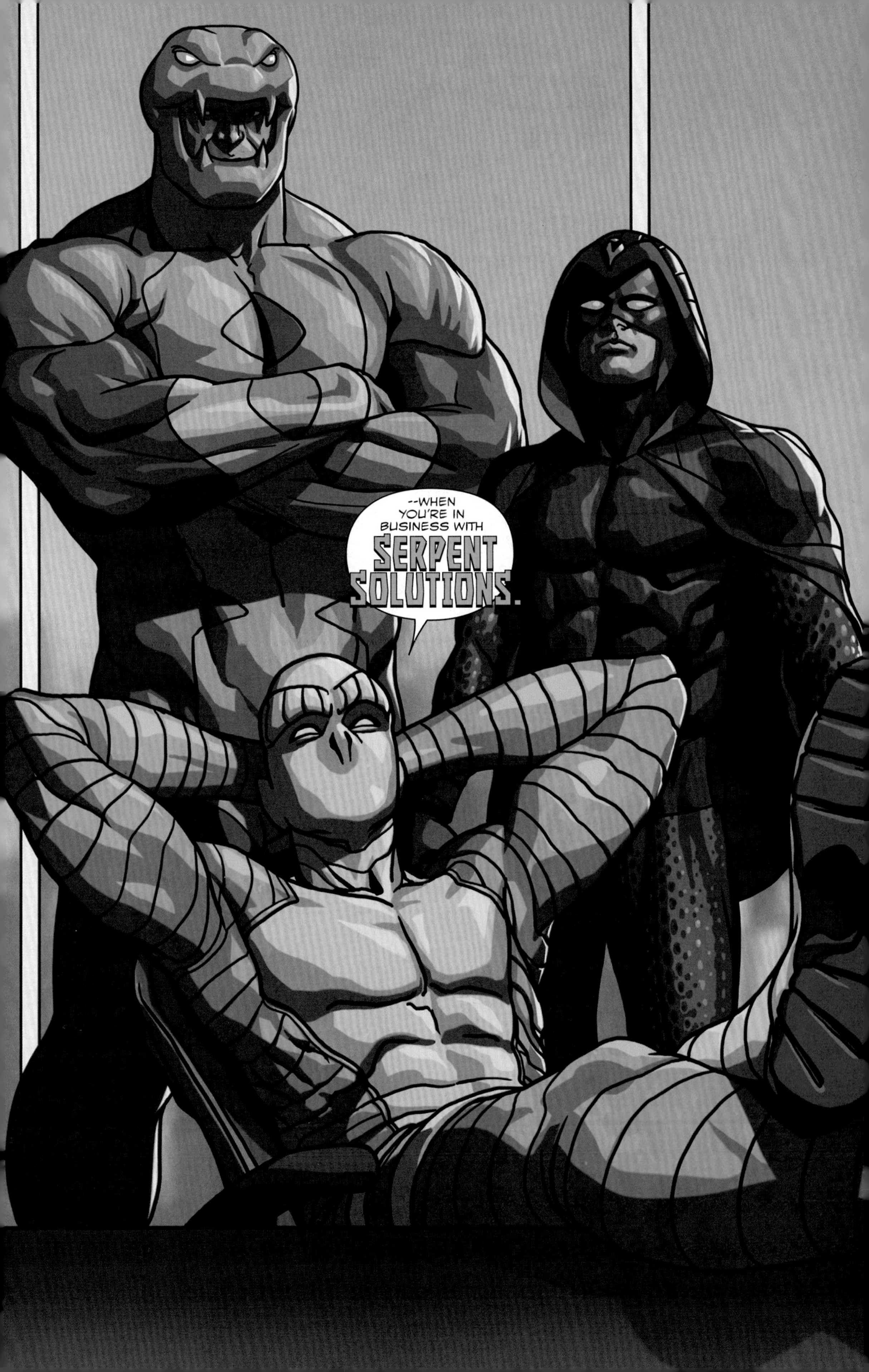
--WHEN YOU'RE IN BUSINESS WITH SERPENT SOLUTIONS.

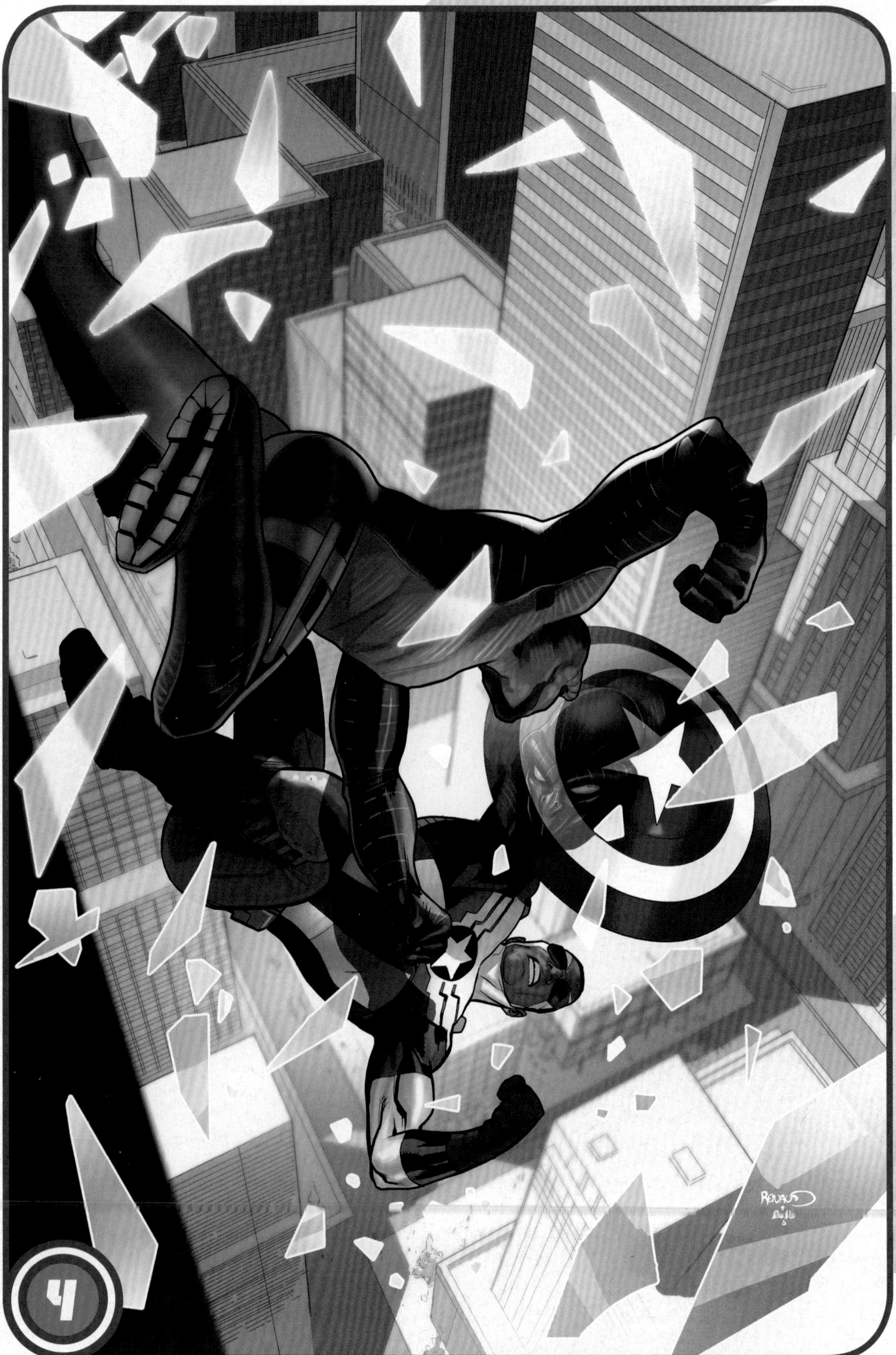

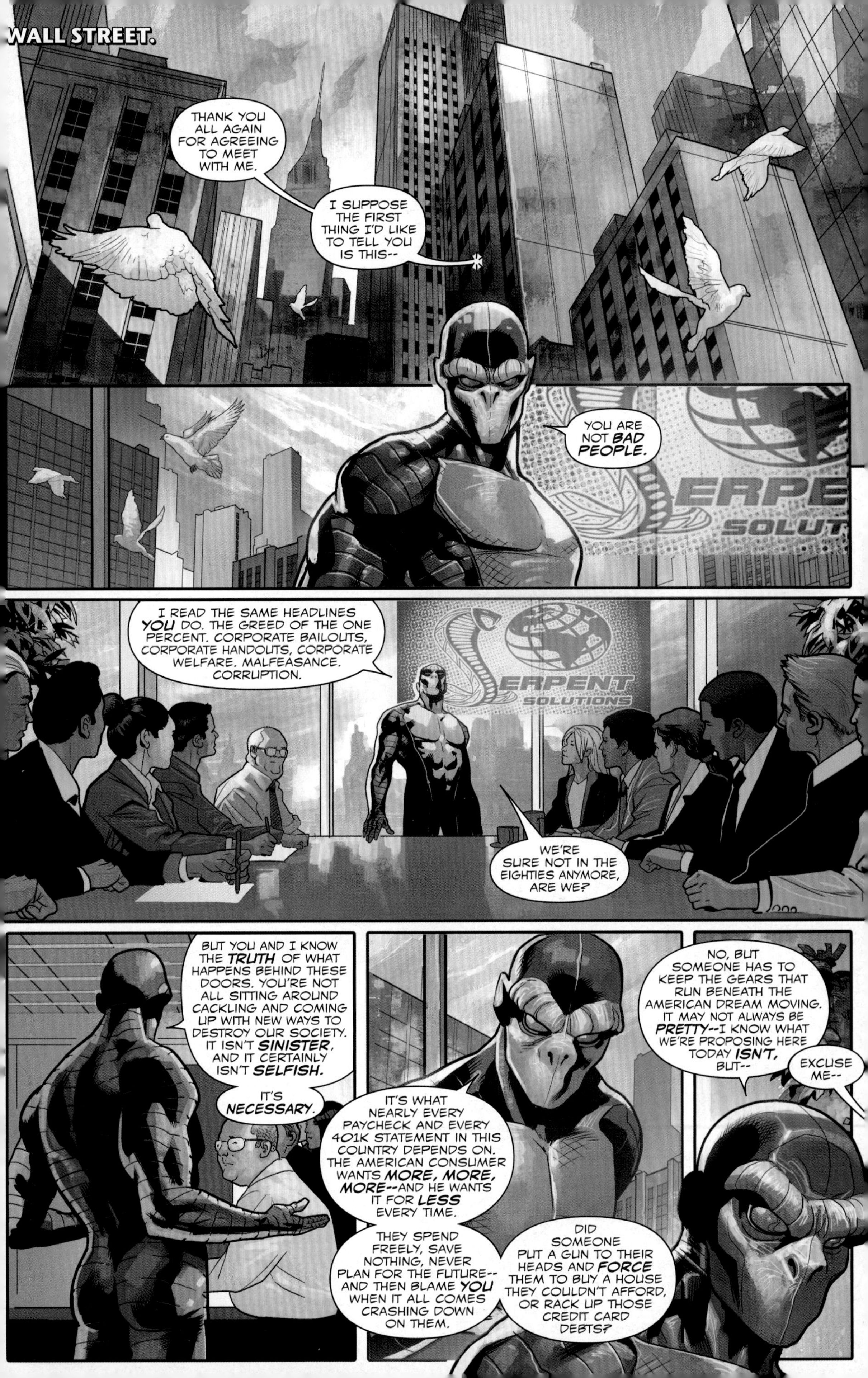
WALL STREET.
THANK YOU ALL AGAIN FOR AGREEING TO MEET WITH ME.
I SUPPOSE THE FIRST THING I'D LIKE TO TELL YOU IS THIS--
YOU ARE NOT BAD PEOPLE.
I READ THE SAME HEADLINES YOU DO. THE GREED OF THE ONE PERCENT. CORPORATE BAILOUTS, CORPORATE HANDOUTS, CORPORATE WELFARE. MALFEASANCE. CORRUPTION.
SERPENT SOLUTIONS
WE'RE SURE NOT IN THE EIGHTIES ANYMORE, ARE WE?
BUT YOU AND I KNOW THE TRUTH OF WHAT HAPPENS BEHIND THESE DOORS. YOU'RE NOT ALL SITTING AROUND CACKLING AND COMING UP WITH NEW WAYS TO DESTROY OUR SOCIETY. IT ISN'T SINISTER, AND IT CERTAINLY ISN'T SELFISH.
IT'S NECESSARY.
IT'S WHAT NEARLY EVERY PAYCHECK AND EVERY 401K STATEMENT IN THIS COUNTRY DEPENDS ON. THE AMERICAN CONSUMER WANTS MORE, MORE, MORE--AND HE WANTS IT FOR LESS EVERY TIME.
THEY SPEND FREELY, SAVE NOTHING, NEVER PLAN FOR THE FUTURE-- AND THEN BLAME YOU WHEN IT ALL COMES CRASHING DOWN ON THEM.
DID SOMEONE PUT A GUN TO THEIR HEADS AND FORCE THEM TO BUY A HOUSE THEY COULDN'T AFFORD, OR RACK UP THOSE CREDIT CARD DEBTS?
NO, BUT SOMEONE HAS TO KEEP THE GEARS THAT RUN BENEATH THE AMERICAN DREAM MOVING. IT MAY NOT ALWAYS BE PRETTY--I KNOW WHAT WE'RE PROPOSING HERE TODAY ISN'T, BUT--
EXCUSE ME--

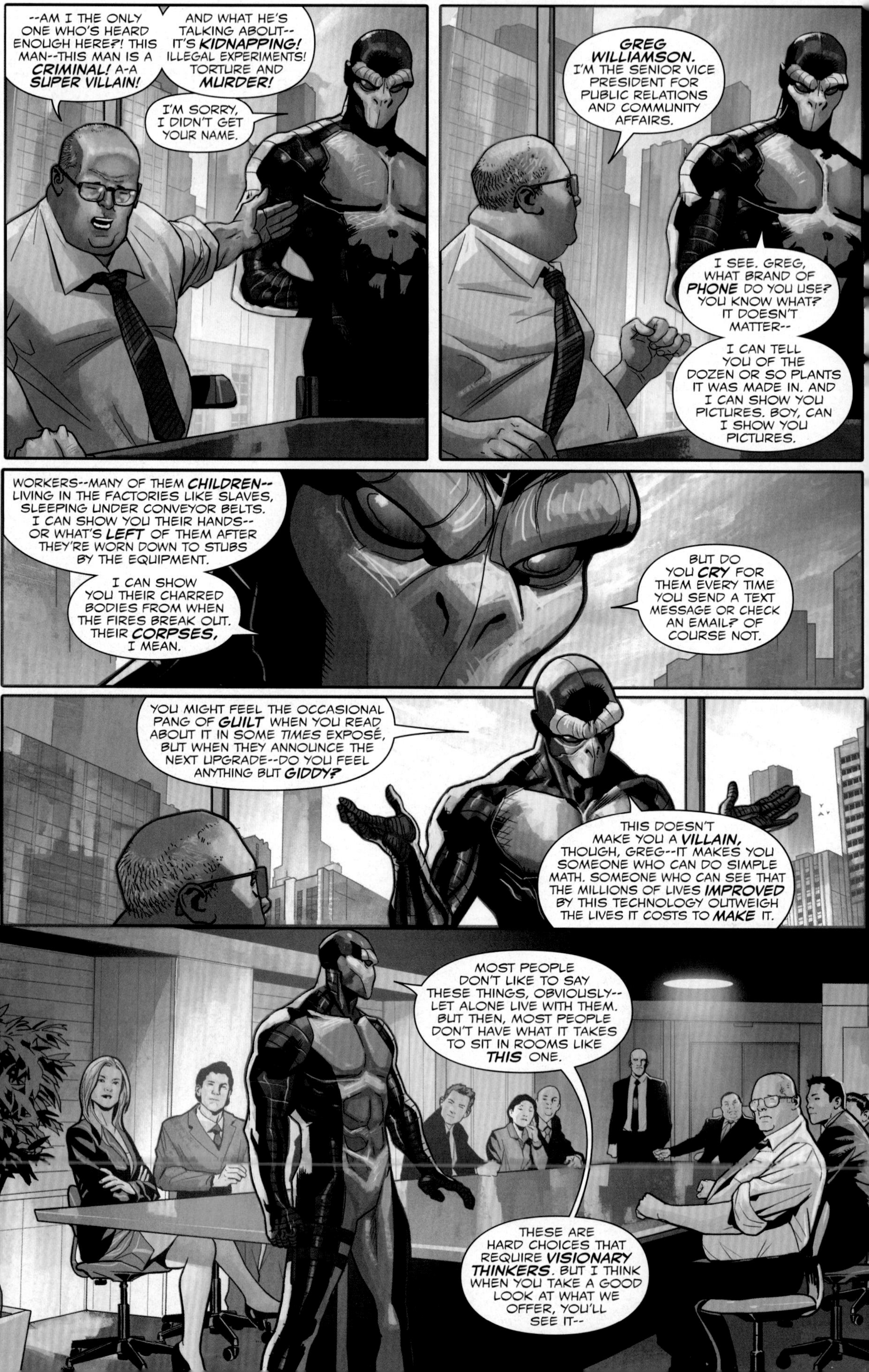
--AM I THE ONLY ONE WHO'S HEARD ENOUGH HERE?! THIS MAN--THIS MAN IS A CRIMINAL! A-A SUPER VILLAIN!
AND WHAT HE'S TALKING ABOUT-- IT'S KIDNAPPING! ILLEGAL EXPERIMENTS! TORTURE AND MURDER!
I'M SORRY, I DIDN'T GET YOUR NAME.
GREG WILLIAMSON. I'M THE SENIOR VICE PRESIDENT FOR PUBLIC RELATIONS AND COMMUNITY AFFAIRS.
I SEE. GREG, WHAT BRAND OF PHONE DO YOU USE? YOU KNOW WHAT? IT DOESN'T MATTER--
I CAN TELL YOU OF THE DOZEN OR SO PLANTS IT WAS MADE IN. AND I CAN SHOW YOU PICTURES. BOY, CAN I SHOW YOU PICTURES.
WORKERS--MANY OF THEM CHILDREN-- LIVING IN THE FACTORIES LIKE SLAVES, SLEEPING UNDER CONVEYOR BELTS. I CAN SHOW YOU THEIR HANDS-- OR WHAT'S LEFT OF THEM AFTER THEY'RE WORN DOWN TO STUBS BY THE EQUIPMENT.
I CAN SHOW YOU THEIR CHARRED BODIES FROM WHEN THE FIRES BREAK OUT. THEIR CORPSES, I MEAN.
BUT DO YOU CRY FOR THEM EVERY TIME YOU SEND A TEXT MESSAGE OR CHECK AN EMAIL? OF COURSE NOT.
YOU MIGHT FEEL THE OCCASIONAL PANG OF GUILT WHEN YOU READ ABOUT IT IN SOME TIMES EXPOSÉ, BUT WHEN THEY ANNOUNCE THE NEXT UPGRADE--DO YOU FEEL ANYTHING BUT GIDDY?
THIS DOESN'T MAKE YOU A VILLAIN, THOUGH, GREG--IT MAKES YOU SOMEONE WHO CAN DO SIMPLE MATH. SOMEONE WHO CAN SEE THAT THE MILLIONS OF LIVES IMPROVED BY THIS TECHNOLOGY OUTWEIGH THE LIVES IT COSTS TO MAKE IT.
MOST PEOPLE DON'T LIKE TO SAY THESE THINGS, OBVIOUSLY-- LET ALONE LIVE WITH THEM. BUT THEN, MOST PEOPLE DON'T HAVE WHAT IT TAKES TO SIT IN ROOMS LIKE THIS ONE.
THESE ARE HARD CHOICES THAT REQUIRE VISIONARY THINKERS. BUT I THINK WHEN YOU TAKE A GOOD LOOK AT WHAT WE OFFER, YOU'LL SEE IT--

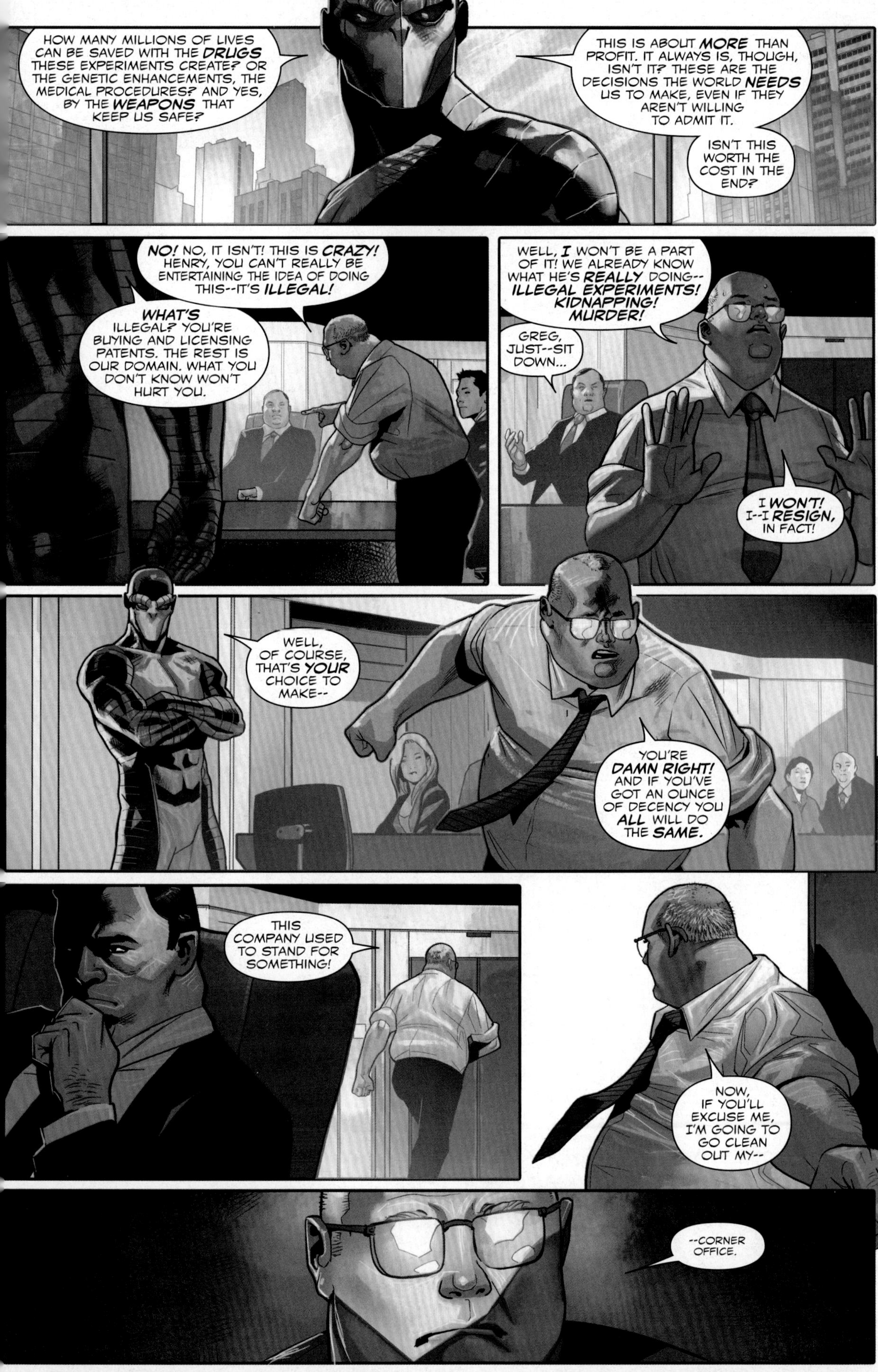
HOW MANY MILLIONS OF LIVES CAN BE SAVED WITH THE DRUGS THESE EXPERIMENTS CREATE? OR THE GENETIC ENHANCEMENTS, THE MEDICAL PROCEDURES? AND YES, BY THE WEAPONS THAT KEEP US SAFE?
THIS IS ABOUT MORE THAN PROFIT. IT ALWAYS IS, THOUGH, ISN'T IT? THESE ARE THE DECISIONS THE WORLD NEEDS US TO MAKE, EVEN IF THEY AREN'T WILLING TO ADMIT IT.
ISN'T THIS WORTH THE COST IN THE END?
NO! NO, IT ISN'T! THIS IS CRAZY! HENRY, YOU CAN'T REALLY BE ENTERTAINING THE IDEA OF DOING THIS--IT'S ILLEGAL!
WHAT'S ILLEGAL? YOU'RE BUYING AND LICENSING PATENTS. THE REST IS OUR DOMAIN. WHAT YOU DON'T KNOW WON'T HURT YOU.
WELL, I WON'T BE A PART OF IT! WE ALREADY KNOW WHAT HE'S REALLY DOING-- ILLEGAL EXPERIMENTS! KIDNAPPING! MURDER!
GREG, JUST--SIT DOWN...
I WON'T! I--I RESIGN, IN FACT!
WELL, OF COURSE, THAT'S YOUR CHOICE TO MAKE--
YOU'RE DAMN RIGHT! AND IF YOU'VE GOT AN OUNCE OF DECENCY YOU ALL WILL DO THE SAME.
THIS COMPANY USED TO STAND FOR SOMETHING!
NOW, IF YOU'LL EXCUSE ME, I'M GOING TO GO CLEAN OUT MY--
--CORNER OFFICE.

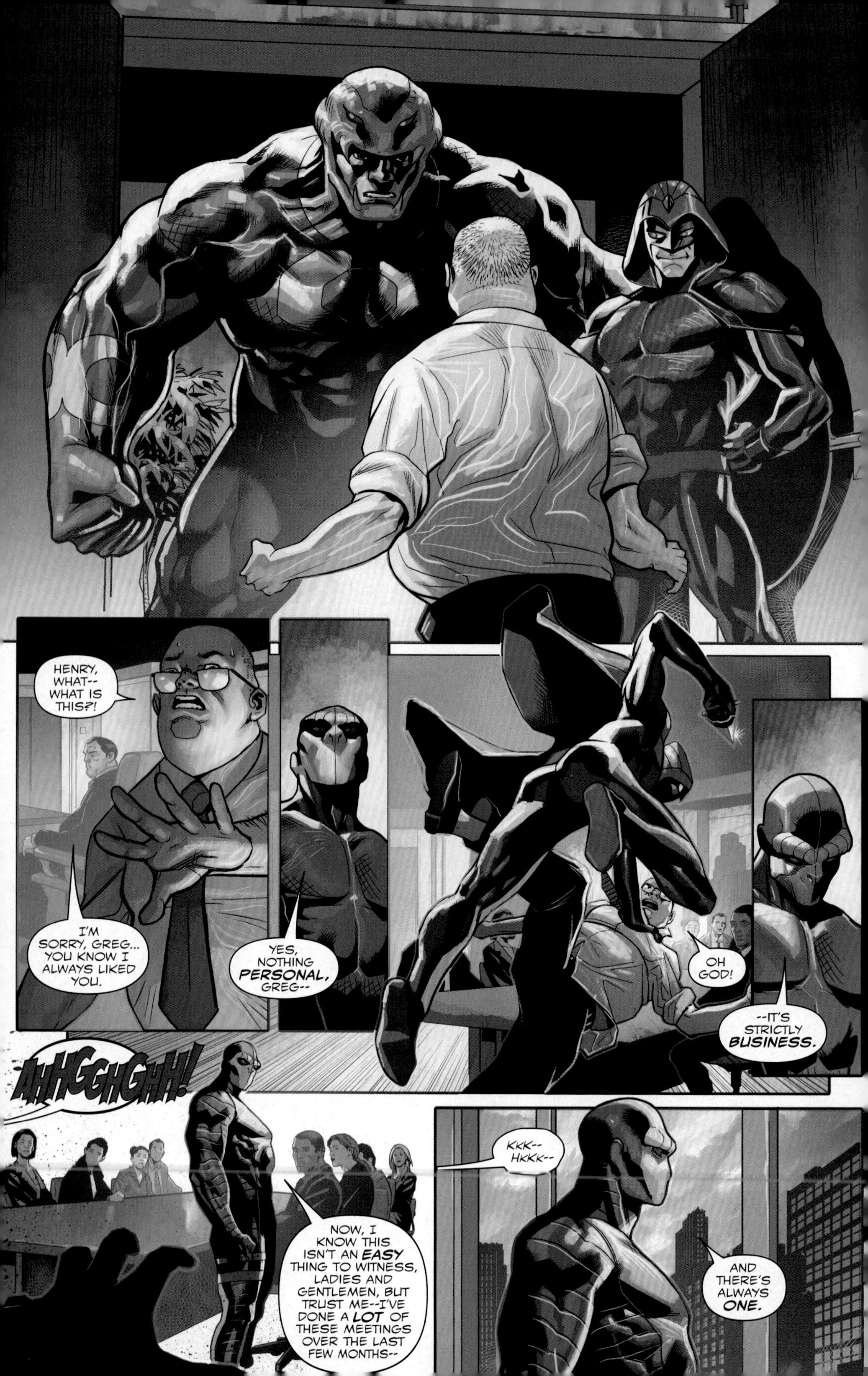
HENRY, WHAT-- WHAT IS THIS?!
I'M SORRY, GREG... YOU KNOW I ALWAYS LIKED YOU.
YES, NOTHING PERSONAL, GREG--
OH GOD!
--IT'S STRICTLY BUSINESS.
AHHGGHGHH!
NOW, I KNOW THIS ISN'T AN EASY THING TO WITNESS, LADIES AND GENTLEMEN, BUT TRUST ME--I'VE DONE A LOT OF THESE MEETINGS OVER THE LAST FEW MONTHS--
KKK-- HKKK--
AND THERE'S ALWAYS ONE.

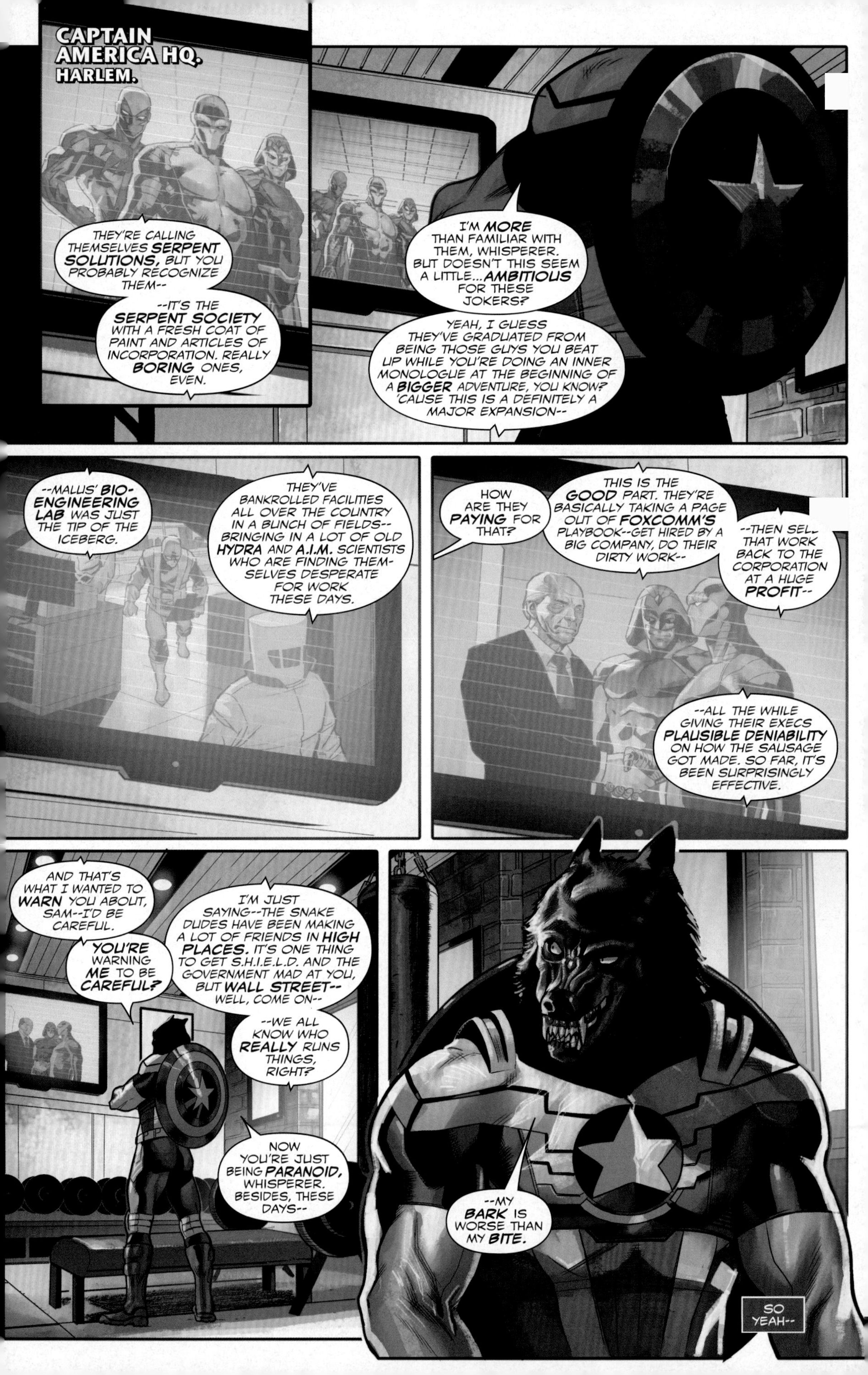
CAPTAIN AMERICA HQ. HARLEM.
THEY'RE CALLING THEMSELVES SERPENT SOLUTIONS, BUT YOU PROBABLY RECOGNIZE THEM--
--IT'S THE SERPENT SOCIETY WITH A FRESH COAT OF PAINT AND ARTICLES OF INCORPORATION. REALLY BORING ONES, EVEN.
I'M MORE THAN FAMILIAR WITH THEM, WHISPERER. BUT DOESN'T THIS SEEM A LITTLE...AMBITIOUS FOR THESE JOKERS?
YEAH, I GUESS THEY'VE GRADUATED FROM BEING THOSE GUYS YOU BEAT UP WHILE YOU'RE DOING AN INNER MONOLOGUE AT THE BEGINNING OF A BIGGER ADVENTURE, YOU KNOW? 'CAUSE THIS IS A DEFINITELY A MAJOR EXPANSION--
--MALUS' BIO-ENGINEERING LAB WAS JUST THE TIP OF THE ICEBERG.
THEY'VE BANKROLLED FACILITIES ALL OVER THE COUNTRY IN A BUNCH OF FIELDS--BRINGING IN A LOT OF OLD HYDRA AND A.I.M. SCIENTISTS WHO ARE FINDING THEMSELVES DESPERATE FOR WORK THESE DAYS.
HOW ARE THEY PAYING FOR THAT?
THIS IS THE GOOD PART. THEY'RE BASICALLY TAKING A PAGE OUT OF FOXCOMM'S PLAYBOOK--GET HIRED BY A BIG COMPANY, DO THEIR DIRTY WORK--
--THEN SELL THAT WORK BACK TO THE CORPORATION AT A HUGE PROFIT--
--ALL THE WHILE GIVING THEIR EXECS PLAUSIBLE DENIABILITY ON HOW THE SAUSAGE GOT MADE. SO FAR, IT'S BEEN SURPRISINGLY EFFECTIVE.
AND THAT'S WHAT I WANTED TO WARN YOU ABOUT, SAM--I'D BE CAREFUL.
YOU'RE WARNING ME TO BE CAREFUL?
I'M JUST SAYING--THE SNAKE DUDES HAVE BEEN MAKING A LOT OF FRIENDS IN HIGH PLACES. IT'S ONE THING TO GET S.H.I.E.L.D. AND THE GOVERNMENT MAD AT YOU, BUT WALL STREET--WELL, COME ON--
--WE ALL KNOW WHO REALLY RUNS THINGS, RIGHT?
NOW YOU'RE JUST BEING PARANOID, WHISPERER. BESIDES, THESE DAYS--
--MY BARK IS WORSE THAN MY BITE.
SO YEAH--

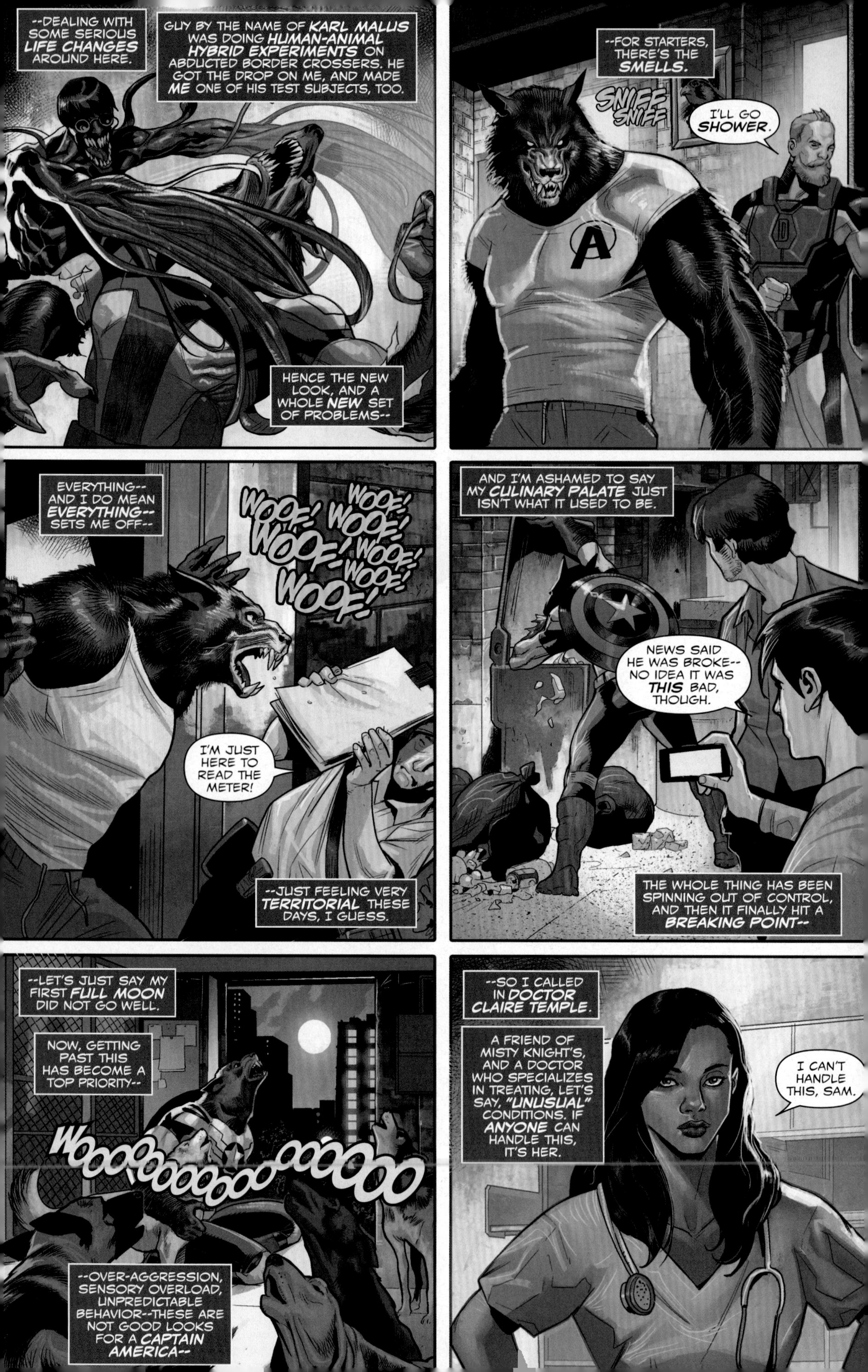
--DEALING WITH SOME SERIOUS LIFE CHANGES AROUND HERE.
GUY BY THE NAME OF KARL MALUS WAS DOING HUMAN-ANIMAL HYBRID EXPERIMENTS ON ABDUCTED BORDER CROSSERS. HE GOT THE DROP ON ME, AND MADE ME ONE OF HIS TEST SUBJECTS, TOO.
HENCE THE NEW LOOK, AND A WHOLE NEW SET OF PROBLEMS--
--FOR STARTERS, THERE'S THE SMELLS.
SNIFF SNIFF
I'LL GO SHOWER.
EVERYTHING-- AND I DO MEAN EVERYTHING-- SETS ME OFF--
WOOF! WOOF! WOOF! WOOF! WOOF! WOOF! WOOF!
I'M JUST HERE TO READ THE METER!
--JUST FEELING VERY TERRITORIAL THESE DAYS, I GUESS.
AND I'M ASHAMED TO SAY MY CULINARY PALATE JUST ISN'T WHAT IT USED TO BE.
NEWS SAID HE WAS BROKE-- NO IDEA IT WAS THIS BAD, THOUGH.
THE WHOLE THING HAS BEEN SPINNING OUT OF CONTROL, AND THEN IT FINALLY HIT A BREAKING POINT--
--LET'S JUST SAY MY FIRST FULL MOON DID NOT GO WELL.
NOW, GETTING PAST THIS HAS BECOME A TOP PRIORITY--
WOOOOOOOOOOOOOOOOOOO
--OVER-AGGRESSION, SENSORY OVERLOAD, UNPREDICTABLE BEHAVIOR--THESE ARE NOT GOOD LOOKS FOR A CAPTAIN AMERICA--
--SO I CALLED IN DOCTOR CLAIRE TEMPLE.
A FRIEND OF MISTY KNIGHT'S, AND A DOCTOR WHO SPECIALIZES IN TREATING, LET'S SAY, "UNUSUAL" CONDITIONS. IF ANYONE CAN HANDLE THIS, IT'S HER.
I CAN'T HANDLE THIS, SAM.

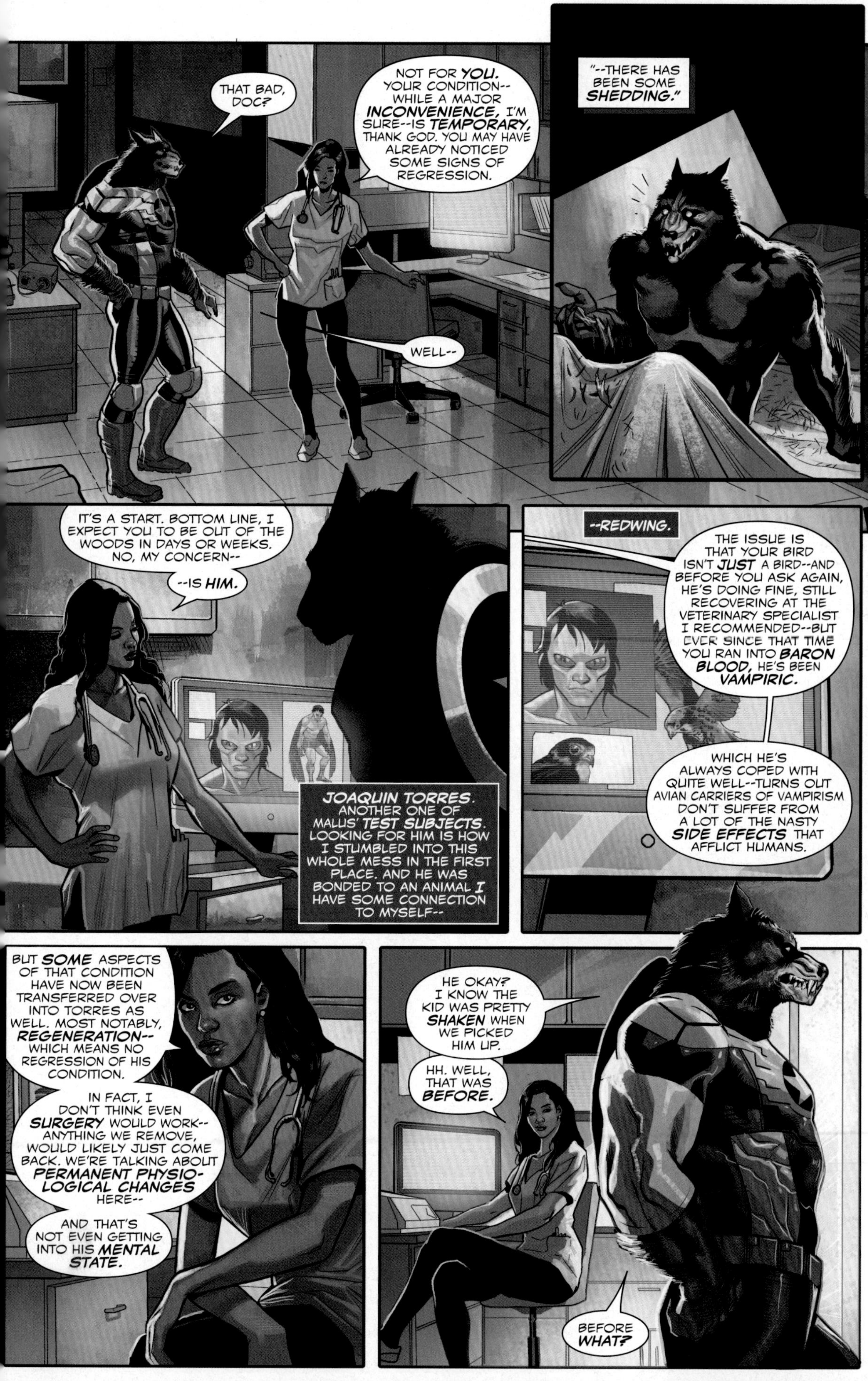

THAT BAD, DOC?
NOT FOR YOU. YOUR CONDITION-- WHILE A MAJOR INCONVENIENCE, I'M SURE--IS TEMPORARY, THANK GOD. YOU MAY HAVE ALREADY NOTICED SOME SIGNS OF REGRESSION.
WELL--
"--THERE HAS BEEN SOME SHEDDING."
IT'S A START. BOTTOM LINE, I EXPECT YOU TO BE OUT OF THE WOODS IN DAYS OR WEEKS. NO, MY CONCERN--
--IS HIM.
JOAQUIN TORRES. ANOTHER ONE OF MALUS' TEST SUBJECTS. LOOKING FOR HIM IS HOW I STUMBLED INTO THIS WHOLE MESS IN THE FIRST PLACE. AND HE WAS BONDED TO AN ANIMAL I HAVE SOME CONNECTION TO MYSELF--
--REDWING.
THE ISSUE IS THAT YOUR BIRD ISN'T JUST A BIRD--AND BEFORE YOU ASK AGAIN, HE'S DOING FINE, STILL RECOVERING AT THE VETERINARY SPECIALIST I RECOMMENDED--BUT EVER SINCE THAT TIME YOU RAN INTO BARON BLOOD, HE'S BEEN VAMPIRIC.
WHICH HE'S ALWAYS COPED WITH QUITE WELL--TURNS OUT AVIAN CARRIERS OF VAMPIRISM DON'T SUFFER FROM A LOT OF THE NASTY SIDE EFFECTS THAT AFFLICT HUMANS.
BUT SOME ASPECTS OF THAT CONDITION HAVE NOW BEEN TRANSFERRED OVER INTO TORRES AS WELL. MOST NOTABLY, REGENERATION-- WHICH MEANS NO REGRESSION OF HIS CONDITION.
IN FACT, I DON'T THINK EVEN SURGERY WOULD WORK-- ANYTHING WE REMOVE, WOULD LIKELY JUST COME BACK. WE'RE TALKING ABOUT PERMANENT PHYSIO-LOGICAL CHANGES HERE--
AND THAT'S NOT EVEN GETTING INTO HIS MENTAL STATE.
HE OKAY? I KNOW THE KID WAS PRETTY SHAKEN WHEN WE PICKED HIM UP.
HH. WELL, THAT WAS BEFORE.
BEFORE WHAT?

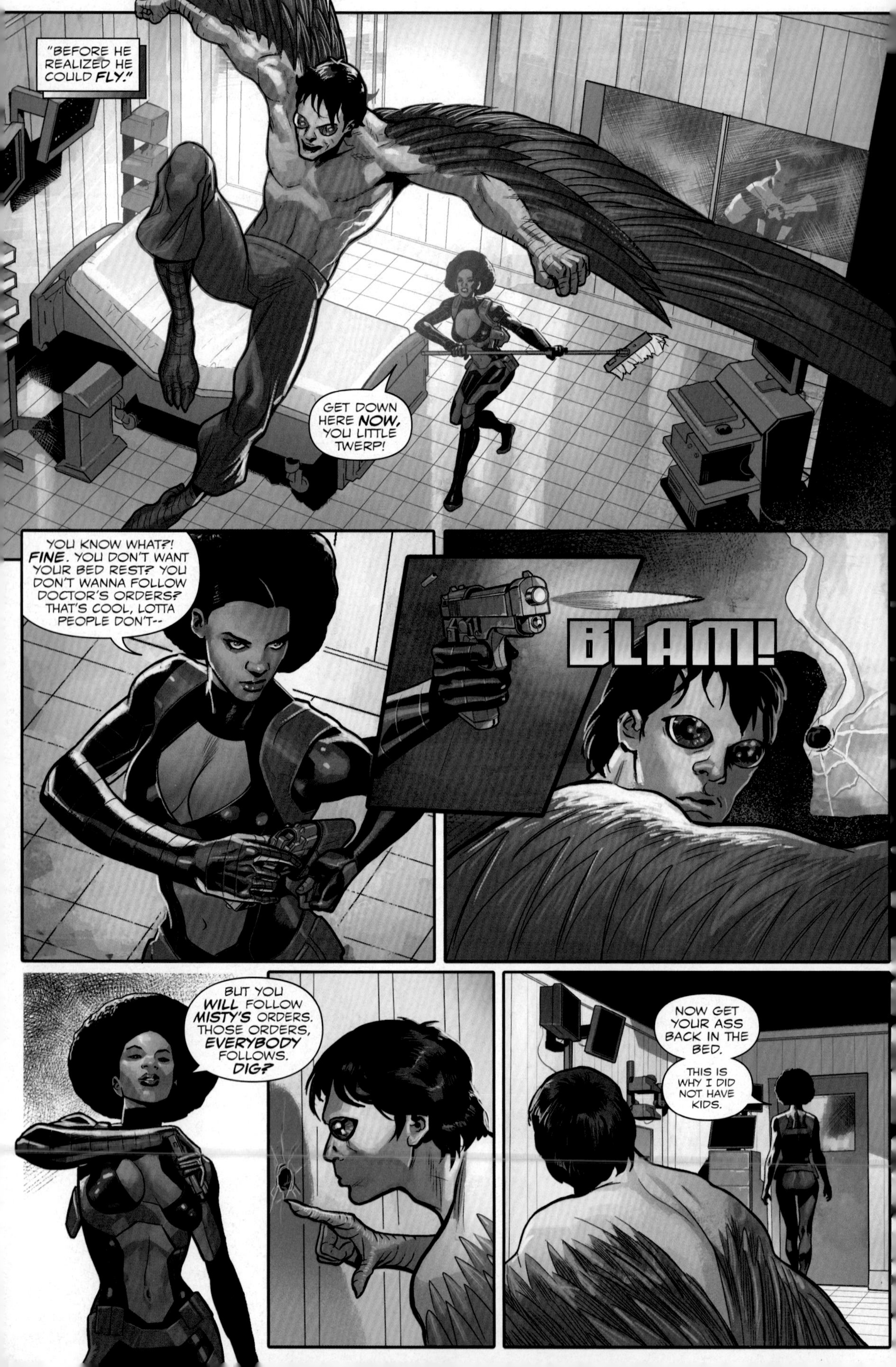
"BEFORE HE REALIZED HE COULD FLY."
GET DOWN HERE NOW, YOU LITTLE TWERP!
YOU KNOW WHAT?! FINE. YOU DON'T WANT YOUR BED REST? YOU DON'T WANNA FOLLOW DOCTOR'S ORDERS? THAT'S COOL, LOTTA PEOPLE DON'T--
BLAM!
BUT YOU WILL FOLLOW MISTY'S ORDERS. THOSE ORDERS, EVERYBODY FOLLOWS. DIG?
NOW GET YOUR ASS BACK IN THE BED.
THIS IS WHY I DID NOT HAVE KIDS.

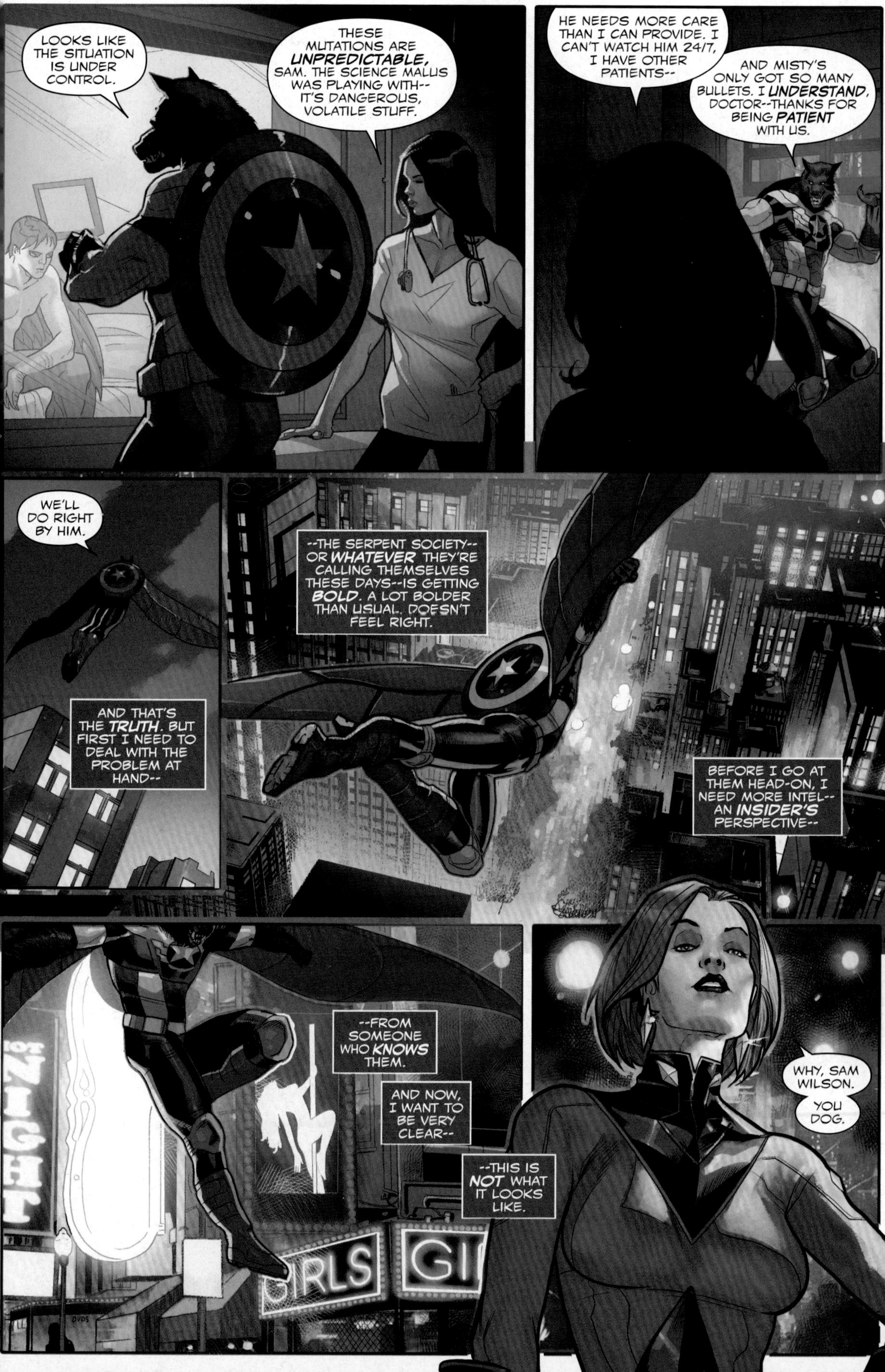
LOOKS LIKE THE SITUATION IS UNDER CONTROL.
THESE MUTATIONS ARE UNPREDICTABLE, SAM. THE SCIENCE MALUS WAS PLAYING WITH-- IT'S DANGEROUS, VOLATILE STUFF.
HE NEEDS MORE CARE THAN I CAN PROVIDE. I CAN'T WATCH HIM 24/7, I HAVE OTHER PATIENTS--
AND MISTY'S ONLY GOT SO MANY BULLETS. I UNDERSTAND, DOCTOR--THANKS FOR BEING PATIENT WITH US.
WE'LL DO RIGHT BY HIM.
--THE SERPENT SOCIETY-- OR WHATEVER THEY'RE CALLING THEMSELVES THESE DAYS--IS GETTING BOLD. A LOT BOLDER THAN USUAL. DOESN'T FEEL RIGHT.
AND THAT'S THE TRUTH. BUT FIRST I NEED TO DEAL WITH THE PROBLEM AT HAND--
BEFORE I GO AT THEM HEAD-ON, I NEED MORE INTEL-- AN INSIDER'S PERSPECTIVE--
--FROM SOMEONE WHO KNOWS THEM.
AND NOW, I WANT TO BE VERY CLEAR--
--THIS IS NOT WHAT IT LOOKS LIKE.
NIGHT
GIRLS
WHY, SAM WILSON.
YOU DOG.

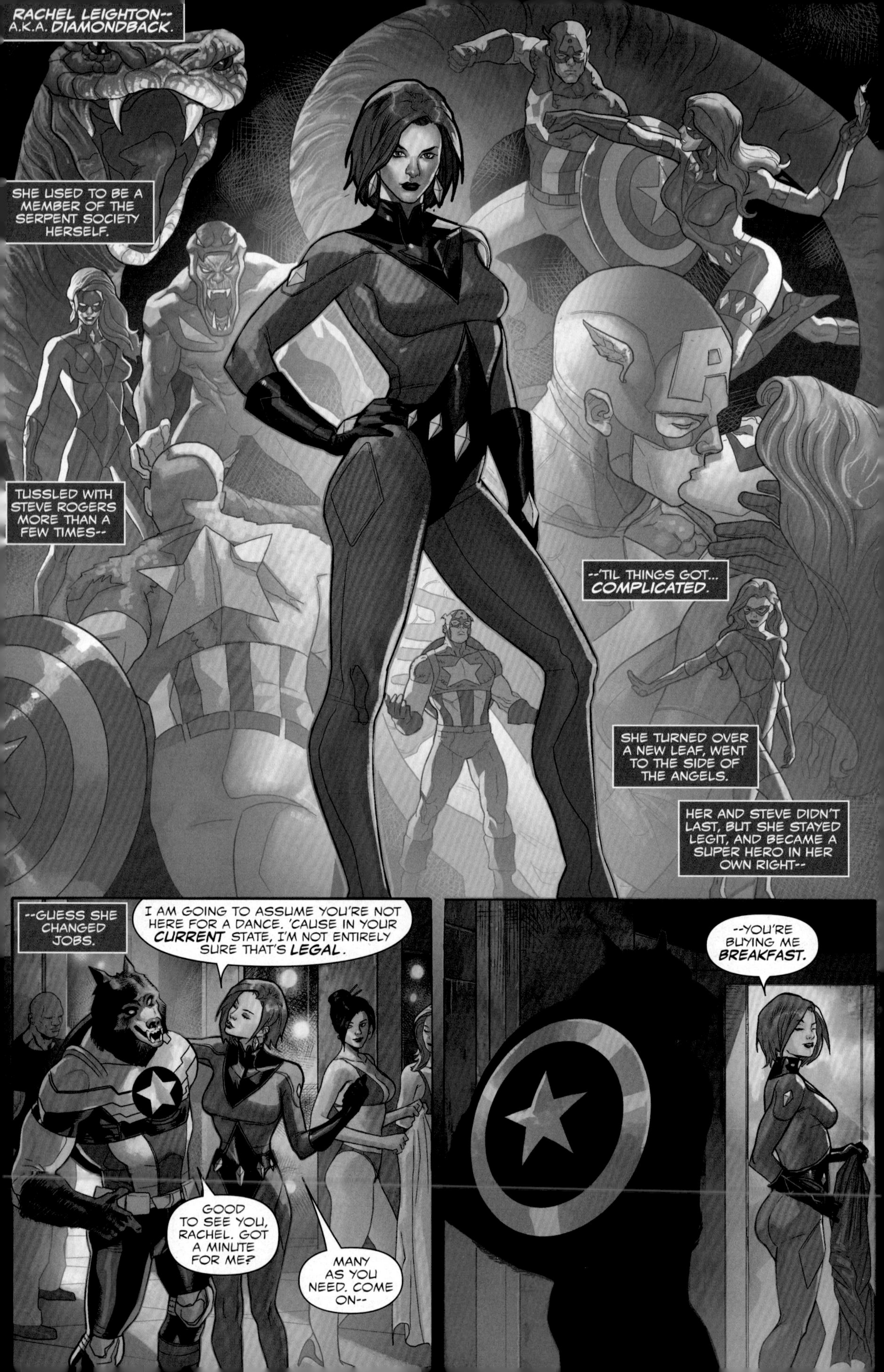
RACHEL LEIGHTON--
A.K.A. DIAMONDBACK.
SHE USED TO BE A MEMBER OF THE SERPENT SOCIETY HERSELF.
TUSSLED WITH STEVE ROGERS MORE THAN A FEW TIMES--
--'TIL THINGS GOT... COMPLICATED.
SHE TURNED OVER A NEW LEAF, WENT TO THE SIDE OF THE ANGELS.
HER AND STEVE DIDN'T LAST, BUT SHE STAYED LEGIT, AND BECAME A SUPER HERO IN HER OWN RIGHT--
--GUESS SHE CHANGED JOBS.
I AM GOING TO ASSUME YOU'RE NOT HERE FOR A DANCE. 'CAUSE IN YOUR CURRENT STATE, I'M NOT ENTIRELY SURE THAT'S LEGAL.
GOOD TO SEE YOU, RACHEL. GOT A MINUTE FOR ME?
MANY AS YOU NEED. COME ON--
--YOU'RE BUYING ME BREAKFAST.

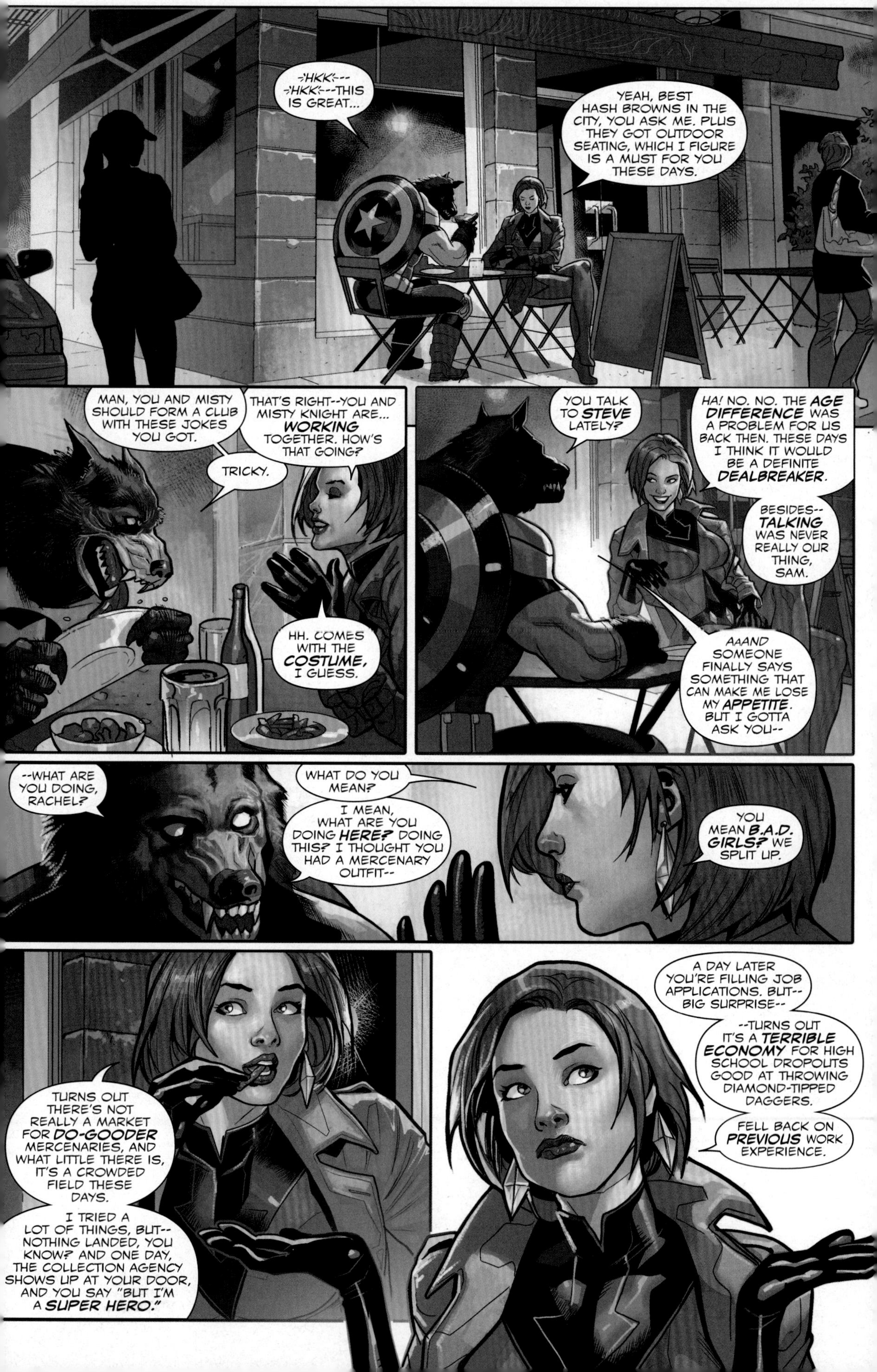
-HKK---
-HKK---THIS IS GREAT...
YEAH, BEST HASH BROWNS IN THE CITY, YOU ASK ME. PLUS THEY GOT OUTDOOR SEATING, WHICH I FIGURE IS A MUST FOR YOU THESE DAYS.
MAN, YOU AND MISTY SHOULD FORM A CLUB WITH THESE JOKES YOU GOT.
THAT'S RIGHT--YOU AND MISTY KNIGHT ARE... WORKING TOGETHER. HOW'S THAT GOING?
TRICKY.
HH. COMES WITH THE COSTUME, I GUESS.
YOU TALK TO STEVE LATELY?
HA! NO. NO. THE AGE DIFFERENCE WAS A PROBLEM FOR US BACK THEN. THESE DAYS I THINK IT WOULD BE A DEFINITE DEALBREAKER.
BESIDES-- TALKING WAS NEVER REALLY OUR THING, SAM.
AAAND SOMEONE FINALLY SAYS SOMETHING THAT CAN MAKE ME LOSE MY APPETITE. BUT I GOTTA ASK YOU--
--WHAT ARE YOU DOING, RACHEL?
WHAT DO YOU MEAN?
I MEAN, WHAT ARE YOU DOING HERE? DOING THIS? I THOUGHT YOU HAD A MERCENARY OUTFIT--
YOU MEAN B.A.D. GIRLS? WE SPLIT UP.
TURNS OUT THERE'S NOT REALLY A MARKET FOR DO-GOODER MERCENARIES, AND WHAT LITTLE THERE IS, IT'S A CROWDED FIELD THESE DAYS.
I TRIED A LOT OF THINGS, BUT-- NOTHING LANDED, YOU KNOW? AND ONE DAY, THE COLLECTION AGENCY SHOWS UP AT YOUR DOOR, AND YOU SAY "BUT I'M A SUPER HERO."
A DAY LATER YOU'RE FILLING JOB APPLICATIONS. BUT-- BIG SURPRISE--
--TURNS OUT IT'S A TERRIBLE ECONOMY FOR HIGH SCHOOL DROPOUTS GOOD AT THROWING DIAMOND-TIPPED DAGGERS.
FELL BACK ON PREVIOUS WORK EXPERIENCE.

THERE'S GOTTA BE SOMETHING ELSE, THOUGH--SOMETHING **BETTER** THAN THIS--

PFFT--YOU HAVEN'T SEEN WHAT I CAN MAKE IN **TIPS** IN A NIGHT. WEIRD AS IT MAY SOUND, I DON'T ALWAYS MISS GETTING INTO FISTFIGHTS WITH PSYCHO-KILLERS AND NEARLY GETTING KILLED ALL THE TIME.

COMPARED TO THAT, THIS JOB IS DOWNRIGHT **TAME**. WELL, **MOST** DAYS.

WE COULD **USE** YOU OUT THERE, THOUGH, RACHEL--YOU'RE A **HERO**. COUNTRY NEEDS PEOPLE LIKE YOU.

DO THEY? LOOK AT ME, SAM. I'M A **RELIC**. THE WOMEN OUT THERE DOING THIS NOW--THEY GET TAKEN SERIOUSLY. THEY WEAR COSTUMES THEY CAN ACTUALLY **BREATHE** IN.

I MEAN, CAPTAIN MARVEL RUNS A **SPACE STATION**. THOR'S A WOMAN NOW! AND DON'T GET ME WRONG, NOBODY'S HAPPIER TO SEE IT THAN **I** AM.

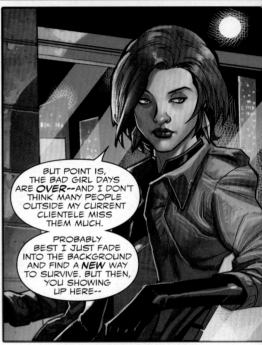

BUT POINT IS, THE BAD GIRL DAYS ARE **OVER**--AND I DON'T THINK MANY PEOPLE OUTSIDE MY CURRENT CLIENTELE MISS THEM MUCH.

PROBABLY BEST I JUST FADE INTO THE BACKGROUND AND FIND A **NEW** WAY TO SURVIVE. BUT THEN, YOU SHOWING UP HERE--

"--SOMETHING TELLS ME YOU'VE GOT SURVIVING ON THE MIND, TOO."

--AND SO I TOLD THE FOLKS AT BAIN, COME BACK TO ME IN **SIX** MONTHS!

HA HA HA HA HA

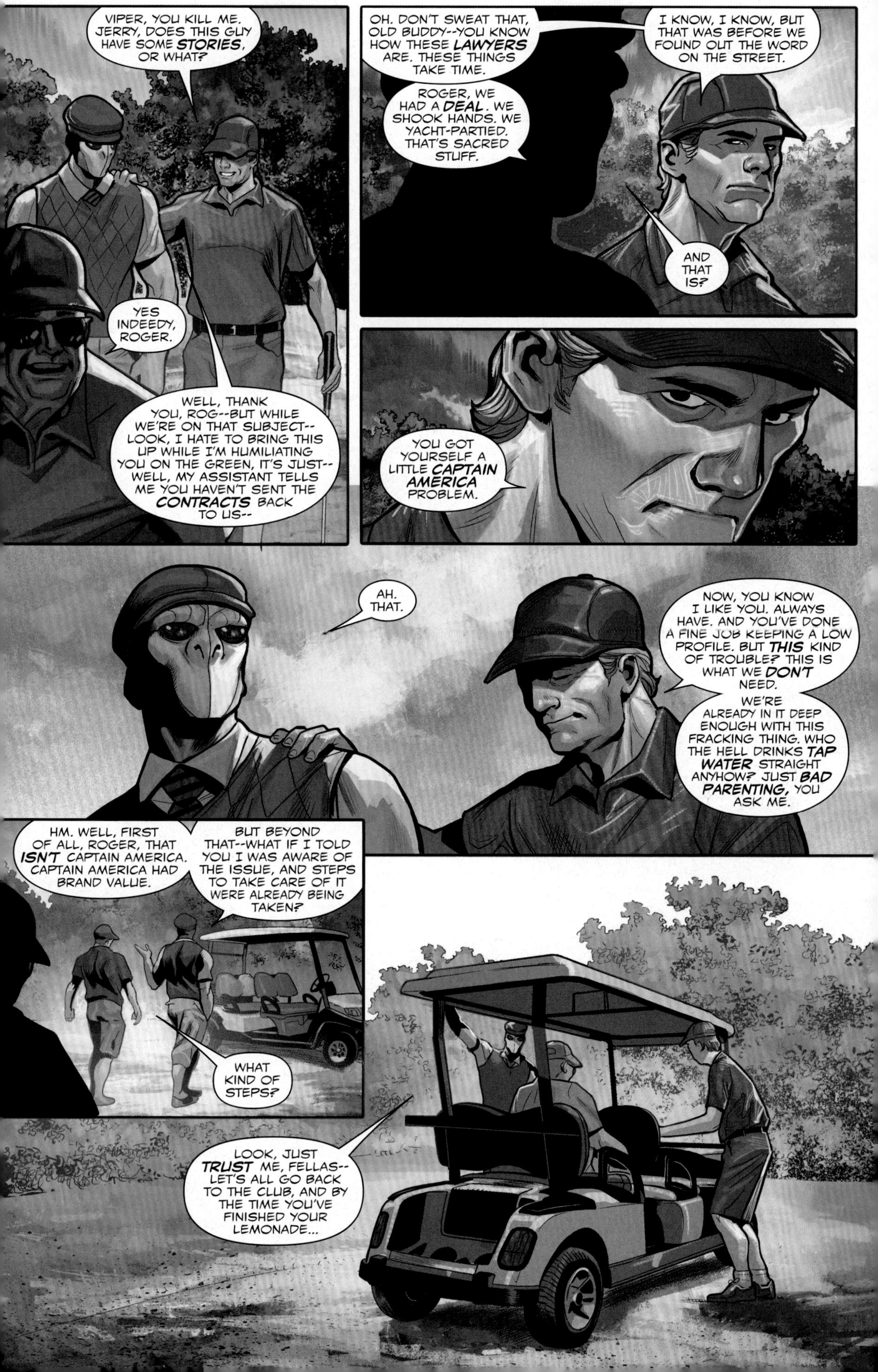
VIPER, YOU KILL ME. JERRY, DOES THIS GUY HAVE SOME STORIES, OR WHAT?
YES INDEEDY, ROGER.
WELL, THANK YOU, ROG--BUT WHILE WE'RE ON THAT SUBJECT--LOOK, I HATE TO BRING THIS UP WHILE I'M HUMILIATING YOU ON THE GREEN, IT'S JUST--WELL, MY ASSISTANT TELLS ME YOU HAVEN'T SENT THE CONTRACTS BACK TO US--
OH. DON'T SWEAT THAT, OLD BUDDY--YOU KNOW HOW THESE LAWYERS ARE. THESE THINGS TAKE TIME.
ROGER, WE HAD A DEAL. WE SHOOK HANDS. WE YACHT-PARTIED. THAT'S SACRED STUFF.
I KNOW, I KNOW, BUT THAT WAS BEFORE WE FOUND OUT THE WORD ON THE STREET.
AND THAT IS?
YOU GOT YOURSELF A LITTLE CAPTAIN AMERICA PROBLEM.
AH. THAT.
NOW, YOU KNOW I LIKE YOU. ALWAYS HAVE. AND YOU'VE DONE A FINE JOB KEEPING A LOW PROFILE. BUT THIS KIND OF TROUBLE? THIS IS WHAT WE DON'T NEED.
WE'RE ALREADY IN IT DEEP ENOUGH WITH THIS FRACKING THING. WHO THE HELL DRINKS TAP WATER STRAIGHT ANYHOW? JUST BAD PARENTING, YOU ASK ME.
HM. WELL, FIRST OF ALL, ROGER, THAT ISN'T CAPTAIN AMERICA. CAPTAIN AMERICA HAD BRAND VALUE.
BUT BEYOND THAT--WHAT IF I TOLD YOU I WAS AWARE OF THE ISSUE, AND STEPS TO TAKE CARE OF IT WERE ALREADY BEING TAKEN?
WHAT KIND OF STEPS?
LOOK, JUST TRUST ME, FELLAS--LET'S ALL GO BACK TO THE CLUB, AND BY THE TIME YOU'VE FINISHED YOUR LEMONADE...

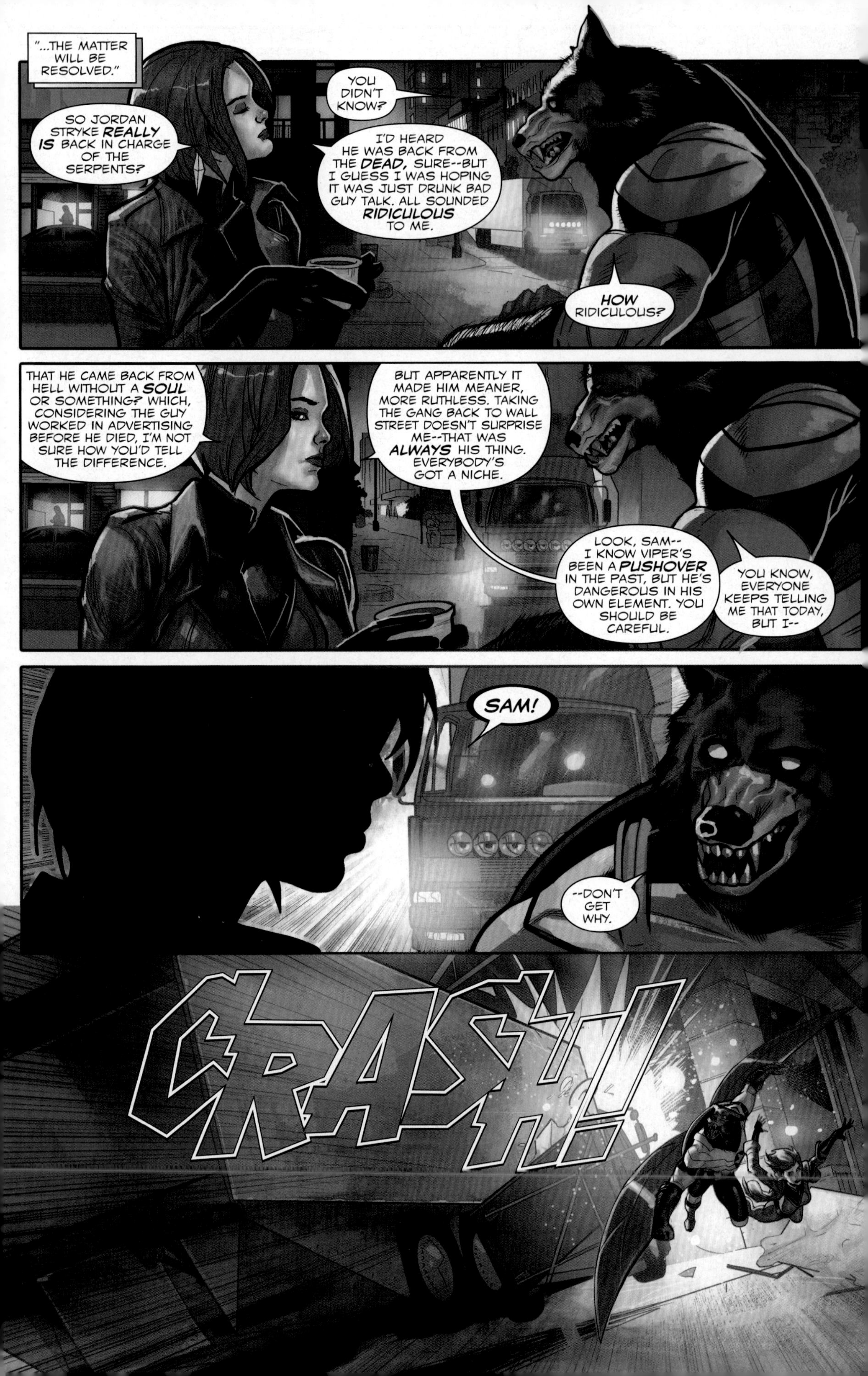
"...THE MATTER WILL BE RESOLVED."
SO JORDAN STRYKE **REALLY IS** BACK IN CHARGE OF THE SERPENTS?
YOU DIDN'T KNOW?
I'D HEARD HE WAS BACK FROM THE **DEAD,** SURE--BUT I GUESS I WAS HOPING IT WAS JUST DRUNK BAD GUY TALK. ALL SOUNDED **RIDICULOUS** TO ME.
HOW RIDICULOUS?
THAT HE CAME BACK FROM HELL WITHOUT A **SOUL** OR SOMETHING? WHICH, CONSIDERING THE GUY WORKED IN ADVERTISING BEFORE HE DIED, I'M NOT SURE HOW YOU'D TELL THE DIFFERENCE.
BUT APPARENTLY IT MADE HIM MEANER, MORE RUTHLESS. TAKING THE GANG BACK TO WALL STREET DOESN'T SURPRISE ME--THAT WAS **ALWAYS** HIS THING. EVERYBODY'S GOT A NICHE.
LOOK, SAM-- I KNOW VIPER'S BEEN A **PUSHOVER** IN THE PAST, BUT HE'S DANGEROUS IN HIS OWN ELEMENT. YOU SHOULD BE CAREFUL.
YOU KNOW, EVERYONE KEEPS TELLING ME THAT TODAY, BUT I--
SAM!
--DON'T GET WHY.
CRASH!!

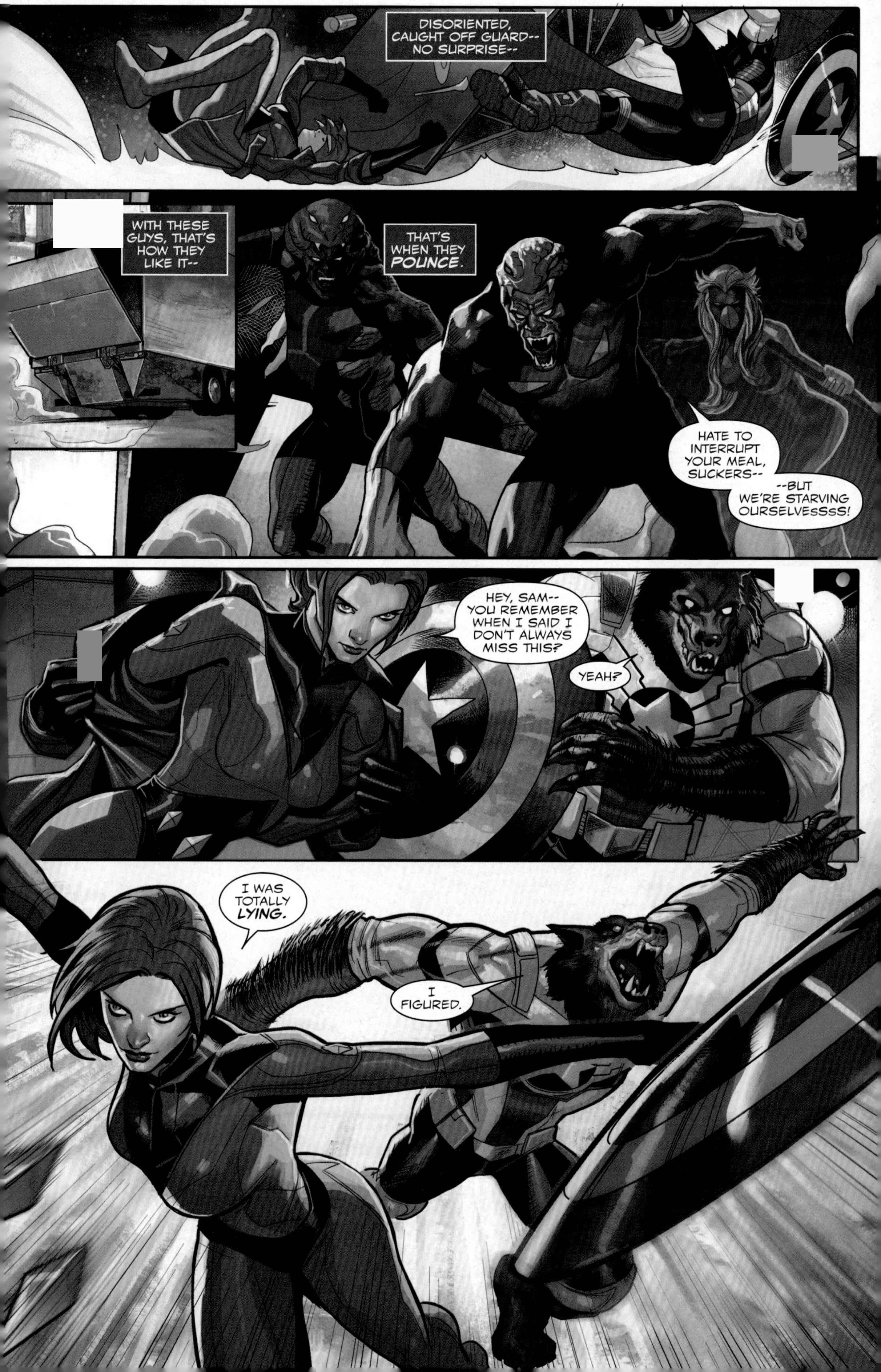
DISORIENTED, CAUGHT OFF GUARD-- NO SURPRISE--
WITH THESE GUYS, THAT'S HOW THEY LIKE IT--
THAT'S WHEN THEY POUNCE.
HATE TO INTERRUPT YOUR MEAL, SUCKERS--
--BUT WE'RE STARVING OURSELVESSSS!
HEY, SAM-- YOU REMEMBER WHEN I SAID I DON'T ALWAYS MISS THIS?
YEAH?
I WAS TOTALLY LYING.
I FIGURED.

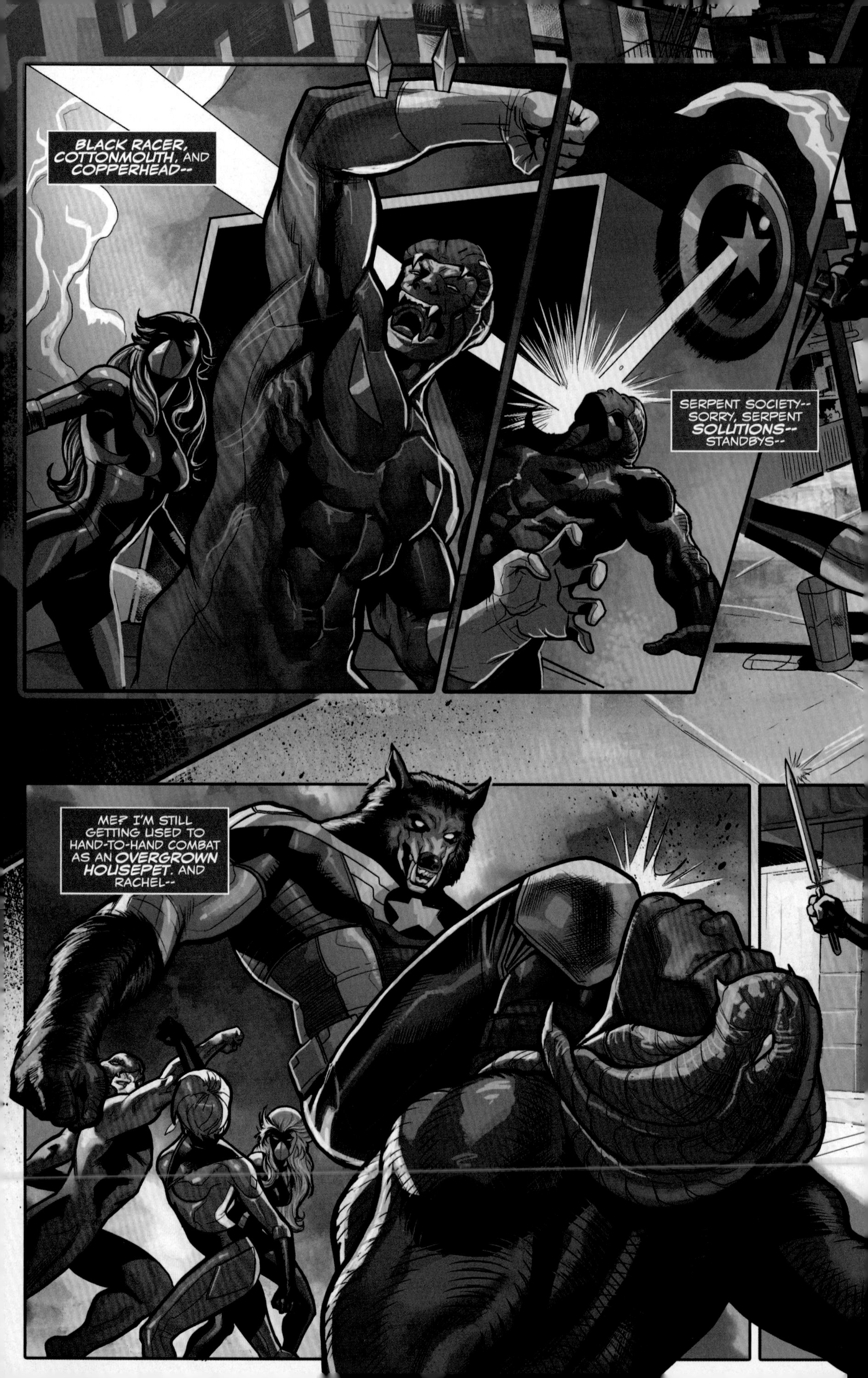
BLACK RACER, COTTONMOUTH, AND COPPERHEAD--
SERPENT SOCIETY-- SORRY, SERPENT SOLUTIONS-- STANDBYS--
ME? I'M STILL GETTING USED TO HAND-TO-HAND COMBAT AS AN OVERGROWN HOUSEPET. AND RACHEL--

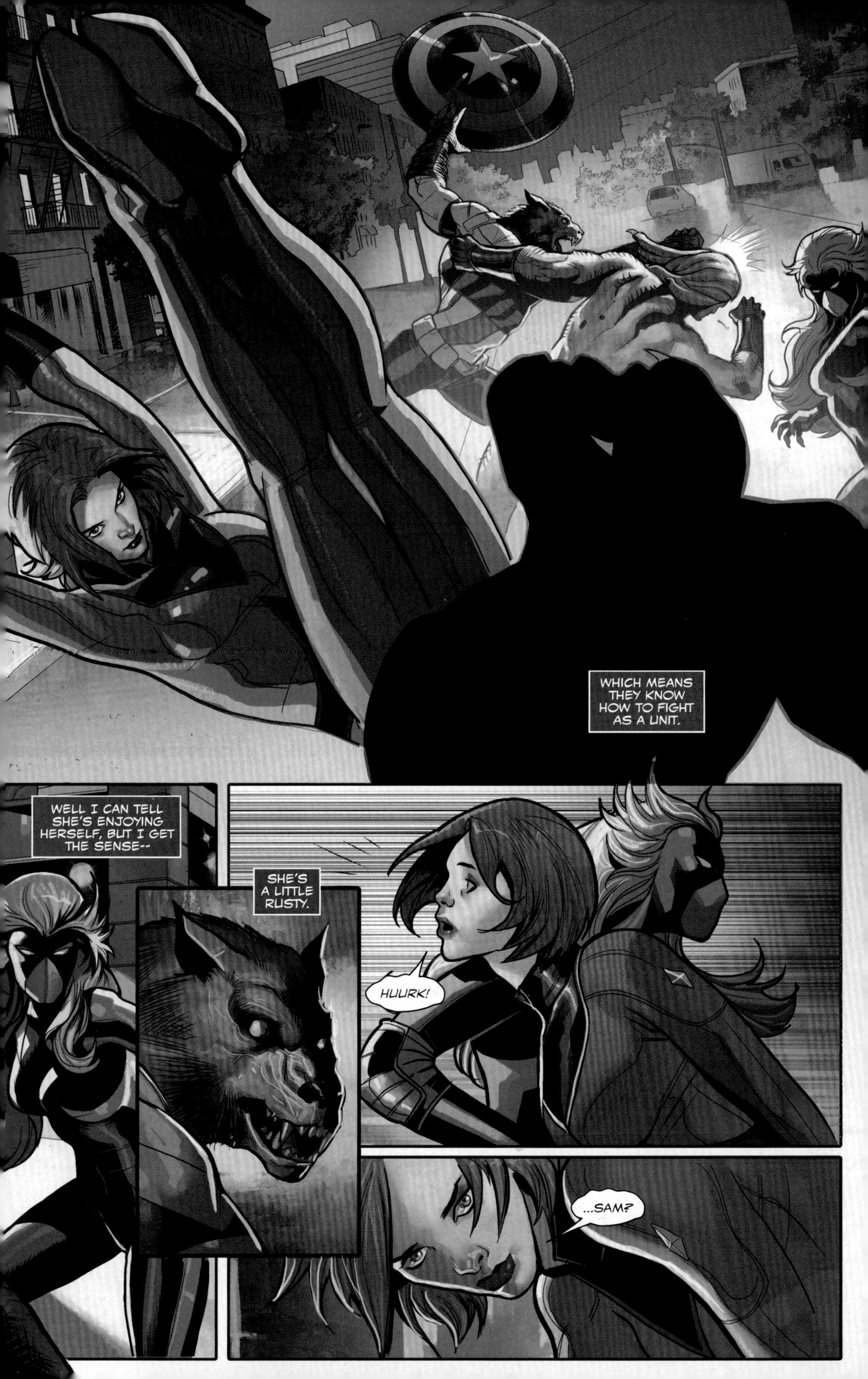
WHICH MEANS THEY KNOW HOW TO FIGHT AS A UNIT.
WELL I CAN TELL SHE'S ENJOYING HERSELF, BUT I GET THE SENSE--
SHE'S A LITTLE RUSTY.
HUURK!
...SAM?

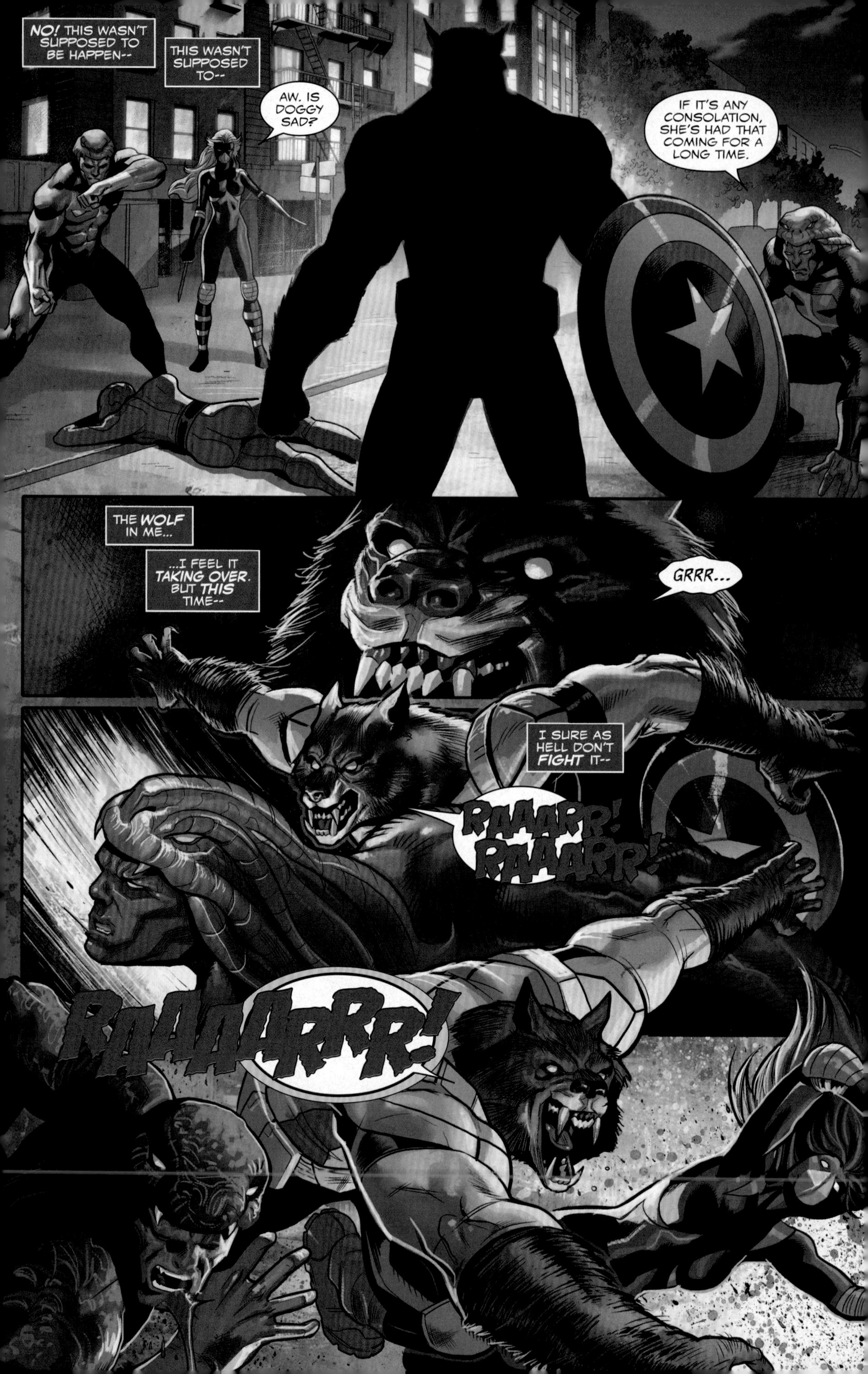
NO! THIS WASN'T SUPPOSED TO BE HAPPEN--
THIS WASN'T SUPPOSED TO--
AW. IS DOGGY SAD?
IF IT'S ANY CONSOLATION, SHE'S HAD THAT COMING FOR A LONG TIME.
THE WOLF IN ME...
...I FEEL IT TAKING OVER. BUT THIS TIME--
GRRR...
I SURE AS HELL DON'T FIGHT IT--
RAAARR! RAAARR!
RAAAARRR!

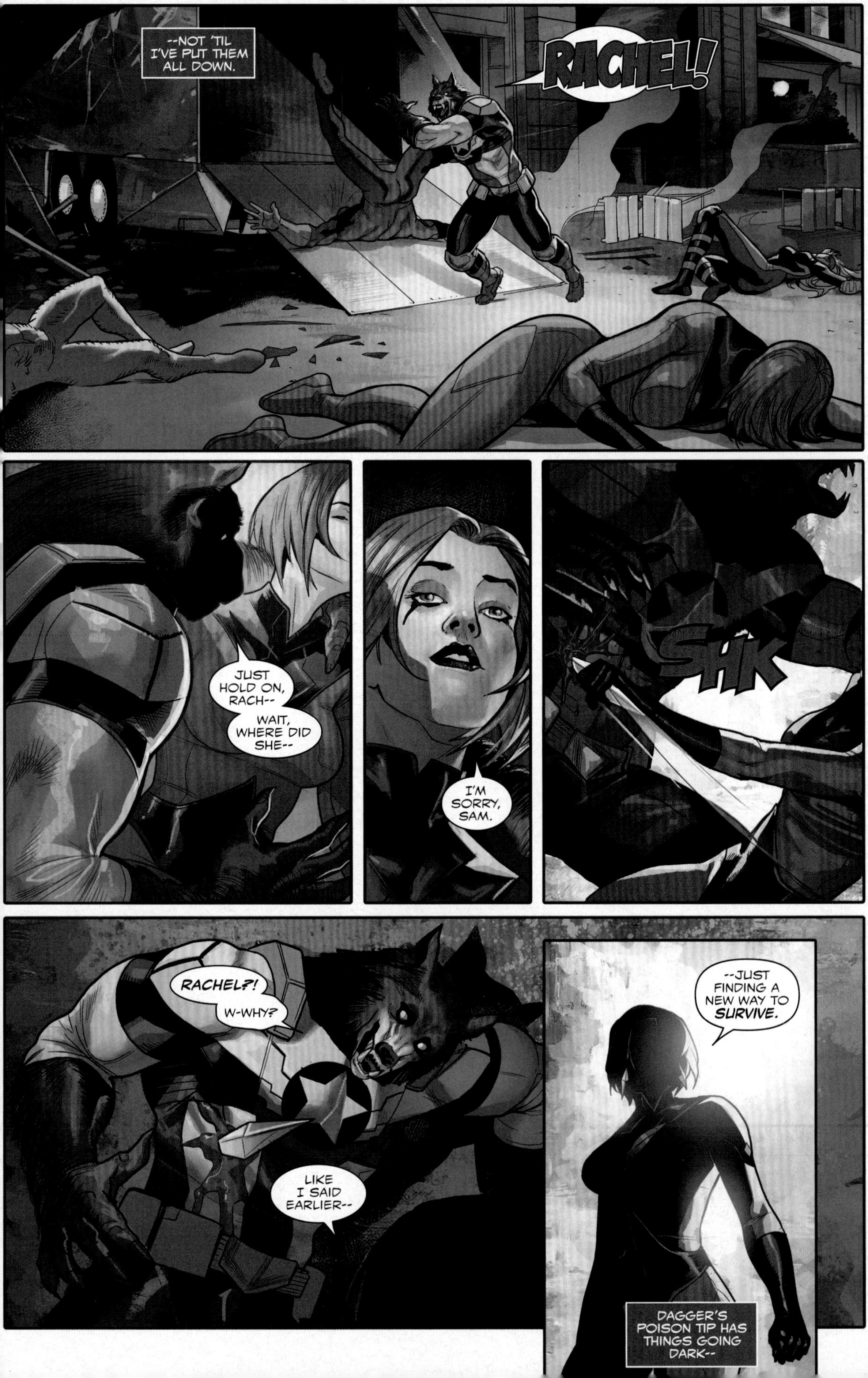
--NOT 'TIL I'VE PUT THEM ALL DOWN.
RACHEL!
JUST HOLD ON, RACH--
WAIT, WHERE DID SHE--
I'M SORRY, SAM.
SHK
RACHEL?!
W-WHY?
LIKE I SAID EARLIER--
--JUST FINDING A NEW WAY TO SURVIVE.
DAGGER'S POISON TIP HAS THINGS GOING DARK--

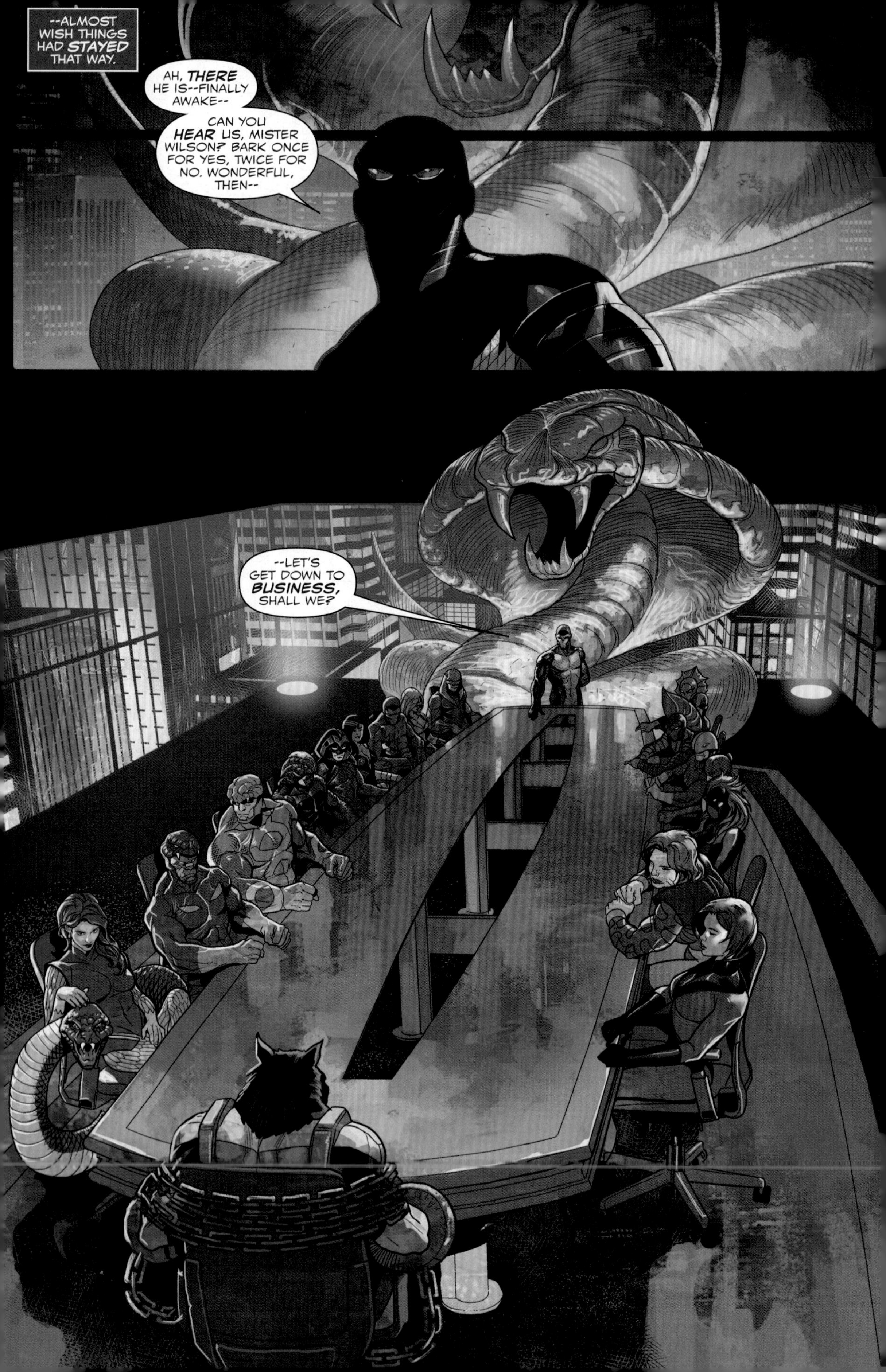
--ALMOST WISH THINGS HAD STAYED THAT WAY.
AH, THERE HE IS--FINALLY AWAKE--
CAN YOU HEAR US, MISTER WILSON? BARK ONCE FOR YES, TWICE FOR NO. WONDERFUL, THEN--
--LET'S GET DOWN TO BUSINESS, SHALL WE?

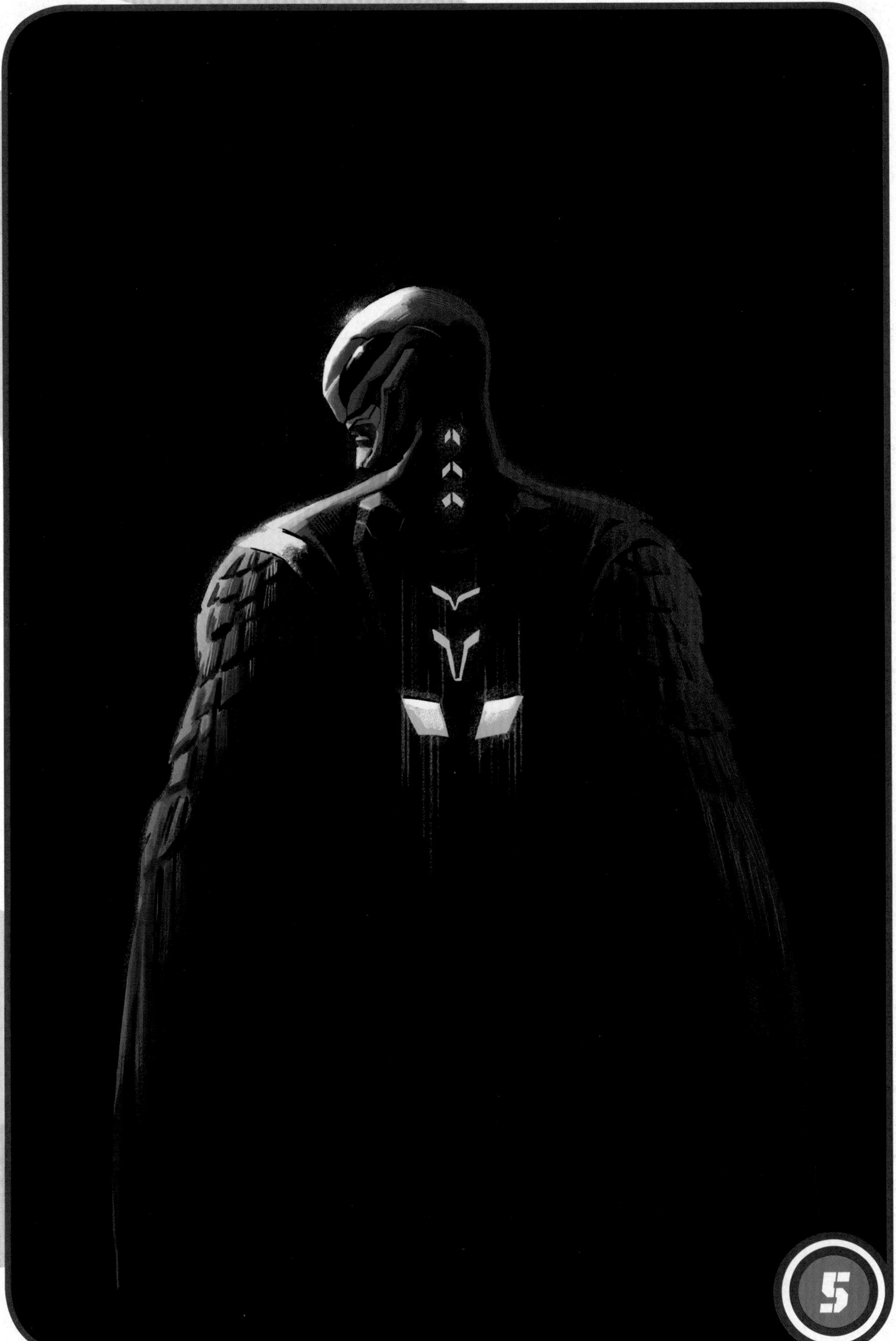
5

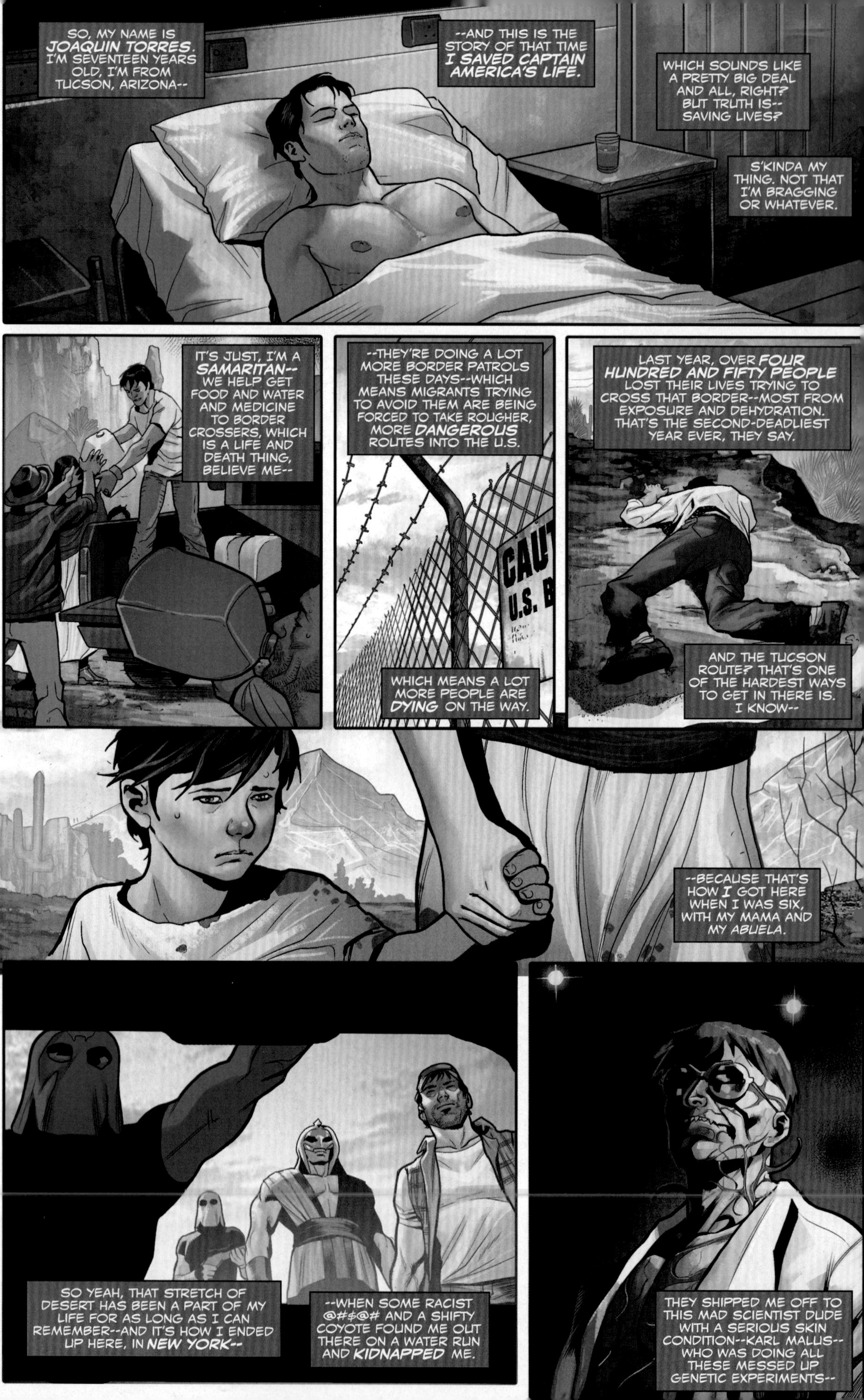
SO, MY NAME IS JOAQUIN TORRES. I'M SEVENTEEN YEARS OLD, I'M FROM TUCSON, ARIZONA--
--AND THIS IS THE STORY OF THAT TIME I SAVED CAPTAIN AMERICA'S LIFE.
WHICH SOUNDS LIKE A PRETTY BIG DEAL AND ALL, RIGHT? BUT TRUTH IS-- SAVING LIVES?
S'KINDA MY THING. NOT THAT I'M BRAGGING OR WHATEVER.
IT'S JUST, I'M A SAMARITAN-- WE HELP GET FOOD AND WATER AND MEDICINE TO BORDER CROSSERS, WHICH IS A LIFE AND DEATH THING, BELIEVE ME--
--THEY'RE DOING A LOT MORE BORDER PATROLS THESE DAYS--WHICH MEANS MIGRANTS TRYING TO AVOID THEM ARE BEING FORCED TO TAKE ROUGHER, MORE DANGEROUS ROUTES INTO THE U.S.
CAUT
U.S. B
WHICH MEANS A LOT MORE PEOPLE ARE DYING ON THE WAY.
LAST YEAR, OVER FOUR HUNDRED AND FIFTY PEOPLE LOST THEIR LIVES TRYING TO CROSS THAT BORDER--MOST FROM EXPOSURE AND DEHYDRATION. THAT'S THE SECOND-DEADLIEST YEAR EVER, THEY SAY.
AND THE TUCSON ROUTE? THAT'S ONE OF THE HARDEST WAYS TO GET IN THERE IS. I KNOW--
--BECAUSE THAT'S HOW I GOT HERE WHEN I WAS SIX, WITH MY MAMA AND MY ABUELA.
SO YEAH, THAT STRETCH OF DESERT HAS BEEN A PART OF MY LIFE FOR AS LONG AS I CAN REMEMBER--AND IT'S HOW I ENDED UP HERE, IN NEW YORK--
--WHEN SOME RACIST @#$@# AND A SHIFTY COYOTE FOUND ME OUT THERE ON A WATER RUN AND KIDNAPPED ME.
THEY SHIPPED ME OFF TO THIS MAD SCIENTIST DUDE WITH A SERIOUS SKIN CONDITION--KARL MALUS-- WHO WAS DOING ALL THESE MESSED UP GENETIC EXPERIMENTS--

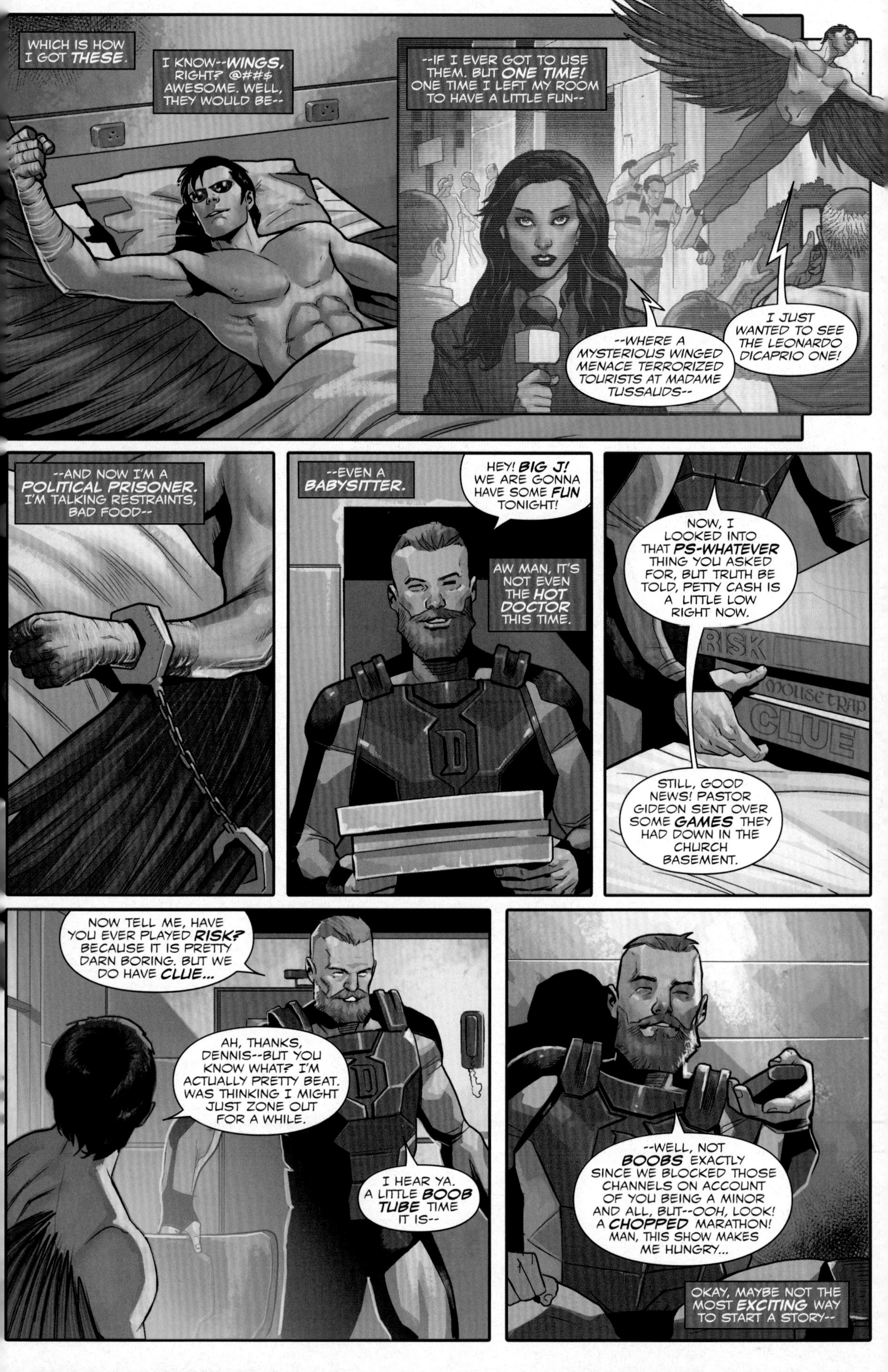
WHICH IS HOW I GOT THESE.
I KNOW--WINGS, RIGHT? @##$ AWESOME. WELL, THEY WOULD BE--
--IF I EVER GOT TO USE THEM. BUT ONE TIME! ONE TIME I LEFT MY ROOM TO HAVE A LITTLE FUN--
--WHERE A MYSTERIOUS WINGED MENACE TERRORIZED TOURISTS AT MADAME TUSSAUDS--
I JUST WANTED TO SEE THE LEONARDO DICAPRIO ONE!
--AND NOW I'M A POLITICAL PRISONER. I'M TALKING RESTRAINTS, BAD FOOD--
--EVEN A BABYSITTER.
HEY! BIG J! WE ARE GONNA HAVE SOME FUN TONIGHT!
AW MAN, IT'S NOT EVEN THE HOT DOCTOR THIS TIME.
NOW, I LOOKED INTO THAT PS-WHATEVER THING YOU ASKED FOR, BUT TRUTH BE TOLD, PETTY CASH IS A LITTLE LOW RIGHT NOW.
RISK
MOUSETRAP
CLUE
STILL, GOOD NEWS! PASTOR GIDEON SENT OVER SOME GAMES THEY HAD DOWN IN THE CHURCH BASEMENT.
NOW TELL ME, HAVE YOU EVER PLAYED RISK? BECAUSE IT IS PRETTY DARN BORING. BUT WE DO HAVE CLUE...
AH, THANKS, DENNIS--BUT YOU KNOW WHAT? I'M ACTUALLY PRETTY BEAT. WAS THINKING I MIGHT JUST ZONE OUT FOR A WHILE.
I HEAR YA. A LITTLE BOOB TUBE TIME IT IS--
--WELL, NOT BOOBS EXACTLY SINCE WE BLOCKED THOSE CHANNELS ON ACCOUNT OF YOU BEING A MINOR AND ALL, BUT--OOH, LOOK! A CHOPPED MARATHON! MAN, THIS SHOW MAKES ME HUNGRY...
OKAY, MAYBE NOT THE MOST EXCITING WAY TO START A STORY--

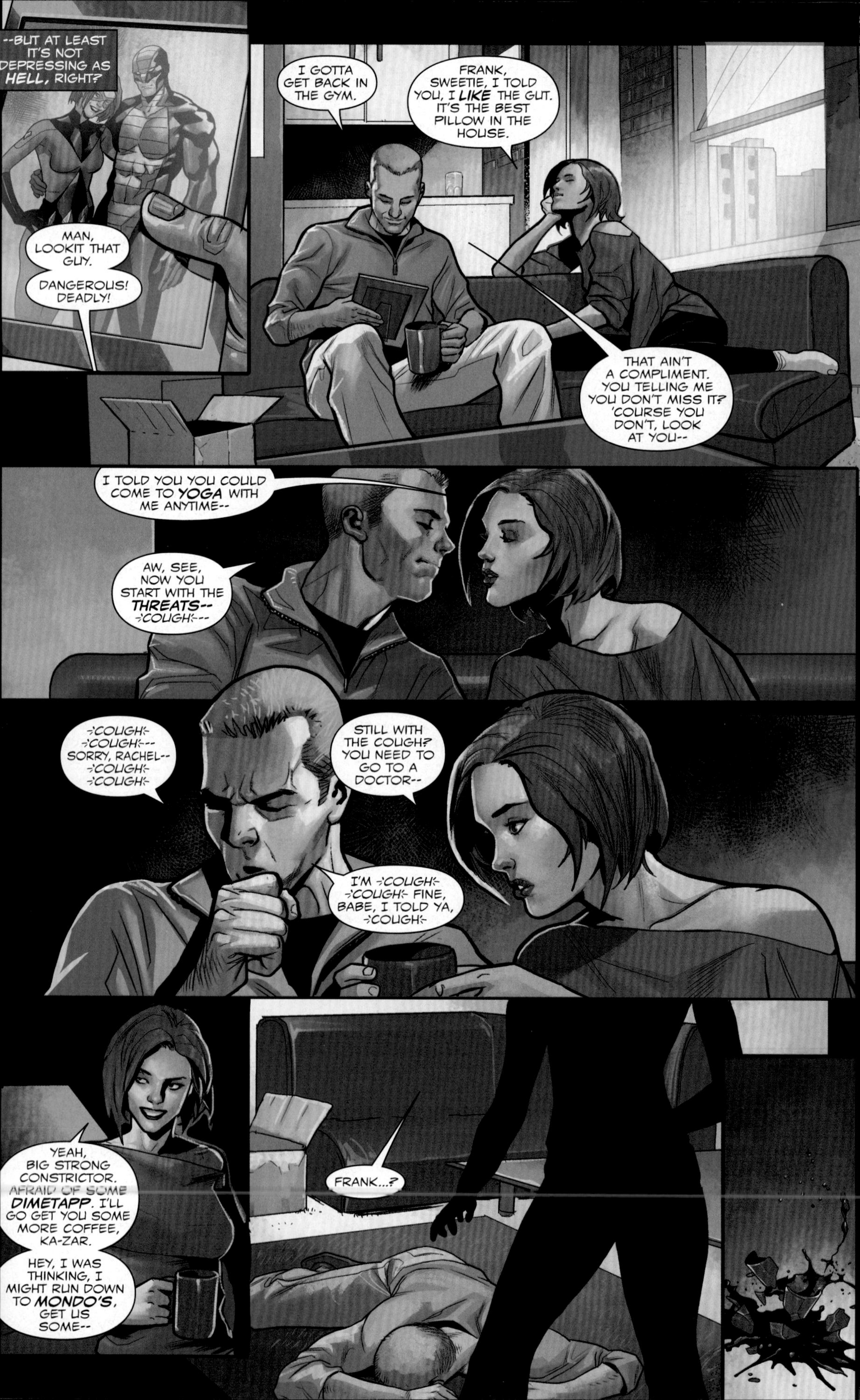
--BUT AT LEAST IT'S NOT DEPRESSING AS HELL, RIGHT?
MAN, LOOKIT THAT GUY.
DANGEROUS! DEADLY!
I GOTTA GET BACK IN THE GYM.
FRANK, SWEETIE, I TOLD YOU, I LIKE THE GUT. IT'S THE BEST PILLOW IN THE HOUSE.
THAT AIN'T A COMPLIMENT. YOU TELLING ME YOU DON'T MISS IT? 'COURSE YOU DON'T, LOOK AT YOU--
I TOLD YOU YOU COULD COME TO YOGA WITH ME ANYTIME--
AW, SEE, NOW YOU START WITH THE THREATS-- COUGH--
COUGH COUGH-- SORRY, RACHEL-- COUGH COUGH
STILL WITH THE COUGH? YOU NEED TO GO TO A DOCTOR--
I'M COUGH COUGH FINE, BABE, I TOLD YA, COUGH
YEAH, BIG STRONG CONSTRICTOR. AFRAID OF SOME DIMETAPP. I'LL GO GET YOU SOME MORE COFFEE, KA-ZAR.
HEY, I WAS THINKING, I MIGHT RUN DOWN TO MONDO'S, GET US SOME--
FRANK...?

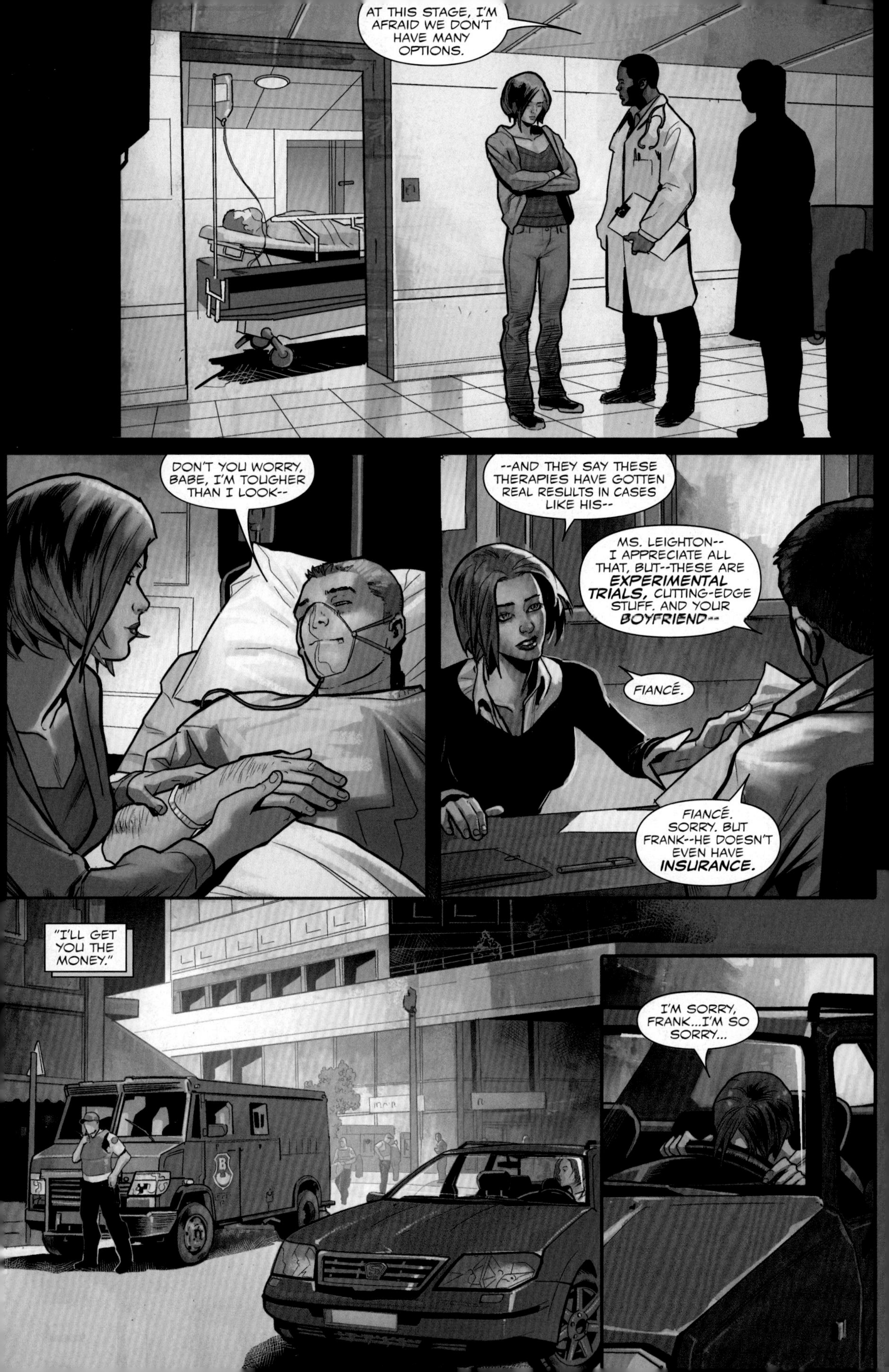
AT THIS STAGE, I'M AFRAID WE DON'T HAVE MANY OPTIONS.
DON'T YOU WORRY, BABE, I'M TOUGHER THAN I LOOK--
--AND THEY SAY THESE THERAPIES HAVE GOTTEN REAL RESULTS IN CASES LIKE HIS--
MS. LEIGHTON-- I APPRECIATE ALL THAT, BUT--THESE ARE **EXPERIMENTAL TRIALS,** CUTTING-EDGE STUFF. AND YOUR **BOYFRIEND--**
FIANCÉ.
FIANCÉ. SORRY. BUT FRANK--HE DOESN'T EVEN HAVE **INSURANCE.**
"I'LL GET YOU THE MONEY."
I'M SORRY, FRANK...I'M SO SORRY...

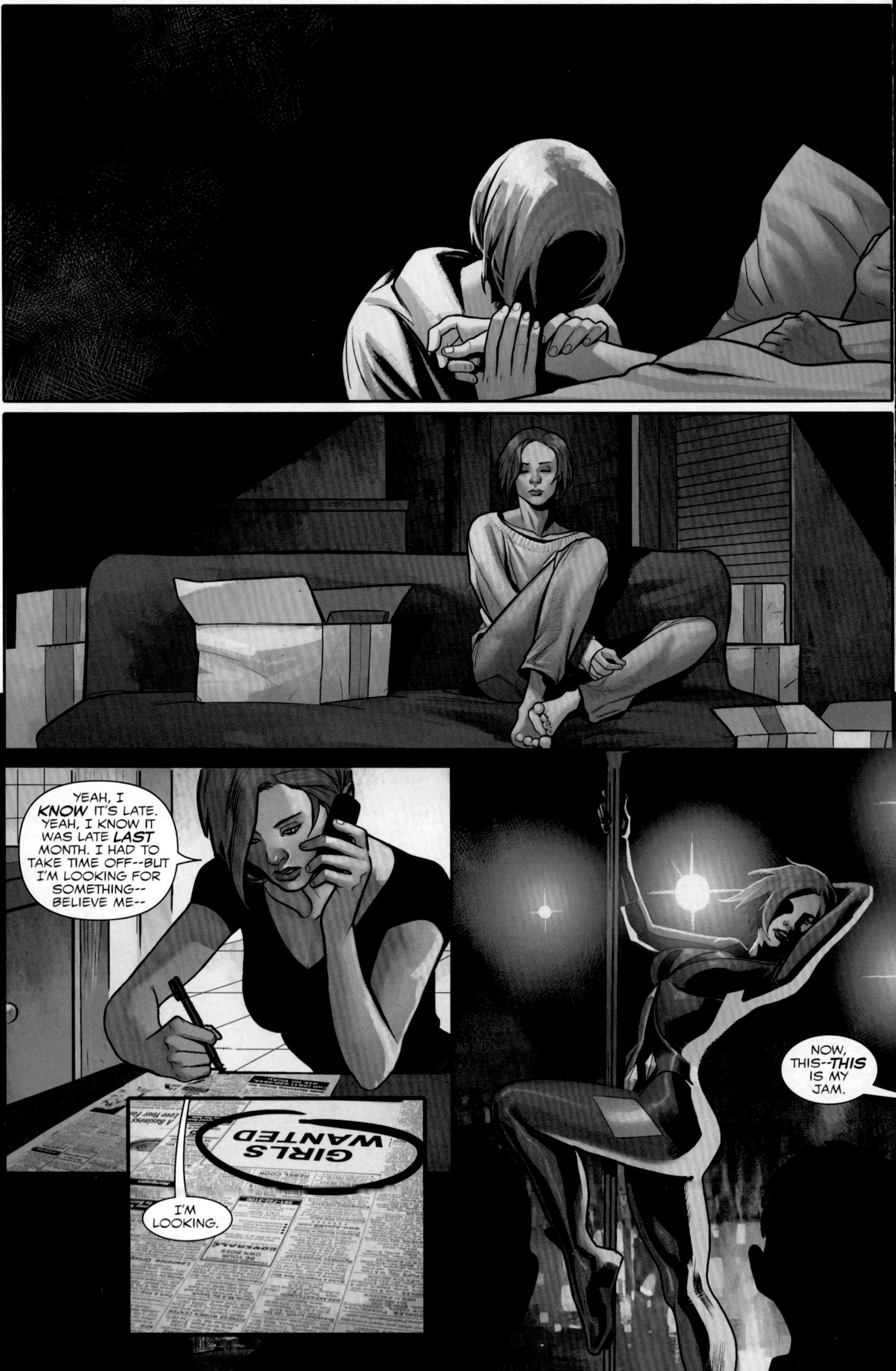
YEAH, I KNOW IT'S LATE. YEAH, I KNOW IT WAS LATE LAST MONTH. I HAD TO TAKE TIME OFF--BUT I'M LOOKING FOR SOMETHING-- BELIEVE ME--
GIRLS WANTED
I'M LOOKING.
NOW, THIS--THIS IS MY JAM.

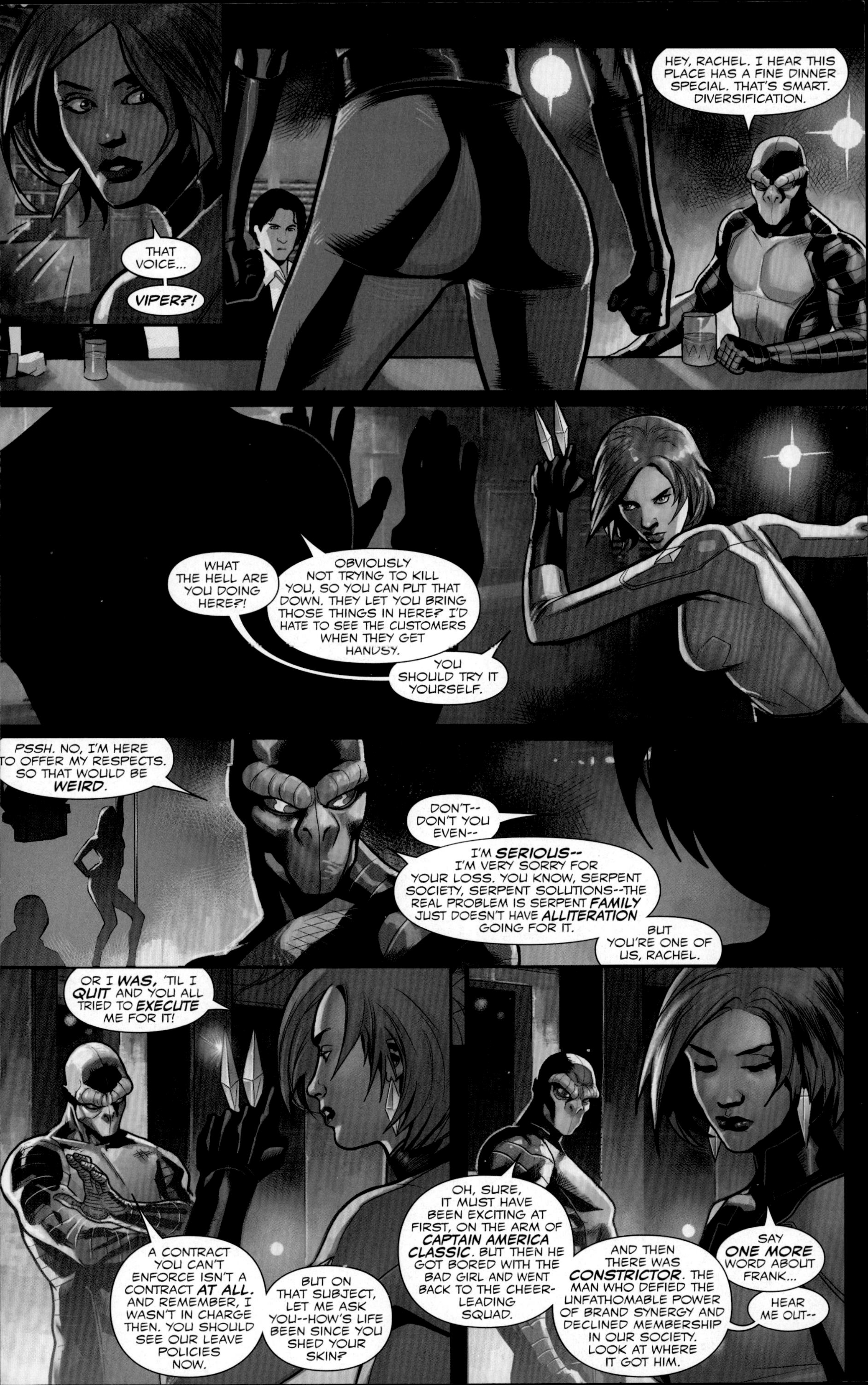
HEY, RACHEL. I HEAR THIS PLACE HAS A FINE DINNER SPECIAL. THAT'S SMART. DIVERSIFICATION.
THAT VOICE... VIPER?!
WHAT THE HELL ARE YOU DOING HERE?!
OBVIOUSLY NOT TRYING TO KILL YOU, SO YOU CAN PUT THAT DOWN. THEY LET YOU BRING THOSE THINGS IN HERE? I'D HATE TO SEE THE CUSTOMERS WHEN THEY GET HANDSY.
YOU SHOULD TRY IT YOURSELF.
PSSH. NO, I'M HERE TO OFFER MY RESPECTS. SO THAT WOULD BE WEIRD.
DON'T-- DON'T YOU EVEN--
I'M SERIOUS-- I'M VERY SORRY FOR YOUR LOSS. YOU KNOW, SERPENT SOCIETY, SERPENT SOLUTIONS--THE REAL PROBLEM IS SERPENT FAMILY JUST DOESN'T HAVE ALLITERATION GOING FOR IT.
BUT YOU'RE ONE OF US, RACHEL.
OR I WAS, 'TIL I QUIT AND YOU ALL TRIED TO EXECUTE ME FOR IT!
A CONTRACT YOU CAN'T ENFORCE ISN'T A CONTRACT AT ALL. AND REMEMBER, I WASN'T IN CHARGE THEN. YOU SHOULD SEE OUR LEAVE POLICIES NOW.
BUT ON THAT SUBJECT, LET ME ASK YOU--HOW'S LIFE BEEN SINCE YOU SHED YOUR SKIN?
OH, SURE, IT MUST HAVE BEEN EXCITING AT FIRST, ON THE ARM OF CAPTAIN AMERICA CLASSIC. BUT THEN HE GOT BORED WITH THE BAD GIRL AND WENT BACK TO THE CHEER-LEADING SQUAD.
AND THEN THERE WAS CONSTRICTOR. THE MAN WHO DEFIED THE UNFATHOMABLE POWER OF BRAND SYNERGY AND DECLINED MEMBERSHIP IN OUR SOCIETY. LOOK AT WHERE IT GOT HIM.
SAY ONE MORE WORD ABOUT FRANK...
HEAR ME OUT--

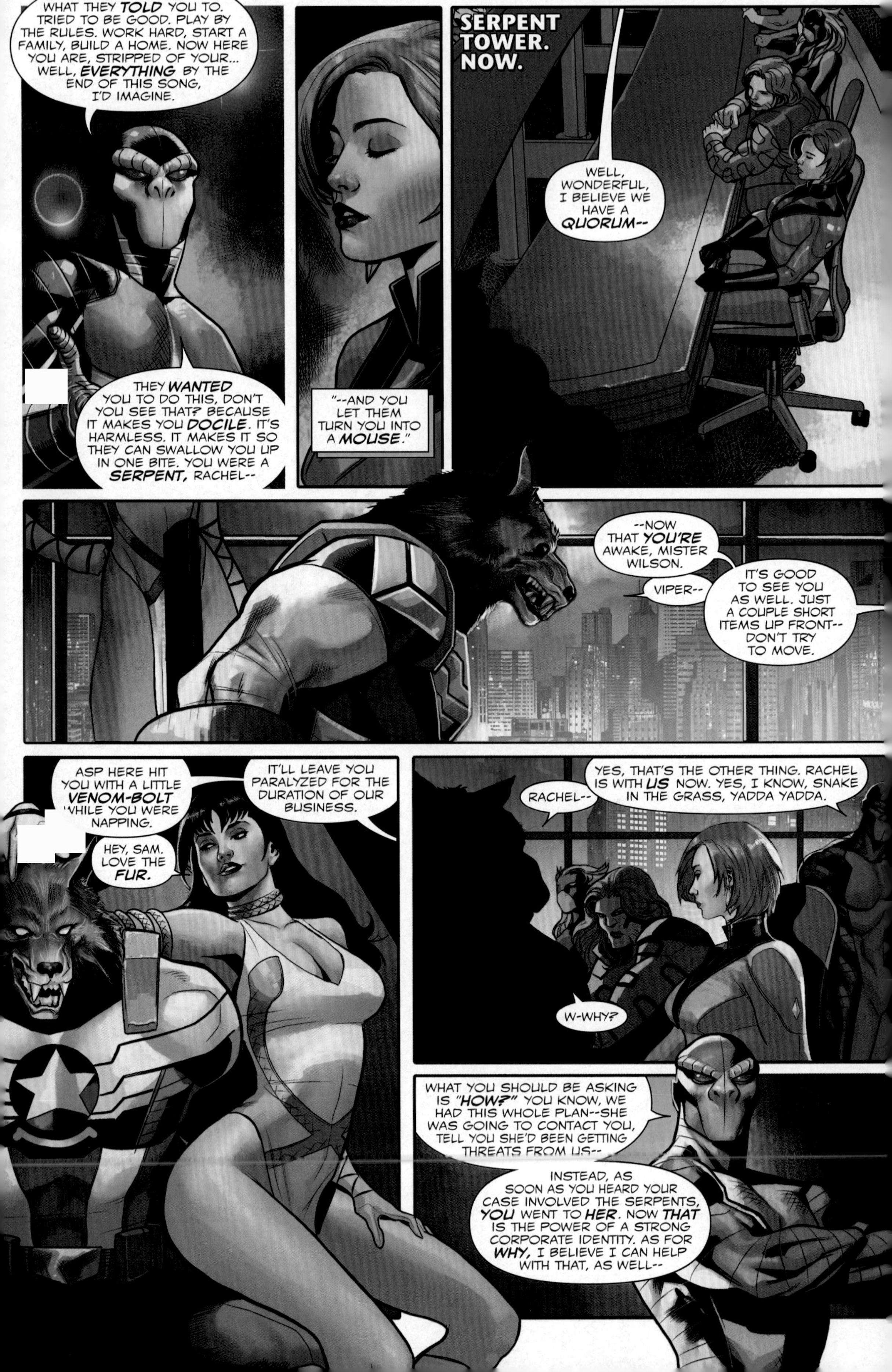

YOU DID WHAT THEY TOLD YOU TO. TRIED TO BE GOOD. PLAY BY THE RULES. WORK HARD, START A FAMILY, BUILD A HOME. NOW HERE YOU ARE, STRIPPED OF YOUR... WELL, EVERYTHING BY THE END OF THIS SONG, I'D IMAGINE.
THEY WANTED YOU TO DO THIS, DON'T YOU SEE THAT? BECAUSE IT MAKES YOU DOCILE. IT'S HARMLESS. IT MAKES IT SO THEY CAN SWALLOW YOU UP IN ONE BITE. YOU WERE A SERPENT, RACHEL--
"--AND YOU LET THEM TURN YOU INTO A MOUSE."
SERPENT TOWER. NOW.
WELL, WONDERFUL, I BELIEVE WE HAVE A QUORUM--
--NOW THAT YOU'RE AWAKE, MISTER WILSON.
VIPER--
IT'S GOOD TO SEE YOU AS WELL. JUST A COUPLE SHORT ITEMS UP FRONT-- DON'T TRY TO MOVE.
ASP HERE HIT YOU WITH A LITTLE VENOM-BOLT WHILE YOU WERE NAPPING.
IT'LL LEAVE YOU PARALYZED FOR THE DURATION OF OUR BUSINESS.
HEY, SAM. LOVE THE FUR.
RACHEL--
YES, THAT'S THE OTHER THING. RACHEL IS WITH US NOW. YES, I KNOW, SNAKE IN THE GRASS, YADDA YADDA.
W-WHY?
WHAT YOU SHOULD BE ASKING IS "HOW?" YOU KNOW, WE HAD THIS WHOLE PLAN--SHE WAS GOING TO CONTACT YOU, TELL YOU SHE'D BEEN GETTING THREATS FROM US--
INSTEAD, AS SOON AS YOU HEARD YOUR CASE INVOLVED THE SERPENTS, YOU WENT TO HER. NOW THAT IS THE POWER OF A STRONG CORPORATE IDENTITY. AS FOR WHY, I BELIEVE I CAN HELP WITH THAT, AS WELL--

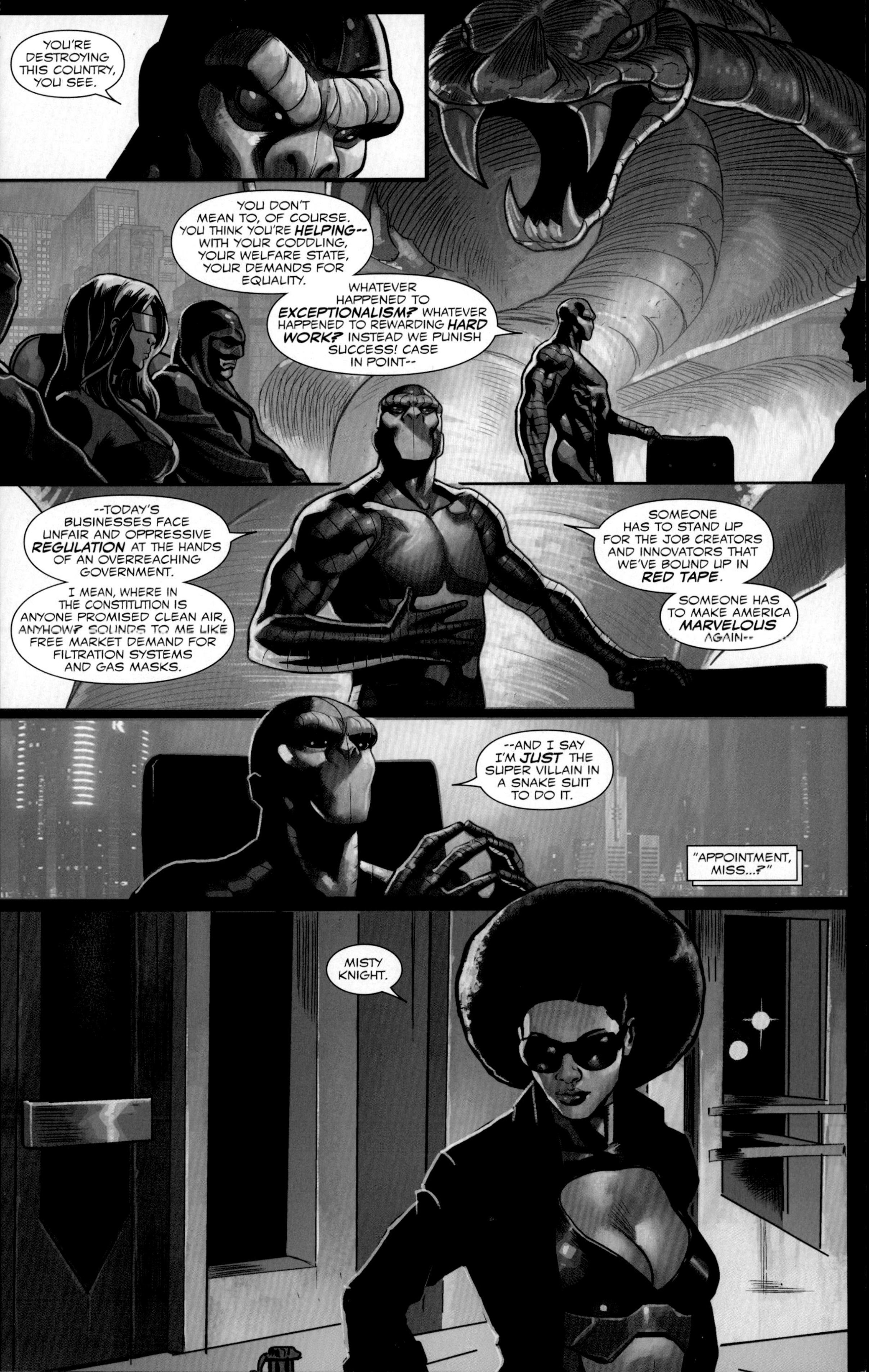
YOU'RE DESTROYING THIS COUNTRY, YOU SEE.
YOU DON'T MEAN TO, OF COURSE. YOU THINK YOU'RE HELPING-- WITH YOUR CODDLING, YOUR WELFARE STATE, YOUR DEMANDS FOR EQUALITY.
WHATEVER HAPPENED TO EXCEPTIONALISM? WHATEVER HAPPENED TO REWARDING HARD WORK? INSTEAD WE PUNISH SUCCESS! CASE IN POINT--
--TODAY'S BUSINESSES FACE UNFAIR AND OPPRESSIVE REGULATION AT THE HANDS OF AN OVERREACHING GOVERNMENT.
I MEAN, WHERE IN THE CONSTITUTION IS ANYONE PROMISED CLEAN AIR, ANYHOW? SOUNDS TO ME LIKE FREE MARKET DEMAND FOR FILTRATION SYSTEMS AND GAS MASKS.
SOMEONE HAS TO STAND UP FOR THE JOB CREATORS AND INNOVATORS THAT WE'VE BOUND UP IN RED TAPE.
SOMEONE HAS TO MAKE AMERICA MARVELOUS AGAIN--
--AND I SAY I'M JUST THE SUPER VILLAIN IN A SNAKE SUIT TO DO IT.
"APPOINTMENT, MISS...?"
MISTY KNIGHT.

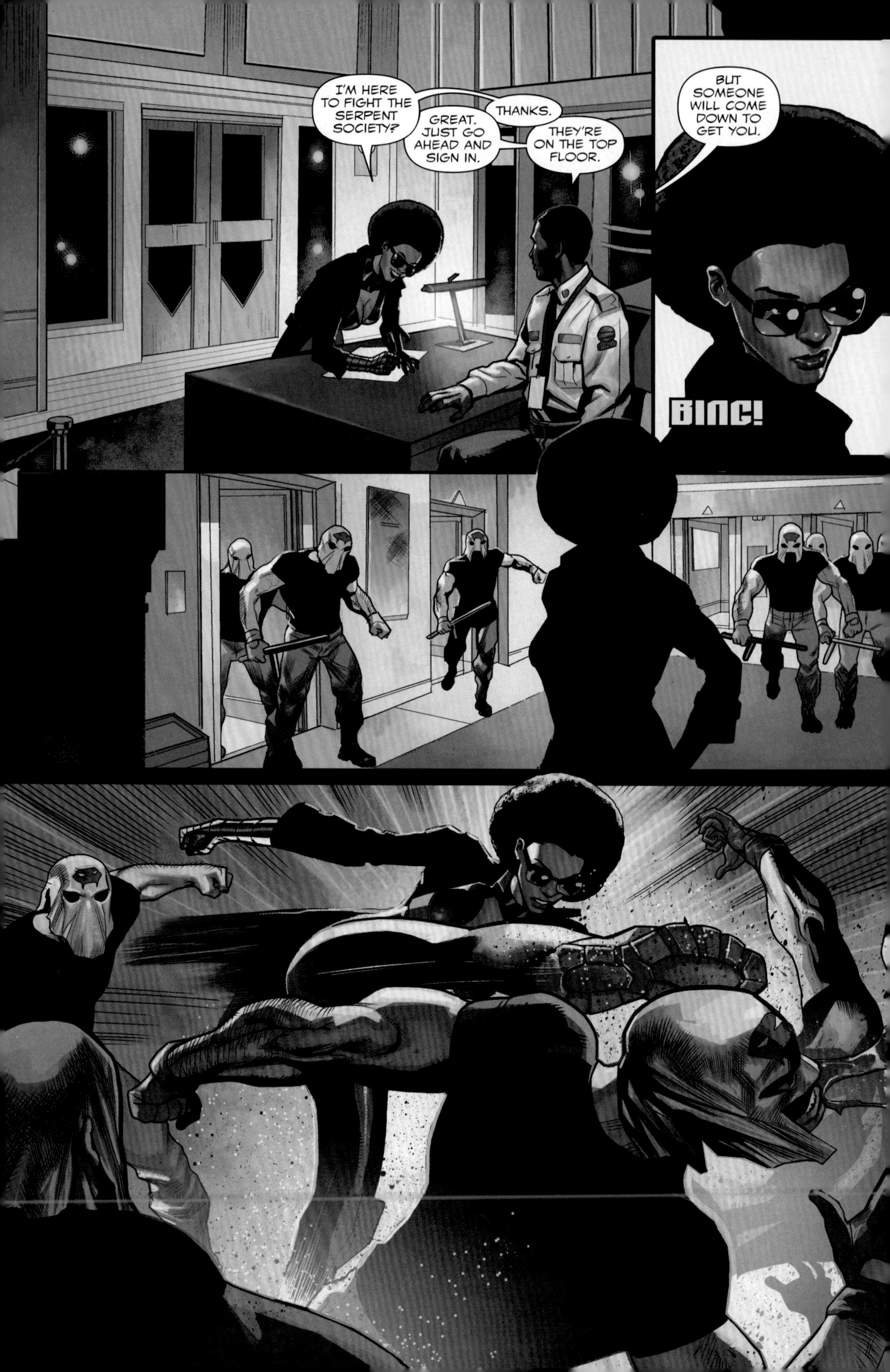
I'M HERE TO FIGHT THE SERPENT SOCIETY?
GREAT. JUST GO AHEAD AND SIGN IN.
THANKS.
THEY'RE ON THE TOP FLOOR.
BUT SOMEONE WILL COME DOWN TO GET YOU.
BING!

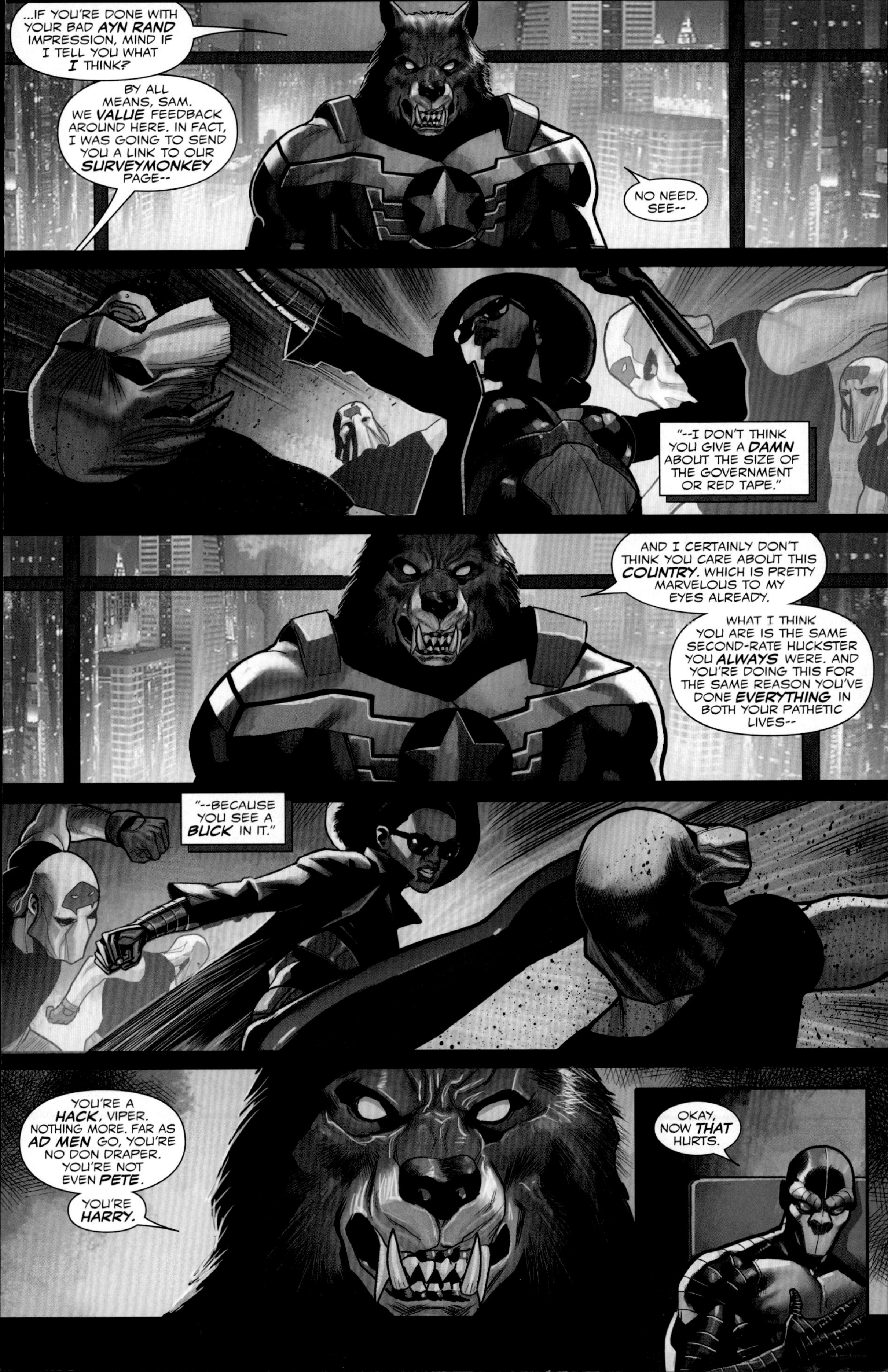
...IF YOU'RE DONE WITH YOUR BAD AYN RAND IMPRESSION, MIND IF I TELL YOU WHAT I THINK?
BY ALL MEANS, SAM. WE VALUE FEEDBACK AROUND HERE. IN FACT, I WAS GOING TO SEND YOU A LINK TO OUR SURVEYMONKEY PAGE--
NO NEED. SEE--
"--I DON'T THINK YOU GIVE A DAMN ABOUT THE SIZE OF THE GOVERNMENT OR RED TAPE."
AND I CERTAINLY DON'T THINK YOU CARE ABOUT THIS COUNTRY. WHICH IS PRETTY MARVELOUS TO MY EYES ALREADY.
WHAT I THINK YOU ARE IS THE SAME SECOND-RATE HUCKSTER YOU ALWAYS WERE. AND YOU'RE DOING THIS FOR THE SAME REASON YOU'VE DONE EVERYTHING IN BOTH YOUR PATHETIC LIVES--
"--BECAUSE YOU SEE A BUCK IN IT."
YOU'RE A HACK, VIPER. NOTHING MORE. FAR AS AD MEN GO, YOU'RE NO DON DRAPER. YOU'RE NOT EVEN PETE.
YOU'RE HARRY.
OKAY, NOW THAT HURTS.

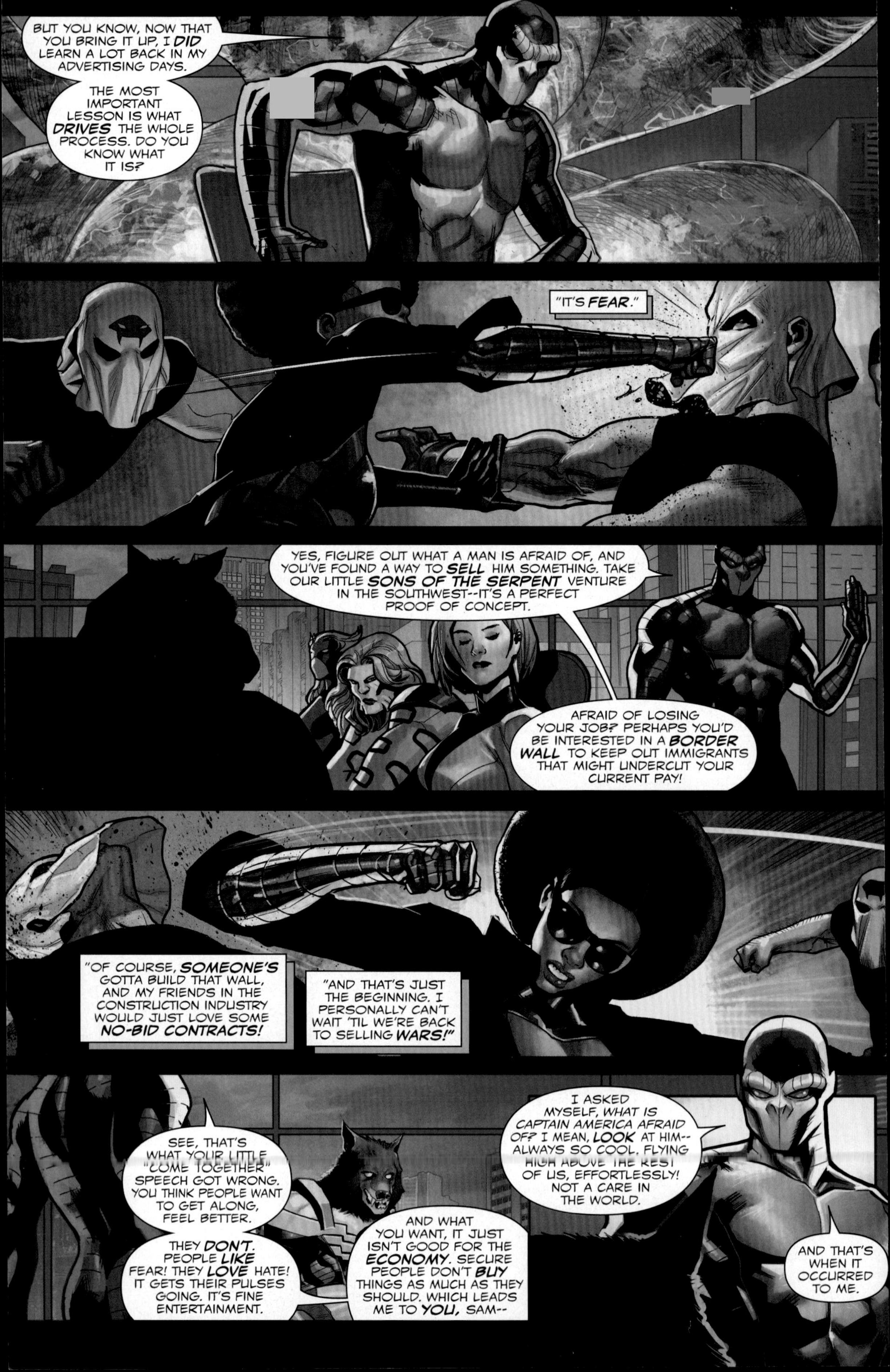
BUT YOU KNOW, NOW THAT YOU BRING IT UP, I DID LEARN A LOT BACK IN MY ADVERTISING DAYS.
THE MOST IMPORTANT LESSON IS WHAT DRIVES THE WHOLE PROCESS. DO YOU KNOW WHAT IT IS?
"IT'S FEAR."
YES, FIGURE OUT WHAT A MAN IS AFRAID OF, AND YOU'VE FOUND A WAY TO SELL HIM SOMETHING. TAKE OUR LITTLE SONS OF THE SERPENT VENTURE IN THE SOUTHWEST--IT'S A PERFECT PROOF OF CONCEPT.
AFRAID OF LOSING YOUR JOB? PERHAPS YOU'D BE INTERESTED IN A BORDER WALL TO KEEP OUT IMMIGRANTS THAT MIGHT UNDERCUT YOUR CURRENT PAY!
"OF COURSE, SOMEONE'S GOTTA BUILD THAT WALL, AND MY FRIENDS IN THE CONSTRUCTION INDUSTRY WOULD JUST LOVE SOME NO-BID CONTRACTS!
"AND THAT'S JUST THE BEGINNING. I PERSONALLY CAN'T WAIT 'TIL WE'RE BACK TO SELLING WARS!"
SEE, THAT'S WHAT YOUR LITTLE "COME TOGETHER" SPEECH GOT WRONG. YOU THINK PEOPLE WANT TO GET ALONG, FEEL BETTER.
THEY DON'T. PEOPLE LIKE FEAR! THEY LOVE HATE! IT GETS THEIR PULSES GOING. IT'S FINE ENTERTAINMENT.
AND WHAT YOU WANT, IT JUST ISN'T GOOD FOR THE ECONOMY. SECURE PEOPLE DON'T BUY THINGS AS MUCH AS THEY SHOULD. WHICH LEADS ME TO YOU, SAM--
I ASKED MYSELF, WHAT IS CAPTAIN AMERICA AFRAID OF? I MEAN, LOOK AT HIM--ALWAYS SO COOL, FLYING HIGH ABOVE THE REST OF US, EFFORTLESSLY! NOT A CARE IN THE WORLD.
AND THAT'S WHEN IT OCCURRED TO ME.

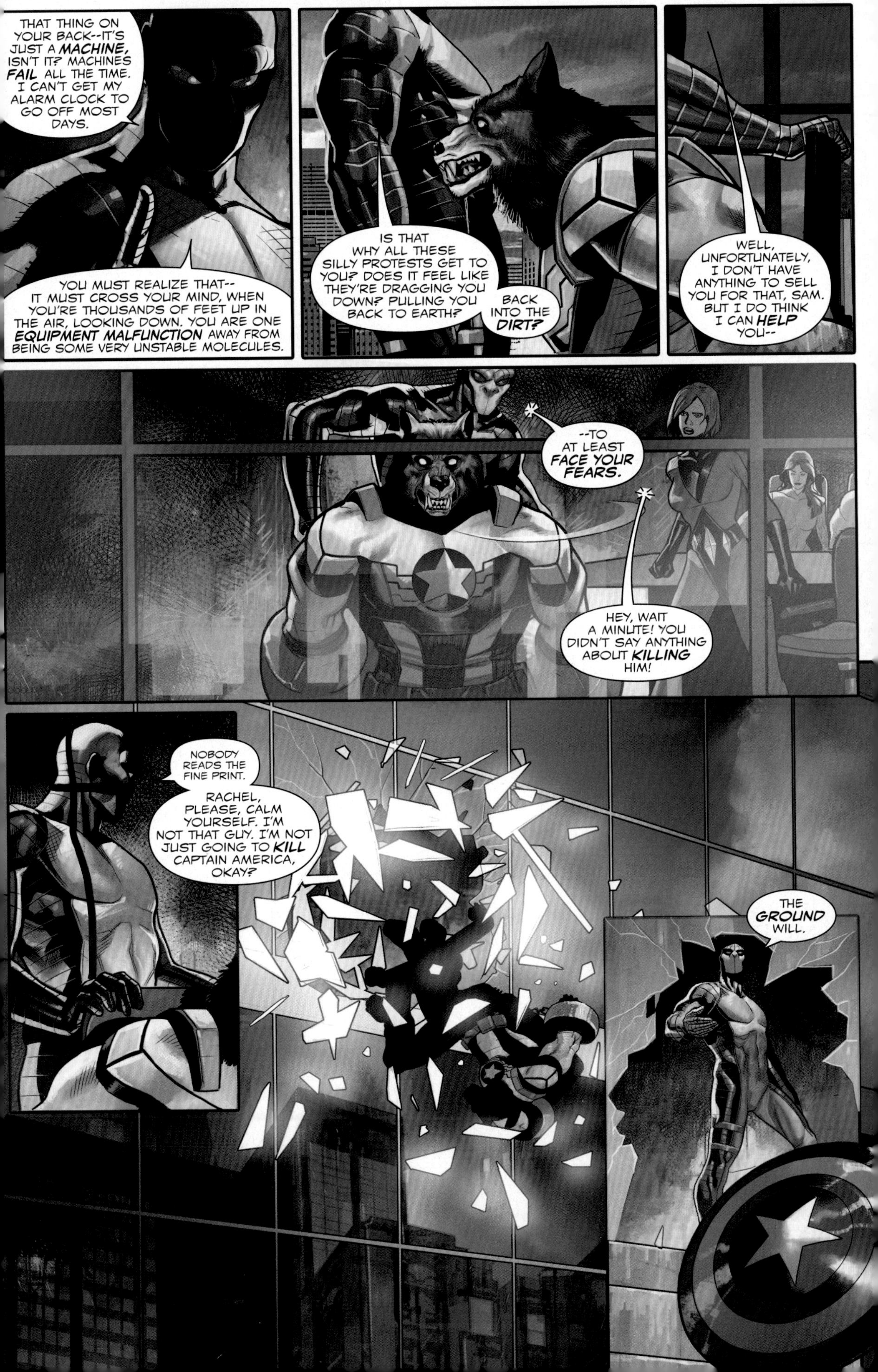
THAT THING ON YOUR BACK--IT'S JUST A MACHINE, ISN'T IT? MACHINES FAIL ALL THE TIME. I CAN'T GET MY ALARM CLOCK TO GO OFF MOST DAYS.
YOU MUST REALIZE THAT-- IT MUST CROSS YOUR MIND, WHEN YOU'RE THOUSANDS OF FEET UP IN THE AIR, LOOKING DOWN. YOU ARE ONE EQUIPMENT MALFUNCTION AWAY FROM BEING SOME VERY UNSTABLE MOLECULES.
IS THAT WHY ALL THESE SILLY PROTESTS GET TO YOU? DOES IT FEEL LIKE THEY'RE DRAGGING YOU DOWN? PULLING YOU BACK TO EARTH?
BACK INTO THE DIRT?
WELL, UNFORTUNATELY, I DON'T HAVE ANYTHING TO SELL YOU FOR THAT, SAM. BUT I DO THINK I CAN HELP YOU--
--TO AT LEAST FACE YOUR FEARS.
HEY, WAIT A MINUTE! YOU DIDN'T SAY ANYTHING ABOUT KILLING HIM!
NOBODY READS THE FINE PRINT.
RACHEL, PLEASE, CALM YOURSELF. I'M NOT THAT GUY. I'M NOT JUST GOING TO KILL CAPTAIN AMERICA, OKAY?
THE GROUND WILL.

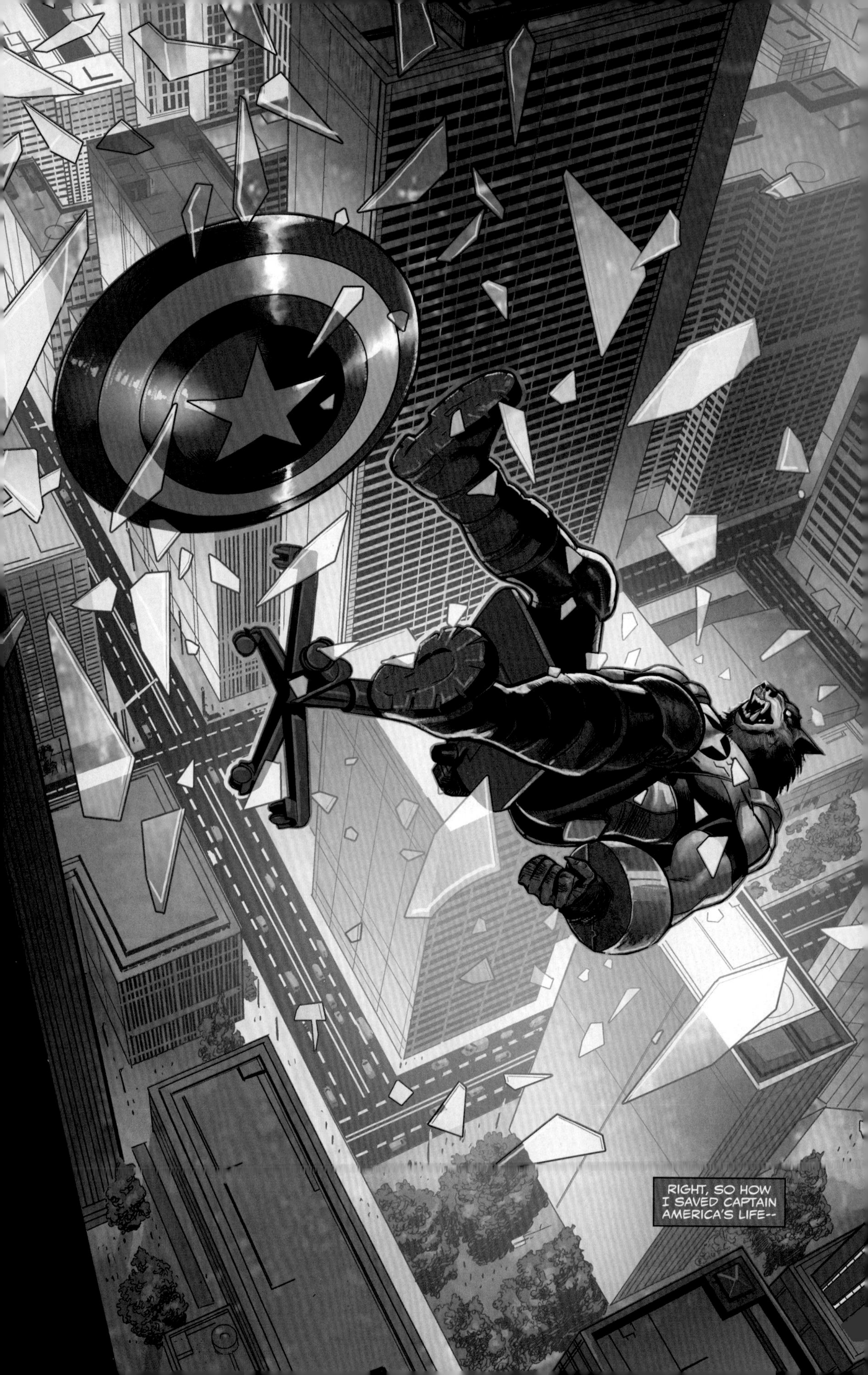
RIGHT, SO HOW I SAVED CAPTAIN AMERICA'S LIFE--

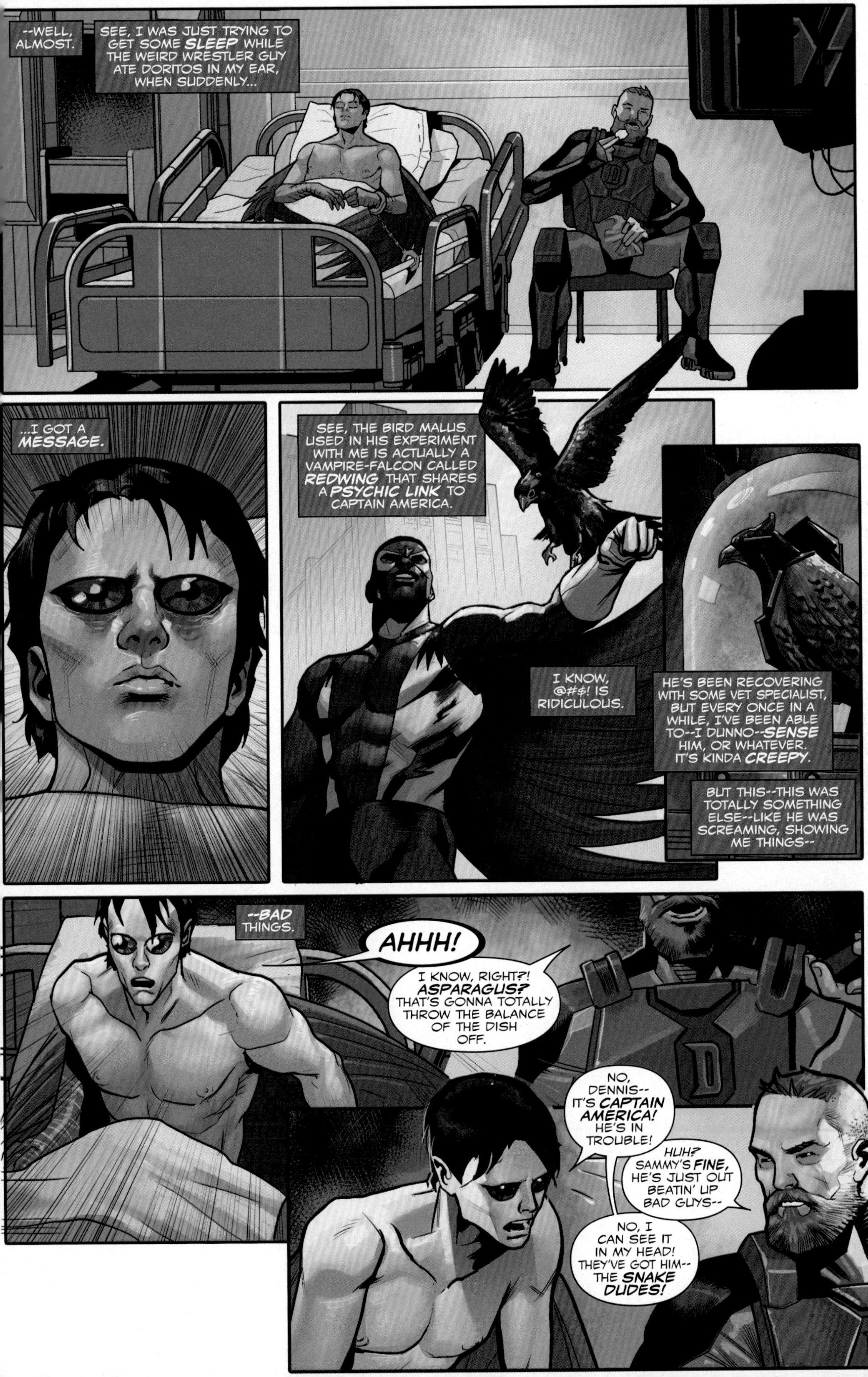
--WELL, ALMOST.
SEE, I WAS JUST TRYING TO GET SOME SLEEP WHILE THE WEIRD WRESTLER GUY ATE DORITOS IN MY EAR, WHEN SUDDENLY...
...I GOT A MESSAGE.
SEE, THE BIRD MALUS USED IN HIS EXPERIMENT WITH ME IS ACTUALLY A VAMPIRE-FALCON CALLED REDWING THAT SHARES A PSYCHIC LINK TO CAPTAIN AMERICA.
I KNOW, @#$! IS RIDICULOUS.
HE'S BEEN RECOVERING WITH SOME VET SPECIALIST, BUT EVERY ONCE IN A WHILE, I'VE BEEN ABLE TO--I DUNNO--SENSE HIM, OR WHATEVER. IT'S KINDA CREEPY.
BUT THIS--THIS WAS TOTALLY SOMETHING ELSE--LIKE HE WAS SCREAMING, SHOWING ME THINGS--
--BAD THINGS.
AHHH!
I KNOW, RIGHT?! ASPARAGUS? THAT'S GONNA TOTALLY THROW THE BALANCE OF THE DISH OFF.
NO, DENNIS-- IT'S CAPTAIN AMERICA! HE'S IN TROUBLE!
HUH? SAMMY'S FINE, HE'S JUST OUT BEATIN' UP BAD GUYS--
NO, I CAN SEE IT IN MY HEAD! THEY'VE GOT HIM-- THE SNAKE DUDES!

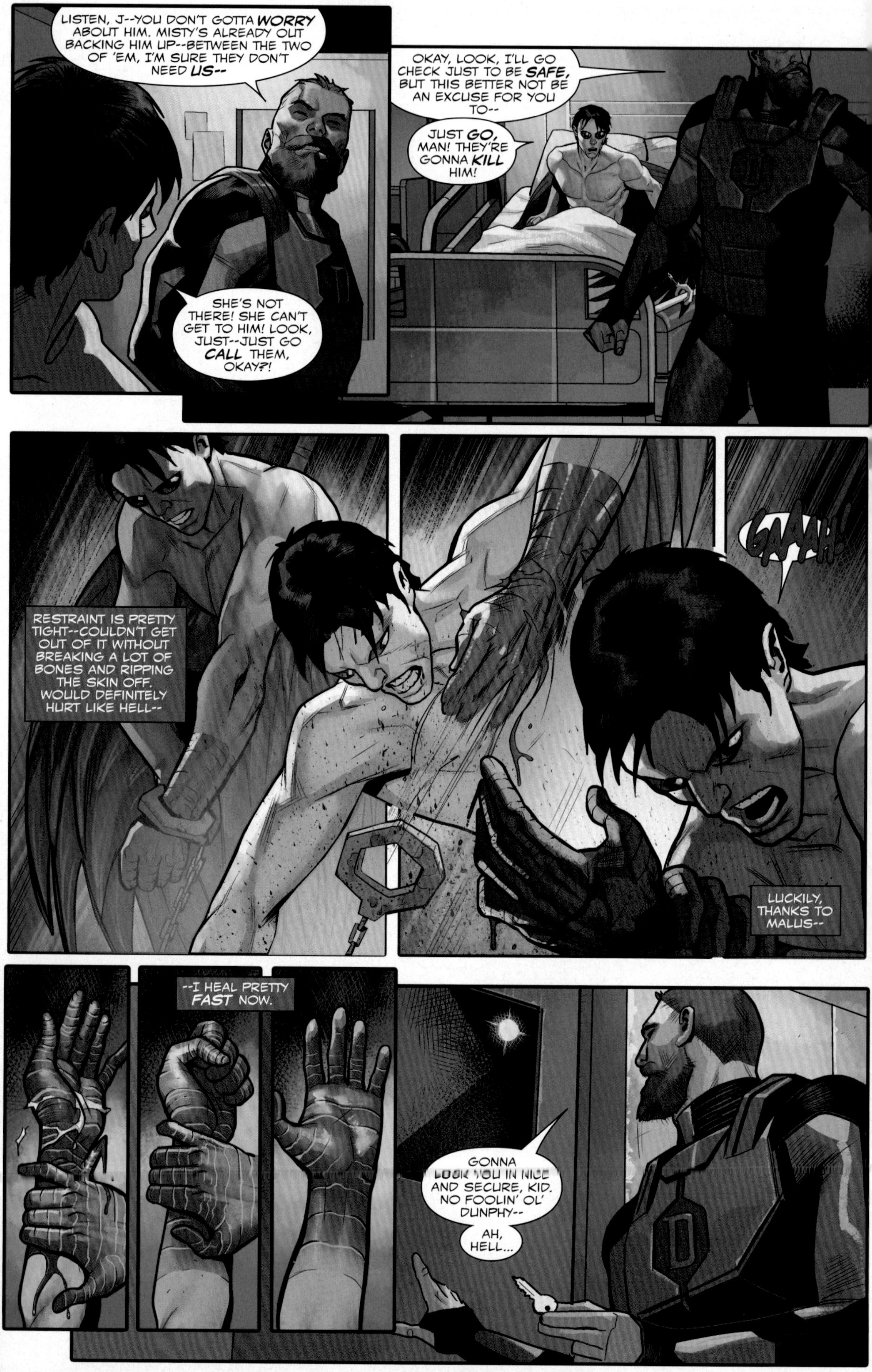

LISTEN, J--YOU DON'T GOTTA WORRY ABOUT HIM. MISTY'S ALREADY OUT BACKING HIM UP--BETWEEN THE TWO OF 'EM, I'M SURE THEY DON'T NEED US--
SHE'S NOT THERE! SHE CAN'T GET TO HIM! LOOK, JUST--JUST GO CALL THEM, OKAY?!
OKAY, LOOK, I'LL GO CHECK JUST TO BE SAFE, BUT THIS BETTER NOT BE AN EXCUSE FOR YOU TO--
JUST GO, MAN! THEY'RE GONNA KILL HIM!
RESTRAINT IS PRETTY TIGHT--COULDN'T GET OUT OF IT WITHOUT BREAKING A LOT OF BONES AND RIPPING THE SKIN OFF. WOULD DEFINITELY HURT LIKE HELL--
GAAAH!
LUCKILY, THANKS TO MALUS--
--I HEAL PRETTY FAST NOW.
GONNA LOCK YOU IN NICE AND SECURE, KID. NO FOOLIN' OL' DUNPHY--
AH, HELL...

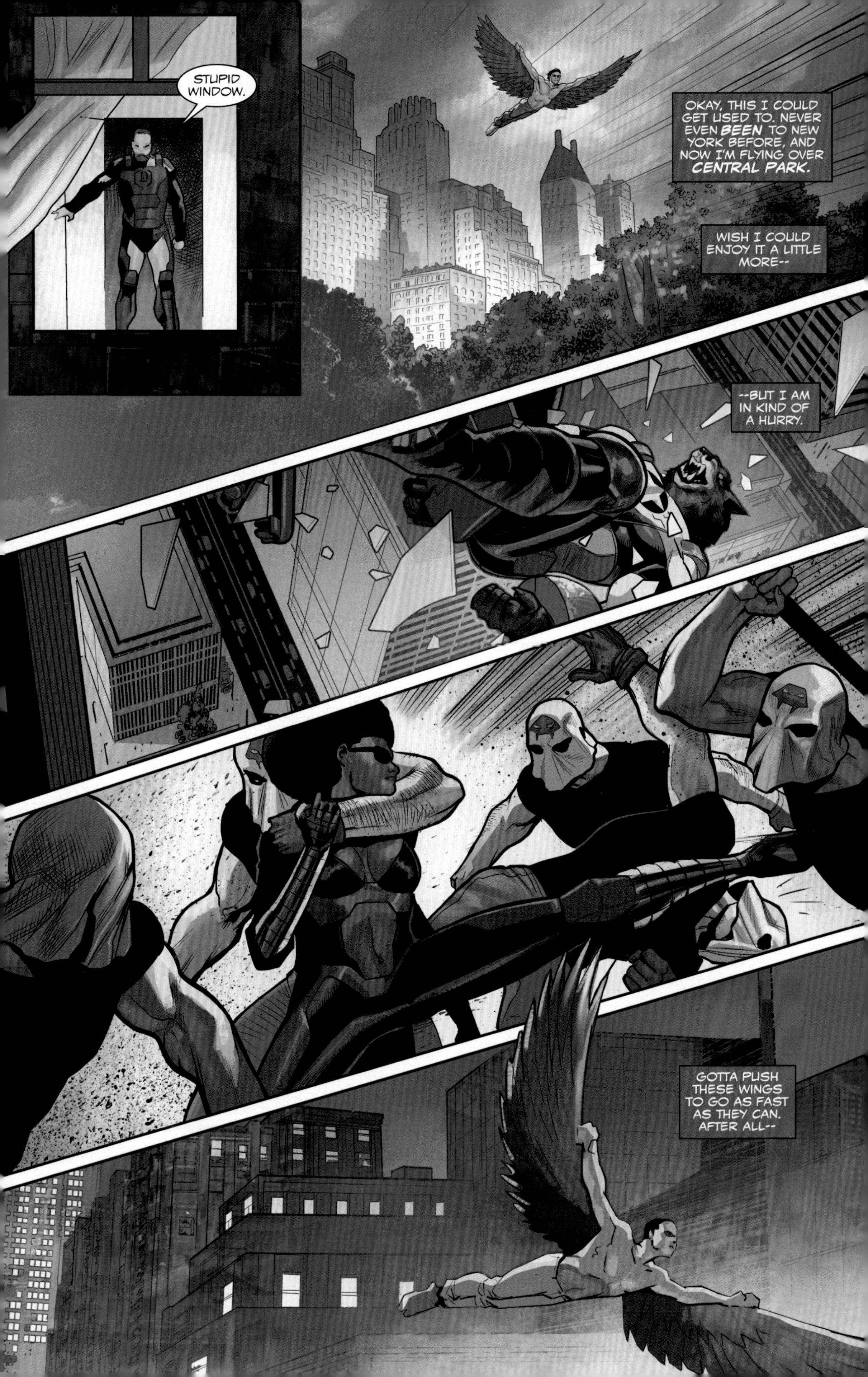
STUPID WINDOW.
OKAY, THIS I COULD GET USED TO. NEVER EVEN BEEN TO NEW YORK BEFORE, AND NOW I'M FLYING OVER CENTRAL PARK.
WISH I COULD ENJOY IT A LITTLE MORE--
--BUT I AM IN KIND OF A HURRY.
GOTTA PUSH THESE WINGS TO GO AS FAST AS THEY CAN. AFTER ALL--

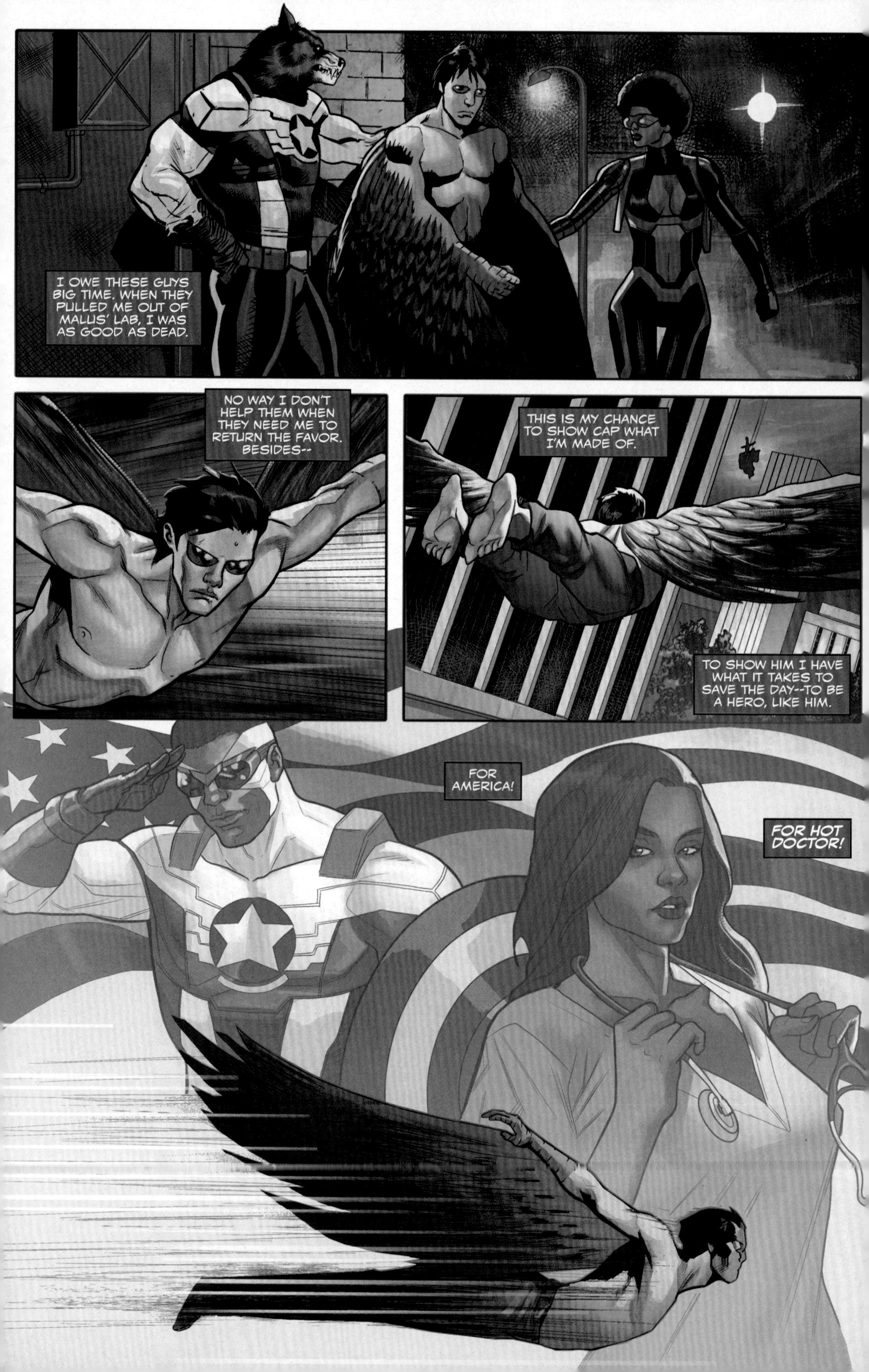
I OWE THESE GUYS BIG TIME. WHEN THEY PULLED ME OUT OF MALUS' LAB, I WAS AS GOOD AS DEAD.
NO WAY I DON'T HELP THEM WHEN THEY NEED ME TO RETURN THE FAVOR. BESIDES--
THIS IS MY CHANCE TO SHOW CAP WHAT I'M MADE OF.
TO SHOW HIM I HAVE WHAT IT TAKES TO SAVE THE DAY--TO BE A HERO, LIKE HIM.
FOR AMERICA!
FOR HOT DOCTOR!

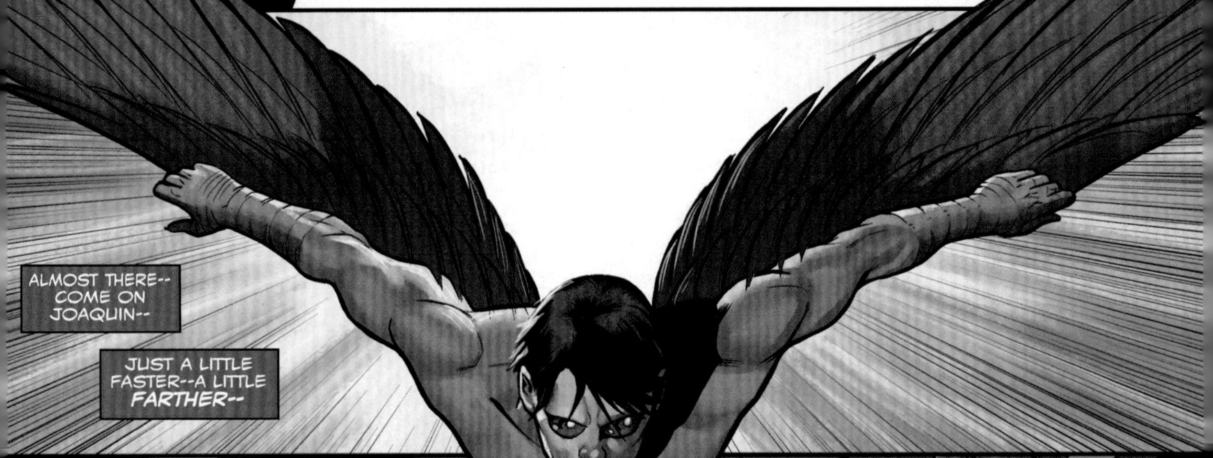
ALMOST THERE--
COME ON
JOAQUIN--
JUST A LITTLE
FASTER--A LITTLE
FARTHER--
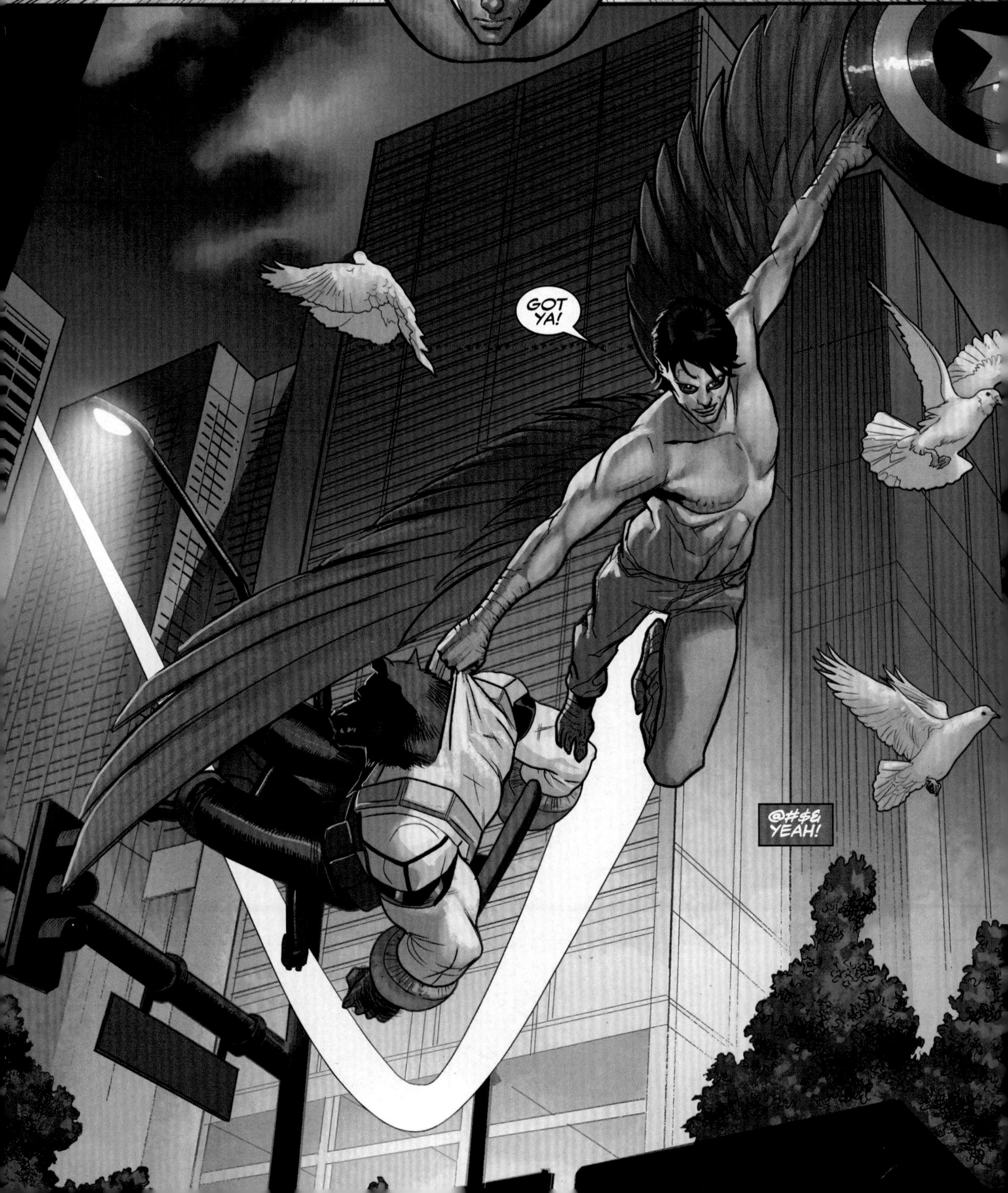
GOT
YA!
@#$&
YEAH!

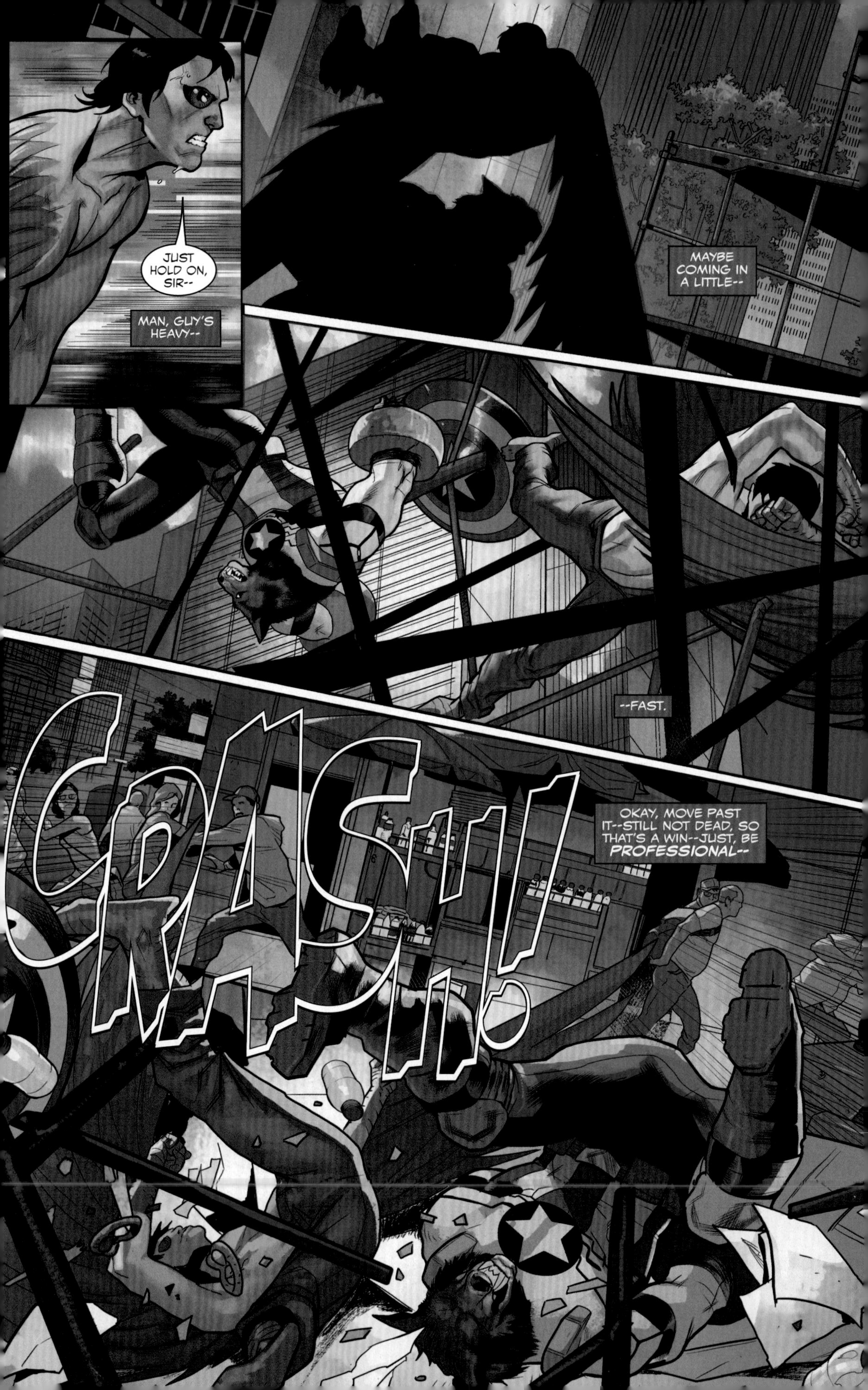
JUST HOLD ON, SIR--
MAN, GUY'S HEAVY--
MAYBE COMING IN A LITTLE--
--FAST.
CRASH
OKAY, MOVE PAST IT--STILL NOT DEAD, SO THAT'S A WIN--JUST, BE *PROFESSIONAL*--

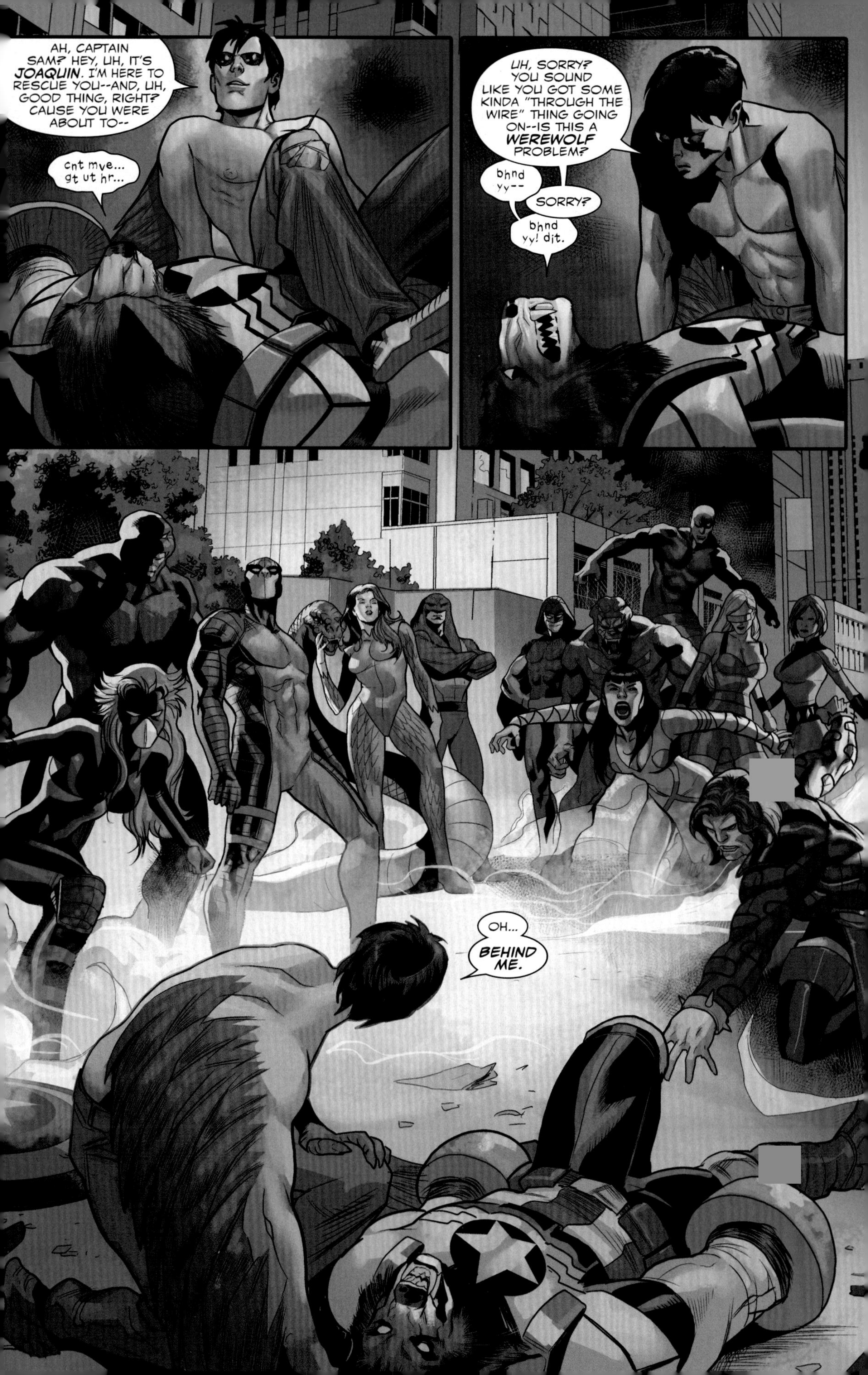
AH, CAPTAIN SAM? HEY, UH, IT'S JOAQUIN. I'M HERE TO RESCUE YOU--AND, UH, GOOD THING, RIGHT? CAUSE YOU WERE ABOUT TO--
cnt mve... gt ut hr...
UH, SORRY? YOU SOUND LIKE YOU GOT SOME KINDA "THROUGH THE WIRE" THING GOING ON--IS THIS A WEREWOLF PROBLEM?
bhnd yy--
SORRY?
bhnd yy! dit.
OH... BEHIND ME.

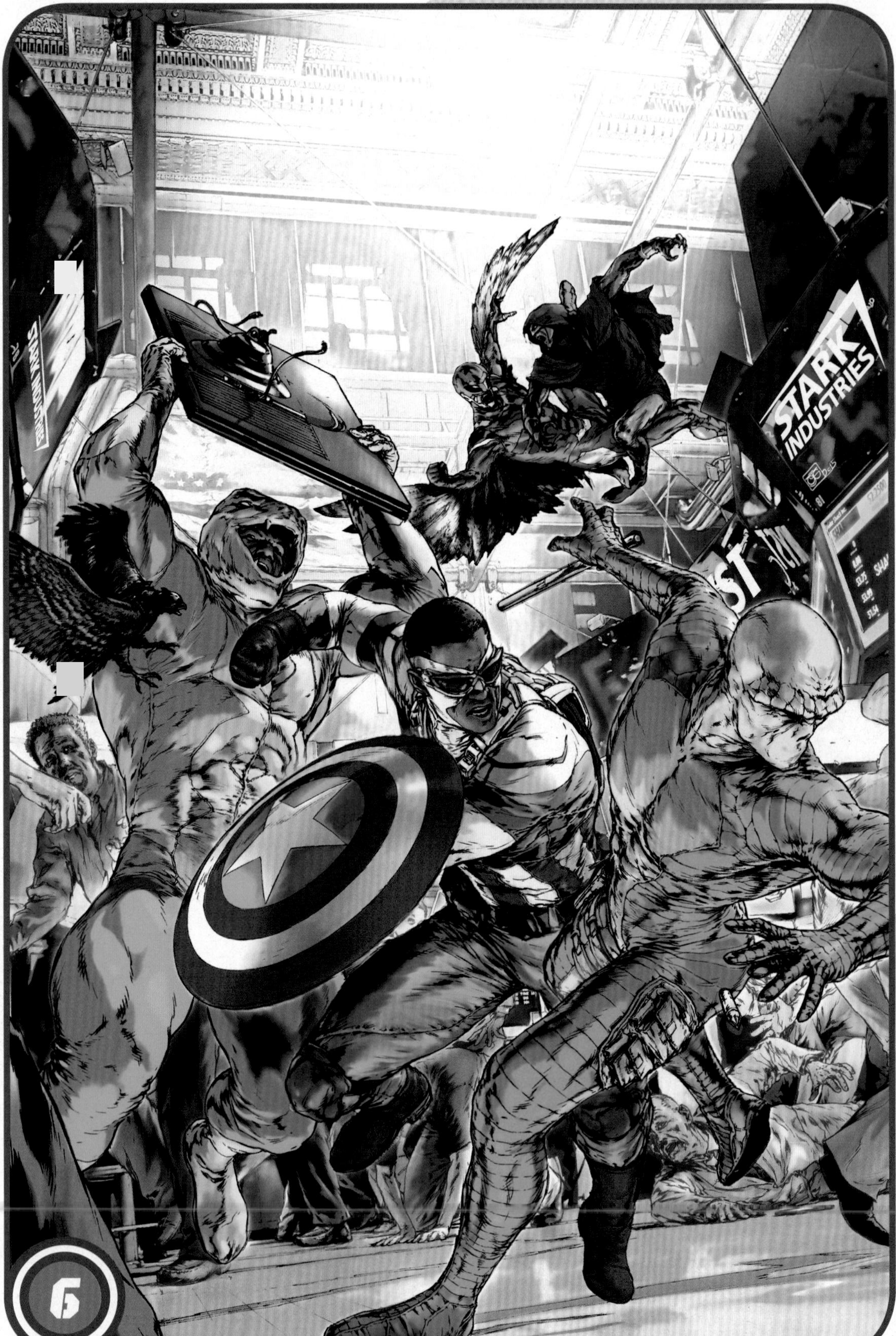
STARK
INDUSTRIES
6

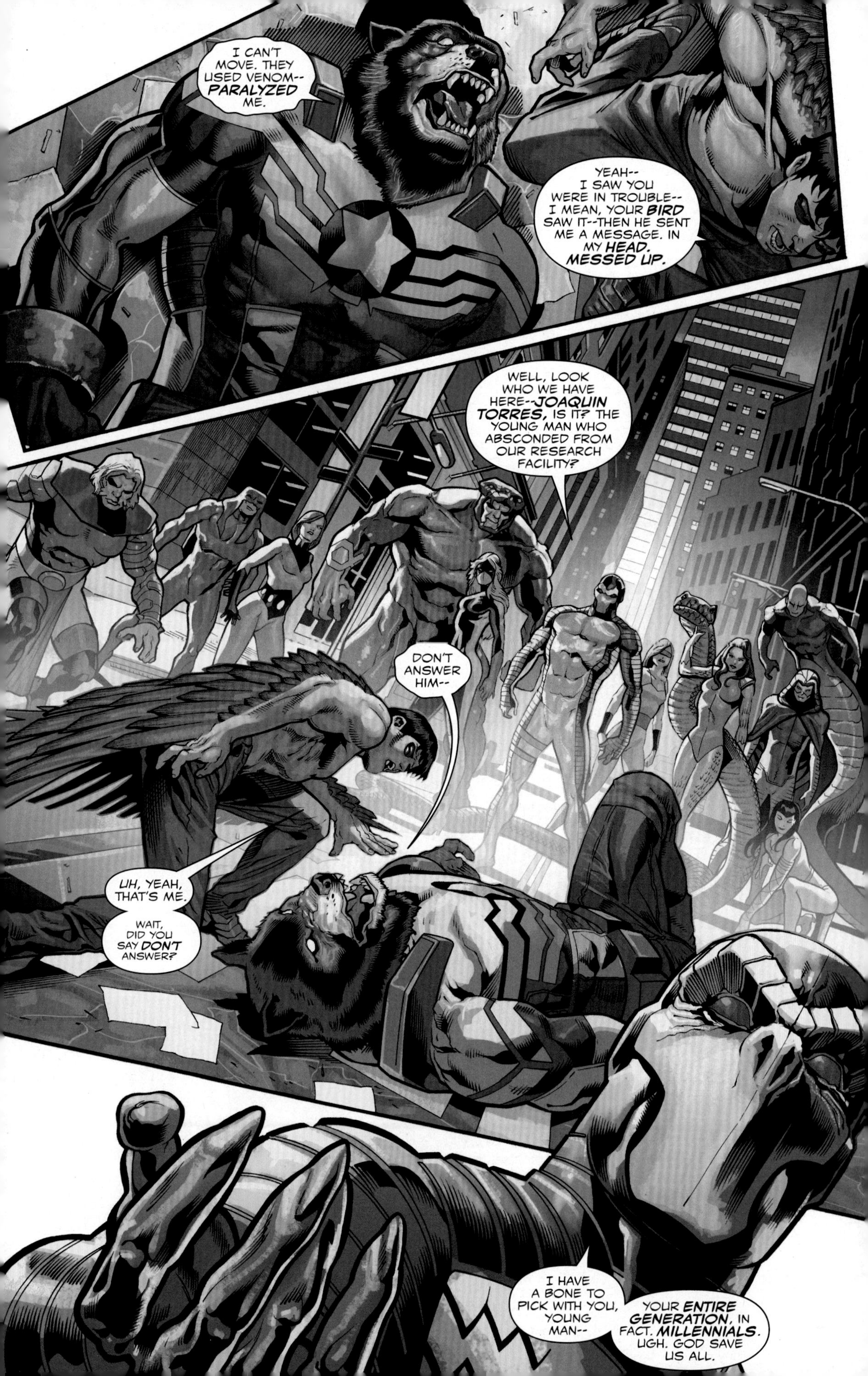
I CAN'T MOVE. THEY USED VENOM--PARALYZED ME.
YEAH-- I SAW YOU WERE IN TROUBLE-- I MEAN, YOUR BIRD SAW IT--THEN HE SENT ME A MESSAGE. IN MY HEAD. MESSED UP.
WELL, LOOK WHO WE HAVE HERE--JOAQUIN TORRES, IS IT? THE YOUNG MAN WHO ABSCONDED FROM OUR RESEARCH FACILITY?
DON'T ANSWER HIM--
UH, YEAH, THAT'S ME.
WAIT, DID YOU SAY DON'T ANSWER?
I HAVE A BONE TO PICK WITH YOU, YOUNG MAN--
YOUR ENTIRE GENERATION, IN FACT. MILLENNIALS. UGH. GOD SAVE US ALL.

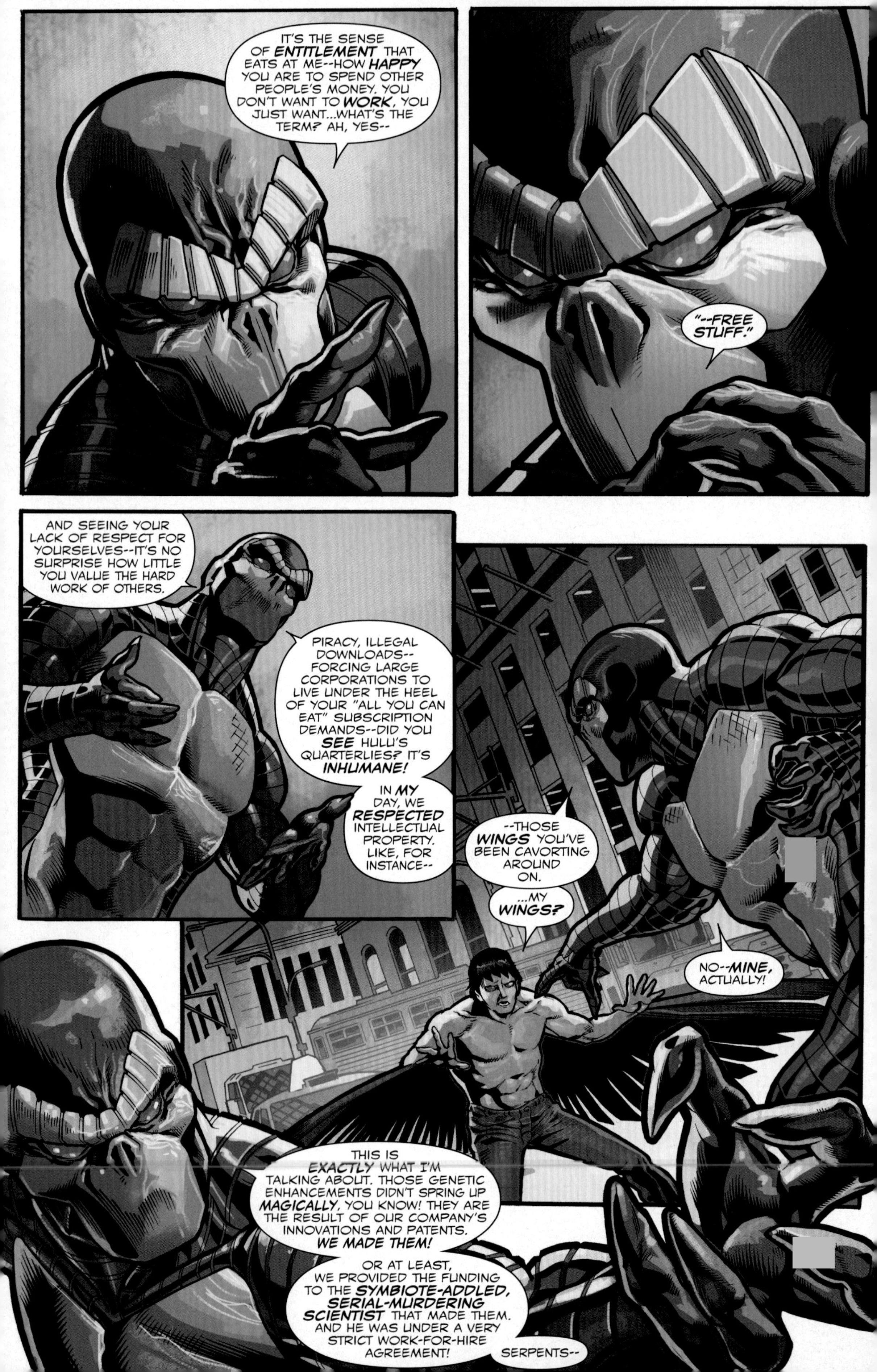
IT'S THE SENSE OF ENTITLEMENT THAT EATS AT ME--HOW HAPPY YOU ARE TO SPEND OTHER PEOPLE'S MONEY. YOU DON'T WANT TO WORK, YOU JUST WANT...WHAT'S THE TERM? AH, YES--
"--FREE STUFF."
AND SEEING YOUR LACK OF RESPECT FOR YOURSELVES--IT'S NO SURPRISE HOW LITTLE YOU VALUE THE HARD WORK OF OTHERS.
PIRACY, ILLEGAL DOWNLOADS--FORCING LARGE CORPORATIONS TO LIVE UNDER THE HEEL OF YOUR "ALL YOU CAN EAT" SUBSCRIPTION DEMANDS--DID YOU SEE HULU'S QUARTERLIES? IT'S INHUMANE!
IN MY DAY, WE RESPECTED INTELLECTUAL PROPERTY. LIKE, FOR INSTANCE--
--THOSE WINGS YOU'VE BEEN CAVORTING AROUND ON.
...MY WINGS?
NO--MINE, ACTUALLY!
THIS IS EXACTLY WHAT I'M TALKING ABOUT. THOSE GENETIC ENHANCEMENTS DIDN'T SPRING UP MAGICALLY, YOU KNOW! THEY ARE THE RESULT OF OUR COMPANY'S INNOVATIONS AND PATENTS. WE MADE THEM!
OR AT LEAST, WE PROVIDED THE FUNDING TO THE SYMBIOTE-ADDLED, SERIAL-MURDERING SCIENTIST THAT MADE THEM. AND HE WAS UNDER A VERY STRICT WORK-FOR-HIRE AGREEMENT!
SERPENTS--

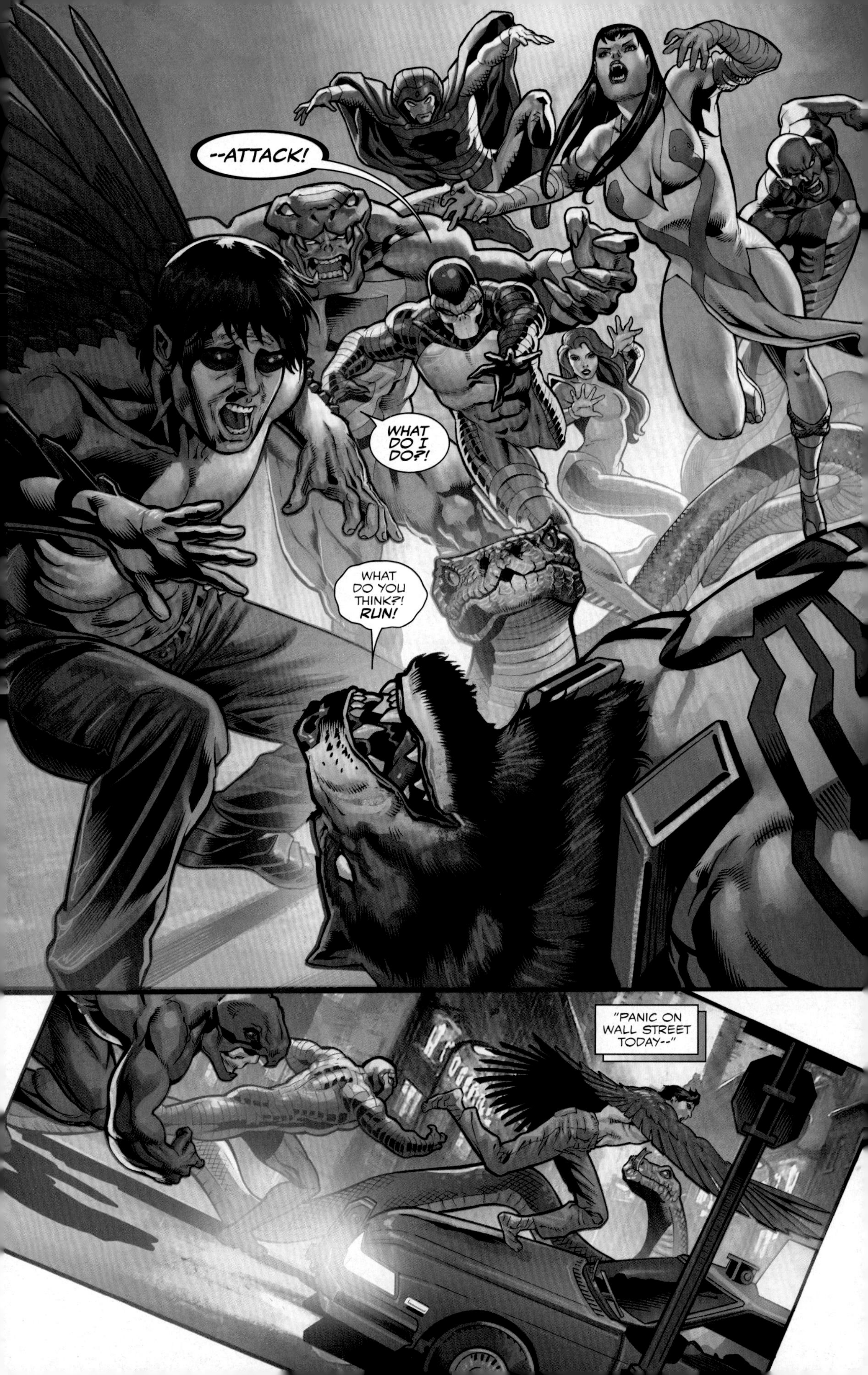
--ATTACK!
WHAT DO I DO?!
WHAT DO YOU THINK?! RUN!
"PANIC ON WALL STREET TODAY--"

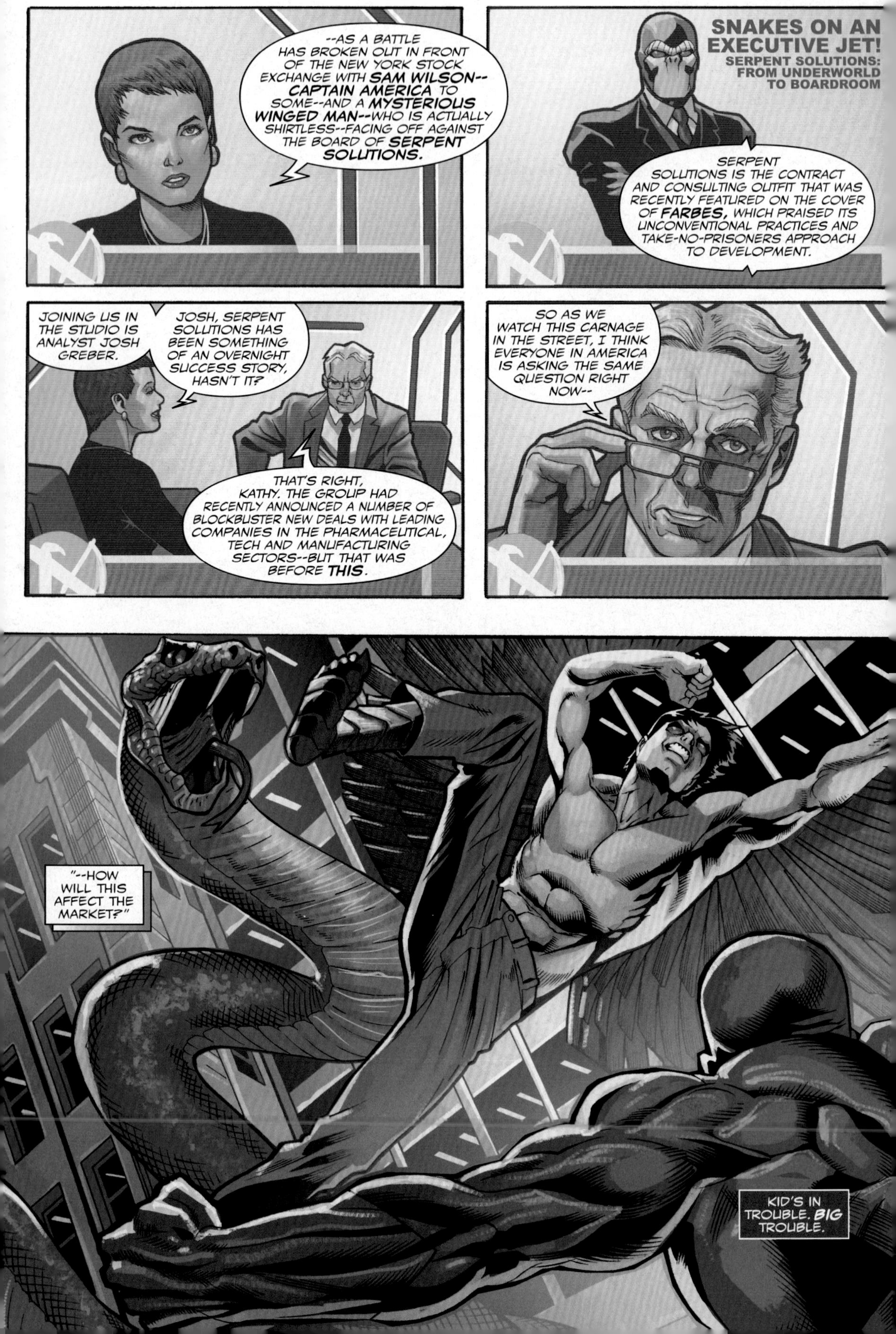
--AS A BATTLE HAS BROKEN OUT IN FRONT OF THE NEW YORK STOCK EXCHANGE WITH SAM WILSON--CAPTAIN AMERICA TO SOME--AND A MYSTERIOUS WINGED MAN--WHO IS ACTUALLY SHIRTLESS--FACING OFF AGAINST THE BOARD OF SERPENT SOLUTIONS.
SNAKES ON AN EXECUTIVE JET!
SERPENT SOLUTIONS: FROM UNDERWORLD TO BOARDROOM
SERPENT SOLUTIONS IS THE CONTRACT AND CONSULTING OUTFIT THAT WAS RECENTLY FEATURED ON THE COVER OF FARBES, WHICH PRAISED ITS UNCONVENTIONAL PRACTICES AND TAKE-NO-PRISONERS APPROACH TO DEVELOPMENT.
JOINING US IN THE STUDIO IS ANALYST JOSH GREBER.
JOSH, SERPENT SOLUTIONS HAS BEEN SOMETHING OF AN OVERNIGHT SUCCESS STORY, HASN'T IT?
THAT'S RIGHT, KATHY. THE GROUP HAD RECENTLY ANNOUNCED A NUMBER OF BLOCKBUSTER NEW DEALS WITH LEADING COMPANIES IN THE PHARMACEUTICAL, TECH AND MANUFACTURING SECTORS--BUT THAT WAS BEFORE THIS.
SO AS WE WATCH THIS CARNAGE IN THE STREET, I THINK EVERYONE IN AMERICA IS ASKING THE SAME QUESTION RIGHT NOW--
"--HOW WILL THIS AFFECT THE MARKET?"
KID'S IN TROUBLE. BIG TROUBLE.

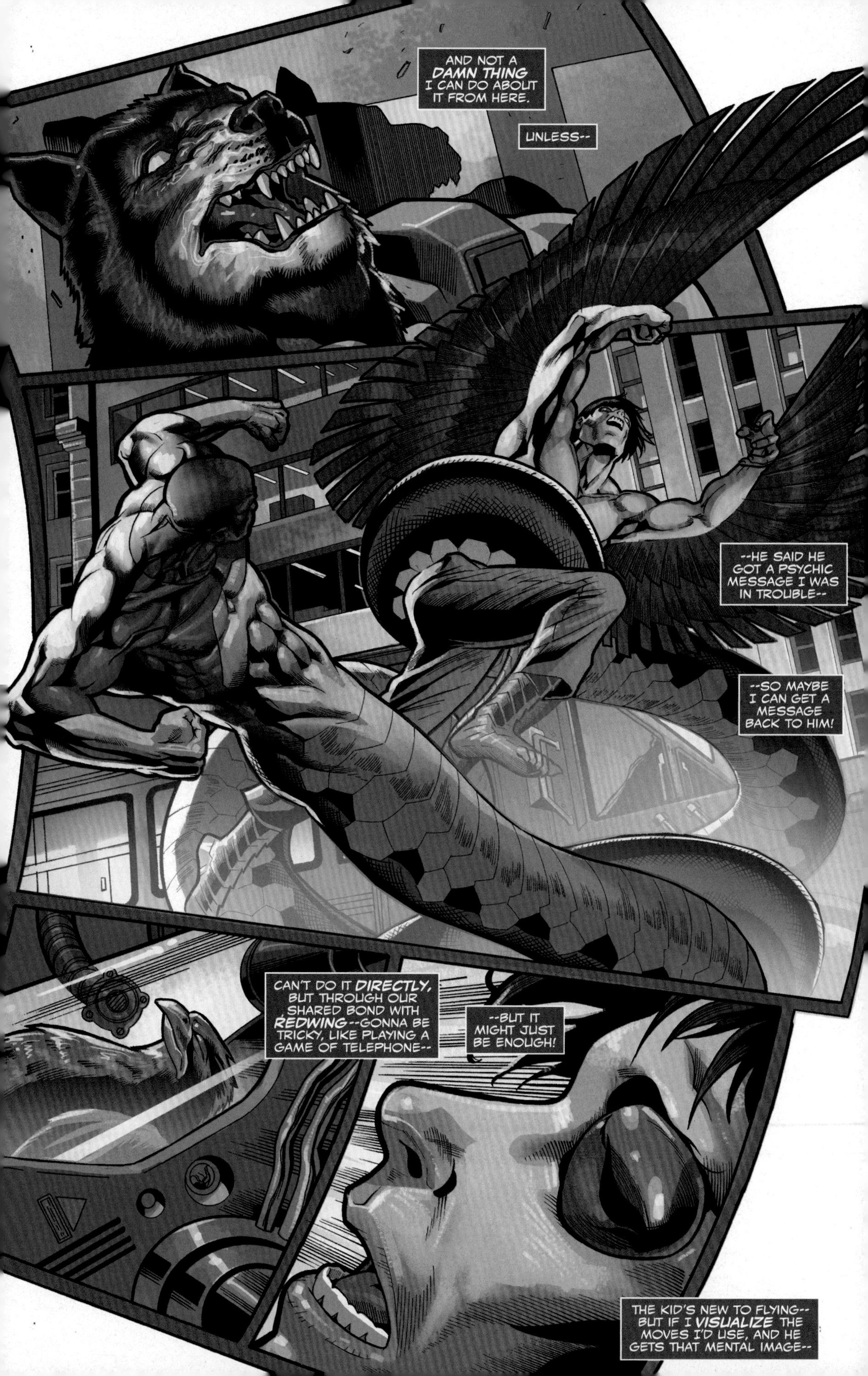
AND NOT A DAMN THING I CAN DO ABOUT IT FROM HERE.
UNLESS--
--HE SAID HE GOT A PSYCHIC MESSAGE I WAS IN TROUBLE--
--SO MAYBE I CAN GET A MESSAGE BACK TO HIM!
CAN'T DO IT DIRECTLY, BUT THROUGH OUR SHARED BOND WITH REDWING--GONNA BE TRICKY, LIKE PLAYING A GAME OF TELEPHONE--
--BUT IT MIGHT JUST BE ENOUGH!
THE KID'S NEW TO FLYING--BUT IF I VISUALIZE THE MOVES I'D USE, AND HE GETS THAT MENTAL IMAGE--

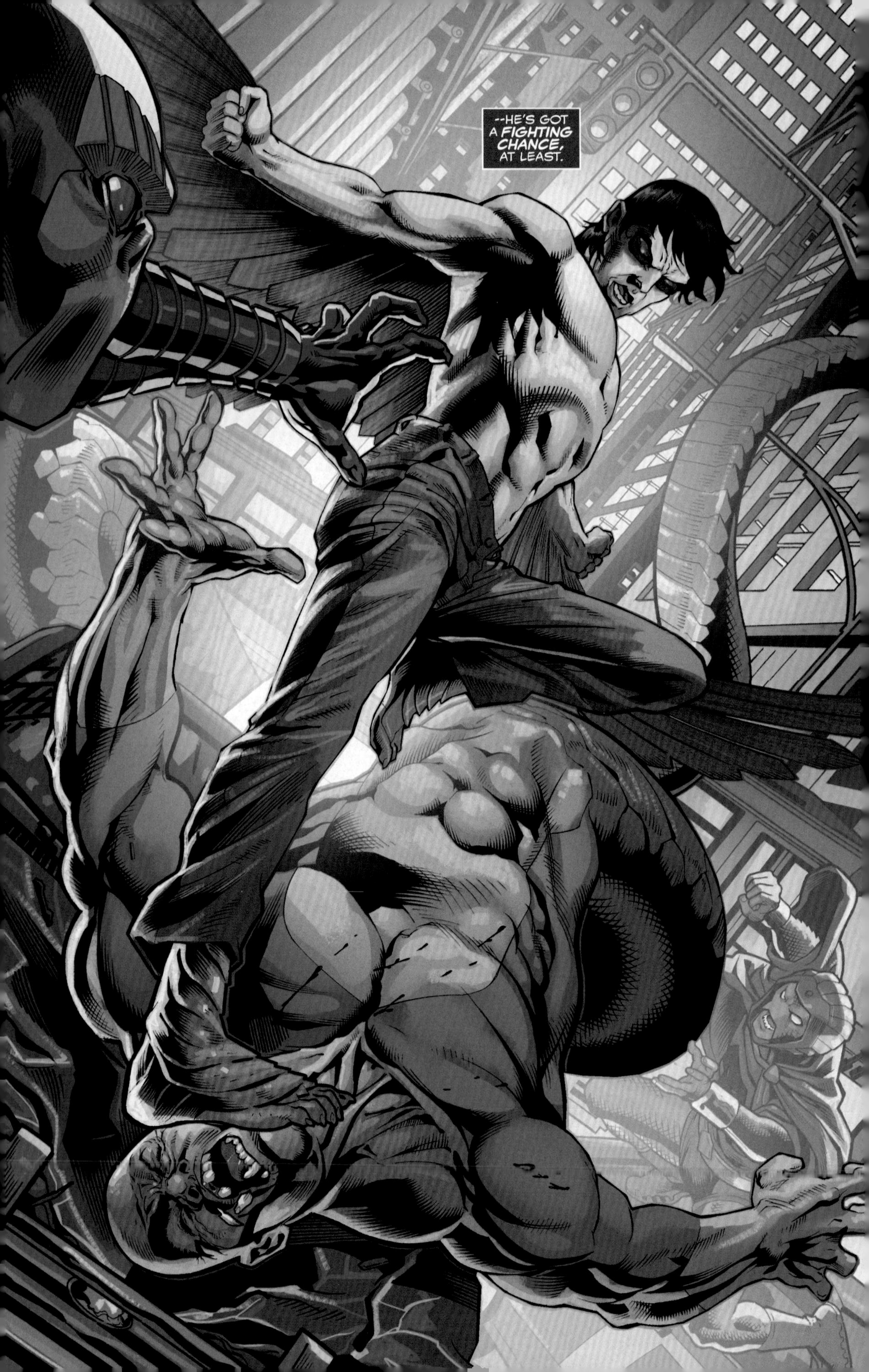
--HE'S GOT A FIGHTING CHANCE, AT LEAST.

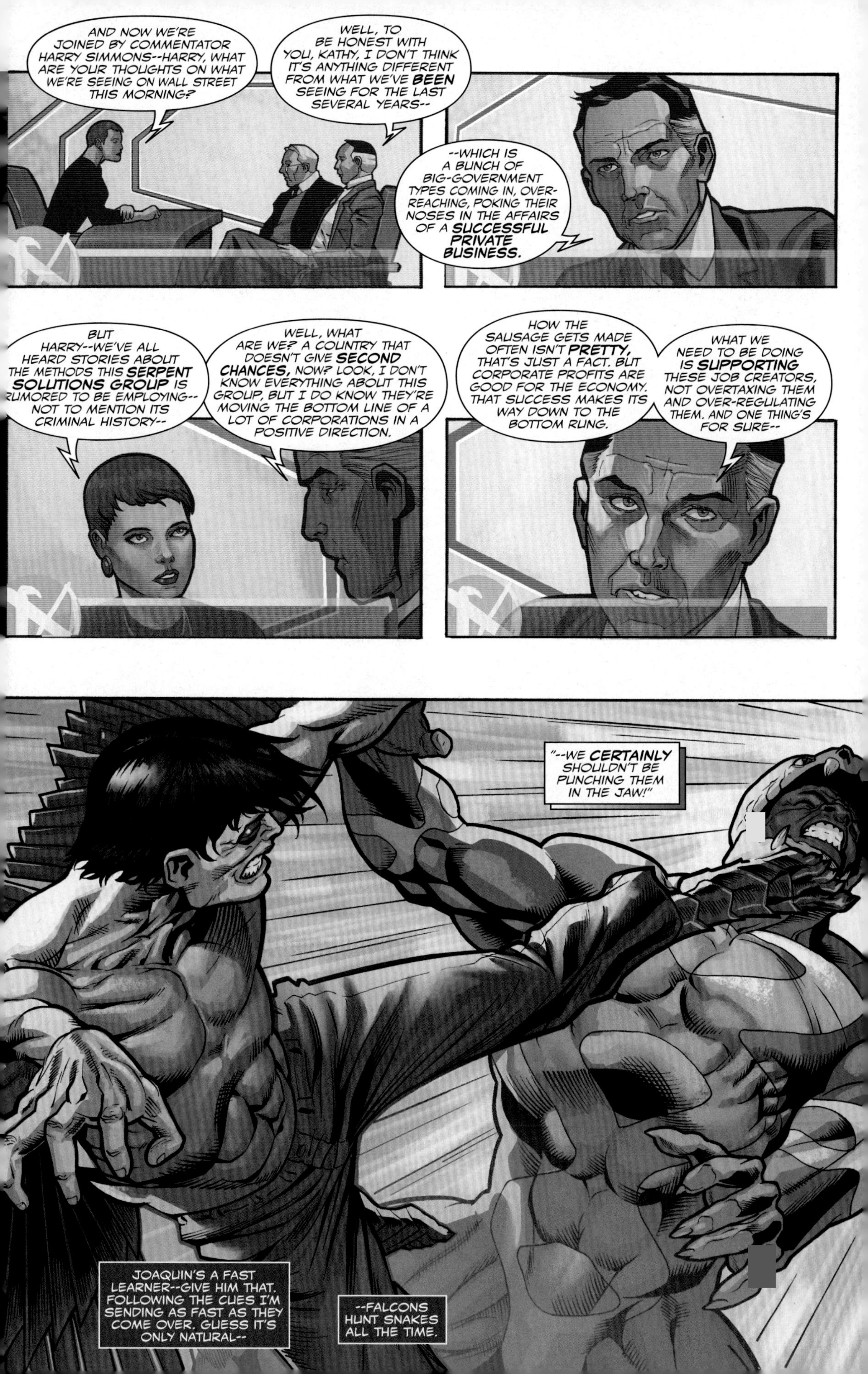

AND NOW WE'RE JOINED BY COMMENTATOR HARRY SIMMONS--HARRY, WHAT ARE YOUR THOUGHTS ON WALL STREET THIS MORNING?
WELL, TO BE HONEST WITH YOU, KATHY, I DON'T THINK IT'S ANYTHING DIFFERENT FROM WHAT WE'VE BEEN SEEING FOR THE LAST SEVERAL YEARS--
--WHICH IS A BUNCH OF BIG-GOVERNMENT TYPES COMING IN, OVER-REACHING, POKING THEIR NOSES IN THE AFFAIRS OF A SUCCESSFUL PRIVATE BUSINESS.
BUT HARRY--WE'VE ALL HEARD STORIES ABOUT THE METHODS THIS SERPENT SOLUTIONS GROUP IS RUMORED TO BE EMPLOYING--NOT TO MENTION ITS CRIMINAL HISTORY--
WELL, WHAT ARE WE? A COUNTRY THAT DOESN'T GIVE SECOND CHANCES, NOW? LOOK, I DON'T KNOW EVERYTHING ABOUT THIS GROUP, BUT I DO KNOW THEY'RE MOVING THE BOTTOM LINE OF A LOT OF CORPORATIONS IN A POSITIVE DIRECTION.
HOW THE SAUSAGE GETS MADE OFTEN ISN'T PRETTY, THAT'S JUST A FACT. BUT CORPORATE PROFITS ARE GOOD FOR THE ECONOMY. THAT SUCCESS MAKES ITS WAY DOWN TO THE BOTTOM RUNG.
WHAT WE NEED TO BE DOING IS SUPPORTING THESE JOB CREATORS, NOT OVERTAXING THEM AND OVER-REGULATING THEM. AND ONE THING'S FOR SURE--
"--WE CERTAINLY SHOULDN'T BE PUNCHING THEM IN THE JAW!"
JOAQUIN'S A FAST LEARNER--GIVE HIM THAT. FOLLOWING THE CUES I'M SENDING AS FAST AS THEY COME OVER. GUESS IT'S ONLY NATURAL--
--FALCONS HUNT SNAKES ALL THE TIME.

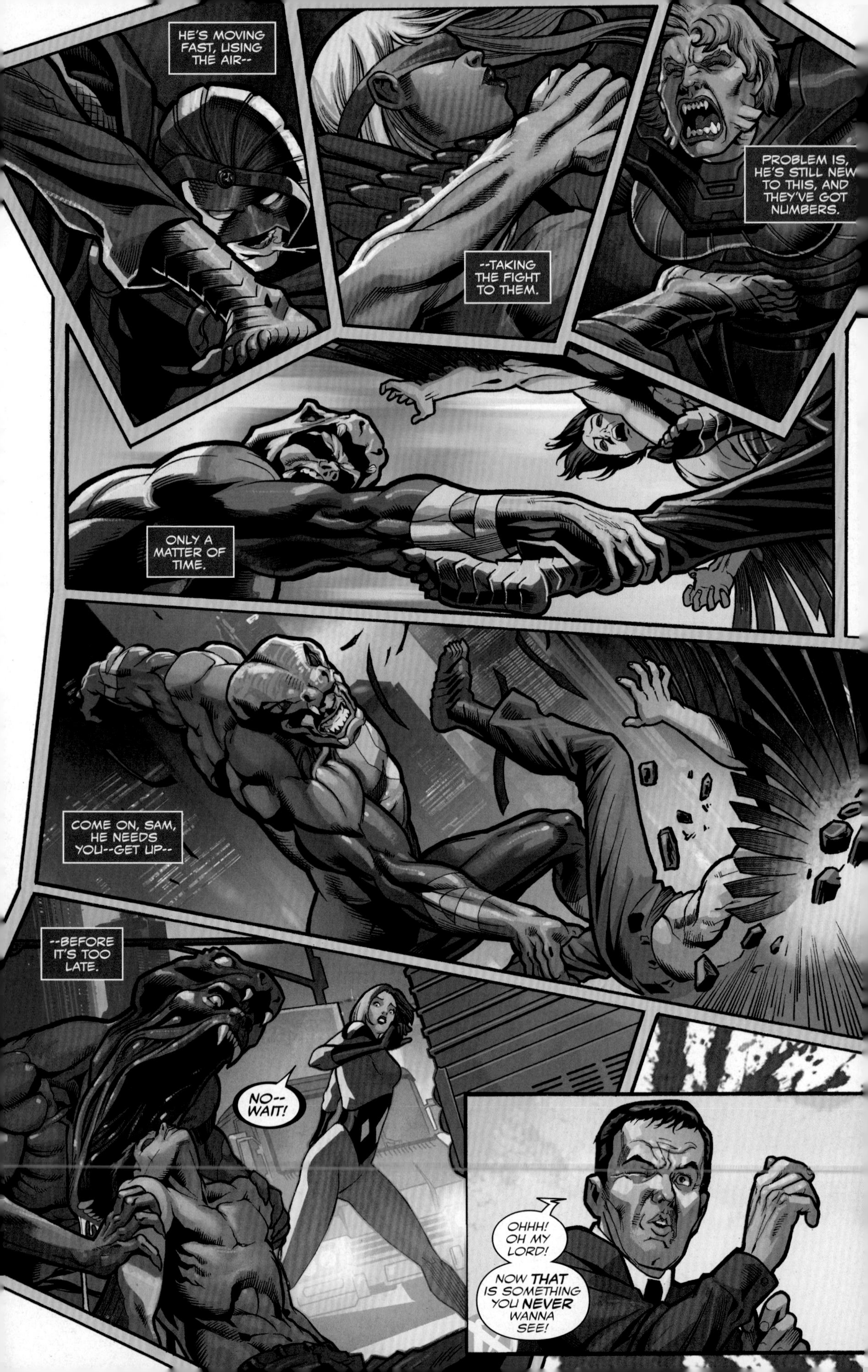
HE'S MOVING FAST, USING THE AIR--
--TAKING THE FIGHT TO THEM.
PROBLEM IS, HE'S STILL NEW TO THIS, AND THEY'VE GOT NUMBERS.
ONLY A MATTER OF TIME.
COME ON, SAM, HE NEEDS YOU--GET UP--
--BEFORE IT'S TOO LATE.
NO--WAIT!
OHHH! OH MY LORD!
NOW THAT IS SOMETHING YOU NEVER WANNA SEE!

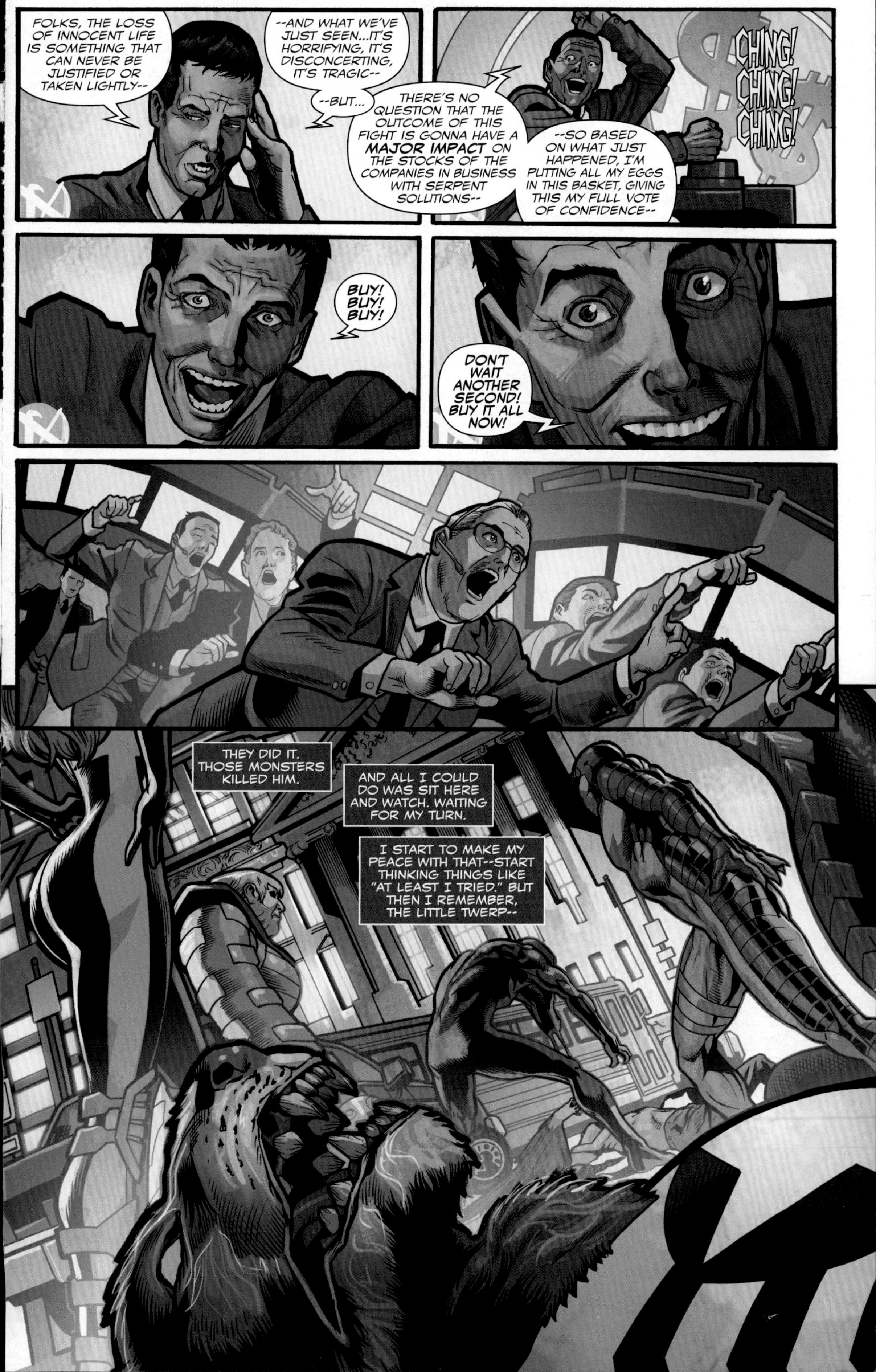
FOLKS, THE LOSS OF INNOCENT LIFE IS SOMETHING THAT CAN NEVER BE JUSTIFIED OR TAKEN LIGHTLY--
--AND WHAT WE'VE JUST SEEN...IT'S HORRIFYING, IT'S DISCONCERTING, IT'S TRAGIC--
--BUT...
THERE'S NO QUESTION THAT THE OUTCOME OF THIS FIGHT IS GONNA HAVE A MAJOR IMPACT ON THE STOCKS OF THE COMPANIES IN BUSINESS WITH SERPENT SOLUTIONS--
CHING! CHING! CHING!
--SO BASED ON WHAT JUST HAPPENED, I'M PUTTING ALL MY EGGS IN THIS BASKET, GIVING THIS MY FULL VOTE OF CONFIDENCE--
BUY! BUY! BUY!
DON'T WAIT ANOTHER SECOND! BUY IT ALL NOW!
THEY DID IT. THOSE MONSTERS KILLED HIM.
AND ALL I COULD DO WAS SIT HERE AND WATCH. WAITING FOR MY TURN.
I START TO MAKE MY PEACE WITH THAT--START THINKING THINGS LIKE "AT LEAST I TRIED." BUT THEN I REMEMBER, THE LITTLE TWERP--

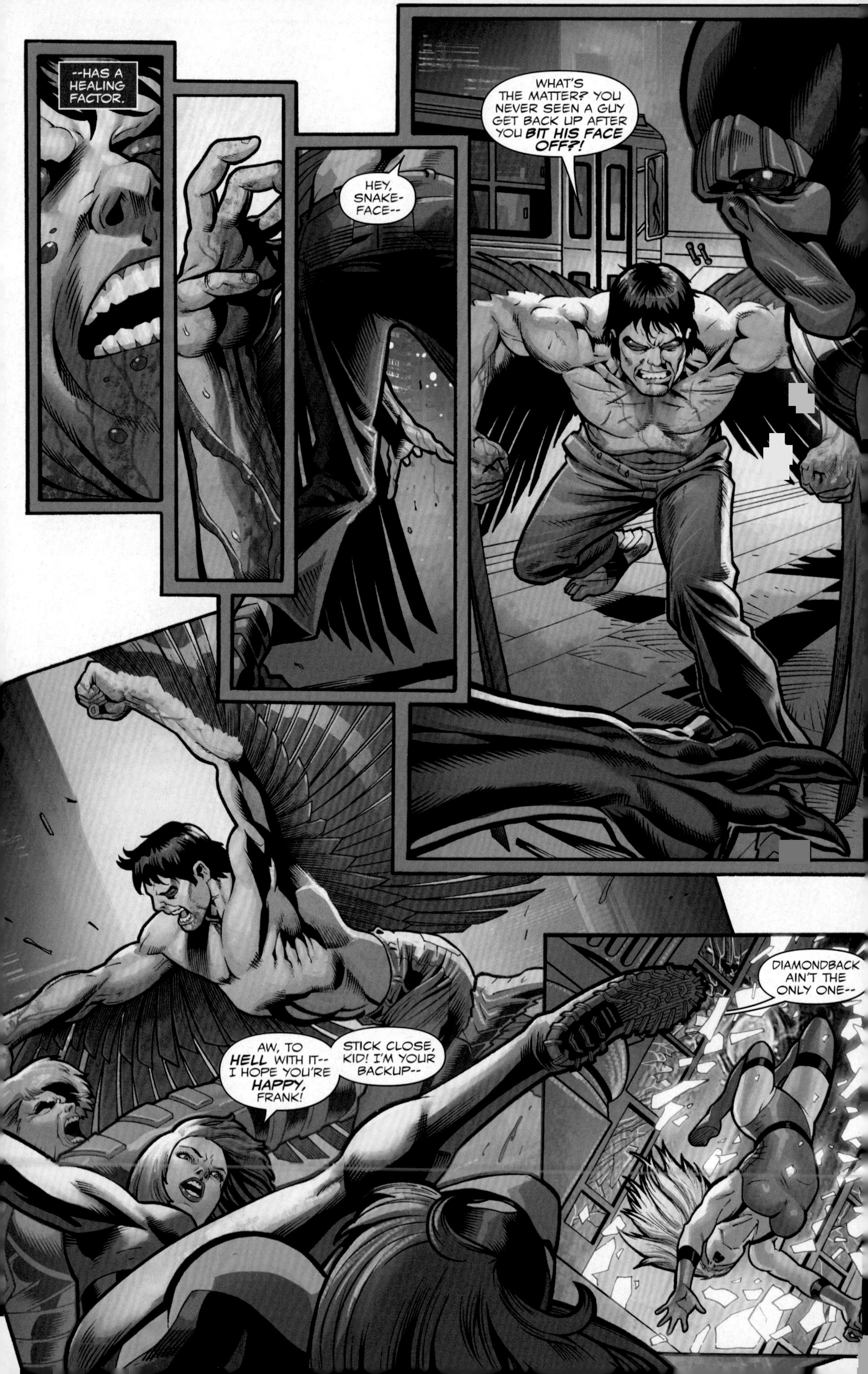
--HAS A HEALING FACTOR.
HEY, SNAKE-FACE--
WHAT'S THE MATTER? YOU NEVER SEEN A GUY GET BACK UP AFTER YOU **BIT HIS FACE OFF?!**
AW, TO **HELL** WITH IT-- I HOPE YOU'RE **HAPPY,** FRANK!
STICK CLOSE, KID! I'M YOUR BACKUP--
DIAMONDBACK AIN'T THE ONLY ONE--

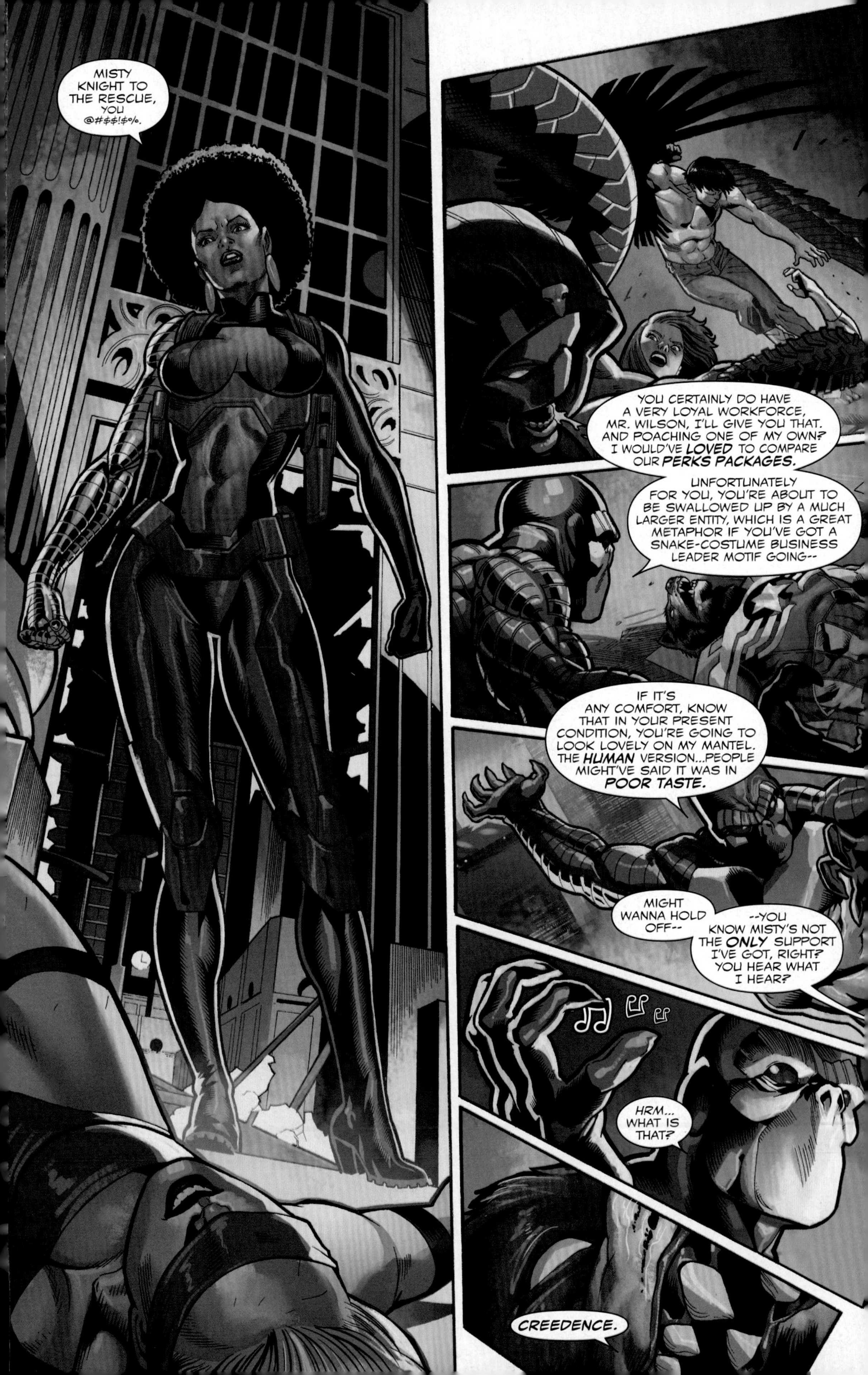
MISTY KNIGHT TO THE RESCUE, YOU @#$$!$%.
YOU CERTAINLY DO HAVE A VERY LOYAL WORKFORCE, MR. WILSON, I'LL GIVE YOU THAT. AND POACHING ONE OF MY OWN? I WOULD'VE LOVED TO COMPARE OUR PERKS PACKAGES.
UNFORTUNATELY FOR YOU, YOU'RE ABOUT TO BE SWALLOWED UP BY A MUCH LARGER ENTITY, WHICH IS A GREAT METAPHOR IF YOU'VE GOT A SNAKE-COSTUME BUSINESS LEADER MOTIF GOING--
IF IT'S ANY COMFORT, KNOW THAT IN YOUR PRESENT CONDITION, YOU'RE GOING TO LOOK LOVELY ON MY MANTEL. THE HUMAN VERSION...PEOPLE MIGHT'VE SAID IT WAS IN POOR TASTE.
MIGHT WANNA HOLD OFF--
--YOU KNOW MISTY'S NOT THE ONLY SUPPORT I'VE GOT, RIGHT? YOU HEAR WHAT I HEAR?
HRM... WHAT IS THAT?
CREEDENCE.

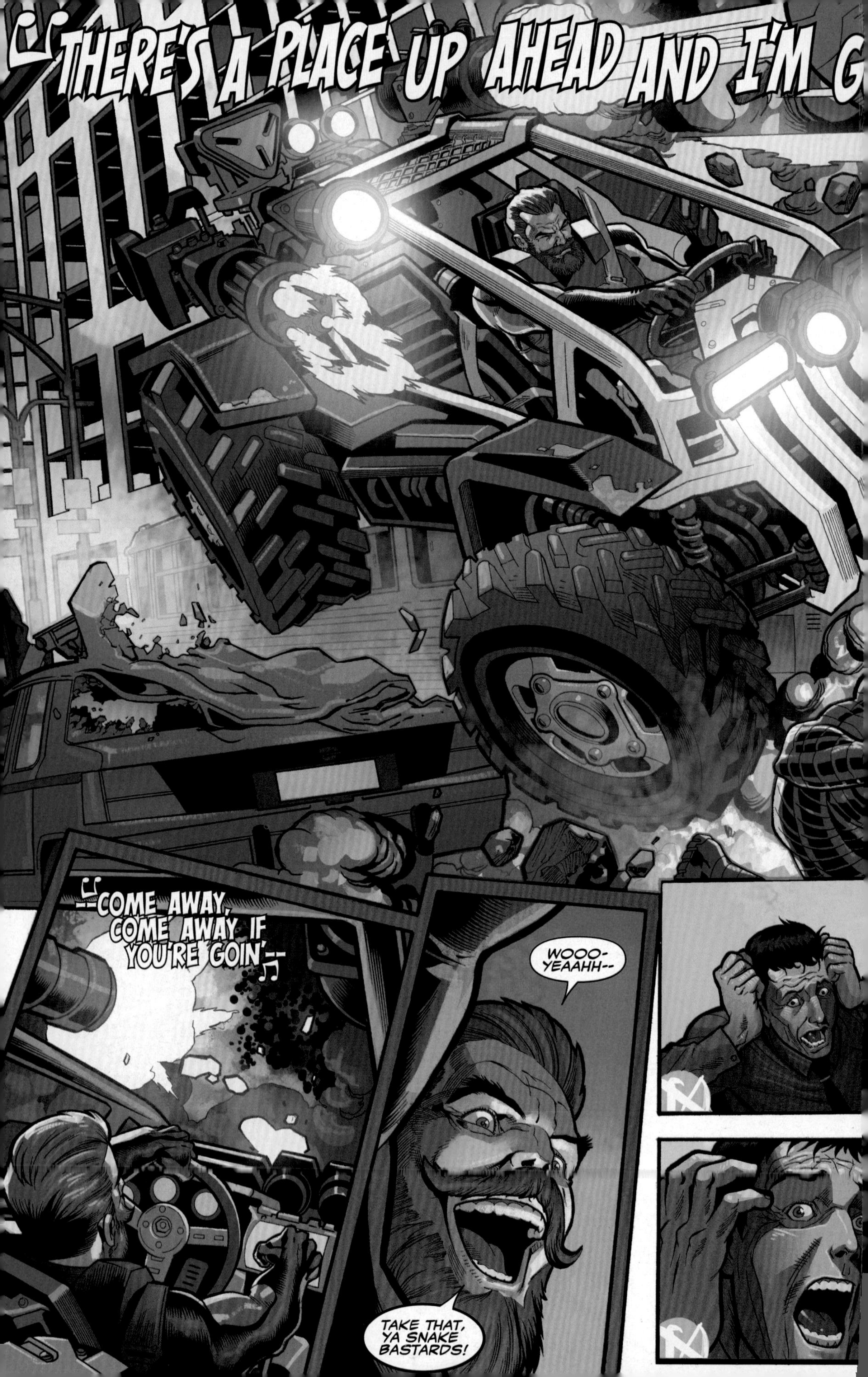
THERE'S A PLACE UP AHEAD AND I'M G
--COME AWAY, COME AWAY IF YOU'RE GOIN'--
WOOO-YEAAHH--
TAKE THAT, YA SNAKE BASTARDS!

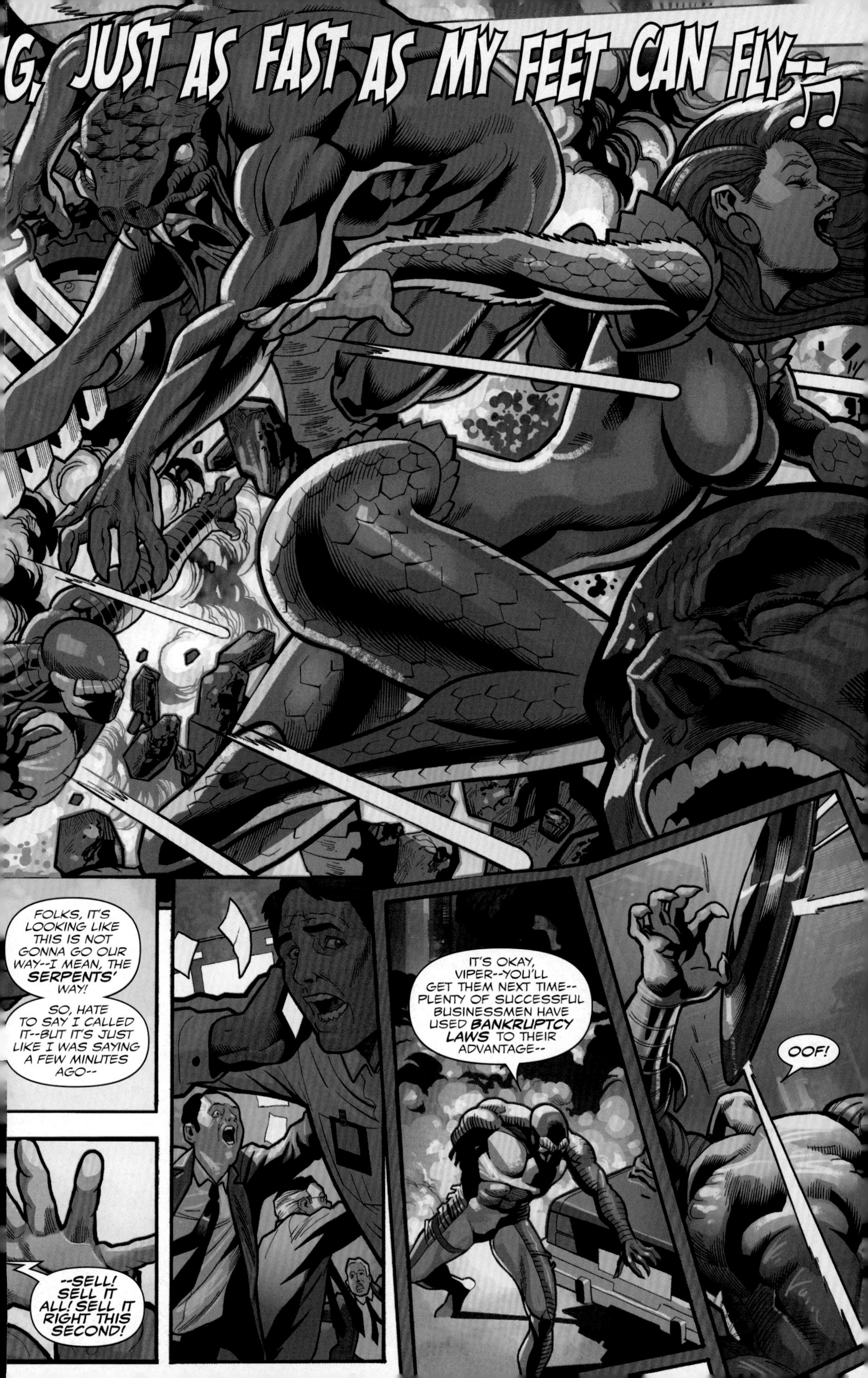
G, JUST AS FAST AS MY FEET CAN FLY--♫
FOLKS, IT'S LOOKING LIKE THIS IS NOT GONNA GO OUR WAY--I MEAN, THE SERPENTS' WAY!
SO, HATE TO SAY I CALLED IT--BUT IT'S JUST LIKE I WAS SAYING A FEW MINUTES AGO--
--SELL! SELL IT ALL! SELL IT RIGHT THIS SECOND!
IT'S OKAY, VIPER--YOU'LL GET THEM NEXT TIME--PLENTY OF SUCCESSFUL BUSINESSMEN HAVE USED BANKRUPTCY LAWS TO THEIR ADVANTAGE--
OOF!

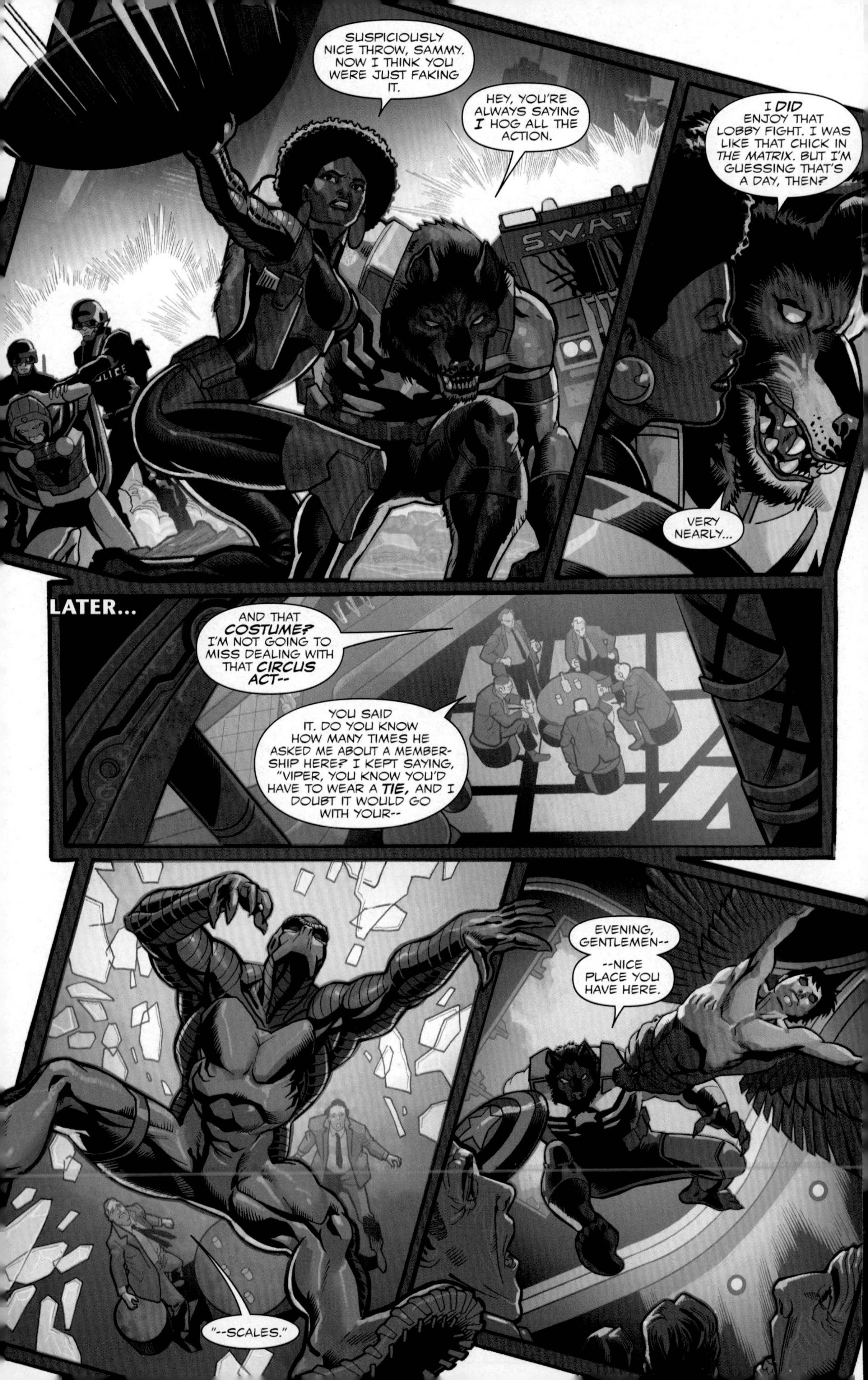
SUSPICIOUSLY NICE THROW, SAMMY. NOW I THINK YOU WERE JUST FAKING IT.
HEY, YOU'RE ALWAYS SAYING I HOG ALL THE ACTION.
S.W.A.T.
I DID ENJOY THAT LOBBY FIGHT. I WAS LIKE THAT CHICK IN THE MATRIX. BUT I'M GUESSING THAT'S A DAY, THEN?
VERY NEARLY...
LATER...
AND THAT COSTUME? I'M NOT GOING TO MISS DEALING WITH THAT CIRCUS ACT--
YOU SAID IT. DO YOU KNOW HOW MANY TIMES HE ASKED ME ABOUT A MEMBERSHIP HERE? I KEPT SAYING, "VIPER, YOU KNOW YOU'D HAVE TO WEAR A TIE, AND I DOUBT IT WOULD GO WITH YOUR--
"--SCALES."
EVENING, GENTLEMEN--
--NICE PLACE YOU HAVE HERE.

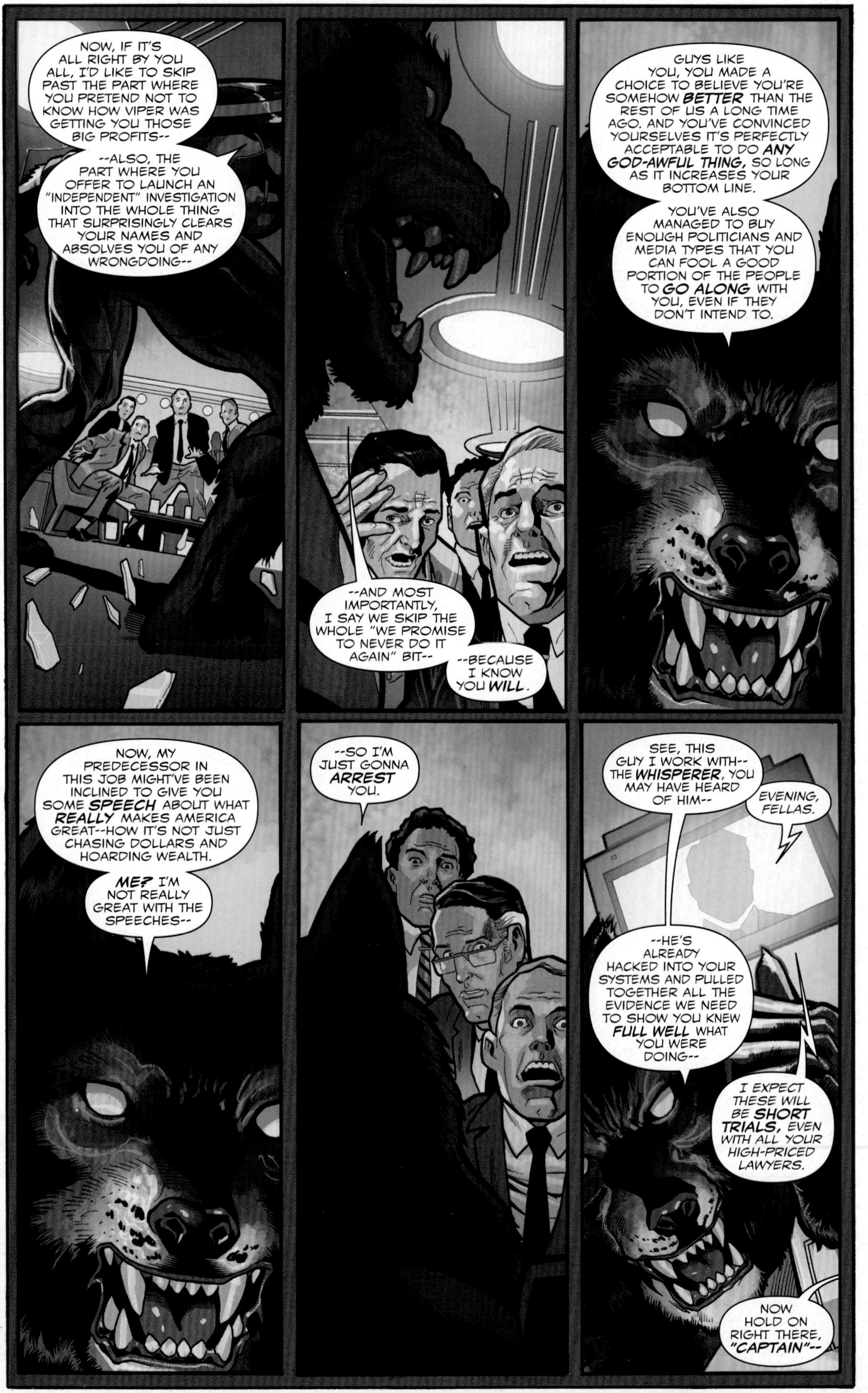
NOW, IF IT'S ALL RIGHT BY YOU ALL, I'D LIKE TO SKIP PAST THE PART WHERE YOU PRETEND NOT TO KNOW HOW VIPER WAS GETTING YOU THOSE BIG PROFITS--
--ALSO, THE PART WHERE YOU OFFER TO LAUNCH AN "INDEPENDENT" INVESTIGATION INTO THE WHOLE THING THAT SURPRISINGLY CLEARS YOUR NAMES AND ABSOLVES YOU OF ANY WRONGDOING--
--AND MOST IMPORTANTLY, I SAY WE SKIP THE WHOLE "WE PROMISE TO NEVER DO IT AGAIN" BIT--
--BECAUSE I KNOW YOU **WILL**.
GUYS LIKE YOU, YOU MADE A CHOICE TO BELIEVE YOU'RE SOMEHOW **BETTER** THAN THE REST OF US A LONG TIME AGO. AND YOU'VE CONVINCED YOURSELVES IT'S PERFECTLY ACCEPTABLE TO DO **ANY GOD-AWFUL THING,** SO LONG AS IT INCREASES YOUR BOTTOM LINE.
YOU'VE ALSO MANAGED TO BUY ENOUGH POLITICIANS AND MEDIA TYPES THAT YOU CAN FOOL A GOOD PORTION OF THE PEOPLE TO **GO ALONG** WITH YOU, EVEN IF THEY DON'T INTEND TO.
NOW, MY PREDECESSOR IN THIS JOB MIGHT'VE BEEN INCLINED TO GIVE YOU SOME **SPEECH** ABOUT WHAT **REALLY** MAKES AMERICA GREAT--HOW IT'S NOT JUST CHASING DOLLARS AND HOARDING WEALTH.
ME? I'M NOT REALLY GREAT WITH THE SPEECHES--
--SO I'M JUST GONNA **ARREST** YOU.
SEE, THIS GUY I WORK WITH--THE **WHISPERER**, YOU MAY HAVE HEARD OF HIM--
EVENING, FELLAS.
--HE'S ALREADY HACKED INTO YOUR SYSTEMS AND PULLED TOGETHER ALL THE EVIDENCE WE NEED TO SHOW YOU KNEW **FULL WELL** WHAT YOU WERE DOING--
I EXPECT THESE WILL BE **SHORT TRIALS,** EVEN WITH ALL YOUR HIGH-PRICED LAWYERS.
NOW HOLD ON RIGHT THERE, **"CAPTAIN"**--

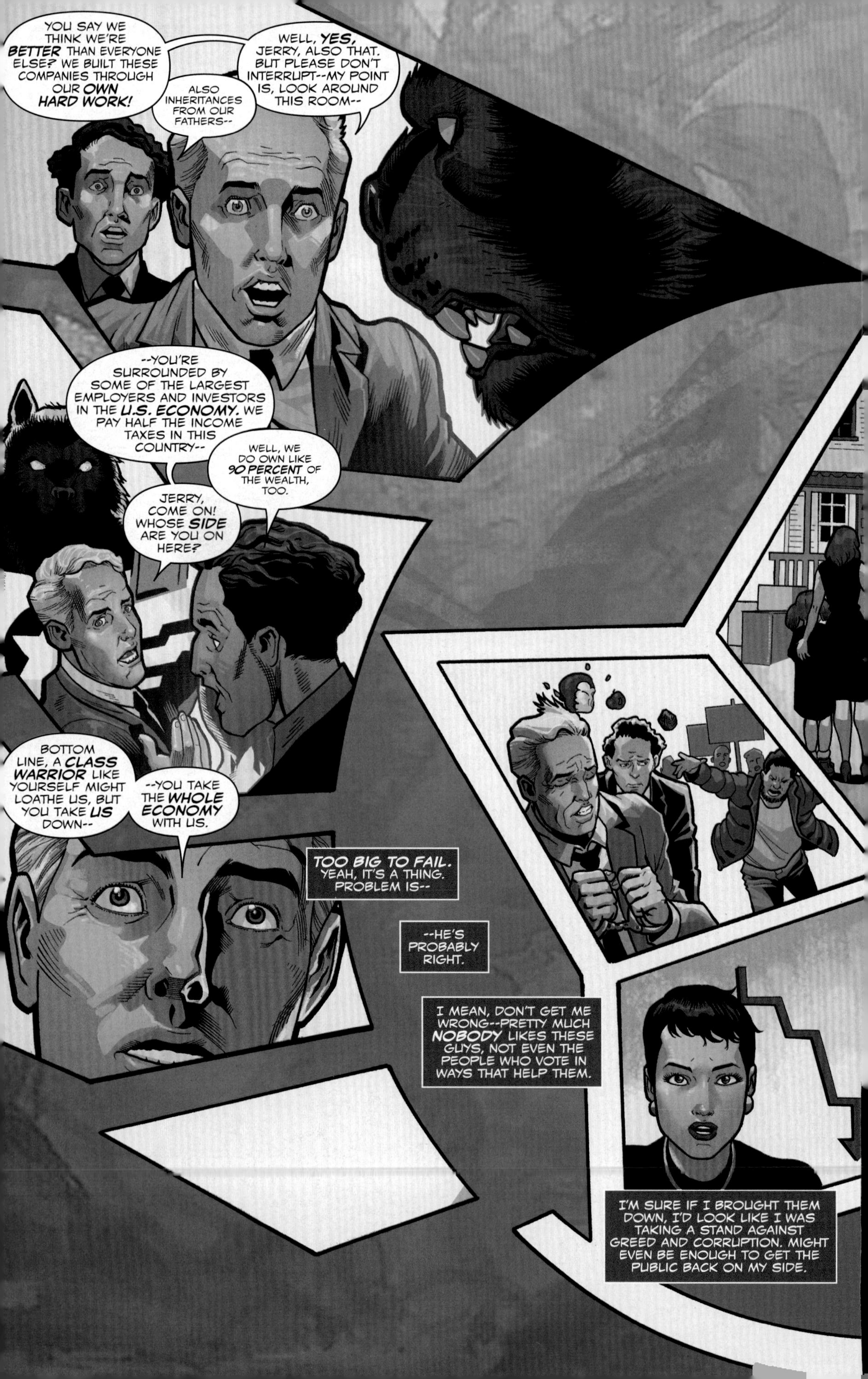
YOU SAY WE THINK WE'RE BETTER THAN EVERYONE ELSE? WE BUILT THESE COMPANIES THROUGH OUR OWN HARD WORK!
ALSO INHERITANCES FROM OUR FATHERS--
WELL, YES, JERRY, ALSO THAT. BUT PLEASE DON'T INTERRUPT--MY POINT IS, LOOK AROUND THIS ROOM--
--YOU'RE SURROUNDED BY SOME OF THE LARGEST EMPLOYERS AND INVESTORS IN THE U.S. ECONOMY. WE PAY HALF THE INCOME TAXES IN THIS COUNTRY--
WELL, WE DO OWN LIKE 90 PERCENT OF THE WEALTH, TOO.
JERRY, COME ON! WHOSE SIDE ARE YOU ON HERE?
BOTTOM LINE, A CLASS WARRIOR LIKE YOURSELF MIGHT LOATHE US, BUT YOU TAKE US DOWN--
--YOU TAKE THE WHOLE ECONOMY WITH US.
TOO BIG TO FAIL. YEAH, IT'S A THING. PROBLEM IS--
--HE'S PROBABLY RIGHT.
I MEAN, DON'T GET ME WRONG--PRETTY MUCH NOBODY LIKES THESE GUYS, NOT EVEN THE PEOPLE WHO VOTE IN WAYS THAT HELP THEM.
I'M SURE IF I BROUGHT THEM DOWN, I'D LOOK LIKE I WAS TAKING A STAND AGAINST GREED AND CORRUPTION. MIGHT EVEN BE ENOUGH TO GET THE PUBLIC BACK ON MY SIDE.

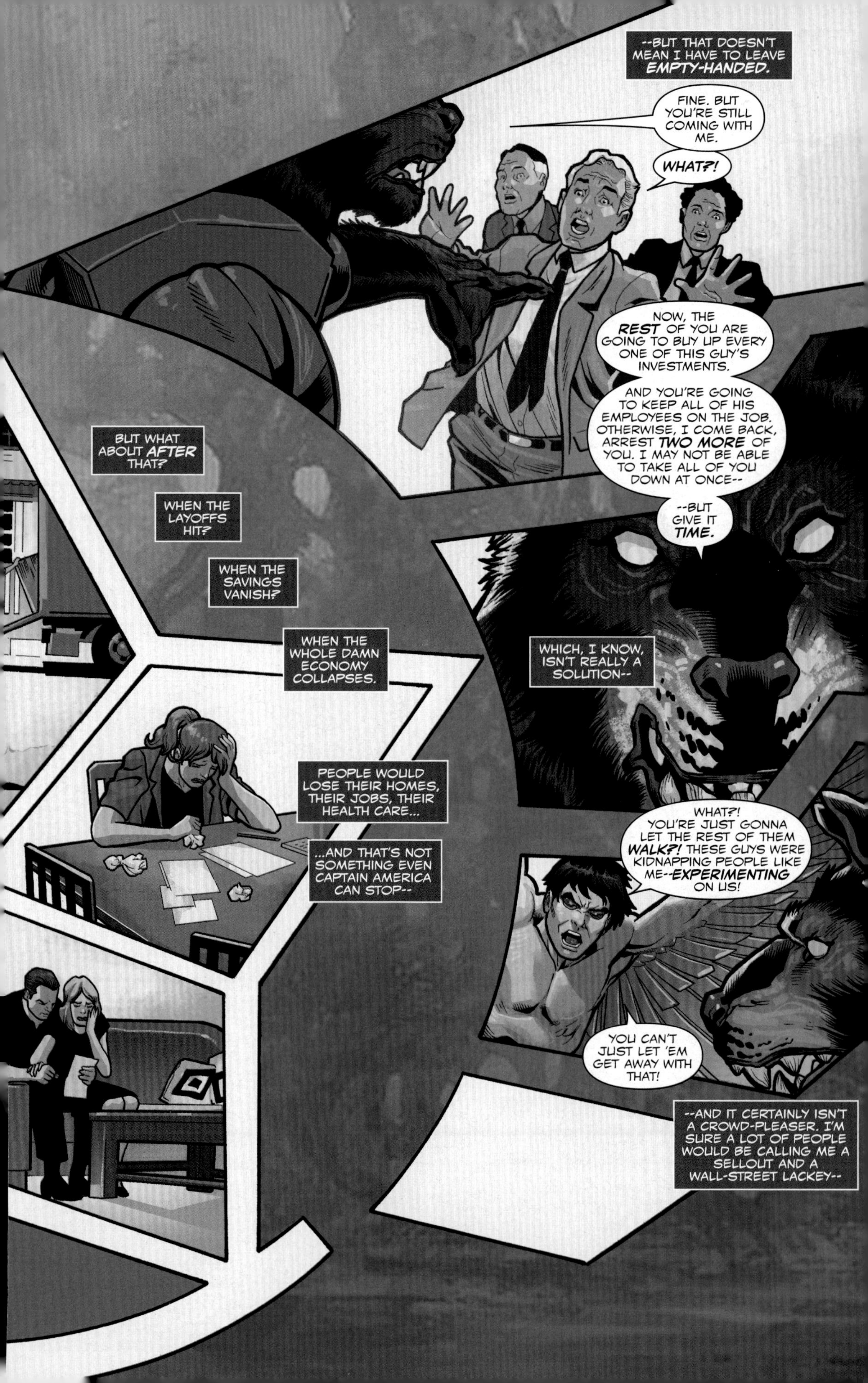

--BUT THAT DOESN'T MEAN I HAVE TO LEAVE EMPTY-HANDED.
FINE. BUT YOU'RE STILL COMING WITH ME.
WHAT?!
NOW, THE REST OF YOU ARE GOING TO BUY UP EVERY ONE OF THIS GUY'S INVESTMENTS.
AND YOU'RE GOING TO KEEP ALL OF HIS EMPLOYEES ON THE JOB. OTHERWISE, I COME BACK, ARREST TWO MORE OF YOU. I MAY NOT BE ABLE TO TAKE ALL OF YOU DOWN AT ONCE--
--BUT GIVE IT TIME.
WHICH, I KNOW, ISN'T REALLY A SOLUTION--
BUT WHAT ABOUT AFTER THAT?
WHEN THE LAYOFFS HIT?
WHEN THE SAVINGS VANISH?
WHEN THE WHOLE DAMN ECONOMY COLLAPSES.
PEOPLE WOULD LOSE THEIR HOMES, THEIR JOBS, THEIR HEALTH CARE...
...AND THAT'S NOT SOMETHING EVEN CAPTAIN AMERICA CAN STOP--
WHAT?! YOU'RE JUST GONNA LET THE REST OF THEM WALK?! THESE GUYS WERE KIDNAPPING PEOPLE LIKE ME--EXPERIMENTING ON US!
YOU CAN'T JUST LET 'EM GET AWAY WITH THAT!
--AND IT CERTAINLY ISN'T A CROWD-PLEASER. I'M SURE A LOT OF PEOPLE WOULD BE CALLING ME A SELLOUT AND A WALL-STREET LACKEY--

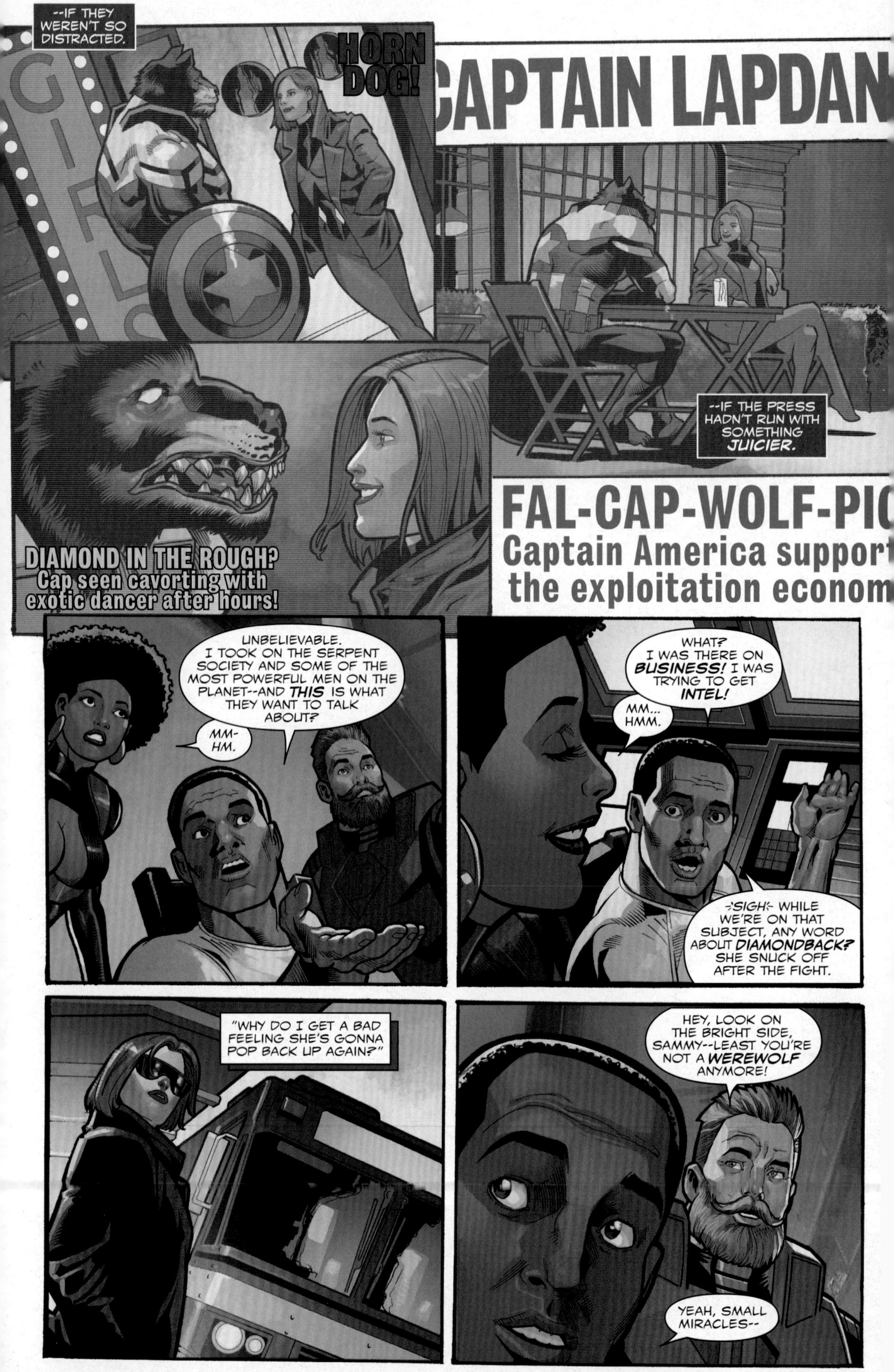
--IF THEY WEREN'T SO DISTRACTED.
HORN DOG!
CAPTAIN LAPDAN
DIAMOND IN THE ROUGH? Cap seen cavorting with exotic dancer after hours!
--IF THE PRESS HADN'T RUN WITH SOMETHING JUICIER.
FAL-CAP-WOLF-PIC
Captain America support the exploitation econom
UNBELIEVABLE. I TOOK ON THE SERPENT SOCIETY AND SOME OF THE MOST POWERFUL MEN ON THE PLANET--AND THIS IS WHAT THEY WANT TO TALK ABOUT?
MM-HM.
WHAT? I WAS THERE ON BUSINESS! I WAS TRYING TO GET INTEL!
MM... HMM.
-SIGH- WHILE WE'RE ON THAT SUBJECT, ANY WORD ABOUT DIAMONDBACK? SHE SNUCK OFF AFTER THE FIGHT.
"WHY DO I GET A BAD FEELING SHE'S GONNA POP BACK UP AGAIN?"
HEY, LOOK ON THE BRIGHT SIDE, SAMMY--LEAST YOU'RE NOT A WEREWOLF ANYMORE!
YEAH, SMALL MIRACLES--

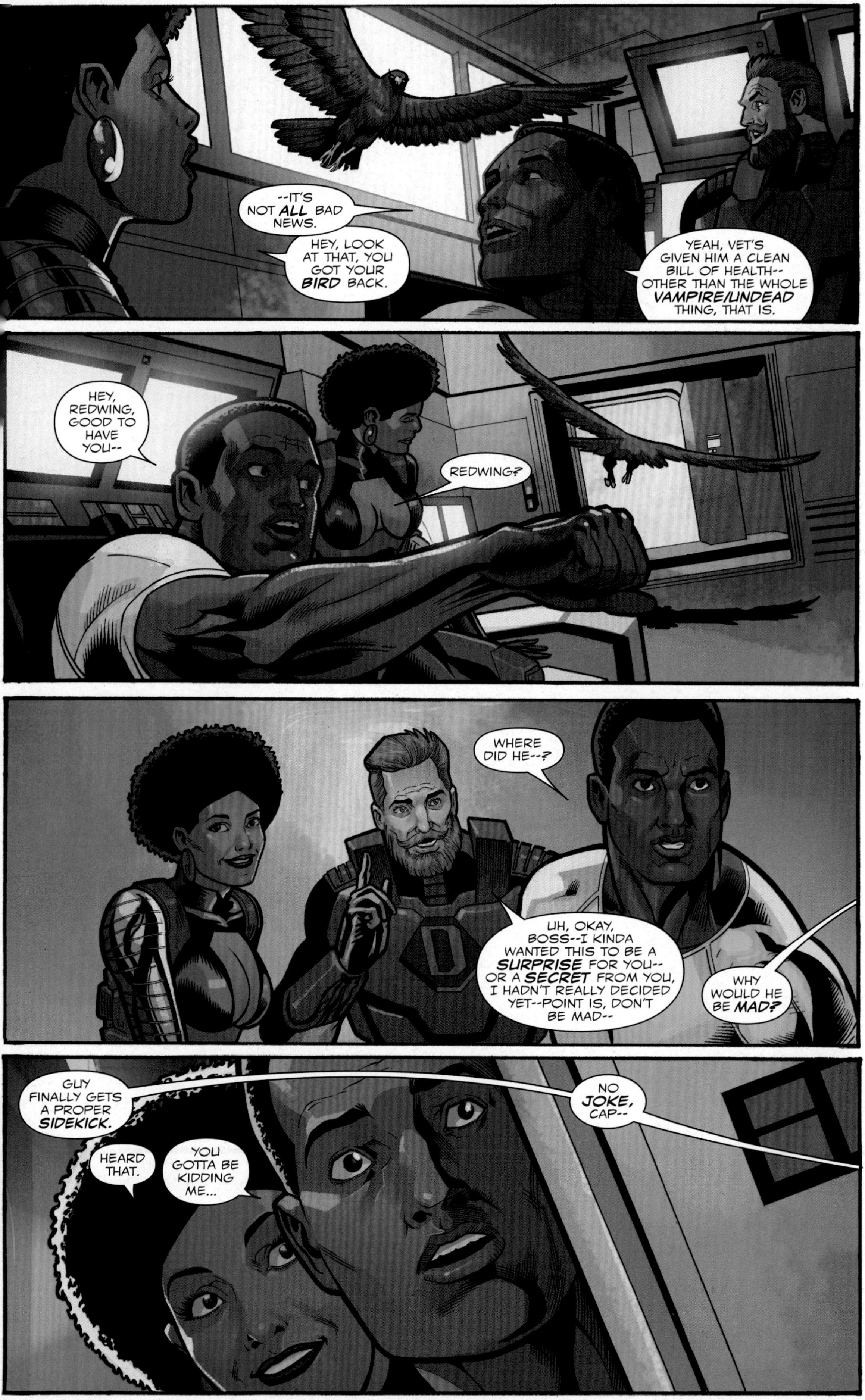
--IT'S NOT ALL BAD NEWS.
HEY, LOOK AT THAT, YOU GOT YOUR BIRD BACK.
YEAH, VET'S GIVEN HIM A CLEAN BILL OF HEALTH--OTHER THAN THE WHOLE VAMPIRE/UNDEAD THING, THAT IS.
HEY, REDWING, GOOD TO HAVE YOU--
REDWING?
WHERE DID HE--?
UH, OKAY, BOSS--I KINDA WANTED THIS TO BE A SURPRISE FOR YOU--OR A SECRET FROM YOU, I HADN'T REALLY DECIDED YET--POINT IS, DON'T BE MAD--
WHY WOULD HE BE MAD?
GUY FINALLY GETS A PROPER SIDEKICK.
NO JOKE, CAP--
HEARD THAT.
YOU GOTTA BE KIDDING ME...

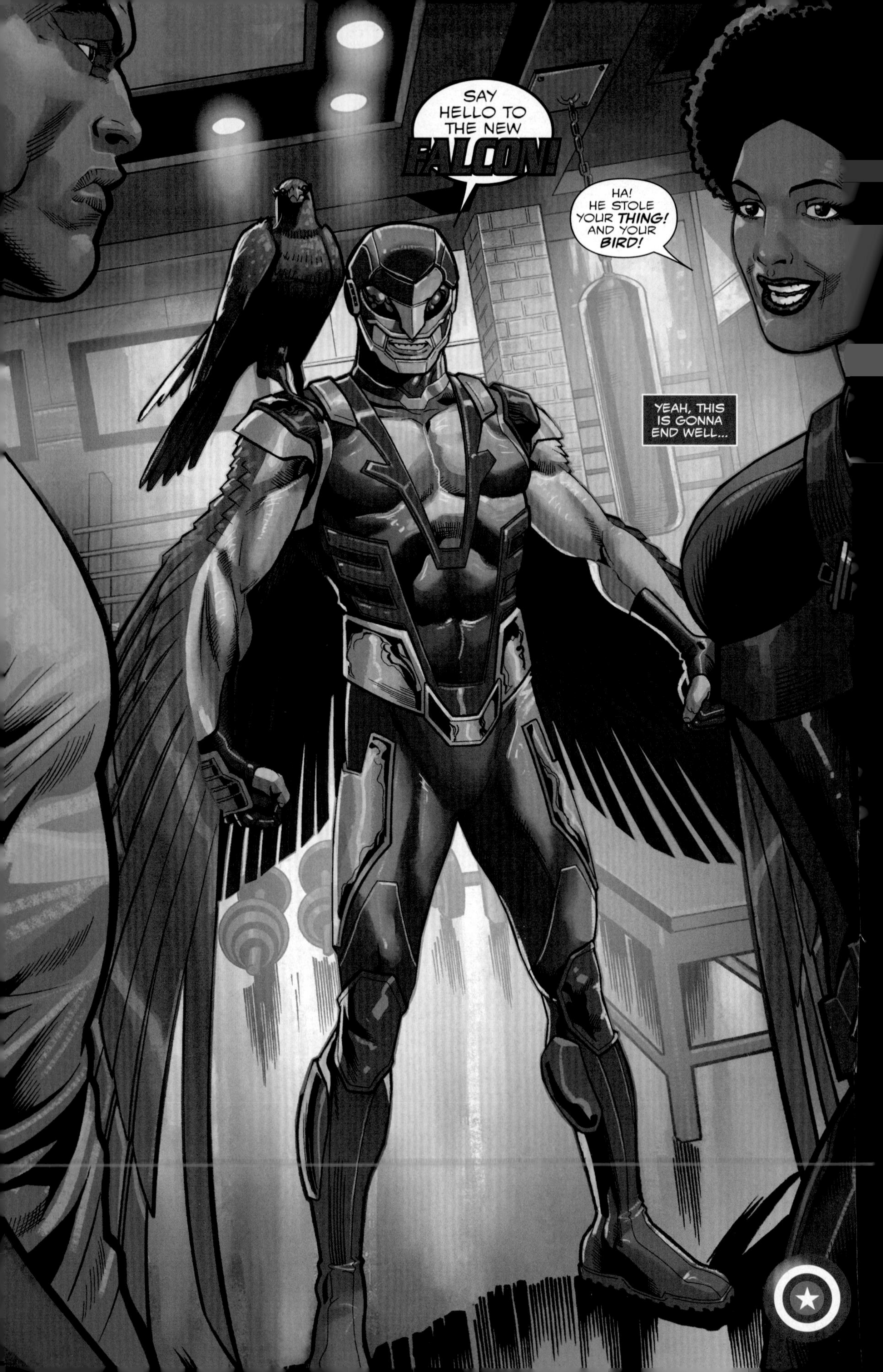
SAY HELLO TO THE NEW FALCON!
HA! HE STOLE YOUR THING! AND YOUR BIRD!
YEAH, THIS IS GONNA END WELL...

#1 variant by
JOHN CASSADAY &
LAURA MARTIN

#1 design variant by
DANIEL ACUNA

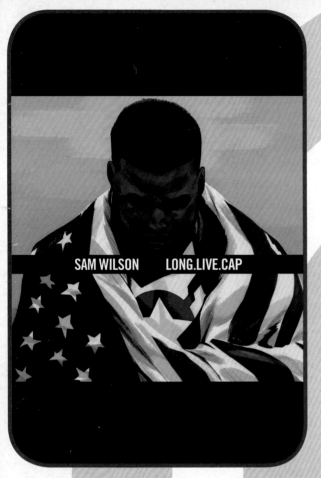

SAM WILSON   LONG.LIVE.CAP

#1 hip-hop variant by
MAHMUD ASRAR

#2 variant by
EVAN "DOC" SHANER